Intersectional Advocacy

What happens to those living at the margins of US politics and policy –
trapped between multiple struggles: gender-based violence, poverty,
homelessness, unaffordable healthcare, mass incarceration, and immigration? In this book, Margaret Perez Brower offers the concept of
"intersectional advocacy" to reveal how select organizations addressing
gender-based violence are closing policy gaps that perpetuate inequalities by gender, race, ethnicity, and class. Intersectional advocacy is a
roadmap for rethinking public policy. The book captures how advocacy
groups strategically contest, reimagine, and reconfigure policy institutions using comprehensive new strategies that connect issues
together. As these groups challenge traditional ways of addressing the
most pressing social issues in the United States, they uncover deep
inequities that are housed within these institutions. Ultimately, organizations practicing intersectional advocacy illuminate how to redraw
the boundaries of policies in ways that transform US democracy to be
more representative, equitable, and just.

Margaret Perez Brower is Assistant Professor of Political Science and
Gender, Women, and Sexuality Studies at the University of Washington.
Her work focuses on the politics of race, ethnicity, and gender and how
these politics shape US institutions, advocacy, policymaking, and social
movements.

Cambridge Studies in Gender and Politics

Cambridge Studies in Gender and Politics addresses theoretical, empirical, and normative issues at the intersection of politics and gender. Books in this series adopt incisive and comprehensive approaches to key research themes concerning the construction and impact of sex and gender, as well as their political and social consequences, across all subfields of political science.

General Editors

Lisa Baldez, *Dartmouth College* (Lead)
Karen Beckwith, *Case Western Reserve University*
Christina Wolbrecht, *University of Notre Dame*

Editorial Advisory Board

Philip Ayoub, *University College London*
Abby Cordova, *University of Notre Dame*
Kristin Goss, *Duke University*
Chryl Laird, *University of Maryland, College Park*
Danielle Thomsen, *University of California, Irvine*
Vesla Weaver, *Johns Hopkins University*
Laurel Weldon, *Simon Fraser University*

Books in the Series

Intersectional Advocacy

Redrawing Policy Boundaries around Gender, Race, and Class

MARGARET PEREZ BROWER
University of Washington

CAMBRIDGE
UNIVERSITY PRESS

CAMBRIDGE
UNIVERSITY PRESS

Shaftesbury Road, Cambridge CB2 8EA, United Kingdom

One Liberty Plaza, 20th Floor, New York, NY 10006, USA

477 Williamstown Road, Port Melbourne, VIC 3207, Australia

314–321, 3rd Floor, Plot 3, Splendor Forum, Jasola District Centre, New Delhi – 110025, India

103 Penang Road, #05–06/07, Visioncrest Commercial, Singapore 238467

Cambridge University Press is part of Cambridge University Press & Assessment, a department of the University of Cambridge.

We share the University's mission to contribute to society through the pursuit of education, learning and research at the highest international levels of excellence.

www.cambridge.org
Information on this title: www.cambridge.org/9781009433099

DOI: 10.1017/9781009433075

First published 2024

A catalogue record for this publication is available from the British Library

Library of Congress Cataloging-in-Publication Data
NAMES: Brower, Margaret Perez, author.
TITLE: Intersectional advocacy : redrawing policy boundaries around gender, race, and class / Margaret Perez Brower.
DESCRIPTION: Cambridge, United Kingdom ; New York, NY : Cambridge University Press, 2024. | Series: Cambridge studies in gender and politics | Includes bibliographical references and index.
IDENTIFIERS: LCCN 2023027777 (print) | LCCN 2023027778 (ebook) | ISBN 9781009433099 (hardback) | ISBN 9781009433044 (paperback) | ISBN 9781009433075 (ebook)
SUBJECTS: LCSH: Women – Violence against – United States. | Intersectionality (Sociology) – United States. | Marginality, Social – United States. | Social service – United States. | United States – Social policy.
CLASSIFICATION: LCC HV6250.4.W65 B758 2024 (print) | LCC HV6250.4.W65 (ebook) | DDC 362.88082–dc23/eng/20231024
LC record available at https://lccn.loc.gov/2023027777
LC ebook record available at https://lccn.loc.gov/2023027778

ISBN 978-1-009-43309-9 Hardback
ISBN 978-1-009-43304-4 Paperback

To Mom and Tasha
For showing me the power of
La Colectiva.

Intersectional Advocacy: The Poem

The law
was never created in her image.
It was meant to confine her.
Erase her.
So that the only trace of her
could be found:
at the margins
that she shared with others.
Their bodies defining the boundaries
Of what was white.
What was man.
What was right.
What was love.
What was
human.
She found herself
somewhere between here
and the arms of her sisters,
brothers, mothers, and daughters.
There is something about being hidden
in plain sight that allows you to move
like no one's watching.
You may have missed her.
Overlooked her.
But that doesn't make her
any less powerful.
She's an artist.
Imaginative.
Creative.
She knows a canvas can
be painted over.
But she never forgets
what's underneath it.
You see impossibilities
Where she sees necessities.
You see separations
Where she sees bridges.
You see stability
Where she sees innovation.
Everything you want to protect
She is ready to dismantle.
It doesn't serve her.
For she's already redesigning,
Redrawing,
Recreating,
Transforming –
You're just missing it.

By Margaret Perez Brower

Contents

Figures

Tables

Acknowledgments

I believe that we produce our best work with a community – people who inspire you, believe in your vision, validate your talents, push back constructively, build ideas with you, and trust you to tell their stories. This book is a product of what it looks like to do work in community, and mine is very special to me. I am most grateful to the organizational leaders and staff featured in this book. Among those I interviewed, they gave up their lunch breaks, set aside time for me at the end of a long workday, and trusted me to tell their stories. They inspired me to write a book that would elevate their incredible courage, creativity, and determination to use policies as tools to build a world we can all live in together freely and equitably. If it were not for the generosity of these organizations, there would be no book to write. I am especially thankful for Women Employed. When I was a graduate student, they invited me to join their advisory board and, in doing so, reminded me of the power of organizing. When I did not have research funds, they donated their own resources to help me field the survey experiment presented in Chapter 6. There were no rewards or incentives to support me, but they believed in uplifting all women no matter what it took. Thank you Judy Miyashita, Amanda Sousa, and Mary Kay Devine for working with me till the very end of the project and making sure I got it right. I also want to give a special thank you to survivors of violence over the years who confided in me and trusted me with their stories. I have held these experiences close to my heart and let them guide me to here, to these advocates, and to this book.

The ideas presented in this book started out as seeds planted by my mother, who dragged me to protests on the gender pay gap, who created feminist spaces for Boricuas, and who made it her life mission that I would be the first in my family to go to college. As a first-generation college student and Latina, I encountered several professors and students who told me not to apply for research opportunities or graduate school or to become an academic. And then I met Joe and Pat Wagner. Joe, thank you for always believing in me and never underestimating me. You are the reason I became a political scientist, and even though you are no longer with us, your spirit and compassion continue to live in me and in this book. Pat, thank you for also constantly believing in me. Your love and encouragement kept me moving forward with the writing of this book. The Office of Undergraduate Studies (OUS) at Colgate also provided me with a supportive community that reassured me early on that the types of experiences I highlight in this book needed to be shared. I am also grateful for the Institute for Recruitment of Teachers (IRT), which opened doors for me in higher education I never dreamed of walking through before their coaching and summer program. Because of IRT, I was able to attend graduate school twice and write the book I always knew lived deep within me.

My supportive family has also made this book possible. I want to recognize my sister Natasha who gave me the courage to write this book. Natasha, thank you for being the fearless one who inspires me to set new precedents in the hope that one day things will be better for everyone. Natasha also designed the cover art for this book. Natasha, you are such a talented artist and graphic designer. Thank you for sharing your gift with me and helping me design a cover that is as powerful as the work inside the book. I want to thank my husband, Anthony, who proudly brags about my work to strangers. When I snuck away to the office on weekends because I was inspired to write this book, you are the one who understood and brought me snacks to sustain my muse. You love me as my authentic self and that gives me the courage to be true to myself in this book. To the Perez family, thank you for welcoming an academic into your community and supporting me. Herb, thank you for loving me in the same language: writing. Jonathan, thank you for giving me reason to be a person you can look up to because it ensured that I wrote with integrity. Traci, thanks for being the first writer in the family and for always supporting my dream to write my own book. Yussef, thank you for being the person that encouraged me to follow my passions wherever they led me, because they led me to this book. Leila, thanks for your enthusiasm and pride in me that make me strive to be my best version of myself in this work.

I was fortunate to have an incredible dissertation committee. Cathy Cohen, thank you for always expecting more from me. Your guidance pushed me to places in my work that were unimaginable before I met you. Thank you for paving the path for young junior scholars like me; your book *The Boundaries of Blackness* continues to be the place that I go to for guidance and inspiration. Michael Dawson, thank you for your patience as I brainstormed with you several ideas before settling with those presented in this book. Will Howell, thank you for your unwavering encouragement and endless support. You continue to be an important cheerleader in my life who has no doubt helped get me to publishing my first book. Jamie Druckman, thank you for validating me and for seeing the potential of my work and perspective, even when it was very different than others. Dara Strolovitch, thank you for setting the bar high with your book *Affirmative Advocacy*, which gave me a starting point for my own work.

I am grateful to my academic community, who introduced me to incredible Black feminist scholars, a tool kit of terms to help me identify "intersectional advocacy," and new ways of thinking. I am grateful to Jamila Michener, Mala Htun, Nadia Brown, and Laurel Weldon for reading this entire book and guiding me in making it the best that it could be. This incredible community of women encouraged me to go above and beyond in capturing the story and presence of "intersectional advocacy." Mala, thank you for early on supporting me as a junior scholar and always pushing me to do my best work. Laurel, thank you for your deep perspective that helped me tighten the empirical work in this book. Nadia, thank you for being a fellow humanist in this work with me and reminding me how important it is to let it into our writing and work. I especially thank Jamila, who has been by my side throughout this process offering valuable perspectives, leading by example, and holding my hand when I needed it. Thank you, Jamila, for always helping me find my way.

I would also like to thank the incredible young women who worked on this project alongside me: Janaki Devendra Kapadia for her enthusiasm in combing through nuanced and overlapping histories of the gender-based violence movement, Madi Norman for her incredible attention to detail and helping me build the hearings dataset on VAWA, and Ali Zimmer for her great intuition in identifying organizations in this movement and supporting me in thinking through their leadership. I know that all of these young and brilliant women will take what they learned from this project and go on to do impactful and important work.

Along the way, people read segments of this work and encouraged me to keep pursuing this book project. Kristin Goss gave me early feedback when this book only encompassed Chapter 3, and she really helped me think through how I wanted to present the advocacy organizations presented in these pages. Christina Bejarano also read an early draft of this chapter and encouraged me to own what I was calling "intersectional advocacy." Jane Junn read my first draft of Chapter 1 on the theory of intersectional advocacy and constructively pushed me to think through its different characteristics, which inspired me to revise it until it truly reflected the actions on the ground. Tabitha Bonilla heard about my work and asked me to present a chapter of it to her undergraduate class; both her and their excitement encouraged me to finish the book. Finally, I am grateful to the dissertation award committee at the Association of Political Science that awarded me "the best dissertation in Public Policy." Sarah Reckhow, David Konisky, and Michael Gusmano, thank you for recognizing the dissertation that this book is based on. Your recognition gave me the confidence I needed to turn it into a book. Across the country and institutions, these very different scholars read my work, validated my project, and helped shape it to become the book it is today.

As I wrote and finished this book, there are several academic friends who supported me on this journey and who often read different chapters and sections. Matt Nelsen and Amanda d'Urso, thank you for reading several of the chapters beforehand and always making my work better. David Knight and Jordie Davies, thank you for reading early drafts of the theory before I knew exactly what intersectional advocacy would become. Devin Judge Lord and Sophie Jacobson, thank you for the workshops during our postdoctoral fellowship at Harvard together that kept me sane and focused. Your feedback really pushed me to the finish line. I am also grateful for the Inequality in America Initiative at Harvard, which granted me a postdoc and the time I needed to finish this book. Elsy Gonzalez, thank you for always knowing this book was within me if I was brave enough to be vulnerable and open with the world. Your friendship has inspired me to be courageous in this book. Patricia Posey, thank you for allowing me to be proud of the book I produced. Noah Schouela, thank you for being the friend that constantly cheered me on even though we study and do very different things. Bianca D'Giovanni, thank you for being my outlet for constantly processing this book experience and seeing me through till the end of it. I am especially grateful to Nancy Thomas, who took me under her wing until it was my time to fly away to the University of Chicago and pursue this book project.

I want to thank my University of Michigan community: David Schoem, Betty Overton, and John Burkhardt. Betty and John, thank you for inspiring me early during graduate school and motivating me to write a book that aligned with my personal theory of change model. David, thank you for making me believe I could do anything that I put my mind to and for encouraging me to dream big.

Finally, I want to give a special thanks to my friend Kumar Ramanathan who read multiple drafts of chapters in this book and stayed as my thought partner till the end of it. Kumar, I am grateful to share an academic world with you in which we build bridges together to the broader public. This book reached its full potential because of you. Behind this book is this entire community of people who made it possible.

INTRODUCTION

Movements to End Gender-Based Violence and Rethinking Feminist Advocacy

> My Master had power and law on his side; I had a determined will. There is might in each.
>
> Harriet Jacobs

In 1996, a headline in the *Washington Post* read: "Abused Immigrant Slain After Plea for Legal Services Help Is Denied" (Claiborne, 1996). The article reported the story of Mariella Batista, who was killed by her intimate partner after she was denied legal services and an order of protection based on her immigration status. Mariella's story highlighted an important gap in public policy on gender-based violence: although survivors qualified for legal services and orders of protection under the recently passed Violence Against Women Act (VAWA), people like Mariella were excluded from such protections due to their immigration status. Legal services, though, were not the only policy benefits Mariella could not access. She was also excluded from public assistance under the 1996 welfare law and was not eligible for public housing benefits through the United States Housing Act. Without legal services, public assistance, and housing options, Mariella struggled to find protection and economic independence from her abuser.

These kinds of policy gaps exacerbate inequalities among women by race, ethnicity, and citizenship status. In the case of VAWA, there were several policy gaps that prevented women like Mariella from being able to access protection and resources under the law. As with many other pieces of legislation in the United States, the Act was structured to address one single issue (i.e., gender-based violence) and did not account for how gender-based violence intersected with other issues such as immigration, poverty, and racism. In doing so, VAWA further marginalized women whose experiences with violence overlapped with these other issues.

However, policies like VAWA changed over the next twenty-seven years to better serve women like Mariella. Since 2014, immigrant women who experience domestic violence are eligible for legal services, can apply for a U Visa for legal immigrant status, are eligible for public housing, and can access public benefits such as welfare. Why does VAWA change over time and what accounts for this transformation? In this book, I argue that "intersectional advocacy" helps explain these transformations and that they are occurring within and beyond VAWA on behalf of intersectionally marginalized groups. I define intersectional advocacy as *advocacy for linkages between policies and issues that reflect the experiences of intersectionally marginalized groups positioned between more than one problem area.* Throughout the pages of this book, I show how intersectional advocacy transforms the US policy system to be more equitable and effective in solving public issues.

I spoke with 43 organizational leaders and examined the behaviors of more than 100 others who participated in congressional hearings on VAWA and it is clear that these advocacy organizations are leading these efforts and in the process are challenging traditional approaches to policymaking. For example, Margarita and Margie from the Latina Network (LN)[1] are constantly thinking about women like Mariella and how traditional law and policy systems fail to fully serve them. Margarita says, "we do not believe that there are master recipes or one-size-fits-all type[s] of [policy] solution[s] to the issue of domestic violence. When other folks come up with those type of models or type of solutions, we're skeptical ... when we're working with communities of color." Instead, Margarita and Margie advocate for issue and policy linkages between domestic violence and other issues such as poverty, housing, immigration, and racism. Margie explains why they advocate for these policy connections: "when people ask me what do [these other issues] have do with domestic violence? [I say] it does in a lot of ways. Because we're thinking about empowerment; we're thinking about creativity; we're thinking about those are the women and moms that support their children when the father or the abusive partner is deported."

Margie and Margarita are not alone. Jada, the director of Sisters Against Violence (SAV),[2] is also advocating for linkages between issues to better serve survivors who are marginalized by both their gender and their race/ethnicity. She says, "women of color have a very – we have a very difficult road because we're always caught in between [issues] ... we cannot have racial justice without gender justice, right? ... [This type of advocacy] can be very difficult, but it's worthwhile." These are the people behind intersectional advocacy, and they are using it to pressure policymakers to adopt issue and policy linkages between gender-based violence and other traditionally distinct

---

[1] This is a pseudonym to protect the organization that participated in this research.
[2] This is a pseudonym to protect the organization that participated in this research.

policy areas: housing, immigration, minimum wage, paid leave, tribal rights, welfare, incarceration, and healthcare.

Examining these practices of intersectional advocacy helps to answer the central question posed in this book: How do advocacy groups intervene in policymaking processes to represent intersectionally marginalized populations? To fully answer this question, I first consider the counterfactual: How do groups that *do not* represent these populations engage in policymaking? By examining these groups' advocacy during the legislative development of the VAWA, I identify how they constructed and reinforced boundaries between problem areas that harmed intersectionally marginalized women. This harm illuminates how the structure of public policy can contribute to growing inequality in the United States and why there is a need to change this existing structure. I then compare this traditional public policy approach with those led by organizations that represent intersectionally marginalized populations. I find that select organizations engage in a distinctive form of advocacy: they establish linkages between VAWA and policies on welfare, immigration rights, and tribal rights (i.e., intersectional advocacy). These linkages address how intersectionally marginalized groups are positioned between more than one policy problem. The remainder of the book presents research on this practice in additional political settings, at varying levels of government, and among different advocacy groups.

Intersectional advocacy in this text is primarily explored within the context of movements to end gender-based violence. These movements are a critical space for understanding the challenges and possibilities of advocating for an issue that often intersects with other problems such as poverty, racism, mass incarceration, immigration, and unaffordable housing. This overlapping feature with other issues makes this movement an ideal observation site for how advocacy groups represent people who are positioned between multiple issues. While this is the primary context for the book, intersectional advocacy as a concept can travel to other policy spaces, additional issues, and alternative state contexts. Intersectional advocacy is ultimately a framework for deciphering a nuanced approach to policymaking and the strategies, leadership, and tactics among those that effectively use it to transform policy and law institutions.

THE POLITICS OF GENDER-BASED VIOLENCE

Gender-based violence is a long-standing problem in the United States. It refers to harm against a person or group of people because of their perceived sex, gender, sexual orientation, and/or gender identity. The advocacy organizations presented in this book focus on two types of gender-based violence: domestic or intimate partner violence and sexual assault. These forms of violence are particularly pervasive in the United States, where more than 10 million adults experience domestic violence each year and a person is sexually assaulted every

68 seconds (Department of Justice, 2020). Between 2016 and 2018, the number of incidences of intimate or domestic partner violence increased by 42 percent (Smith et al., 2018), and in 2018 partner violence accounted for 20 percent of all violent crime (Morgan, 2018). At the same time, the number of reported sexual assaults increased by 146 percent, affecting one in five women (Morgan, 2018). Among people who are marginalized by more than one identity (e.g., gender, sexual orientation, ability, race, ethnicity, immigration status), rates of domestic violence and sexual assault are even greater (The National Center for Victims of Crime, 2018). Current efforts to address gender-based violence are falling short as millions of people become survivors of one of these forms of violence.

Movements to end gender-based violence in the United States have emerged, overlapped, contradicted each other, disappeared, and resurfaced on several occasions over the course of US history. There is not a sole or cohesive movement that addresses gender-based violence but rather a long history of struggles, resistance, organized activism, and advocacy led by different groups of women in varying contexts. The resistance against gender-based violence has taken a variety of forms across different groups of women, because a woman's vulnerability to sexual misconduct, her recourse, her rights recognized by the government, her capacity to resist violence, and the activism, coalitions, and organized groups that she mobilizes to address this issue are all deeply shaped by gender, class, race, and ethnicity.

Carving out a policy space to address gender-based violence is a difficult task that activists and advocacy groups have struggled to create over the last 100 years. It is a difficult task because gender-based violence is enabled and validated by several interlocking practices, norms, laws, and policies that allow people to abuse their power over others. In the following sections, I explain how systems of subordination historically and contemporarily create environments and opportunities for gender-based violence. Advocacy groups respond to these systems in different ways depending on the other identities their members hold. I explain why that is the case by showing how interlocking systems of oppression create variations in gender-based violence by gender, class, race, and ethnicity. I then briefly discuss how individuals and groups respond to these systems with different forms of resistance and what makes the structure of advocacy groups unique in how they respond to these issues. Advocacy groups are not monolithic and are in tension with one another when they differ in the types of changes and impacts that they aim to have on political institutions and US democracy more broadly. I highlight these tensions to carve out the stakes of intersectional advocacy – what happens in its absence to public policy and why it matters for populations of survivors who are marginalized across more than one identity. Finally, I discuss my approach to studying and defining the term "intersectional advocacy" and provide a road map for the remaining chapters that follow.

PATRIARCHAL SYSTEMS AND GENDER-BASED VIOLENCE

Patriarchal systems exist all around the world and have been in place for thousands of years. These systems are consistent laws, policies, practices, values, expectations, cultural norms, relationships, and ideologies that all define and enforce gender inequality. Before 1920 in the United States, these systems granted white men the right to own property, open a bank account or credit card, join the workforce, hold appointments in elected office, vote, and make decisions for the household. Meanwhile, not only were women not granted these same opportunities but, under the doctrine of coverture (marriage law), the husband had ownership rights over his wife and legally was entitled to control her income, property, and residence (Calvo, 2004). While women could vote starting in 1920, it was not until 1970 that they could legally take out a credit card or have property in their own name (Pateman, 2018). Women's subordination to and economic dependence on heterosexual white men allowed for the control and domination of women through gender-based violence (Pateman, 2018). This control was institutionalized among spouses; marital sexual assault was not recognized by law and domestic violence was viewed as a private matter among family members (Alvarez, 1990).

Movements to Confront Patriarchy

As activists and advocacy groups confronted these systems, they did so without institutionalized power. Without this power, several coalitions, activist groups, and advocacy organizations organized what is now referred to as the "anti-rape and battered women's movement." White, middle-class, and heterosexual women predominantly led this movement, which emerged out of feminist consciousness-raising groups, when white housewives would gather together and discuss their common experiences with sexual and domestic violence (Schechter, 1982). White women who participated in these discussions started to change how they talked about violence. Instead of rationalizing acts of violence as private incidents in the home, women from these groups began discussing sexual violence within the context of male-dominated institutions – institutions like the congressional body that passed laws that made men legally superior to women (Koss & Harvey, 1991). At this time, there was not a policy space for gender-based violence, and these groups wanted to change that.

Advocacy groups in this movement sought to create laws that would identify sexual violence as a crime, protect survivors from men, and provide them with medical attention (Arnold, 2017). To provide survivors with medical attention, feminist groups in California and Washington, DC established the first Rape Crisis Centers (RCCs) in 1971. The first domestic violence shelters opened in Arizona and California between 1973 and 1974 (Arnold, 2017). The establishment of RCCs and shelters pressured the federal government by the mid-1970s to provide funding for RCCs through the Law Enforcement Assistance Administration (LEAA) and the Department of Labor's Comprehensive Employment and Training Act (CETA). However, only RCCs that had traditional hierarchical structures and credentialed staff qualified for the available funds (Arnold, 2017). These restrictions meant that grassroots organizations and community health centers that predominantly serviced survivors of color and low-income women with medical care could not access these resources (Wilkes, 2019).

While predominantly white feminists successfully pressured the government to identify sexual violence as a public issue that deserved federal funding, their efforts primarily benefited white, middle-class women who were able to access these types of mainstream institutions. Without these resources, advocacy groups representing American Indian women sought to fill these gaps. For example, the Indian Law Resource Center, the Minnesota Indian Women's Resource Center, and Mending the Sacred Hoop established the first outpatient treatments for American Indian women so that they would not be removed from their land to seek medical help and could access culturally specific healing practices (Le May, 2018).

Meanwhile, other coalitions, such as the Combahee River Collective, were in tension with this movement. The Combahee River Collective was a Black feminist collective among activists in the Boston area in 1974 that brought attention to how both the white feminist movement and the civil rights movement failed to address their needs and interests as Black women and, in particular, as Black lesbians (Taylor, 2017). Even though the "anti-rape and battered women's movement" advanced institutional support for gender-based violence, Black feminists in this collective highlighted the dangers of confronting patriarchal systems without attention to other forms of oppression. Barbara Smith, Demita Frazier, and Beverly Smith were the primary authors of the Combahee River Collective statement, which articulated the difficulties that queer and trans Black women faced due to the multiple forms of oppression they encountered and proposed a new approach to addressing issues such as sexual violence, police brutality, and school segregation that was oriented toward their positionalities. Why was the Combahee River Collective unable to fully support the broader anti-rape movement without attention to multiple forms of oppression? In the next section, I briefly explain how patriarchal systems are interconnected with additional systems of oppression that, together, uniquely impact how people experience gender-based violence by race, ethnicity, and class.

INTERLOCKING SYSTEMS OF OPPRESSION AND VIOLENCE

Patriarchal systems are not alone in inequitably distributing power among the population by identity characteristics; additional systems are similarly engrained into the US fabric of policies, laws, practices, cultural expectations, and values that allow select groups to abuse their power and dominate others. In this section, I highlight a few of these additional systems – colonialism, slavery, white supremacy and capitalism – that all magnify gender-based violence for certain populations by gender, class, race, and ethnicity. These systems are interlocking. They reinforce one another to produce institutionalized gender-based violence against women of color, in ways that are different from other populations such as white middle-class women, LGBTQ women, or men of color. While systems of slavery or colonialism in the United States can be viewed as archaic systems, I argue that they have long-lasting impacts on gender-based violence for these groups today. Understanding how these systems interlock to produce conditions of gender-based violence that are different for low-income women and women of color is important for grasping why intersectional advocacy emerges to connect multiple issue areas together in order to better serve these populations.

Colonialism and Gender-Based Violence

In the initial phase of European colonialism in the Americas, sexual violence against American Indian women was a primary tool of colonialization. These sexual acts of colonialization are recorded as early as the 1500s when Michele de Cuneo wrote in his diary about capturing and sexually assaulting an American Indian woman (Castillo & Schweitzer, 2001). Systematic sexual violence against American Indian women continued for centuries, as colonizers intervened in the reproductive lives of American Indians and sought to gain control of their communities and land (McClintock, 2013). By the 1800s, laws were in place that reinforced and supported this maltreatment of American Indian women. For example, the Indian Act of 1850 allowed white people to indenture American Indian women and children as domestic servants, making them more vulnerable to instances of sexual and domestic violence (Reséndez, 2016).

The interconnectedness between patriarchal systems and colonialism for American Indian women meant the issue of gender-based violence was deeply connected to other issues such as land rights. Thus, it is not surprising that activism led by American Indian women around gender-based violence was intertwined with reclaiming land rights that protected them from colonizers and the US federal government. For example, in the 1800s, Cherokee women organized against the Indian Removal Act and successfully pushed the US government to renegotiate the Treaty of 1819 by providing more sovereignty rights to the Cherokee tribe and protections for American Indian women from sexual and physical abuse by Americans (Miles, 2009).

Colonialism today continues to impact the experiences of American Indian women with gender-based violence. Those living on reservations cannot access the resources or medical attention they need because of the way that the United States structures resources for gender-based violence around sovereignty.

American Indian survivors then are expected to choose between accessing resources they need and appealing to a foreign government for assistance (Jacobs, 2009; Smith, 2001). When violence occurs on reservations, American Indian women have limited access to legal or social service responses, especially when violence is committed on reservations by non-Indians, due to jurisdictional problems and lack of funding (Deer, 2006; Whittier, 2016). Additionally, leaders advocating for these types of changes, such as Winona LaDuke, Louise Erdrich, Eve Ensler, and Patina Park, explicitly linked the gender-based violence of American Indian women with issues of land sovereignty when they filed a submission requesting United Nations (UN) intervention to support the human rights of American Indian women by addressing US colonialism (Le May, 2018). Among this population, addressing gender-based violence cannot be severed from issues of land sovereignty or US colonialism.

In Puerto Rico, advocacy groups such as the Colectiva Feminista en Construcción also underscore how gender-based violence on the island is a product of colonialism. Puerto Rico is a commonwealth territory of the United States; US forces invaded Puerto Rico in 1898 and occupied it during the Spanish-American War. It was not until 1952 that US Congress approved that Puerto Ricans could elect their own governor. The territory and colonial state relationship between Puerto Rico and the United States limits the power and representation of Puerto Ricans to make decisions about how resources on the island are allocated and protected (Roure, 2011). These restrictions impact gender-based violence for Puerto Rican women by creating conditions of poverty that lead to greater instances of femicide and limit Puerto Rico's agency in deciding how to address this issue (Ortiz-Blanes, 2021). Contemporary and historical systems of colonialism uniquely impact American Indian women and Puerto Rican women's experiences with and recourse for gender-based violence in ways that are not applicable to other groups. Moreover, among these populations, gender-based violence is not a standalone issue but one that is interrelated with land sovereignty and a commonwealth status.

Slavery and Gender-Based Violence

From the early colonial period, Black women were subjugated through sexual violence as part of the system of chattel slavery. Paying attention to how Black women historically resisted slavery highlights how sexual violence was deeply interconnected with this system. During chattel slavery, it was a common and legal practice to rape and abuse enslaved women (Feinstein, 2018). Within this oppressive context, Black women resisted these violent practices. For example, Harriet Jacobs, an enslaved Black woman from North Carolina, wrote about her experiences with sexual violence in *Incidents in the Life of a Slave Girl*, documenting the ways she resisted her sexual exploitation and bringing awareness to the violent experiences of enslaved Black women (Jacobs, 1861).

At a time when Black women had little to no sovereignty over their bodies, others, such as Celia Newsom and Margaret Gardner, also engaged in acts of resistance that challenged the laws and practices that had left enslaved women vulnerable to acts of sexual violence. In an act of resistance to avoid her children returning to the abuse that a life of slavery would hold, Margaret Gardner killed her own children (Weisenburger, 1999). Celia Newsom killed her slave master after years of sexual violence, and her trial was the first in which a lawyer attempted to defend a woman by citing the 1845 law in Missouri that declared it a crime "to take any women unlawfully against her will and by force, menace, or duress, compel her to be defiled" (McLaurin, 1991). Newsom's case pioneered the notion that rape could be a defense in a murder case and prompted the question of whether the law could protect enslaved women from sexual assault by their masters. Unfortunately, her experiences with forced intercourse were stricken from the record, and the Missouri Supreme Court denied the appeal of her guilty verdict and sentence (McLaurin, 1991). These examples of Black women's resistance illuminate how their experiences with gender-based violence were deeply tied to the ways in which slavery was used to control them.

Even after the end of chattel slavery in the United States, this system had long-term implications for how and why Black women were continually targeted for sexual and physical violence. After the Civil War and emancipation, white mobs – especially members of the Ku Klux Klan who were in opposition to emancipation – organized and committed acts of sexual violence against Black women (Wade, 1998). In 1866, one of the earliest organized anti-rape efforts occurred when a group of Black women testified before Congress that a white mob engaged in gang rape during the Memphis Riot (Ryan, 1977). Black women such as Lucy Smith, who was sixteen years old at the time, testified about the sexual violence she and others experienced during the riots. These were the first known testimonial experiences with sexual assault delivered in the US Congress (Rosen, 2009). Black women such as Ida B. Wells, Anna Julia Cooper, Fannie Barrier Williams, and others formed Black women's clubs to organize anti-rape and anti-lynching campaigns (Giddings, 2009). These efforts established some of the first Black women's clubs and organizations to address gender-based violence, such as the National Association of Colored Women's Clubs (NACWC), the National League for the Protection of Colored Women, and the National Coalition Against Domestic Violence (Hine, 1989). These groups addressed sexual violence alongside a range of issues important to Black women's experiences, including health, sanitation, education, racism, and women's suffrage (Appiah & Gates, 2005). For Black women, gender-based violence was interconnected with these other issues, because they all stemmed from the historical legacy of slavery.

White Supremacy and Violence

Slavery in the United States in part contributed to broader systems of white supremacy that likewise impacted Black women's experiences with gender-based violence. These systems also impacted women marginalized by other racial and ethnic identities such as Asian American, American Indian, and Latina women. Systems of white supremacy reproduced racial hierarchies that were part of slavery: allocating the most power to white people in the United States and the least amount of power to Black people; other racially and ethnically marginalized groups are then situated in this hierarchy between white and Black people (Omi & Winant, 2014). For example, post-slavery Jim Crow laws, state and local statutes that legalized racial segregation until 1968, explicitly provided more resources, better facilities, opportunities for employment, and education to white people while denying them to African Americans (Ryan, 1977). These laws also reproduced ideologies and beliefs about African Americans as being less deserving of individual rights, benefits, and equal treatment (Lopez, 1994). Black women during the time of Jim Crow were especially vulnerable to acts of sexual violence, which is a tool of domination to reinforce this racial hierarchy.

There were several cases of sexual violence against Black women in the time of Jim Crow that mobilized activist and advocacy groups, especially in 1919 when Recy Taylor and Flossie Hardman were sexually assaulted. When Flossie Hardman's supervisor was found not guilty of committing sexual assault, Black activists organized a boycott that put her employer's grocery store out of business (McGuire, 2010). During these boycotts and twelve years before sparking the Alabama Bus Boycotts, Rosa Parks launched the Alabama Committee for Equal Justice to address sexual violence among women of color. These anti-rape efforts and organizing tactics played a pivotal role in helping to establish organizational infrastructure and strategies of resistance for the civil rights movement (McGuire, 2010).

Systems of white supremacy impact all racially and ethnically marginalized groups in the United States, but they uniquely shape women of color's vulnerabilities to gender-based violence. As Black leaders established organizations such as the National Association for the Advancement of Colored People (NAACP), women like Rosa Parks attempted to influence these organizations to address sexual misconduct and represent Black survivors of sexual violence (Theoharis, 2015). This task was not easy; organizations like the NAACP were not structured to address both racism and sexism, and thus Black women leaders had to persuade other organizational members that issues like sexual violence aligned with the NAACP's mission and goals (Sartain, 2007).

Today, advocacy and activist groups continue to face systems of white supremacy and to emphasize how these systems impact Black women's experiences with gender-based violence differently than other groups. For example, a 100 years later there are still Black women like Flossie Hardman who are segregated in industries that lack financial security and make them more vulnerable to predatory practices of sexual harassment and assault (Conley, 2010; Dozier, 2010; Katznelson, 2005). While Jim Crow is no longer an institution, state-sanctioned violence against Black people is considered the "New Jim Crow" (Alexander, 2020) and continues to further legitimize violence against Black women. Black women's access to social service programs and economic benefits continues to be disproportionately limited, making them more likely to be financial dependent on family members and partners that can abuse this power (Keane & Wolpin, 2010; Wacquant, 2009; Wallace, 2002). For Black women, gender-based violence cannot be separated from police, military, and economic violence against Black communities (Collins, 1998a; C. M. West, 2002; T. C. West, 1999; Wyatt, 1992). This is why advocacy groups representing Black people often identify state violence (i.e., police brutality, incarceration, discrimination) and economic violence (social services and programs that are racially and economically exclusionary) as closely related to intimate partner violence – because they shape the conditions of subordination that provoke violence among communities of color (Beal et al., 1970; hooks, 2014a).

Some of these groups today are part of the Black Lives Matter (BLM) movement. The BLM movement comprises groups that center the leadership of Black women and queer and trans people in seeking the liberation of Black people. Part of this movement encompasses campaigns and efforts to bring awareness to Black women's experiences with state-sanctioned violence, such as the "Say Her Name" campaign, which names Black women who have experienced violence and murder by police officers (Crenshaw et al., 2015; Ransby, 2018). Groups outside this movement are also challenging that gender-based violence is confined to systems of patriarchy. For example, "INCITE!" is a group that advocates for adopting anti-violence strategies that address the broader structures of violence (e.g., colonialism, white supremacy, racism) that shape the conditions of gender-based violence that trans, queer, and women of color experience (INCITE!, 2017). Black women activists and advocates continue to straddle different movements as they voice the ways their experiences with gender-based violence are motivated by interlocking systems of oppression.

Systems of white supremacy also impact other racial and ethnic groups in the United States in ways that intersect with gender-based violence. For example, there is a long history in the United States of institutionalizing sexual narratives about Asian American women. In 1875, the Page Act prevented Chinese women in particular from entering the United States because they were believed to be "lewd" prostitutes, even though many were coming to reunite with their husbands who had already immigrated (Peffer, 1999). Moreover, in the mid-twentieth century, US wars and military bases, particularly in China, Japan, the Philippines, Korea, and Vietnam, introduced American soldiers to Asian women as sex workers or on-base service workers (L. Wong, 2018). Many American troops would come home with perceptions of Asian women as submissive and sexually exploitative (L. Wong, 2018). These perceptions were then normalized via popular culture, especially through two binary and highly sexualized tropes known as the Lotus Flower and the Dragon Lady – both of which reinforced the expectation that Asian women were submissive, sexually subservient, and sexually exotic (Shimizu, 2007). These characters highlight how systems of white supremacy are not just laws or policies embedded in the state but also cultural references, beliefs, and stereotypes enmeshed in US norms.

In 2021, the killing of six Asian Americans – Soon Chung Park, Hyun Jung Grant, Suncha Kim, Yong Yue, Xiaojie Tan, and Daoyou Feng – is interconnected with this history and these engrained systems of white supremacy that reinforce violence against Asian American women. Similar to other examples in this section, advocacy and activist groups such as the Red Canary Song and the Asian American Pacific Islander Coalition Against Hate organized protests to "Stop AAPI Hate" and are contextualizing these sexual and violent acts along this longer history of racism, gender, and migration to the United States (Namkung, 2021). In addition to this activism, advocacy groups such as Kan-Win continue to forge issue connections between sexual violence, racism against Asian Americans, human trafficking, and immigration when advocating against gender-based violence.

Issues of immigration in particular continue to make Asian Americans without US citizenship vulnerable to gender-based violence. This vulnerability determines their options for escaping intimate partner violence and, similar to immigration law from the Page Act of 1875, political institutions reinforce these vulnerabilities. For example, Congress strengthened the power of the male spouse in immigration law, giving him unilateral control over the alien spouse's immigration status, and this control enables abusive spouses to exploit the threat of deportation (Chen, 2000; Sokoloff & Dupont, 2005). Abusers can exploit this legal vulnerability by destroying the survivor's immigration papers, threatening to withdraw their petitions for immigration, and threatening to call authorities to have them deported (Dutton et al., 2000; Orloff & Kaguyutan, 2002; Salcido & Adelman, 2004; Villalón, 2010). Similar to Black women, the gender-based violence of Asian Americans cannot be severed from interconnected issues such as immigration or racism that are products of interlocking systems between patriarchy and white supremacy.

Capitalism and Gender-Based Violence

Capitalism in the United States includes many different types of systems that determine the ownership and control of labor, property, and goods. Here, I focus on the distribution, cost, and management of labor to highlight how capitalism engenders environments for sexual exploitation among the most socioeconomic vulnerable populations. Capitalist systems are reinforced by an absence of public policies and laws to regulate market conditions. Deregulation of the economy enables private actors to make decisions about the free-market economy often at the expense of vulnerable and marginalized workers (Fleming & Morris, 2015; Leong, 2013; Omi & Winant, 2014). For example, private actors can prioritize profit margins instead of paying workers a living wage, offering health benefits, and providing paid-leave options, as well as cutting hours or wages, which affects people's livelihoods (Jayaraman, 2021). Without reliable wages and benefits in these industries, workers are more likely to experience financial instability, poverty, debt, and health issues due to unaffordable treatment (Jayaraman, 2021).

These economic outcomes disproportionately impact low-income women and especially Black and Latina women, the groups most concentrated in these low-wage industries (Woody, 1992). The structure of the distribution of labor by gender and race within low-wage industries is in part explained by racialized history in which people themselves were and are used as capital (i.e., chattel slavery) for the state's economic gains (Dawson, 2014, 2016). In the workforce, poor working conditions enable predatory practices among these workers, such as sexual exploitation among low-wage women workers and especially women of color (Aizer, 2010; Browne, 2000; Kilbourne et al., 1994; Tangri et al., 1982). Because there are fewer protections within these industries for workers, these groups have limited options for recourse, making them prime targets for sexual exploitation (Jayaraman, 2021).

Outside the workforce, these economic circumstances determine the disproportionate distribution of economic resources by gender, race, and class and limit low-income women's financial resources, which heightens their economic reliance on partners, thus diminishing their ability to leave abusive relationships (Ake & Arnold, 2017; Websdale & Johnson, 1997). This economic vulnerability cannot be alleviated among low-income women "as long as poverty denie[s] them safe neighborhoods, adequate health care, decent housing, good childcare, and efficient transportation" (Kessler-Harris, 2003, p. 268). The US capitalist system provides the incentives, conditions, and laws for the free-market economy to monetize goods and services without having to account for the extent to which they are unaffordable or inaccessible to people by gender, class, and race. As low-income women navigate low-wage industries that suppress their wages, do not provide healthcare benefits, lack childcare options, and do not offer consistent hours of work, they are increasingly at risk for both economic and sexual exploitation inside and outside the workforce. Capitalism and patriarchal systems thus reinforce one another by coproducing the conditions for economic and gender inequality.

As early as the late 1800s, several organizations and activists addressed patriarchal and capitalist systems together through labor policy advocacy (Kessler-Harris, 2003). In 1844, the Lowell Female Labor Reform Association testified before the Massachusetts legislature for new labor requirements that would improve women's physical well-being (Mattina, 1986). Since this historical moment, advocacy organizations such as the Women's Trade Union League, the National Federation of Business and Professional Women's Clubs, Ladies' Auxiliaries (LA) of the International Union of Mine, Mill and Smelter Workers (IUMMSW), and the National Council of Negro Women emerged throughout the twentieth century to focus on gender, class, and racial inequality through labor policy changes. Today, organizations are connecting these work conditions additionally to the issue of gender-based violence. For example, Women Employed advocates for paid-leave laws, affordable caregiving policies and programs, and eliminating the tipped minimum wage in relation to their policy advocacy to address sexual violence in the workplace. Women Employed is an advocacy organization based in Chicago that seeks to address economic inequality among women through policymaking and advocacy. For Women Employed advocates, it is impossible for them to address gender-based violence in the workforce without also changing laws, policies, and programs that address how capitalist practices reinforce economic inequality by gender, class, race, and ethnicity. One policy area alone cannot address the multitude of ways that economic inequality is embedded throughout normalized and accepted capitalistic practices. In Chapter 6, I share how Women Employed pursues policy linkages between these issues and how these connections mobilize their supporters around these policy initiatives that undercut these systems.

There are additional systems of oppression that interlock with patriarchy that uniquely shape how different groups by race, ethnicity, class, ability, and sexual orientation are vulnerable to, experience, and are able to access recourse for gender-based violence. I briefly highlight in this section on "Interlocking Systems of Oppression and Violence" a few of these systems to illustrate Four different points: (1) historical systems of oppression connect to contemporary conditions of gender-based violence; (2) different systems of oppression uniquely impact groups by gender, class, race, and ethnicity; (3) interlocking systems of oppression reveal how issues become interconnected with gender-based violence; and finally, (4) activist and advocacy groups have been making these connections for hundreds of years. In Chapters 1 and 2, I delve deeper into these points as I show how public policy can be a mechanism for reproducing and maintaining these interlocking systems of oppression. Each of these points is relevant to how advocacy groups are oriented today around the issue of gender-based violence and why select groups engage in what I am calling "intersectional advocacy."

ADVOCACY GROUPS

Advocacy groups play a particular role in these movements to end gender-based violence and, at some level, accept the structure of US institutions in that they often do not propose completely dismantling or rebuilding them. Instead, they propose changes in laws, policies, the representation of political officials, and how political categories are defined, implemented, and regulated by the state. These strategies have advantages and limitations. Advocacy organizations are able to influence legal and policy changes to some degree, but they cannot eliminate the structures or the systems of inequality that produced them.

In considering the change these groups can affect through public policy, I follow the approach in Roth (2004) for understanding advocacy organizations by identifying the nuances of how these groups approach and view US institutions differently. In doing so, the "recognition of feminist organizing in different communities allows us to ask questions about who came to feminism, how they came to feminism, and how feminism was done in different social spaces" (Roth, 2004, p. 4). I apply this gradient approach to understanding advocacy groups by considering a variation in how organizations engage in what Strolovitch (2007) calls "affirmative advocacy." Affirmative advocacy is a framework of representational redistribution that recognizes equitable representation for disadvantaged groups (e.g., women of color, immigrants) and requires proactive efforts to overcome biases and inequalities within American political institutions. According to Strolovitch (2007), advocacy organizations engage in this practice "to redistribute resources and attention to issues affecting intersectionally disadvantaged subgroups in order to level the playing field among groups" (p. 10). In this book, I build off Strolovitch's (2007) conceptualization of affirmative advocacy by examining not only how these groups represent disadvantaged groups and redistribute resources among them but also how they directly engage with US policy institutions to advance these outcomes.

Scholars have used the term "intersectional advocacy" in a broad way to identify advocacy that "occurs on behalf of multiply disadvantaged subgroups" (Dwidar, 2021; English, 2021; Marchetti, 2014). This growing body of research focuses on who organizations represent (English, 2021; Marchetti, 2014; Strolovitch, 2007) and how they advocate for these interests, especially through lobbying (Dwidar, 2021; Junk, 2019; Lorenz, 2020; Marchetti, 2014) and rulemaking (English, 2021). These studies tend to characterize all advocacy undertaken on behalf of multiply disadvantaged groups as intersectional. While this work has contributed valuable insights, especially for our understanding of the politics of representation, it has not engaged with how these very systems, institutions, and processes can contribute to the oppression and marginalization of the very populations these groups are representing. In these pages, governance structures (e.g., Congress, federalism), policymaking processes (e.g., problem definition, lobbying, rulemaking), and responses to policy outcomes (e.g., policy feedback, social movements) that all influence policymaking are contested by the advocacy groups presented here. *By illuminating the American state's policies throughout this book, I highlight advocacy groups that not only represent multiply disadvantaged subgroups but also intervene in the policymaking process in ways that directly challenge and transform these structures.*

In my analysis of advocacy groups, I consider Strolovitch's (2007) distribution of resources to these groups across policy issues, and in the process capture the types of policy institutions that can be reconfigured to serve these purposes. I argue this engagement is unique to organizations representing groups that are marginalized by more than one identity. This positionality motivates a distinct form of advocacy that I refer to as "intersectional advocacy." I argue that organizations engaging in this practice operate very differently from traditional organizations in that they challenge the political boundaries of policies. In Chapter 2, I show that these traditional groups do not contest these boundaries but instead reinforce them. Organizations practicing intersectional advocacy, on the other hand, are reimagining the function and structure of policy institutions by challenging these boundaries. This approach to policymaking is innovative, imaginative, and more representative of the needs of intersectionally marginalized communities. Although intersectional advocacy alone will not eliminate sexism, racism, and inequality in America, it does provide new infrastructures that reduce the impact of these inequalities in concrete ways for intersectionally marginalized groups today. It is also a practice that benefits not only survivors of violence but other groups who are similarly positioned between multiple issues.

DEFINING INTERSECTIONAL ADVOCACY

I offer a specified definition of intersectional advocacy to help us understand an innovative and important practice to transform the US policy system, but "intersectional advocacy" is also a collective project. This concept grows out of Black feminist literature, social movement scholarship, gender and sexuality studies theories, research in political science on advocacy groups and representation, and theories of institutional change in public policy. In Chapter 1, I take the time to credit and highlight the ways these different scholars have contributed to this work and concept. Briefly here, though, I also want to capture their contributions.

Black feminist thought grounds the concept of intersectional advocacy because "the necessity of addressing all oppressions is one of the hallmarks of Black feminist thought" (King, 1988, p. 43). Black feminists articulate how interlocking systems of oppression produce conditions of marginalization by especially race and ethnicity but also by sexual orientation and class (Cohen, 2005; Collins, 1998a, 1998b; Crenshaw, 1997; Davis, 2011; hooks, 2014a, 2014b; Morga & Anzaldua, 2015; White, 1999). Social movement scholars build on this work by examining how groups respond to these conditions of oppression and marginalization with activism and social movements (Tormos, 2017; Townsend-Bell, 2011; Weldon, 2012; Yuval-Davis, 2006).

Intersectionality in this context is studied in lots of different forms: intersectional synthesis (Cole 2008; Curtin et al., 2015; Greenwood, 2008; Irvine et al., 2019), intersectional praxis (Tormos-Aponte, 2019), intersectional consciousness (Roberts & Jesudason, 2013; Tormos-Aponte, 2019; Weldon, 2006), and political intersectionality (Crenshaw, 1997). These different concepts of intersectionality are meant to identify how groups build a consciousness around intersectionality, address power asymmetries within their organizations, and identify their organizing approaches to overlapping forms of oppression.

The concept of "intersectional advocacy" is added to this collection of terms to help specify how advocacy groups engage with public policy institutions that represent intersectionally marginalized populations. What the concept of "intersectional advocacy" adds to this growing and substantial literature is how advocacy organizations reconfigure public policy institutions to better serve intersectionally marginalized groups. In this book, I argue that issue and policy linkages are key to this reconfiguration, which is why I am using the term "intersectional advocacy" to precisely mean *advocacy for linkages between policies and issues that reflect the experiences of intersectionally marginalized groups positioned between more than one problem area.* By offering up this definition, my hope is that this concept more precisely identifies the connections between marginalization, intersectionality, and systems of oppression that these scholars and I all highlight as fundamental to addressing inequality in the United States.

INTERSECTIONALLY MARGINALIZED GROUPS

I use the term "intersectionally marginalized" to reference people who are marginalized across more than one axis of their identity. These groups are "intersectionally marginalized" in that they experience marginalization and oppression at the intersection of multiple identities that uniquely shape their experiences. There are many different ways these identities can intersect, and thus several groups that fit within this term such as women of color, low-income women, immigrant women, LGBTQ people of color, and disabled women. These examples include groups marginalized across identity categories of gender, race, ethnicity, class, ability, and sexual orientation. In this book, I primarily focus on survivors who are intersectionally marginalized by gender, class, race, and ethnicity. By homing in on their experiences, I am better able to clearly articulate how public policy is structured to produce inequalities among this group. There are a few reasons for this choice. Since this book is situated within movements to address gender-based violence, gender is a focal point for this work. Gender is an identity in these movements that has organized collective actions among advocates and activists. Gender has also remained a contentious identity in these movements, as activists and advocacy groups have wrestled with "who" the term "women" represents (Carruthers, 2018; Crenshaw, 1997; hooks, 2014b; Taylor, 2017).

Considerable attention by activists, advocates, and scholars focuses on how the collective identity of "women" in these movements favored the lived experiences of cis, white, heterosexual, and middle-class women while leaving out the experiences of all women of color, and especially Black queer women (Babcox & Belkin, 1971; Beal et al., 1970; hooks, 2000; McGuire, 2010; Richie, 2000; Sokoloff & Dupont, 2005). Within this void, advocacy organizations emerged primarily around the collective identities of race or ethnicity and gender. This history of advocacy and the wide range of advocacy groups today that still organize their efforts around class, gender, race, and ethnicity are another reason why I focus on advocacy groups that represent these marginalized identities in this text.

Advocacy organizations that represent intersectionally marginalized groups such as women with disabilities, LGBTQ women, queer Black women, nonbinary people of color, and LGBTQ youth are all important groups that require prioritization and depth that I am not able to provide in this book. While I posit that intersectional advocacy should also apply to these groups, the empirical work presented in this book does not provide evidence that this is the case. It is my hope that this book's research can inform and inspire others to consider how intersectional advocacy can serve these additional groups and the ways in which organizations serving these groups might expand, contest, and revise the practices that I examine here. Meanwhile, I reference these other axes of marginalization when I can draw from other scholarship that centers their experiences and focus most of my attention on low-income women and women of color. When I use the term "women" to reference these intersectionally marginalized groups, I am using it to include all people that identify in this way (i.e., nonbinary, cis and trans women).

POLICIES AS SITES OF CONTESTATION

I focus on advocacy groups within the context of policymaking because they are a primary lever through which governments operate to reproduce inequalities. I will argue in the following chapters that these policymaking processes reveal the relationships between the structure of the state and the concrete realities of gender, racial, and economic inequalities that survivors of violence face. For example, at the time of the New Deal, Old Age Insurance (OAI), which is now Social Security, included provisions that disqualified workers in the agricultural and domestic industries (Gordon, 2012; Lieberman & Lapinski, 2001; Mettler & Soss, 2004; Williams, 2004). These industries were predominantly comprised of Black women workers (Mettler, 1998). Although OAI was intended to be a policy that improved the economic welfare of Americans, the structure of the policy (i.e., its provisions and eligibility requirements) produced gender and racial inequities when Black women were not eligible for these resources.

Decades later, the VAWA included similar types of exclusionary provisions. When VAWA was enacted, the policy was intended to provide women with additional safety, protection, and resources from violence by establishing shelters, orders of protection, and public benefits for survivors of violence. However, as mentioned, immigrant survivors without formal citizenship status were disqualified (Villalón, 2010). Similar to OAI, the structure of VAWA produced gender and racial inequities, where immigrant women were not eligible for these resources and protections by the state. Moreover, since immigration law is located outside the boundaries of VAWA, this Act alone did not completely protect or serve immigrant women without citizenship status. These are the additional policy structures maintained by the government that reproduce and maintain these inequalities. The advocacy groups that I study in this book are acutely aware of these policy structures, which is why policy institutions are a primary site of contestation for them. At the same time, these groups view policy institutions as redeemable and as key levers for social change. They do not seek to fully dismantle them but instead to repurpose them for intersectionally marginalized groups.

To advocate for these changes, groups and individuals practicing intersectional advocacy intervene in the policymaking process at different stages and at different levels to create issue and policy linkages between seemingly separate problems, laws, and policies. Issue linkages occur when these groups successfully persuade policymakers to adopt rhetorical and conceptual connections between one problem (e.g., gender-based violence) and another (e.g., mass incarceration). Policy linkages include amendments that connect separate legislation, laws, and policies to one another. These linkages can also be newly proposed policies, statutes, and laws that bring together stakeholders working across multiple problem areas. Throughout the remaining chapters, I argue that, to effectively persuade policymakers to adopt issue and policy linkages, these advocates establish policy infrastructure to hold these interventions. Policy infrastructure can be new coalitions, precedents for establishing policy linkages advocates can point back to, or networks with legislatures that support these linkages and participate in committees across issues. Both issue and policy linkages are presented throughout the book to showcase how this practice varies depending on the level of government advocacy groups are targeting for their efforts (e.g., municipal, state, federal), the types of institutional boundaries they face in making these connections (e.g., restricted funding, precedents set for laws and policies that are written separately from one another, issues pitted against each another in the problem definition of the policy), where they intervene in the policy process (e.g., problem definition, policy proposal, implementation), and which intersectionally marginalized groups they represent (e.g., Black women, Latinas, low-income women). I will return to these terms throughout the book and show how they help us understand the strategies advocacy groups use to intervene in policymaking processes in ways that fundamentally challenge how we approach policymaking in the United States.

REDEFINING POLICY EFFECTIVENESS

The research presented throughout the chapters of this book challenges traditional and accepted ideas of how we evaluate the effectiveness of public policy. For example, in Chapter 2, I present an analysis of the congressional hearings on the VAWA that illustrates the harms this Act had in the 1990s on women of color as well as immigrant and low-income women survivors. I also reference work from scholars like Bumiller (2009), Richie (2012), and Whittier (2016) that illustrates how some of these harms were facilitated by tethering the VAWA to the Violent Crime Control and Enforcement Act of 1994. This 1994 Act allocated nearly 10 billion dollars for new prison construction and the authorization of the expansion of mass incarceration of people of color, including many survivors of sexual and domestic violence (Bumiller, 2009; Whittier, 2016). If a policy mass-incarcerates the US population disproportionately by class, race, and ethnicity – which includes survivors of violence themselves – is it an effective policy? Were there alternative policies that could have been tethered to the VAWA in 1996 that would have addressed gender-based violence but not resulted in the same types of harmful consequences? These are the questions I answer in Chapters 2 and 3.

The US policy system is designed to evaluate effectiveness in terms of whether it impacts the majority of a target population. One of the arguments I make in this book is that if we continue to evaluate policies in this way, they will have disproportionate effects on the most marginalized and vulnerable populations. Additionally, I make the case in Chapter 4 that this policy approach will also never fully address social issues such as gender-based violence, poverty, homelessness, or unfordable healthcare. Intersectional advocacy is an alternative approach to policymaking that I argue more comprehensively addresses these social problems. By linking policies across social issues to intentionally address how these problems overlap in the lives of intersectionally marginalized groups, we close policy gaps and start to address the underlying systems that perpetuate inequalities in the United States.

MY APPROACH

Provided that there are these nuanced and layered aspects to advocacy groups, I take a mixed-method approach to peel back these layers one by one to get at the core of intersectional advocacy. Each of these layers necessitates a tailored methodological approach that fits the context and activities of these organizations. Thus I draw from several different types of methods and sources: archival textual analyses, qualitative interviews, and survey experiments. I use these methods to study how advocacy organizations advocate for intersectionally marginalized populations in varying policy contexts.

Advocacy is a multifaceted phenomenon. It includes an ecosystem of complex organizations with varying structures, staff, sizes, descriptive representation, budgets, mission statements, origins, leadership styles, visions, and orientations to politics (Berry, 2003; Gen & Wright, 2020b, 2020c; Gronbjerg, 1991). This ecosystem is situated within a broader landscape of movements, politics, and current events (Cobble, 2004; Cohen, 1985; Hidalgo, 2015; Weldon, 2006). Within organizations, there are unique dynamics that include conflicts, disagreements, leadership processes, subgroups of supporters that are prioritized or marginalized, organizational growth, leadership changes, and staff turnover (Chen & Graddy, 2010; Child & Grønbjerg, 2007; Jang & Feiock, 2007; Vanner & Dugal, 2020). The relationships between advocacy organizations and their supporters are evolving and constantly changing as both inform one another's goals, visions, and expectations for the organizational work (Brower, 2022; Simonofski et al., 2021). These organizations use political strategies to advance their policy goals, including tactics for pressuring political officials; framing approaches for making their proposals convincing; relationship building with other coalitions, politicians, and allies; and infrastructure building as they imagine new structures that can hold their interventions (Dwidar, 2021; English, 2021; Junk, 2019; Lorenz, 2020; Marchetti, 2014; Strolovitch, 2018). Additionally, the tangible impacts these groups have on national conversations, the design and implementation of public policy, how public officials are elected, when laws are overturned or enacted, and how the structure of political institutions changes over time are also important for understanding these groups (Bonner, 2009; Clemens, 1997; Lorenz, 2020; Phinney, 2017).

Each chapter presented in this book offers a unique lens to view these groups in action as they make strategic decisions to engage in intersectional advocacy. To fully understand why organizations participate in this practice, I open the book by bringing the American state into full view in Chapter 1 and show the ways in which its policies reinforce gender, economic, and racial inequality. I situate this institutional function within a larger historical context of patriarchal systems that I argue reproduce these inequalities in ways that must be understood when it comes to addressing gender-based violence. The chapter then introduces the concept and theoretical underpinnings of intersectional advocacy, which is an outgrowth of Black feminism theory, social movement scholarship, race and ethnic politics, and gender and sexuality studies, as well as the empirical work that follows.

To fully understand the innovative potential of intersectional advocacy, one needs to understand the traditional policymaking process that it confronts. In Chapter 2, I make a case that policy boundaries contribute to inequality in the United States. Drawing from a textual analysis of the congressional hearings on the VAWA and newspaper articles covering the Act, I present evidence that the policy boundaries in the VAWA harmed intersectionally marginalized groups. Moreover, I show how advocacy organizations that did not represent intersectionally marginalized groups contributed to the setting of these policy boundaries by participating in the policymaking process. By showing how advocacy groups that do *not* represent intersectionally marginalized populations intervene in the policymaking process, I illustrate what is at stake with traditional approaches and the ways that mainstream advocacy groups have participated in it.

In Chapter 3, I start to answer the overarching question of this book: How do advocacy groups intervene in policymaking processes to represent intersectionally marginalized populations? Here, I examine how advocacy organizations representing intersectionally marginalized groups have participated in this policymaking process. Analyzing the testimony and statements from advocacy groups during congressional hearings on the reauthorization of VAWA over the past twenty-five years, I find that select organizations were successfully advocating for linkages between policies and issues that reflected the experiences of intersectionally marginalized groups positioned between more than one problem area. These linkages were between VAWA and policies on welfare, immigration, and tribal rights. In this chapter, I identify this practice as "intersectional advocacy" and explain how advocacy groups in this setting engaged in it to change VAWA policy over time. I found that VAWA changes in remarkable ways that better represent and serve intersectionally marginalized groups.

In Chapter 4, I consider the applicability of this practice by asking to what extent does participation in intersectional advocacy vary depending on the level of government or political context where the advocacy takes place? Drawing from a qualitative analysis of forty-three interviews with organizational leaders, I examine how intersectional advocacy was applied at the municipal, state, and federal levels. I find that these organizational leaders strategically established policy connections between gender-based violence and unaffordable housing, inaccessible healthcare, and mass incarceration. I explain how issue and policy linkages vary across these problem areas and the level of government that advocates are situated within. I also describe the types of institutional boundaries they encountered as they intervened in these policymaking processes. Ultimately, I find the practice of intersectional advocacy transcended these three different levels of government and that groups deployed unique strategies depending on these varying contexts.

What explains why these groups take on the practice of intersectional advocacy? In Chapter 5, I answer this question from an organizational perspective. Drawing again from the qualitative analysis of interviews with organizational leaders, I examine the features of their advocacy organizations. I find that there are four constitutive features of their organizations that were related to their engagement in intersectional advocacy. Despite a commitment to intersectional feminism, one of these organizations did not have all of these features and it also did not fully participate in intersectional advocacy. By discussing this case, I demonstrate how an analysis of the four organizational features also helps to identify why groups such as these do not fully take on this practice. I then explain how organizations with commitments to intersectionally marginalized groups but that have not actualized them through intersectional advocacy can change their varying organizational structures to take on this approach.

What remains then from this organizational analysis is an examination of the role of supporters in intersectional advocacy. While membership in women's advocacy organizations has decreased over the years (Skocpol, 2013), supporters who volunteer their time to advocacy organizations to advance their policy goals have been largely overlooked. Having volunteered on an advocacy board for a women's organization for five years, I was struck by how important supporters are to these organizations. In Chapter 6, I present two original survey experiments with the supporters of this organization that also engages in intersectional advocacy. Each experiment contained authentic policy platforms that presented either an intersectional advocacy approach or a traditional single-issue policy alternative to supporters. The findings from these experiments answer my final question: Does intersectional advocacy resonate with the intersectionally marginalized populations it aims to serve, and if so, to what extent does it mobilize them to participate in the policymaking process? I find that, yes, intersectional advocacy will mobilize supporters, especially intersectionally marginalized women of color, but only if these groups perceive a connection between the two issues linked by the policy platform. I also find evidence that there is a tool that organizations can use to ensure supporters make these connections. This chapter highlights the role of supporters in advancing these policy efforts while showcasing tangible and practical approaches organizations can use today to engage in intersectional advocacy.

Finally, while I study intersectional advocacy in the context of movements to end gender-based violence, this concept transcends across other movements and additional policy spaces. The book concludes with a discussion of the current state of policymaking in the United States and how intersectional advocacy illuminates the many policy gaps that contribute to inequality. Throughout this discussion, I reference the challenges and the possibilities of applying this practice in US politics. If we are invested in addressing inequality and oppression, we need to take a closer look at these policy systems and reimagine them. Intersectional advocacy provides a road map for rethinking these institutions and policymaking practices.

Together, these chapters provide an examination of the policymaking process from the vantage point of advocacy organizations – how they understand it, participate in it, challenge it, and how some advocate for transforming it. Those that aim to transform it by advocating for linkages between problem areas, policies, laws, and statutes are what I call "intersectional advocates." Throughout this book, I explain several different factors that motivate this participation in the policymaking process and the strategies these groups deploy to successfully make these connections. As these advocates contest and reimagine policy, they encounter several institutional boundaries that reinforce a policy system where issues are separated from one another. I show how they traverse these boundaries and, in the process, fundamentally influence the reconfiguration of these policy institutions. These reconfigurations seek to close gaps in public policies that affect millions of people in the United States.

Before engaging in this research, I spent more than five years working directly with nonprofit advocacy groups and four of those years serving on an advisory board for a women's advocacy organization. Today, I continue to work directly with dozens of these groups. I share this experience because it provides me with an up-close-and-personal look into the activities, challenges, and innovation that take place within these organizations. The people leading these groups are working at overcapacity, are poorly funded, and are overextended as they try to solve nationally pressing social issues with limited resources and power. And yet, they are extraordinary in their drive, creativity, innovation, perseverance, direct impact on the communities they serve, and persuasiveness to policy and lawmakers as well as inspiring, especially to me. It is my hope that, after reading this book, you feel compelled to support them in this work. Whether you are a policymaker, lawmaker, politician, activist, educator, social worker, student, or concerned denizen, it is my hope that these groups compel you to be a part of this change. The stakes of not supporting these organizations and intersectional advocacy are high: growing inequality, public issues that worsen over time, and people that continue to be trapped within policy gaps. These advocacy groups cannot do it all alone.

I

Theory of Intersectional Advocacy

> There is no such thing as a single-issue struggle because we do not live single-issue lives.
>
> Audre Lorde

What does bail bond reform have to do with gender-based violence? For the organization Communities for Survivors (CFS), these two issues are interlocking. The executive director, Angela, shared why she is coleading a campaign for a bail bond reform bill. She says there is a need for "a good bill that would make the criminal justice system fairer for people of color in general and people who do not have the economic means to bail themselves out ... racial justice is part of survivor justice ... it helps us fight back on the narrative that tough on crime is supportive of victims of violence." While Angela may see the connections between the criminal justice system, bail bond reform, and justice for survivors of violence, the US policy system is not structured in a way that embraces these multi-issue interventions. Across levels of governance, these issues are separated from each other through institutions and practices such as policy design, bureaucratic organizations, and budget appropriations (Thurston, 2018; Weir et al., 1988). This separation makes it difficult to address these multiple issues simultaneously. Angela is undertaking an uphill political battle that requires her to strategically consider how to (1) redraw issue boundaries to reflect the issue connections between gender-based violence, racial justice, and the criminal justice system; (2) develop policy linkages that address these issues together; and (3) change the institutions and structures that reinforce these problems. Angela's undertaking is a form of advocacy that is practically and theoretically distinct from other types of political engagement. I refer to it in this book as "intersectional advocacy."

I define intersectional advocacy as *advocacy for linkages between policies and issues that reflect the experiences of intersectionally marginalized groups positioned between more than one problem area.* Intersectional advocates like Angela seek to change how the US policy system defines, categorizes, and constructs policies around issue areas to better reflect how intersectionally marginalized groups are positioned between more than one problem. Throughout this book, I use the term "intersectionally marginalized" to describe populations that are marginalized across more than one axis of their identity (e.g., gender, race, ethnicity, class, sexual orientation). Angela seeks to change how the policy system responds to Black women by intervening in the policymaking process to propose linkages between racial justice, criminal justice reform, and gender-based violence. Sometimes these linkages are conceptual: defining and framing these problems in relation to one another. Other times these linkages are policies in the forms of amendments, provisions, and new legislation that connect a policy on criminal justice reform to another on gender-based violence. Intersectional advocates like Angela are strategic in how they confront the US policy system to propose and push for these linkages.

We can understand her strategies, behaviors, and motivations through the lens of several scholars from political science, public policy, sociology, gender and sexuality, race and ethnic studies, and Black feminism. The concept of intersectional advocacy emerges from bridging the work of these scholars across disciplines to understand how advocacy groups like CFS, which Angela represents, intervene in the policymaking process to represent intersectionally marginalized populations. In this chapter, I draw from this scholarship to explain a distinct form of advocacy that fundamentally aims to change the US policy system in ways that we need to understand if we are committed to developing and implementing policies that are inclusive, equitable, and just. To fully communicate this radical shift in policymaking, in the next few sections I explain how existing US policies and governmental systems produce inequality among people across race, ethnicity, class, and gender.

THE AMERICAN STATE

The concept of intersectional advocacy necessitates an understanding of the United States as a "state," which highlights the different layers of government and statehood that shape policymaking. The state as a concept has been theorized by scholars in different ways. Early scholars defined the state predominantly as a political organization associated with violence, "a human community that claims the monopoly of the legitimate use of physical force within a given territory" (Weber, 1965, p. 33). Within this definition, Weber (1965) outlines the functions of a state: legislative action, protection and public order, administration of justice, administrative branches to cultivate education, social welfare or other cultural interests, and a military. These administrative features and taxation as a mechanism to maintain these functions legitimize state power (Tilly, 1993). Institutional arrangements then regulate the lives of civil society through governance, laws, and policies (Levi, 1989). These conceptions of the state are largely materialistic, emphasizing the power of statehood through force and its many institutional arrangements. Yet state power is not solely derived from physical forces.

State formation illuminates the ways in which the state is also immaterial – and these features are critically important for intersectional advocacy, which contests their meaning. Through state formation, institutional arrangements are codified and embedded with immaterial concepts of administration, ideology, concepts of family rights, beliefs about race and gender, and power dynamics in civil society (Adams, 2007; Corrigan & Sayer, 1991; Day, 2002; Gorski, 2003; Ikegami, 1997; Wong, 2018). As Gorski (2003) underscores: "states are not only administrative, policing, and military organizations. They are also pedagogical, corrective, and ideological organizations" (p. 165). These immaterial components of the state are central to processes of state formation that account for how the state reinforces or changes the meaning of these ideologies over time. Indeed, statehood is a culmination of this process by which "species of capital" are established (e.g., fiscal systems, citizenship requirements, school systems, police force) that allow the state to be "the holder of a sort of meta-capital granting power over other species of capital or their holders" (Bourdieu, 1998, p. 67). It is through this "meta-capital granting power" that the state elevates the status of some groups while diminishing those of others. This disproportionate distribution of power, status, and resources often occurs through law and policymaking.

Scholars attuned to how these processes result in racial inequalities argue that the American state is also a "racial state." Omi and Winant (2014) make the case that "through policies that are explicitly or implicitly racial, state institutions organize and enforce the racial politics of everyday life" (p. 105). Lieberman and Lapinski (2001), for example, found that the Aid to Dependent Children (ADC) policy, when it was distributed federally, resulted in large racial disparities: eligible Black people received less coverage than their white counterparts. These outcomes are part of a process of exclusion by the state that are not only racialized but also gendered. Another example is one of the centerpieces of the New Deal, Old Age Insurance (OAI), which included provisions that disqualified workers in the agricultural and domestic industries (Gordon, 2012; Lieberman & Lapinski, 2001; Mettler & Soss, 2004; Williams, 2004). This was an implicit racial and gendered policy; nine out of ten African American women workers were ineligible for OAI based on these criteria (Mettler, 1998). Although OAI never explicitly denied African American women these policy benefits, by excluding industries where they were concentrated, this policy had a racialized and gendered effect. The American state also creates conditions for income inequality through policymaking. Financial deregulation by the government is one example. Financial deregulation policies provide corporations with more discretionary power over their workers; groups such as the Labor Law Reform Group then leveraged this status to develop a strike insurance fund that denied union demands for wage increases (Linder, 1999). Efforts such as these led to the decline of both unions and existing union power, which largely affected low-income workers who depended on these unions to provide them with fair working conditions (Hacker & Pierson, 2010). Thus, the state can also reproduce income inequalities by not implementing policies that would better protect more vulnerable populations.

The state, through these many different functions (e.g., institutions, laws, policies, and financial appropriations), regulates the lives of people by determining their access to opportunities, resources, and power. The federal government's delegation of the implementation of social welfare programs to subnational actors meant that local bureaucrats and policymakers exercised discretion to disproportionately deprive Black people of access to welfare assistance, food stamps, health insurance, and housing assistance. For Black women who retired later in life, the state's exclusion of agricultural and domestic industries from OAI meant that Black women lost thousands of dollars over their lifetime compared to their white counterparts. For blue-collar workers who suffered injuries, the state's financial deregulation of corporations meant some of them did not access unions to advocate for paid leave or disability insurance. Advocates of gender, class, and racial justice recognize how the state functions in these ways through public policies, perceiving the state as "sites of struggle" (Randall & Waylen, 1998, p. 15).

Intersectional advocacy is a response to how the state regulates the lives of marginalized groups through policies, laws, and the distribution of resources that create conditions of inequality by gender, race, and class. Groups practicing this form of advocacy view law and policymaking processes as important sites of intervention, for these sites also open up opportunities to replace old repertoires that are "parochial, direct and segmented" with new ones that are "national, flexible, and based on modular forms of actions" (Tarrow, 2011, p. 55). Intersectional advocacy emerges from an understanding of how the multidimensional state harbors, produces, and reproduces inequalities by differences in identity such as race, ethnicity, class, and gender. In the next section, I focus on how ideologies about gender translate into state policies and laws that reinforce gender-based violence.

PATRIARCHY AND GENDER-BASED VIOLENCE

There are many types of systems, practices, policies, and laws that shape people's vulnerabilities to violence and their recourse for addressing this issue. The concept of patriarchy is useful for understanding underlying ideologies about gender and domination that inform these state functions. Patriarchy captures processes of domination that lead to outcomes in which "men are the powerful, women the powerless; adults the powerful, children the powerless; white people the powerful, Black people and other nonwhite peoples the powerless. In a given situation, whichever party is in power is likely to use coercive authority to maintain that power if it is challenged or threatened" (hooks, 2000, p. 118). The state often enforces this domination through law, public policy, and the distribution of resources, which then shape people's social and institutional lives by gender.

The state's role in reinforcing and reproducing these patriarchal institutions is part of a long history of contracts, laws, and policies that structure economic and legal life by gender (Htun & Jensenius, 2020; Htun & Weldon, 2018; Pateman, 2018). For example, prior to the 1970s, financial laws stipulated that women could not legally take out a credit card or have property in their own name; these laws incentivized marriage between a man and woman, requiring women to be subordinate to their male partners on whom they depended for financial security (Pateman, 2018). Moreover, under the doctrine of coverture (marriage law) the husband had ownership rights over his wife and legally was entitled to control her income, property, and residence (Calvo, 2004). In the 1980s, marriage fraud laws provided the alien male spouse with unilateral control over his female spouse's immigration status (Chen, 2000). Thus, legal rights across marriage, finances, and immigration all were enforced and reproduced by the state to elevate the dominant position of men while subordinating women.

Expectations of heteronormativity are similarly structured into the state;[1] accessing state benefits such as welfare, child support, and marriage rights are all dependent on intimate heteronormative relationships (Koyama, 2001). Social institutions (e.g., marriage, heterosexuality, the family) then reinforce and reproduce these inequalities by gender, sex, and sexual orientation (Collins, 2009; hooks, 2000; Nash, 2018; Pateman, 2018). Patriarchy provides a concept for understanding how the state, through these functions, reinforces norms of female subordination, heterosexuality, and male domination. Identifying patriarchal institutions and policies was important for feminists, especially in the late twentieth century, to identify the state's role in reproducing gender-based violence. Patriarchal legislative institutions relegated cis women's issues to the private sphere;[2] "the political then [was] the domain of [primarily white] men and male issues [whereas issues that affected women] like reproduction, contraception, childcare, rape, sexual abuse and battery and so on are pre-defined as outside the 'proper' realm of politics" (Alvarez, 1990, p. 28). Patriarchy was thus engrained into the legislative processes, and as such,

---

[1] Heteronormativity refers to a worldview that promotes heterosexuality as the normal or preferred sexual orientation.

[2] The prefix "cis" means "on the same side as." Thus, while people who are transgender move "across" genders, people who are cisgender remain on the same side of the gender they were initially identified as at birth.

political officials who were a part of this system were not incentivized to alter the power arrangements that are embedded within it.

Masculine-structured political institutions further reduced the significance of gender-based violence as an issue in the political sphere, because its "devalued status [as an issue was] assigned in social and political life to characteristics and people associated with femininity. In this reading, 'gender' is divisible into *masculinities* and *femininities*, which are 'stereotypes, behavioral norms, and rules' assigned to those people perceived to be men and those people perceived to be women" (Sjoberg, 2006, p. 33; emphases in original). Gender-based violence often ran counter to these expectations of femininity and heteronormativity (Mcdonagh, 2002). For example, being a good wife was couched in the heterosexual norm of taking care of a husband's sexual needs; therefore, an issue such as marital rape, which contests this expectation of a heterosexual woman, lost the political attention of the state under these circumstances (Bergoffen et al., 2010).

Patriarchal institutions also regulated state responses to violence against trans, queer, and lesbian women in its reinforcement of norms, expectations, and power around heterosexual and cisgender categories (Cohen, 2005; Jennings & Andersen, 2003; Johnson & Henderson, 2005). These categories often relegated violence against LGBTQ survivors to the private sphere and allowed for heterosexual categories to be used as a tactic for abuse. For example, abusive partners of LGBTQ survivors were able to use these norms to their advantage by suggesting that others would not believe the relationship between same-sex partners was real – and thus intimate partner violence was invisible. Moreover, abusive partners of LGBTQ survivors could threaten disclosing the sexual orientation of a survivor to their family or community (Calton et al., 2016). By organizing social institutions, laws, and family norms around heterosexuality, the experiences of violence among LGBTQ members are discarded, made invisible, and accompanied by further stigma and alienation. Identifying and recognizing the ways in which patriarchy is enforced and reproduced by the state illuminates why social movements to address gender-based violence have emerged over the course of US history.

MOVEMENTS AND ADVOCACY

Movements to end gender-based violence in the United States have emerged, overlapped, and contradicted each other on several occasions. Starting in the 1960s, though, women's advocacy groups within these movements began to visibly target the US policy system by advocating for new legislation and policies to prevent intimate partner violence and other forms of gender-based violence (Htun & Weldon, 2018; Weldon, 2002). These efforts over decades effectively influenced the passing of state policies (Weldon, 2012) and the enactment of the landmark federal legislation on gender-based violence known as the Violence Against Women Act (VAWA) (Ake & Arnold, 2017). How women's advocacy groups strategically sought these types of policy changes to address a single issue (e.g., gender-based violence) is well-documented (Ake & Arnold, 2017; Banaszak et al., 2003; Clemens, 1997; Goss, 2012; Kessler-Harris, 2003). However, most of these scholars focus on advocacy on behalf of women without disaggregating strategies that represent women who are marginalized across additional axes of their identities. This lack of attention to intersectionally marginalized groups eclipses an understanding of how advocacy organizations serve these populations differently (see Richie, 2012; Strolovitch, 2007; Weldon, 2012).

Attention to the advocacy organizations that represent and prioritize intersectionally marginalized groups reveals different approaches to engaging with the American State and US policy system. For example, advocacy organizations representing women of color often focus on issues that are not traditionally considered racially or gender motivated problems but do disproportionately affect women of color, such as public housing (Williams, 2004), domestic worker conditions (Hondagneu-Soleta, 2007; Nadasen, 2015), welfare benefits (Nadasen, 2012), and immigration (Chen, 2007). This advocacy demonstrates both the pervasiveness of oppression across a continuum of social identities and how different subgroups of women formulate ideologies of resistance that deviate from those of mainstream women's organizations. These ideologies are most certainly related to where low-income women and women of color lie differently on the social hierarchy and how their rights and opportunities are positioned between multiple struggles (Cobble, 2004; Robnett, 1997; Springer, 2005; White, 1999). Thus, there is a fragmentation of women's organizing, especially by race, ethnicity, and class – where multiple groups of women are working on gendered issues but from very different organizations and with varying issue priorities (Richie, 2012; Strolovitch, 2007; Weldon, 2012). How women can be marginalized across these additional identity characteristics is key to understanding why these advocacy groups differ in the issues they underscore, the policies they propose, and the strategies they deploy when trying to influence the US policymaking process.

INTERSECTIONALLY MARGINALIZED GROUPS AND BLACK FEMINISM

Black feminists offer many useful frameworks and concepts for understanding marginalization across multiple axes of identities. As Deborah King notes, "the necessity of addressing all oppressions is one of the hallmarks of Black feminist thought" (King, 1988, p. 43). Black feminism is characterized by its multidimensional approach to liberation that attends to the ways in which sexism, class oppression, and racism are bound together. The ways these systems relate to one another are often understood through the concept of "intersectionality." The Combahee River Collective, a collective of Black feminists who offered a statement of their politics in 1974, are often pointed to as authoring one of the foundational texts of contemporary Black feminism. In their statement, they frame their politics as being "actively committed to struggling against racial, sexual, heterosexual and class oppression, and see[ing] our particular task [as] the development of integrated analysis and practice based upon the fact that the major systems of oppression are interlocking" (Moraga & Anzaldua, 2015, p. 218). By engaging in this practice, Combahee and other Black feminists are "creating alternatives of self-governance and self-determination, and by using it [they] can more effectively prioritize problems and methods that center historically marginalized people in [their] communities" (Carruthers, 2018, p. 10).

As the Combahee Collective statement points out, there have always been Black women activists "who have had a shared awareness of how their sexual identity combined with their racial identity to make their whole life situation and the focus of their political struggles unique" (Moraga & Anzaldua, 2015, p. 218). Black contemporary feminism is thus an evolving product of these projects, interventions, and activism. Early conceptions of Black feminist theory engaged with the concept of the "double bind," which referred to the experience of being both Black and a woman (Feal, 2002). Others have characterized this double-bind experience as a form of oppositional consciousness, the state of belonging to a group (i.e., Black people) while at the same time not belonging to another (i.e., Black men). This dual positioning renders Black women vulnerable to the structural, political, and representational dynamics of both race and gender subordination. This experience is particularly relevant to how Black women experience violence – and contest it.

Some Black feminist scholars theorize resistance within the context of systems of gender and racial domination starting with precolonial experiences of violence. White (1999) discusses how enslaved Black women actively resisted rape, separation from their children on plantations, and forced pregnancy. In doing so, they enacted an early resistance to both gendered and racial oppression aimed at Black women. Harriet Jacobs' emancipation narrative in 1861, for example, is one of the documents written from this perspective that illuminates early Black feminist resistance to both slavery and sexual abuse. She says: "When he told me that I was made for his use, made to obey his command in everything; that I was nothing but a slave, whose will must and should surrender to his, never before had my puny arm felt half so strong" (Jacobs, 1861, p. 39). Following this trace of enslaved Black female as both a subject and an object of violence, Black feminists writing about this period underscore the relationships between violence, race, gender, and political subjectivity under the conditions of slavery and continued Black oppression. In these texts, they demonstrated how separating anti-racist and feminist politics that frequently intersect created new dilemmas for Black women. To theorize, understand, and address the intersecting nature of these structural dimensions of oppression, one tool Black feminists offer is "intersectionality theory."

INTERSECTIONALITY THEORY AND ADVOCACY

Intersectionality is a framework developed by Black feminist scholars to capture how a multiplicity of intersecting social identities determine one's power, life experiences, political interests, and more (Cohen, 1999; Collins, 1998a; Hancock, 2007; Lorde, 2017; Nayak, 2014). This framework is part of a collection of terms that Black feminists have mobilized to examine and understand the interconnectedness of structures of oppression (Nash, 2018). These structures have long been considered by Black feminists. Evelyn Brooks Higginbotham (1992) in particular writes, "race not only tends to subsume other sets of social relations, namely, gender and class, but it blurs and disguises, suppresses and negates its own complex interplay with the very social relations it envelops" (p. 255). Black feminist scholars thus bring attention to the ways in which social categories such as gender and class are given meaning through processes of racial domination. While "intersectionality" is a modern term for describing the experiences of this domination (Crenshaw, 2015), others have used terms such as "multiplicative relationships" (Hancock, 2007; King, 1988), "double jeopardy," "double discrimination" (Beal et al., 1970), and "the matrix of domination" (Collins, 2009) to emphasize Black women's interrelated experiences with racism, sexism, and classism. Thus, intersectionality theory is a product of several scholarly works by Black feminists to conceptualize the lived experiences of women who are vulnerable to varying forms of domination, discrimination, and oppression.

Intersectionality theory is especially helpful for understanding the movement to end gender-based violence. Crenshaw's (1991b) conceptualization of it is particularly useful. She provides three applications of the theory: the structural dimensions of domination (structural intersectionality), the politics engendered by a political system of domination (political intersectionality), and the representations of the dominated (representational intersectionality). These concepts can all be used to understand how women's positionality shapes their experiences with violence. Structural intersectionality illustrates how violence toward women often occurs within a specific context that varies depending on their race, class, sexual orientation, citizenship status, and other social categories. For example, a woman's citizenship status (structural inequality) may prevent her from being able to leave an abusive partner who holds US citizenship and who may threaten her with deportation if she leaves. Political intersectionality captures the various ways that political and discursive practices relating to race, ethnicity, sexuality, gender, or citizenship status overlook the existence of women with identities across these social categories. For example, without a pathway to residency or citizenship, for immigrant women who experience domestic abuse the interests and needs of women with these identities are overlooked by processes that separate citizenship from violence. Finally, representational intersectionality refers to how multiple identities are understood normatively. For example, Latinas and

Black immigrant women who hold dual marginalized identities (i.e., their race and gender) are often oversexualized in media and film (Stockdale, 1996), which overlook the nuances in their experiences with violence.

Intersectionality continues to be a collective project that encompasses a variety of terms we can use to understand the dimensions of marginalization and how these dimensions inform both activism and advocacy on the ground. As part of this collective project, social movement scholars offer conceptual terms to understand how intersectionality informs coalition-building and social movements. Intersectional coalition-building refers to how groups build coalitions across intersectional differences (Collins & Chepp, 2013). Intersectional solidarity occurs when groups are able to establish connections across social group differences by negotiating power asymmetries together (Hancock, 2011; Tormos, 2017). Intersectional praxis refers to organizing within social movements that aim to transform overlapping forms of oppression (Montoya & Seminario, 2022; Tormos-Aponte, 2019; Townsend-Bell, 2011). Intersectional consciousness is when individuals and groups recognize overlapping forms of oppression and build these lived conditions into movement agendas (Cho et al., 2013; Greenwood, 2008; Tormos-Aponte, 2019). In this book, I add to this collection of terms "intersectional advocacy," which more precisely explains how advocacy groups can engage in intersectional consciousness in strategic ways that reconfigure state structures (i.e., a form of intersectional praxis), such as policy institutions. This precise definition of "intersectional advocacy" helps us better understand the strategies and goals of advocacy groups operating within these broader social movements.

These different aspects of intersectionality theory are reflected in the efforts of advocacy groups on the ground that emphasize marginalization across both gender and race/ethnicity in their efforts. For example, in the 1970s, Chicana feminist discourse brought attention to specific issues that affected Chicanas as Latinas, which emerged primarily as a result of the dynamics within the Chicano movement (Garcia, 1989). Similar to Black feminists, Chicana feminists emphasized their multitude of identities – their gender, ethnicity, and citizenship status – to communicate how issues of violence uniquely shaped their lives across these identities. In doing so, they emphasized how cultural nationalism, gender and racial oppression, and classism worked in tandem to oppress Chicana women in particular (Blackwell, 2016). For both Chicana feminists and Asian feminists, thinking critically about how patriarchal family structures intersect with racial oppression was important for understanding the difficulties of removing women from households where they experienced domestic violence (Chen, 2007). For Native feminists, exposing deep connections between policies of settler colonialism, patriarchy, and political sovereignty is necessary for understanding their multiple struggles with violence in their communities (Arvin et al., 2013). These different positionalities underscore the need to address the issue of gender-based violence while accounting for these varying and overlapping identities.

Scholars have also used the framework of intersectionality to study how organizations acknowledge these different positionalities through advocacy groups. Strolovitch (2007) drew from this framework to study a range of different organizations and found that most advocacy groups do not promote the interests of intersectionally marginalized constituents, such as low-income Black women, compared to those of more advantaged constituents, such as middle-class white women. The few organizations that do affirm the interests of intersectionally marginalized populations, Strolovitch (2007) identified as groups that practice "affirmative advocacy." Affirmative advocacy is when organizations "redistribute resources and are attentive to issues affecting intersectionally disadvantaged subgroups in order to level the playing field among groups" (Strolovitch, 2007, p. 10). Other scholarship builds from this work by studying the range of advocacy groups that affirm what Strolovitch (2007) refers to as multiply "disadvantaged subgroups."

To capture a range of strategies in how advocacy organizations represent these groups, scholars use the term "intersectional advocacy" broadly to identify advocacy that occurs on behalf of multiply disadvantaged subgroups (Dwidar, 2021; English, 2021; Marchetti, 2014). These scholars have found that organizations advocate for "multiply disadvantaged subgroups" especially through lobbying (Junk, 2019; Lorenz, 2020), intragroup coalitions (Dwidar, 2021), and rulemaking (English, 2021). These studies primarily focus on how organizations integrate their advocacy into existing policymaking and rulemaking processes on behalf of multiply disadvantaged subgroups (Dwidar, 2021; English, 2021; Junk, 2019; Lorenz, 2020; Marchetti, 2014; Phinney, 2017). While these studies offer important insights about the strategies of these organizations, because they reflect the behaviors of advocacy groups that support and work within existing policy systems, organizations that contest these systems and policymaking processes are overlooked.

Yet policy systems and policymaking processes harbor many of the inequities and inequalities that organizations representing intersectionally marginalized groups are seeking to change (Mettler & Soss, 2004; Michener, 2019; Michener & Brower, 2020; Omi & Winant, 2014). Therefore, differentiating among organizations representing intersectionally marginalized groups is important for understanding the subset of organizations that aim to challenge and reimagine existing policy systems. In this book, I bring attention to how this subset of advocacy organizations representing intersectionally marginalized groups engage with the very structures of US institutions (i.e., policy institutions) that are responsible for the marginalization and inequities these groups experience. This engagement in the policymaking process is distinct and warrants a more developed theory of intersectional advocacy. I build on this previous scholarship to develop a theory of intersectional advocacy that helps identify how advocacy organizations intervene in the policymaking process on behalf of intersectionally marginalized groups and how this engagement fundamentally changes US policy institutions.

THEORY OF INTERSECTIONAL ADVOCACY

Intersectional advocacy is defined in this book as advocacy for linkages between policies and issues that reflect the experiences of intersectionally marginalized groups positioned between more than one problem area. This form of advocacy can be observed across a gradient of strategies, contexts, and time periods, and it is practiced by different types of organizations with varying perceptions of constraints, resources, and transformative justice. Throughout the book, I explore these strategies within varying contexts to illustrate how intersectional advocacy is applied by a wide range of feminist groups. Though its application results in different goals, strategies, and outcomes among advocacy organizations, I argue there are four consistent characteristics that undergird this approach and that this advocacy can lead to policy reconfiguration. In Figure 1.1, I provide an illustration of how these characteristics are part of a sequential process for reconfiguring policies over time.

Firstly, intersectional advocacy only occurs when it represents groups that experience the issue of interest across more than one marginalized identity. It is the experiences of these groups that illuminate the difficulties of addressing issues like gender-based violence without attending to other overlapping issue areas. Secondly, to reflect these experiences of intersectionally marginalized groups in the policymaking process, individuals or organizations aim to establish issue linkages that change how problems are defined, framed, and conceptualized in relation to one another. Thirdly, to transform issue linkages into tangible policy changes, advocates encounter several types of institutional boundaries that separate these issues from one another. These boundaries are structured by the state (e.g., laws, policies, budget appropriations) and state adjacent entities (e.g., corporations, social institutions). To successfully advocate for policy linkages, advocates reinterpret, traverse, and redraw these boundaries by pressuring policymakers to adopt new policies, laws, or institutions; they also sometimes recommend dismantling existing institutions or projects and replacing them with other types of structures. These efforts I show throughout this book reconfigure policies to be more equitable, representative, and supportive of intersectionally marginalized groups. In the next sections, I elaborate on each of these characteristics and explain their importance within the context of the movement to end gender-based violence.

Gender-based violence and movements to address it are a rich case study for examining this concept and its many underlying political strategies for two

FIGURE 1.1 Theoretical model of intersectional advocacy

important reasons. First, we know from existing scholarship that this movement is a contentious space among advocates representing populations that are marginalized across multiple axes of their identities such as race, ethnicity, and citizenship status (Calton et al., 2016; Richie, 2012; Seelman, 2015; Smith, 2004; Weissman, 2013; Weldon & Htun, 2013; Wood, 2004). This allows for the examination of how advocates representing women who are marginalized by more than one identity compare to other advocates who do not take this positionality into account. Second, violence is an issue that crosscuts others such as housing (Ford et al., 2013; James et al., 2016; Kattari & Begun, 2017), poverty (Coker, 2004; Dutton et al., 2000; Mottet & Ohle, 2006; Sokoloff, 2004; Wacquant, 2009), immigration rights (Dutton et al., 2000; Orloff & Kaguyutan, 2002; Shiu-Thornton et al., 2005; Villalón, 2011; Wood, 2004; Wrangle et al., 2008), incarceration (Bumiller, 2009; Chesney-Lind, 2002; Gottschalk, 2006; Miller, 1989; Richie, 2012), and racism (Aszman, 2011; Coker, 2000; Crenshaw, 1997; Richie, 2000; Smith, 2004, 2008; Sokoloff, 2004). This interconnectedness with other issues presents advocates with several opportunities to develop unique strategies for addressing these issues together. While I focus on the movement to end gender-based violence,[3] the framework of intersectional advocacy can be applied to many other issues and movements.

Representing Intersectionally Marginalized Groups

Representing the experiences and interests of an intersectionally marginalized group is a prerequisite for engaging in intersectional advocacy. I use the term "intersectionally marginalized" to refer to a group that is marginalized across more than one axis of their identity (e.g., Black women). Individuals with these multiple identities of marginalization are more vulnerable to interrelated systems of inequality and oppression. In the movement to end gender-based violence, these different positionalities matter for how these groups experience violence and how advocacy organizations represent them. In this section, I provide several examples of why these varying positionalities of marginalization importantly guide advocacy group approaches to policymaking.

Advocacy organizations that represent groups marginalized across two axes of identities – (1) gender and (2) class – often reference how both patriarchal institutions and capitalist policies work in tandem to make this group more vulnerable to domestic and sexual violence.[4] Together, these sets of policies,

---

[3] My reference to the movement to end gender-based violence is broad and includes overlapping movements and activism to address different forms of violence (i.e., domestic violence, sexual abuse, state violence, community violence). I use this terminology because it is how advocacy groups that I study view the political landscape that they are working within, but these initiatives and advocacy are not limited to women. They often are also for children, men, and trans people.

[4] Capitalism is referred to here as a system of economic inequality and exploitation. It is supported by structures that allow the market to regulate capital often at the expense of vulnerable and

which determine the distribution of economic resources by gender and class, limit women's financial resources, which heighten their economic reliance on partners and diminish their ability to leave these relationships (Ake & Arnold, 2017; Websdale & Johnson, 1997). The outcomes of these policies by both gender and class are striking when violence is considered among women who are not marginalized by their class status. Middle-class or high-income women have access to resources that help keep abuse private, such as safe shelters and private physicians who guard them from other institutions such as the police or social service agencies. Meanwhile low-income women who lack these resources are more likely to be subjected to state coercion and privacy invasion as they seek help from social service agencies (Chesney-Lind, 2002; Miller, 1989). In these instances, advocacy groups highlight how marginalization across two axes of identities (i.e., gender and class) influences both a woman's vulnerability to violence and her ability to escape it, as well as the different resources she can rely on to change these circumstances.

Advocacy groups representing low-income Black women focus on marginalization by axes of gender, class, and race. They draw our attention to how political and social institutions create conditions of inequality that then determine Black women's experiences with violence and their options for recourse. The majority of Black women are occupationally segregated in industries that lack financial security and make them more vulnerable to predatory practices of sexual harassment and assault (Conley, 2010; Dozier, 2010; Katznelson, 2005). State-sanctioned violence against Black people further legitimizes violence against Black women (Ake & Arnold, 2017; Crenshaw, 1991a; Richie, 1996; Thompson, 2002; Thuma, 2019). Finally, by limiting Black women's access to social service programs, they are more likely to be financially dependent on family members and partners who can abuse this power (Keane & Wolpin, 2010; Wacquant, 2009; Wallace, 2002). For Black women, gender-based violence cannot be separated from police, military, and economic violence against Black communities (Collins, 1998b; C. M. West, 2002; T. C. West, 1999; Wyatt, 1992). This is why advocacy groups representing Black survivors often identify state violence (i.e., police brutality, incarceration, discrimination) and economic violence (social services and programs that are racially and economic exclusionary) as closely related to intimate partner violence – because they shape the conditions of subordination that provoke violence among communities of color (Beal et al., 1970; hooks, 2014b). Moreover, these groups face the unique challenge of combating interpersonal and state violence simultaneously, while ensuring safety for survivors (Smith,

marginalized groups (Fleming & Morris, 2015; Leong, 2013; Omi & Winant, 2014). These structures are part of a racialized history in which people themselves were and are used as capital for the state's economic gains (Dawson, 2014, 2016). Capitalism is also represented by laws and policies that determine the unequal and disproportionate allocation of resources to people by race, ethnicity, gender, and class (Conley, 2010; Dawson, 2014; Katznelson, 2005).

2001). Black women advocates underscore the intersections of these various social and political institutions that shape the experience of violence and recourse available for Black women (Bograd, 1999; Collins, 1998b; Crenshaw, 1994; Richie, 1996; West, 2002).

Indigenous women who are marginalized across axes of gender, race, and class are similarly situated between multiple struggles that shape their experiences with violence, their resources to heal, and legal actions to take against perpetrators. Settler colonialism refers to the process of displacement and replacement of Indigenous populations by a settler state that over time develops a distinct identity and sovereignty (Arvin et al., 2013; Blackhawk, 2009; Bruyneel, 2007). Indigenous women advocates call attention to how violence against Indigenous women is historically related to settler colonialism, which is linked to the commodification and appropriation of land (Reséndez, 2016; Smith, 2001). For Native women living on reservations, the way the state structures resources around sovereignty positions them between accessing resources they need and appealing to a foreign government for assistance (Jacobs, 2009; Smith, 2001). Moreover, when violence occurs on reservations, they have minimal access to legal or social service responses, especially when violence is committed on reservations by non-Indians, due to jurisdictional challenges and inadequate funding for these services (Deer, 2006; Whittier, 2016b). Thus, advocacy groups representing Indigenous women must consider how these policies work together to reduce the autonomy of Indigenous communities, which has direct implications for how survivors of violence access resources, support, and recourse.

Advocacy groups representing Latina and Asian noncitizen women are similarly concerned with issues of autonomy as the state regulates and reduces their citizenship rights. For these groups, their marginalized identities across axes of gender, ethnicity, and citizenship status make them particularly vulnerable to immigration laws. This vulnerability determines their options for escaping intimate partner violence and their resources. For example, Congress strengthened the power of the male spouse in immigration law, giving him unilateral control over the alien spouse's immigration status, and this institutionalized control enables abusive spouses to exploit the threat of deportation (Chen, 2000; Sokoloff & Dupont, 2005). Advocacy groups have drawn attention to how abusers exploit this legal vulnerability by destroying their immigration papers, threatening to withdraw their petitions for immigration, and threatening to call authorities to have them deported (Dutton et al., 2000; Orloff & Kaguyutan, 2002, 2002; Salcido & Adelman, 2004; Villalón, 2010). Abusers often have more leverage over women with children, as these women contend with the possibility of state-sanctioned separation from their children (Kasturirangan et al., 2004; Wood, 2004).

Citizenship status also intersects with other identities such as ethnicity and class to create additional challenges for noncitizen women experiencing violence, such as social isolation from American culture and family members who are not in the country (Bhuyan & Senturia, 2005; Erez & Hartly, 2003; Kasturirangan et al., 2004; Salcido & Adelman, 2004; Villalón, 2011). They are also vulnerable to financial insecurity, which makes women dependent on their spouses (Erez & Hartly, 2003; Kasturirangan et al., 2004; Salcido & Adelman, 2004). Noncitizen immigrants also have negative experiences with law enforcement. To these groups, law enforcement is often associated with its deportation function, which disrupts a family unit, sends family members to detention centers, and worsens the economic circumstances of the family (Shiu-Thornton et al., 2005; Silva-Martínez, 2016). Deportation is a real concern; there are many instances in which reporting intimate partner abuse has resulted in Immigration and Customs Enforcement (ICE) involvement (Raj & Silverman, 2002). Noncitizen women are rightfully concerned that relying on law enforcement will result in deportation; police enforcement as a mechanism for reporting violence is then problematic for noncitizen women (Erez & Hartly, 2003). These advocates highlight how social institutions (e.g., family structures, language), economic relief policies (e.g., eligibility for social services), bureaucratic institutions (e.g., police force), and laws (e.g., laws on immigration) are all interwoven to determine the capacity of noncitizen, immigrant women to avoid, address, and escape violence.

These examples highlight why the experiences of violence among intersectionally marginalized populations lead advocates to consider additional and overlapping issue areas in their advocacy. They also illustrate the direct role of the state in determining the conditions of inequality that these groups face. While these examples are not all encompassing of the many ways in which identities map onto these experiences, they do communicate the relationships between identity, marginalization, state interventions, and advocacy. Intersectional advocacy emerges in response to these relationships as it seeks to address an issue (i.e., gender-based violence) that is shaped by these many conditions. To do so, advocacy organizations representing these groups develop and advocate for issue linkages.

Issue Linkages

Issue linkages are rhetoric, framing, and problem definitions that identify one issue in relation to another. In this section, I draw from existing literature to describe one example of how advocates on the ground advocate for an issue linkage between gender-based violence, state-sanctioned violence, and mass incarceration. Advocacy groups representing queer Black women and low-income Black women such as Women of Color Against Violence, The Defense of Battered women, and INCITE! have built campaigns to solidify issue linkages between gender-based violence and mass incarceration. These groups view the mainstream movement approach to end gender-based violence by criminalizing the action to be a problem. Relying on and expanding the criminal legal system is seen among these groups as an outcome that further criminalizes communities of color, especially Black men and Latinos (Bumiller, 2009; Coker, 2004; Dasgupta, 2003; Goodmark, 2013; Haney, 2010; Miller et al., 2011; Richie, 2000). Organizations such as these underscore how these laws and policies add to existing community violence and state harm.

Black cis, trans, and queer advocates sought to address this issue by organizing campaigns that aimed to dismantle the criminal justice system often under the framework of abolition. They did so by linking abuses of the carceral state with the struggle to eradicate sexual and domestic violence (Richie, 2012; Smith et al., 2006; Thuma, 2019). For example, advocacy groups such as Love & Protect, INCITE!, and the California Coalition for Women Prisoners (CCWP) developed the campaign "Survived and Punished" to coalesce existing defense campaigns and build a larger movement to support survivors and abolish gender violence, policing, prisons, and deportations. Other campaigns like "Say Her Name" were also created to call attention to police violence against Black women and girls while also promoting changes in the legal cases of survivor-defendants (Thuma, 2019). These efforts all aim to reconceptualize and redefine gender-based violence in relation to mass incarceration and state-sanctioned violence. These issue linkages can also change how resources are allocated. For example, advocacy groups affiliated with the Audre Lorde Project and the Anti-Violence Project representing Black transwomen advocated for redirecting resources from the criminal legal system to the development of alternative violence prevention and intervention strategies (Jordan et al., 2019).

These examples highlight the strategic decisions of advocacy organizations to link together the issues of gender violence to state-sanctioned violence and mass incarceration. What this literature does not provide, however, is how these groups transform issue linkages into policy outcomes that change how the state responds to these problems. This is the added value of a study on intersectional advocacy. In the next section, I explain how these agendas and broader campaigns to advocate for issue linkages are translated into actionable policies and laws.

Boundary Crossing and Policy Linkages

As these advocates push for policy linkages between issues, they encounter a variety of different institutional boundaries that they often have to confront and traverse. Policy linkages are amendments, new policies, and funding that link one policy to another. This is a strategic endeavor that I capture in my study of advocacy organizations. For example, in Chapter 4 of this book, I explain how the organization Communities for Survivors (CFS) transformed its issue linkages between gender-based violence and criminal justice into a policy linkage that was part of a bail bond reform initiative. Working in collaboration with other organizations, they wrote a bill that would take away the bond requirement for defendants pending trial. Advocates from CFS view bail bonds as a product of mass incarceration, incarcerating people (which includes survivors of violence) because they are too poor to afford cash bail. Gender-based violence has often been an issue that political groups historically used to justify bail bond reform (Bumiller, 2009; Richie, 1996); thus, presenting these two issues as interconnected in the form of this policy is peculiar to most politicians and advocates. In this example, CFS is crossing issue boundaries to reform policies around incarceration – connections that legally do not exist. This instance of boundary crossing is often an action these groups have to take to establish policy linkages.

Why is intersectional advocacy a difficult approach to practice that underscores the contributions these groups are making by advocating for issue and policy linkages? The state reinforces social policy boundaries that advocates seek to rearrange by maintaining that "various social benefits [remain] operationally, fiscally, and symbolically separate from one another" (Weir et al., 1988, p. 9). These structural boundaries around public policy are established by a long history of a growing administrative state (Lawson, 1994). The welfare state – an extensive institutional set of policies in the United States that promotes the economic and social well-being of its citizens – offers a key example of how and why the state develops rigid policy boundaries. The welfare system in the United States began in the 1930s during the Great Depression when state systems were unprepared to respond to the volume of requests from individuals and families without work or income (Voegeli, 2012). The Emergency Relief and Construction Act of 1932 was then the first welfare initiative that provided an initial state structure for welfare (Howard, 1997). Since then, other welfare policies were layered onto this one: the Social Security Act of 1935, cash assistance programs such as the Aid to Dependent Children, the Temporary Assistance for Needy Families (TANF) program, and so on. As these policies were layered or replaced, the administrative state grew to include new bureaucratic positions, policies, laws, and programs for managing welfare.

These state structures set the boundaries for what welfare policy was – and what it was not. These policy boundaries separated welfare from policies on immigration, crime, housing, policing, and so on through its singular focus on economic well-being (Raphael, 2015). In Chapter 3, I discuss how advocacy organizations contest these boundaries of welfare to include the issue of gender-based violence. Among organizations and individuals practicing intersectional advocacy, addressing the issue of gender-based violence necessitates some type of boundary crossing into state structures that operate outside the scope of their core issue (i.e., gender-based violence).

Scholars theorize "boundary crossing" in a variety of different contexts. I draw mostly from Star and Griesemer's (2016) broader conception of boundary crossing, which is the practice of inhabiting several intersecting worlds that are "both plastic enough to adapt to local needs and the constraints of the several parties employing them, yet robust enough to maintain a common identity across sites. They are weakly structured in common use and become strongly structured in individual site use" (p. 393). Studying boundary crossing thus requires an examination of loosely connected systems (Star & Griesemer, 2016). These loosely connected systems (i.e., policies and laws) provide advocacy groups with "resources for the creative acts of recombination at the heart of innovation" (Sheingate, 2003, p. 192). I posit that, as advocacy groups seek to institute policy linkages, they encounter a variety of structural boundaries. While these boundaries may appear rigid, it is these loosely connected systems of policies and laws that offer pathways for crossing and reconfiguring these boundaries.

In the movement to end gender-based violence, advocacy groups on behalf of intersectionally marginalized populations often cross institutional boundaries to advance their political goals. Sometimes these are legal boundaries, like those between the Violence Against Women Act (VAWA) and welfare policy. Other times these are definitional boundaries, such as budgets allocated at the state and city level to address specific issues such as housing or education, but not violence. And often these are legislative boundaries that reinforce separation between issues such as incarceration, violence, and poverty. While policy linkages reflect the needs of women who experience overlapping instances of oppression, these linkages do not fit into state structures that separate these issues from one another through laws, policies, budget appropriations, and social institutions. Thus, advocates who take on an intersectional advocacy approach are often engaging in this action of boundary crossing in order to connect issues they perceive as interlocking. There is less scholarship detailing this engagement. While scholars study boundary crossing in a few ways – how groups cross boundaries to change market problems to collective action efforts (Thurston, 2018), reconfiguring institutions within a policy area (Rocco et al., 2017), crossing policy boundaries for temporary political goals (Béland, 2009), and borrowing strategies from one regime of policies and applying them to another (Ramanathan, 2021) – none of these scholars consider how crossing boundaries across policies to establish issue and policy linkages can reconfigure the policies themselves. Throughout the book, I bring attention to how advocates cross institutional boundaries to advocate for issue and policy linkages. In the process, I argue that these groups are leading efforts to reconfigure policy boundaries.

Policy Reconfiguration

Advocacy that crosses institutional boundaries to establish issue and policy linkages between gender violence and other issue areas often leads to policy reconfiguration. This reconfiguration is the product of advocates' creative recombination of resources to "develop new ideas, tactical repertoires, and infrastructures to challenge existing policies" (Rocco et al., 2017, p. 14). In Chapter 3, I demonstrate how these policies change incrementally as a product of several issue and policy linkages – what I refer to as policy reconfiguration. I draw on Banaszak, Beckwith, and Rucht's (2003) conceptualization of reconfiguration for capturing the process that leads to this outcome. They argue that the fundamental character of the nation-state involves undergoing state formation, which is a constant state of change. When fundamental changes (e.g., the Great Depression, the Civil Rights Act, the women's movement) occur, formal and informal state powers can be reconfigured to potentially shape a new state model, thereby changing the relationship between states and their polity (Htun & Weldon, 2018). Reconfiguration then occurs in two processes: (1) through structural changes within the state and (2) by the changing relationship between the state and civil society. Together, these two processes reconceptualize the institutional roles of the state (Banaszak et al., 2003).

Intersectional advocacy has the potential to reconfigure one aspect of the state: its policy institutions. Policy institutions "reflect and contribute to power dynamics that reinforce and magnify the position of their creators" (Montoya, 2016, p. 374). By reconfiguring the boundaries of policies, I argue that advocates are transforming the policy function of the state by shifting these power dynamics. This transformation is a process of modifying, eliminating, and reinventing policies to better meet the needs of intersectionally marginalized populations. Intersectional advocacy is then a process of establishing issue and policy linkages between distinct issue areas that modify, eliminate, and reinvent the existing boundaries for policymaking. These changes alter the relationship between the state and these groups by changing how the state represents their interests and how it distributes resources to them through these policies. For example, when the state links together policies through amendments and provisions that grant citizenship rights to immigrant women that experience intimate partner violence, approve their eligibility for welfare, and provide them with access to public housing, these policy linkages all work together to change the distribution of power to intersectionally marginalized populations. Policy institutions are then reconfigured to redistribute resources that not only more comprehensively address a social problem but also change dynamics between "the powerful" and "the powerless" by distributing resources across distinct issue areas. When the state changes how it organizes its policies in this way, people are no longer marginalized across these institutions because they are not trapped within policy gaps that do not account for their unique positionalities. This is a potential outcome of policy reconfiguration that occurs incrementally as a result of several micro-changes and transformative shifts in how policies are connected to one another.

CONCLUSION

Scholars across disciplines provide important insights for understanding marginalization, oppression, social movements, advocacy groups, and policymaking. In this book, I draw from this interdisciplinary scholarship to make sense of a unique form of advocacy that I refer to as "intersectional advocacy" and define as *advocacy for linkages between policies and issues that reflect the experiences of intersectionally marginalized groups positioned between more than one problem area.* As organizations and individuals engage in intersectional advocacy, they encounter the American state, which encompasses several institutions with powerful logics that have "the capacity to conquer, enslave, surveil and imprison" (Morgan & Orloff, 2017, p. 1). As advocacy groups reconfigure policy boundaries, they are contesting the established norm that the state is made up of "static structures of political opportunity" and reinterpreting it as a set of organizations that can "transform the character of states or their constituent institutions" (Morgan & Orloff, 2017, p. 3). And transform *they do.* In the following chapters, I present evidence that advocacy groups are leading efforts to create issue and policy linkages that "transform the character of their constituent institutions." To fully understand these remarkable transformations and the nuances of this approach, in Chapter 2 I present an example of advocacy that reinforces policy boundaries. I then explain the harms of this approach on intersectionally marginalized groups. By doing so, I underscore what is at stake if these policymaking processes and outcomes are maintained, while illuminating policy alternatives that intersectional advocates present to us.

2

Setting the Policy Boundaries of the Violence Against Women Act

[Mariella] wanted protection, but there was nothing the agency could do because under the 1996 Legal Services Corporation Appropriations bill, the agency could not even use private funds to help her, since she was not yet a permanent resident. She was in the protected parole position, as is given to Cubans before there are adjustments of status. What was the result? Her husband killed her. The court-house deputies killed her husband. Her young son is left an orphan. Steps which could have been taken to protect the woman from her abuser were not taken because Congress denied her access to the agencies which could help her.

Senator Kennedy (D-MA), Hearing before the Committee
on the Judiciary, United States Senate, May 15, 1996

In Chapter 1, I presented a theory of intersectional advocacy. Intersectional advocacy challenges boundaries that separate policies from one another by advocating for linkages between them to better serve intersectionally marginalized groups. In this chapter, I turn to the policy case of the Violence Against Women Act (VAWA). Analyzing the policymaking process that created the original version of the VAWA in 1994, I show how policy boundaries were contested and defined by advocacy groups and legislators who participated in the policymaking process. These policy boundaries were singularly constructed around the criminalization of gender-based violence and immediate services to help women temporarily escape from violent situations.

Drawing from an analysis of the congressional hearings on the VAWA between 1990 and 1994, I illustrate how women's advocacy groups validated and contributed to setting these boundaries and why doing so ultimately had dire consequences for intersectionally marginalized groups. These hearings are contextualized within broader movements to address gender-based violence as I describe the political context of the late 1970s and 1980s when there were little to no government interventions or policies focused on gender-based violence.

This context and national support for addressing violent crimes in the United States shaped the window of opportunity for legislation on the VAWA to be attached to a major crime bill.

The chapter ends with a discussion of how these boundaries excluded and disproportionately harmed intersectionally marginalized groups. In Chapter 3, I show how intersectional advocates contested these boundaries in subsequent decades and reconfigured them by establishing policy linkages between the VAWA and other pieces of legislation and laws. Together, these two chapters underscore what is at stake in the US policy system when policies reinforce inequalities and how intersectional advocacy can reconfigure this system to be more just, equitable, and representative of an increasingly diverse US population.

INEQUALITY AND POLICY

Public policies play a fundamental role in producing, reproducing, and maintaining inequalities in the United States. Three features of policies that facilitate this role are (1) exclusions in a given policy (i.e., groups that are ineligible for policy benefits), (2) the divergent implementation of policies by subnational governments under a structure of federalism, and (3) local bureaucratic practices that provide administrators with the discretion to decide who and how people can access the policy benefits. I propose that an additional feature of public policy can exacerbate inequalities: the *boundaries* that separate policies from one another.

The first feature of policies that can lead to inequality is how a given policy excludes particular groups from its benefits. The practice of policymaking in the United States is predicated on including and excluding groups from resources, opportunities, and rights that are distributed by the government. The distribution of these goods affects the everyday lives of people who receive or are excluded from these benefits. For example, the GI Bill established a wide range of benefits to veterans returning from World War II. Some of these benefits included low-cost home loans, education and vocational training, an expansion of healthcare, and unemployment payments. This bill and accompanying policies increased veterans' enrollment in college. As veterans flooded into colleges and universities, these institutions became more diverse and veterans became more civically engaged (Bound & Turner, 2002; Mettler, 2002). In this example, a policy targeted toward one demographic group (i.e., veterans) regulated their social and institutional lives by increasing their access to higher education and changing their civic participation. Social policies often have target groups, which means some portion of the population is excluded from these benefits. When exclusions are included in policies, these can lead to inequalities and inequities by gender, race, and class (among other characteristics). For example, Old Age Insurance (OAI), now called Social Security, excluded agricultural and domestic workers from being eligible for the policy (Gordon, 2012; Lieberman & Lapinski, 2001; Mettler & Soss, 2004; Williams, 2004). Black women were highly concentrated in these industries, resulting in a policy that disproportionately excluded Black women from benefits that were intended to improve the economic welfare of all people (Mettler, 1998).

Secondly, federalism in the implementation of policies also contributes to growing inequalities. Grumbach and Michener (2022) found that American federalism creates inequality in venue selection (i.e., more powerful groups pick what levels of government are politically involved), information asymmetry (i.e., less powerful groups cannot monitor more powerful groups), unequal exit threat (i.e., wealthier groups can threaten to leave or politically pressure governments), and decentralized accountability (i.e., multiple levels of government make it difficult to track accountability). These disproportionate concentrations of power and decentralized processes for policy implementation can lead to vast inequalities in access to healthcare, welfare benefits, and immigration rights (Miller, 2008). For example, Michener (2018) found that Medicaid, through its policy implementation across states, resulted in inconsistencies in healthcare among people of color by localities. Different states provided varying healthcare practices and as a result people of color in particular did not experience consistent care and resources depending on where they lived.

Thirdly, bureaucratic discretion in the administration of policies also contributes to inequalities. Localities very often establish independent practices for administering and working with policy recipients. For example, even though the GI Bill included all veterans on paper, discretionary local practices resulted in racial exclusion of Black veterans from the policy's benefits in Georgia, Alabama, and Mississippi (Onkst, 1998). Similarly, Aid to Dependent Child (ADC), a welfare policy, required local bureaucrats to administer welfare benefits, which also included discretionary power in providing information about the policy, communicating eligibility, and supporting people in applying for welfare benefits. Lieberman and Lapinski (2001) showed that there were considerable racial disparities in the distribution of ADC benefits due to bureaucratic discretion, such that Black people received less welfare coverage than their white counterparts.

In addition to these established and studied features of policies that can lead to inequality, in this chapter I show that the *boundaries* that separate policies from one another can also exacerbate inequities among groups. Boundaries between policies are particularly acute in the US context, where they are consistently operationally, fiscally, and symbolically separate from one another (Weir et al., 1988). These boundaries are constructed as separations or demarcations for the purpose of categorizing policy issues and establishing governmental enforcing agencies that correspond to the policy objectives (Faling et al., 2019). Policy boundaries are often defined during the first phase of the policymaking process, known as problem definition (Jones &

Baumgartner, 2005). In the section "A Policy Window to Address Gender-Based Violence," I show that legislators defined the problem of gender-based violence as a problem of *crime*, thus bounding the VAWA as a crime control policy. While these types of boundaries make policymaking more efficient, the ways in which they are constructed have consequences for how they are implemented and how future policies are developed from these categories. As I show in this chapter, boundaries that defined the VAWA as a crime control and immediate services policy reproduced inequalities by race, ethnicity, class, and gender. In the following sections, I explain the political context that the VAWA legislation was situated within and how advocacy groups intervened in the policymaking process to participate in developing this legislation. Their interventions and the final markup of the VAWA in 1994 tell a cautionary story about bounded policies and the types of inequalities they can produce among intersectionally marginalized groups.

MOVEMENTS TOWARD LEGISLATION

Throughout the nineteenth and twentieth centuries, advocates led movements, created organizations, advanced legal arguments for self-defense against gender-based violence, independently established rape crisis centers, and developed shelters for survivors – all before the US government recognized sexual assault and domestic violence as public problems that needed a policy response. Prior to these efforts, in the 1970s violence against women and children was viewed as a private matter to be adjudicated within heterosexual relationships between a husband and a wife (Goodmark, 2012; Weldon, 2006). During this time, the state and private sector elites granted men considerably more power than women in marriages. For example, women could not hold a credit card or property in their name, making them reliant on a relationship with a man for economic security (Pateman, 2018). Laws such as the doctrine of coverture provided a husband with ownership rights over his wife, enabling men to control their wives' income, property, and livelihood (Calvo, 2004). Thus, not only was gender-based violence relegated to the private sphere by the US government, but laws, financial institutions, and contracts put women in a subordinate position relative to men when violence occurred. The experiences of LGBTQ people facing sexual and domestic violence were invisible to the law as they occurred outside these heteronormative structures recognized by the state. While there were laws regarding rape as a crime, these laws were written to protect men's claims to women as their property. In other words, other men could not use sexual abuse to control another man's wife (Schulhofer, 2000). These entrenched structures all made violence against women, children, and LGBTQ people challenging to address through public policy. Additionally, laws and policies that unfairly distributed resources, public goods, and rights to people by race and ethnicity (Omi & Winant, 2014; Richie, 2000) made it even more difficult for survivors of color to seek recourse, resources, and healing from gender-based violence.

To confront some of these underlying systems of inequality and bring visibility to the issue of gender-based violence, feminists formed groups, coalitions, and clubs to advocate for policy change, many of which were organized around their gender and race/ethnicity. These groups provided resources, organizing capacity, and support structures such as organizations, campaigns, centers, and coalitions. For example, Black leaders such as Ida B. Wells, Anna Julia Cooper, Fannie Barrier Williams, and others formed Black women's clubs to organize anti-rape and anti-lynching campaigns (Giddings, 2009). These efforts established some of the first national Black women's clubs and organizations to address gender-based violence, such as the National Association of Colored Women's Clubs (NACWC), the National League for the Protection of Colored Women, and the National Coalition Against Domestic Violence (NCADV) (Hine, 1989). In the 1970s and 1980s, American Indian leaders were establishing clubs and organizations as venues for advocacy that addressed sexual violence and also included interrelated issues such as sovereignty rights and the economic well-being of American Indian women and their families. Some of these groups were the Indian Law Resource Center, the Minnesota Indian Women's Resource Center, and Mending the Sacred Hoop (Le May, 2018).

Throughout the twentieth century, feminist groups emerged across these identity cleavages, at times they influenced one another, and other times they came into conflict with each other. Some leaders even straddled these different groups. For example, women-of-color advocates worked in white-dominated feminist groups, mixed-gender organizations, and in autonomous Black, Latina, American Indian, and Asian feminist organizations (Thompson, 2002). Within specific factions, there were also disagreements among leaders about the direction of these efforts and whether or not to include them in other movements such as the civil rights movement (McGuire, 2010). As feminists brought considerable public attention to women's different experiences with violence and targeted efforts to address them, these campaigns were not sequential, uniformly coordinated, or similarly motivated. This separate and yet cooccurring organizing, particularly among women of color, strengthened these movements to address gender-based violence by increasing policy responsiveness especially among state governments (Weldon, 2012).

Advocates confronted the policies and legal structures that were perpetuating gender-based violence through clubs, organizations, coalitions, and social movement organizing. Targeting the courts, feminist groups and activists argued for new precedents for adjudicating gender-based violence. In 1974, Joan Little was the first woman, and Black woman, in the United States to be acquitted in a murder case of self-defense from sexual assault of a white jail guard (McConahay et al., 1977). Throughout the 1970s, advocates not only brought individual cases directly into the courts but also coordinated efforts to successfully lobby states to pass laws against marital rape (Bergen & Barnhill, 2006). Feminist groups associated with the battered women's movements in the 1970s advocated for centers designated to survivors who needed medical attention. Led by advocates such as Susan Brownmiller and Susan Griffin, the anti-rape movements in the 1970s helped establish the first rape crisis centers (RCCs) in Seattle, California, and Washington, DC. The first domestic violence shelters opened in Arizona and California between 1973 and 1974 (Richie, 2012). The first national coalitions were also formed at this time, most notably the NCADV in 1978 and the National Coalition Against Sexual Assault (NCASA) in 1979 (Arnold, 2017). Shelters were established by groups across the country, especially through grassroots and local community efforts on behalf of women of color: Casa Myrna Vasquez opened up a shelter in Boston for Latina women, the White Buffalo Calf Women's Society opened up the first tribal shelter in South Dakota, and the Everywoman's Shelter was opened up in Los Angeles to serve Asian women (Ferraro, 1996; Schechter, 1982).

However, when the federal government began to provide funding support for these structures, this came with a criterion that excluded most grassroots and community health centers. The Family Violence Prevention and Services Act (FVPSA) of 1984 provided funding toward shelters and related services, but only centers with traditional hierarchical structures and credentialed staff qualified (Arnold, 2017). These restrictions meant that grassroots organizations and community health centers that predominantly serviced women of color and low-income women survivors with medical care could not access these resources (Wilkes, 2019). This governmental intervention addressed gender-based violence while maintaining existing racial, ethnic, and class power structures, in many ways foreshadowing the politics that would lead to the VAWA.

The overlapping and fragmented nature of feminist movements is a necessary context for understanding the policy window that opened up for these groups, and why, when given the opportunity to pass the first major piece of legislation in the United States on gender-based violence (i.e., the VAWA),[1] there were substantive disagreements among these groups of activists and organizational advocates. These disagreements were primarily around the decision to include the VAWA as part of a major crime bill.

A POLICY WINDOW TO ADDRESS GENDER-BASED VIOLENCE

During the late 1980s and early 1990s, state attention to gender-based violence had changed in a few important ways. The anti-rape and battered women's movements were garnering widespread public attention as feminist groups stormed city halls and district attorney offices, held speak-outs in the streets,

---

[1] The FVPSA was the first piece of legislation to address gender-based violence; however, the Act only provided grants for shelter organizations and did not include policy or legal changes.

and organized conferences on gender-based violence (Jacquet, 2019). By the 1980s, many of the projects established by feminists such as RCCs had been bureaucratized and subject to state control, and "'Co-optation' happened before many women understood the meaning of the term" (Schechter, 1982, p. 42). This process began with the first federal statute on domestic violence, the FVPSA, which was passed in 1984 and granted funding toward immediate services to survivors predominantly in the form of shelters.

Widespread social movement organizing, increased state "co-optation," and a proposal that Joseph Biden – then a senator from Delaware – introduced to the US Congress to address gender-based violence together enabled the opening of a policy window for federal legislation on the issue. Policy windows are "the opportunities for action given initiatives [that] present themselves and stay open for only short periods" (Kingdon, 1995, p. 166). These windows emerge when problems (i.e., gender-based violence), policies (i.e., FVPSA), and politics (i.e., Biden's interest in gender-based violence) converge around an issue area and advocates of a new policy initiative claim their proposal is a solution that addresses it (Kingdon, 1995). Because policy windows emerge in this way, these opportunities often overlap with other political interests. In the case of the VAWA, there was a coalition of law and conservative groups pushing for a major crime bill that would provide the infrastructure for the VAWA (Richie, 2012).

Marrying these two pieces of legislation was a critical point of dissension among feminist groups that occupied these movements; some groups wanted to move forward with attaching the VAWA to a crime bill while others wanted to develop it independently from this legislation. At the time of this policy window, there was a diverse coalition of feminist groups that were advocating for policy approaches that did not rely on the criminal legal system and did not want to attach the VAWA to the crime bill (Richie, 2012). This group identified as radical, anti-racist feminists who argued that "power was at the heart of male violence against women and that only through liberation of women would the problem of male violence end" (Richie, 2012, p. 76). The types of alternative approaches they focused on were the underlying factors that contributed to men's power over women that positioned them to use violence as a tool of subordination. These factors included women's economic reliance on men, divestments in communities that contributed to socioeconomic distress in households, women's citizenship status in cases where her partner held this status above her, and established norms that reinforced these power dynamics (hooks, 2000; Richie, 2012; Thuma, 2019).

To address these underlying issues, policy alternatives would need to include initiatives to increase survivors' financial independence, change their citizenship status, expand the benefits of welfare, reinvest resources and job opportunities into their low socioeconomic community, provide them with long-term affordable housing, and introduce men and women to educational initiatives that changed how they understood their positionality in relation to one another.

Criminalizing gender-based violence as a major policy solution did not reflect these interests or address how this coalition was conceptualizing this problem. However, the limited policy window available was constrained to a crime control approach. This wide coalition of organizations would have to decide whether to support such legislation, which would address gender-based violence, but only to the extent that it could be identified as a "crime." Advocacy organizations predominantly representing women of color, and especially Black women, did not support this legislation; they were concerned about the consequences of ceding so much power to the state, increasing mass incarceration, and redirecting resources away from local grassroots efforts that were part of the survivors' communities (Richie, 2012). These feminist groups viewed their grassroots work as providing an alternative to a male-dominated criminal legal system.

Despite these concerns, a set of mainstream organizations moved forward with drafting this legislation, which would be part of "one of the most comprehensive, far-reaching crime bills in the history of the United States" (Richie, 2012, p. 86). Mainstream women's organizations, predominantly representing white women, allied with law-and-order conservatives to include the VAWA as part of the Violent Crime Control and Law Enforcement Act (VCCLEA) (Richie, 2012). These organizations, such as the National Organization for Women's Legal Defense and Education Fund, were part of the National Task Force to End Sexual and Domestic Violence created in 1990 to collaborate with senators such as Joseph Biden to draft what is now known as the VAWA. Together, the VAWA and the VCCLEA instituted mandatory arrest policies for perpetrators of violence, allocated nearly $10 billion for new prison construction, and authorized the expansion of state violence against marginalized populations, including many survivors of sexual and domestic violence (Bumiller, 2009; Thuma, 2019). Groups such as the Feminist Alliance Against Rape in their newsletter asked: "How is this after-the-fact action helping women? ... If all men who had ever raped were incarcerated tomorrow, rape would continue" (Jacquet, 2019, p. 150). Among these groups, the VAWA would not address the underlying issues they sought to address; and among communities that were already negatively affected by mass incarceration and a weakening of social safety net policies, this Act would only exacerbate these circumstances especially for survivors of violence (Richie, 2012).

Advocacy groups representing intersectionally marginalized survivors (i.e., women of color, immigrant women, low-income women) anticipated the dangers of developing a policy agenda that was heavily punitive and that did not account for the different needs of survivors of violence. Meanwhile, what policies and interventions did the mainstream organizations that participated in this policy process specifically advocate for when developing this piece of legislation? What were the actual consequences of the passage of this legislation on intersectionally marginalized women? In the next section,

I discuss how advocacy groups intervened in legislative processes by presenting testimony and statements in the congressional hearings on the VAWA. In doing so, I highlight their role in establishing a bounded policy to address gender-based violence that had detrimental consequences for intersectionally marginalized groups.

CONGRESSIONAL HEARINGS AND POLICYMAKING

Legislative Politics and the VAWA

Congressional hearings are a pivotal venue for advocacy groups to advance their policy goals. Committee members play a substantial role in setting the policy agenda, particularly in the House (Cox & McCubbins, 2005; Krehbiel, 1991; Lorenz, 2020; Oleszek, 2013; Weingast & Marshall, 1988), and thus which issues, bills, and topics they bring up matters to interest groups (Drutman, 2010; Grossmann, 2012; Lorenz, 2020). Committee and subcommittee hearings offer interest groups an opportunity to shape policy design and legislators' votes by presenting testimony (Andrews & Edwards, 2004a; Holyoke, 2011; King et al., 2007; Sabatier, 1991). Since legislatures often lack expertise, interest groups often fill important knowledge gaps by recommending policy solutions (Burns, 2005; Burstein & Hirsh, 2007; Skrentny, 2006). Women's organizations, in particular, are known to leverage this mechanism (Clemens, 1997; Daniels et al., 1997; Goss, 2012; Skocpol, 2013). Indeed, offering policy expertise in this way has become the major strategy among these organizations to influence politics and policy development (Goss, 2012). Thus, congressional hearings are an ideal venue to observe interest-group advocacy.

There are some limitations to viewing interest groups' political participation from this vantage point. First, only some interest groups are invited by legislators to participate in hearings (Bauer et al., 1972; Hansen, 1991). In the case of the 1990s hearings on the VAWA, participants from women's organizations were mostly selected by members of the National Organization for Women's (NOW)[2] Legal Defense and Education Fund because this organization was initially invited to develop the first version of the bill proposed by Senator Biden (Strebeigh, 2009). This is a common practice; committees often rely on major interest groups to suggest witnesses, language, and data to be presented during hearings (Davidson et al., 2019; Miller, 2004). Members of the NOW Legal Defense and Education Fund produced summaries of the issues for committee members and helped in selecting witnesses for the hearings (Whittier, 2016). The privileged role of the NOW Legal Defense and

---

[2] Note that NOW includes different branches and programs that are distinctly operated by different groups of advocates. These varied groups participated differently in the hearings.

Education Fund is important for interpreting the advocacy that occurs during the hearings.

Because the NOW Legal Defense and Education Fund had considerable influence in deciding witness testimonies, they were the dominant voice in the hearings. It is not surprising that many witnesses echoed the goals, objectives, and core beliefs of this organization. Thus, while the hearings offer a substantial snapshot of advocacy among organizations working to advance legislative change on gender-based violence, they mostly represent a select group of privileged organizations (mainstream, well-resourced, Washington, DC–located groups) whose preferences were fairly aligned with each other.

Second, by only focusing on congressional hearings, we miss other important behaviors for influencing legislators, such as conversations with legislators outside of hearings (Hall & Deardorff, 2006), protests that signal to political officials (Miller, 2016), or later markups of the bill (Lorenz, 2020). Congressional hearings cannot provide a full causal story about advocacy and legislative change. However, they can illustrate how advocacy groups participated in the policymaking process and influenced the VAWA.

Congressional Hearings and Analytical Approach

This chapter and Chapter 3 both draw from a qualitative analysis of congressional hearings on the VAWA. This analysis provides a rich source of data on how witnesses, organizations, and lawmakers framed their positions (Brasher, 2006; Whittier, 2016). I compiled the committee hearings on the VAWA from the first hearing in 1990 to the last in 2014. This yielded thirty hearings across four reauthorization cycles, which I read fully for background understanding. I then created a subsample of the testimony, statements, and letters provided by women's organizations and nonprofit groups that serve women who experience violence. This yielded a variety of organizations: state coalitions (e.g., Nevada Coalition Against Domestic Violence), service and advocacy nonprofits (e.g., shelters, counseling services, hotlines, advocacy groups, combination organizations like the Junior League), and legal services organizations (e.g., Battered Women's Law Project). Testimonies that were excluded from this sample came from law enforcement (e.g., police, prosecutors), governmental agency representatives (e.g., Department of Health and Human Services, crime victim services), academics (e.g., professor of psychiatry), and survivor testimonies that were not explicitly affiliated or on behalf of a women's organization. The subsample that I analyze in this chapter focuses on advocates representing organizations against gender-based violence.

In total, this subsample included testimonies from 125 organizations.[3] This group includes organizations that participated across the hearings and those

---

[3] See the Appendices for criteria and information gathered for each organization and codebook used for analyses.

that newly emerged from time to time. Most of these organizations were added to the testimony list by NOW (Whittier, 2016). I coded the type of organization that each participant represented using the software NVivo. This typology included grassroots organizations (organizations that focus on local communities and develop their advocacy based on the input they receive from these communities), legal organizations (organizations that focus on legal rights, representation, and the law), national organizations (organizations with multiple chapters or national influence), service organizations (organizations that provide direct services to survivors of violence such as hotlines or shelters), and state coalitions (coalitions of organizations that are state-based). These are the categories that advocacy leaders on the ground use to characterize organizations working on issues of violence.[4] Figure 2.1 shows the distribution of testimonies among these organizational types. I used a codebook to capture how these groups intervened in the policy processes through their testimony and hearings. The codebook included codes to capture the proposed policy solutions that scholars identify as the hallmarks of the Act (see Bumiller, 2009; Whittier, 2016). I also coded the strategies, frames, and approaches of interest groups to influence policy processes (see Ake & Arnold, 2017; Alex-Assensoh & Stanford, 1999; Arnold, 2017; Clemens, 1997; Cobble, 2004; Dasgupta, 2003; Markowitz & Tice, 2002; Skocpol, 2013; Strolovitch, 2007; Villalón, 2011; Weldon, 2002; Weldon & Htun, 2013; Wood, 2004).

In this chapter, I focus on hearings that occurred between 1990 and 1994, preceding the initial enactment of the VAWA. These hearings show how organizational leaders and legislators framed and defined the problem of

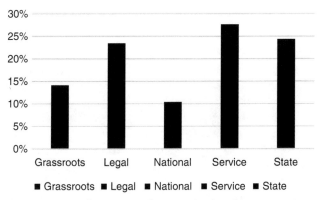

FIGURE 2.1 Testimonies and statements by organizational type

---

[4] While in the field interviewing leaders, I learned that organizations discussed different structures for addressing violence against women, and these are the big five to which leaders often refer to characterize the differences in how organizations approach their work.

gender-based violence and possible policy solutions. These exchanges and the final version of the VAWA that was passed in 1994 illustrate how policy boundaries develop during the policymaking process. Through my analysis of the hearings, I show that the initial boundaries that developed around the VAWA were detrimental to intersectionally marginalized groups such as women of color, low-income women, and immigrant women.

SETTING THE BOUNDARIES OF THE VAWA

Prior to the VAWA, there was no coherent policy response at the federal level to address gender-based violence. This lack of a prior policy legacy shaped how organizations advocated for policy change during hearings on the proposal for the VAWA during the years 1990–4. Advocates spent much of their testimonies and statements defining what constituted violence, referencing the federal government's negligence in addressing it, and offering policy solutions. Because there was a large void in governmental responses to violence, and according to advocates a dire need for immediate services to help especially women escape violent circumstances, much of the policy solutions advocates proposed in the hearings were reactive and immediate: punitive interventions, temporary shelters, hotlines for initial reporting, awareness campaigns, and legal services for survivors of violence to pursue legal action against their abusers. Throughout this section, I will highlight particular testimony and statements from these advocates that illustrates why they proposed these policies and why specific advocates promoted punitive interventions. These recommendations are important for understanding the role advocates played in defining the boundaries of the VAWA. Many of the recommendations made by these organizational leaders (including mandatory arrests, funding for shelters, funding for hotlines, increased time limits for restraining orders, awareness campaigns, educational services, and police training) were included in the final version of the bill.

In the early 1990s, mainstream advocacy organizations predominantly defined "gender-based violence" as a "crime," and crimes needed to be addressed with police intervention. Most of the advocacy organizations that adopted this position were national and state coalitions: NOW, NCADV, Iowa Coalition Against Sexual Assault, and Connecticut Coalition Against Domestic Violence. Leaders from these organizations in their testimony and statements to legislatures framed gender-based violence as a legitimate and significant issue that required government action. When the VAWA was first proposed, there was little to no information available about the violence women were experiencing, and domestic violence in particular was viewed as a private matter between spouses (Arnold, 2017). An advocate from the National Women Abuse Prevention Project shared in her testimony:

Woman abuse – also called domestic violence, family violence, wife-beating – is not a relationship problem and it is not simple pushing, shoving, or a family squabble. It is the use of threat or physical force in order to gain control over a current or former intimate partner, and that use of threat only escalates in seriousness and frequency as time goes on without serious intervention.[5]

In her testimony, she confronted the widespread belief that domestic violence is a private issue and reframed it as a public concern.

How did organizational leaders representing the National Women Abuse Prevention Project recommend the government address this issue? The executive director in particular advocated for establishing a national media campaign that presents domestic violence as a serious problem and to utilize the criminal justice system to intervene.[6] The National Women Abuse Prevention Project among others (e.g., NCADV, Project Safeguard, the Julian Center) in the hearings devote their testimonies to establishing domestic violence against women as a crime that no longer can be adjudicated within a romantic relationship. Leaders from these organizations consistently proposed increasing the visibility of this problem by condemning it, which is why much of their proposed interventions include incentivizing law enforcement to intervene and public efforts to identify it as a crime.

These recommendations conceptually suggested to legislators that they create a tight policy boundary of "crime control" around the content of the VAWA through a layering of law enforcement policies: orders of protection,[7] requiring police officers to make mandatory arrests,[8] and increasing felony penalties.[9] As an advocate from the Julian Center testified: "Everything in your power should be done to encourage state legislatures to improve criminal law so that it truly protects women from battering. For instance, mandatory arrest and sentencing laws have proven to be quite effective, yet very few states have passed them."[10] Organizational leaders from Project Safeguard validated this recommendation, referring to their existing local partnerships with law enforcement in Denver to increase police responses to domestic violence. An advocate from Project Safeguard added her testimony: "Law enforcement sets the tone for the whole community, to approach

---

[5] Hearing before the Subcommittee on Children, Family, Drugs and Alcoholism of the Committee on Labor and Human Relations, April 19, 1990.

[6] Hearing before the Subcommittee on Children, Family, Drugs and Alcoholism of the Committee on Labor and Human Relations, April 19, 1990.

[7] Hearings before the Committee on the Judiciary, Subcommittee on Civil and Constitutional Rights, Crimes of Violence Motivated by Gender, November 16, 1993.

[8] Hearing before a Subcommittee of the Committee on Appropriations United States Senate, Special Hearing, February 12, 1991.

[9] Hearings before the Committee on the Judiciary, Domestic Violence: Not Just a Family Matter, June 30, 1994.

[10] Hearing before the Subcommittee on Children, Family, Drugs and Alcoholism of the Committee on Labor and Human Relations, April 19, 1990.

domestic violence as a family affair to be ignored or as criminal behavior which must be stopped."[11]

In opposition to the mainstream narrative of criminalization, advocates from the Nevada Domestic Crisis Shelter shared their negative experiences with law enforcement responses: police were arresting survivors of violence instead of their abusers. An advocate from this organization warned legislatures:

Domestic violence cannot and will not be prevented by arresting every batterer or sheltering every victim. We must address the fact that we, as a society, bear responsibility for this problem. If a lack of affordable housing, healthcare, or childcare traps some victims in an escalating cycle of violence; if substance abuse, unemployment or a legacy of family violence provide abusers with an excuse to choose violence, then we must address these problems as well.[12]

Her testimony reflects the ineffectiveness of a criminal justice approach to addressing violence for communities of survivors that don't trust police and are more likely to be arrested themselves (Whittier, 2016). Such an approach also allocates resources away from these other issues areas (e.g., affordable housing, healthcare, unemployment) that are often connected to gender-based violence (Smith, 2001). The Nevada Domestic Crisis Shelter stood alone in these early hearings, however: they were one of the only invited organizations to provide a minority perspective that ran counter to crime control policy recommendations and increasing law enforcement.

Beyond framing the VAWA as a crime control policy, early advocates in hearings before its enactment also emphasized a need for immediate services. In many ways, this advocacy mimicked the only legislative precedent in this policy area, the FVPSA. The FVPSA was designed around providing immediate services to survivors. These requests mostly came from service organizations – such as the House of Ruth, the Harriet Tubman Center, and the Chicago Abused Women Coalition – who ran shelters for women, offered counseling services, and operated hotlines. Representatives from these service organizations focused on expanding the pool of resources to address the immediate needs of women who experienced violence. With this focus, their recommendations were often short-term: requesting transitional housing, immediate counseling, increasing hotlines, and so on.[13] For example, an advocate from the Pennsylvania Coalition Against Domestic Violence explained: "What we realized was that there is a huge gap in services, because of funding. We estimate a need of $11.8 million more just in one state. We

---

[11] Hearing before the Subcommittee on Children, Family, Drugs and Alcoholism of the Committee on Labor and Human Relations, April 19, 1990.

[12] Hearing before the Subcommittee on Children, Family, Drugs and Alcoholism of the Committee on Labor and Human Relations, April 19, 1990.

[13] Hearings before the Committee on the Judiciary, Domestic Violence: Not Just a Family Matter, June 30, 1994.

discovered that the need for more shelter space is critical: 25 of the 67 counties in Pennsylvania have no shelter facilities."

Even though these types of organizations concentrated their advocacy in the hearings on increasing shelters, it is clear from their testimonies that they also believed the federal government needed to go beyond providing immediate services. Funding for shelters was the bare minimum requirement for these organizations but also perhaps the most tangible win they could achieve in this political context. An advocate from the House of Ruth made this very point. She said in her testimony: "Safe shelter has been the initial focus of programs throughout the country and really remains the cornerstone of national efforts to end violence against women ... We consider shelters the minimum that a community can provide for battered women; 2/3rds of the counties in this country do not even have that."[14] Similarly, legal services were an immediate and minimum service for which these organizations advocated. For example, an advocate from the Committee to Aid Abused Women shared in her testimony: "Although some legal services are available to those who cannot afford to hire a private attorney to represent them, the services provided are limited ... Affordable legal assistance is practically impossible for them to obtain, and their cases can become more complex."[15]

Together, these sets of advocates in different ways carved out a legitimate space for the VAWA as a crime control and immediate services policy. In doing so, they created tight boundaries around the issue of gender-based violence by defining how the state should respond to it and the resources needed to address the problem immediately. This construction of the issue portrayed violence as a single problem that could be solved with better crime control and immediate services to help people, especially women, leave violent circumstances. In 1994, the recommendations of feminist organizations in these hearings to mandate arrests, provide more shelters for funding, establish a national hotline, initiate restraining orders that were enforced by the courts, and implement pro-arrest programs and police training were all translated into the final version of the bill. By initiating the federal government's response to gender-based violence, the VAWA crystallized definition of the problem of gender-based violence and created a distinct and separate policy area. Figure 2.2 conceptually presents how these policies were layered onto one another to create bounded policy around crime control and immediate services.

---

[14] Hearing before the Committee on the Judiciary United States Senate, Legislation to Reduce the Growing Problem of Violent Crime Against Women, June 20, 1990.

[15] Hearing before a Subcommittee of the Committee on Appropriations United States Senate, Special Hearing, February 12, 1991.

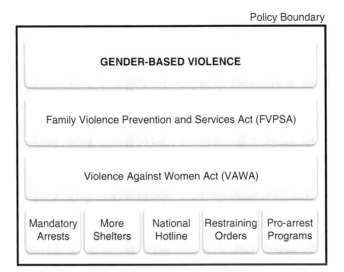

FIGURE 2.2 Bounded Violence Against Women Act (VAWA) 1994

POLICY BOUNDARIES FROM THE PERSPECTIVE OF ADVOCATES

Why did these advocacy groups in the early 1990s reinforce the VAWA's policy boundaries through this policymaking process around criminalization, police interventions, and immediate services to survivors of violence? Moreover, why was it so difficult for other groups, such as the Nevada Domestic Crisis Shelter, to challenge and change the ways these boundaries were being identified when legislators were developing the initial version of the VAWA? To understand these dynamics and perspectives, we have to understand the political context these groups were in at this time as they made these decisions.

In the late 1980s and early 1990s, there was substantial national attention to address violent crime, and police institutions were viewed as a key mechanism for addressing it, especially among white public opinion and white political officials. Indeed, the time period between 1974 and 1990 was referred to as the "crime plateau period" to signify attention to consistently high crime rates (Lafree, 2000). At this time, crime was receiving considerable public attention by the media and political officials. Such attention was reflected and intensified by the 1988 presidential election, during which the criminal record of Willie Horton, a Black man who escaped from prison and kidnapped and assaulted a white couple in their home, was a centerpiece of the Bush campaign's push for increased federal involvement in crime control (Mendelberg, 1997). Campaigns such as these increased racial prejudice (Mendelberg, 1997) and justified more punitive crime control policies especially among the white public (Ackerman et al., 2001). Law enforcement institutions at this time received positive ratings from the public and were viewed as the appropriate responders to instances of violent crime (Roberts et al., 2005). Nevertheless, despite the widespread support for the police among the majority of Americans, people of color and especially Black people rated the ethical standards of police officers much lower than did white Americans (Ackerman et al., 2001). These opinions were "the minority" of public opinion and did not map onto the sweeping national narrative to be "tough on crime." It is also known as the peak of the electoral capture of Black voters, which reduced the incentives of political parties to be responsive to their preferences (Frymer & Skrentny, 1998). Starting in 1991, the scholars of criminal justice refer to the 1990s as the "crime bust period," where crime was a central policy priority that marked steep declines in violent crime (Lafree, 2000).

Advocacy groups concerned about gender-based violence operated in this broader political context characterized by widespread national support for punitive crime control policies and law enforcement institutions. Groups such as the NCADV, Project Safeguard, and the National Women Abuse Prevention Project were determined to add gender-based violence to the list of crimes that needed to be controlled. In an interview I conducted with Susan, the executive director of the organization Women Against Violence Everyday (WAVE), she recalled this period of advocacy.[16] She explained that police officers did not take gender-based violence seriously and there were no organizations to protect women during the 1980s. She said: "[In] the country at the time, there was no facility and no one agency working on rape and incest, and frankly, there wasn't much talk of that anyway. The police blotters at that time showed trespassing or battery and usually not rape when there had been." Without police support, organizations, or shelters for survivors of violence to turn to, and without laws or policies condemning gender-based violence, advocates like Susan were doing everything they could to bring visibility to an issue that no one was taking seriously. Susan shared:

So in those early days, it was all about visibility and voice and being heard and just working really hard to establish ourselves in some kind of mainstream thinking. That required me back then to be a real fighter and a real scrapper for everything. We had no money, no funding, no visibility, very little legislative support.

To Susan, "establishing ourselves in some kind of mainstream thinking" meant bringing public attention to gender-based violence for the first time, and the VAWA provided that opportunity. Susan supported police interventions and establishing gender-based violence as a crime because, from her perspective, police were a trustworthy institution and gendered violence needed to be visible and publicly condemned. Susan has dedicated forty years of her life to addressing gender-based violence. From her positionality as a white woman in predominantly white communities, relationships with police officers were

---

[16] The name and organization are pseudonyms to protect the confidentiality of the leader and her organization.

positive, and thus we can understand why she was supportive of punitive approaches to gender-based violence. In Chapter 4, I explain how WAVE's later advocacy also maintained these types of boundaries around policies outside of the VAWA. For now, her recollections illuminate the political context in which mainstream feminists were situated.

Alongside this mainstream perspective, there were simultaneous minority perspectives, especially among women of color, that challenged a criminal justice approach to gender-based violence. In the previous section, I highlighted the statement of Nevada Domestic Crisis Shelter as one of these minority perspectives that challenged police interventions as a primary response and instead proposed addressing related issues such as affordable housing and healthcare. In addition to groups like these, there were also intersectional advocates at the individual level that were part of the coalitions that pushed for these boundaries. For example, I interviewed Jada who was part of the NCASA, an organization that supported the enactment of the VAWA. She was one of the few women of color in this organization, though she didn't feel she could substantively influence their advocacy. She shared: "You could be in a room of about two representatives each state territory of a hundred people. And there would be maybe five, if we're lucky, women of color, people of color, just period, in the room." Jada later left this coalition and created her own organization to focus on the experiences of women of color. Her perspective suggests that, even within organizations that supported the policy boundaries set in the initial version of the VAWA, there were minority counter-perspectives, but they were not very visible. In Chapters 4 and 5, I will come back to Jada and explain her vision for addressing gender-based violence outside of the VAWA.

Finally, at this time there were other groups that abstained from these hearings and the policymaking process to determine the VAWA and did not support legislation around crime control or service interventions that did not address the underlying power imbalances (Richie, 2012). In tension with these different perspectives, the VAWA was enacted in 1994 and it contained policy boundaries that reproduced inequalities among intersectionally marginalized survivors.

POLICY BOUNDARIES AND INEQUALITY

The policy boundaries that defined the VAWA as a crime control and immediate services policy enabled secondary marginalization among women (Cohen, 1999). By this, I mean that the VAWA as enacted in 1994 "expand[ed] and ma[de] accessible the status quo for more privileged members of marginal groups, while the most vulnerable in our communities continue to be stigmatized and oppressed" (Cohen, 2005, p. 443). The VAWA's boundaries did so by (1) contributing to the mass incarceration of poor people and people of color, which included survivors of violence and their communities; (2) concentrating the VAWA's resources and funding toward police interventions and institutions that women of color as well as low-income and immigrant women were less likely to use; (3) establishing immediate services without accounting for how intersectionally marginalized groups would have difficulty accessing them as a product of their citizenship status, native language, sexual orientation, and gender; (4) investing in short-term services that would not address the long-term needs of survivors without economic stability and independence from their abusers; and (5) not accounting for overlapping issues such as tribal rights, which for American Indian and Alaska Native women are central to determining how they sought recourse and the resources to address gender-based violence. Meanwhile, the most privileged women who were English speakers and had financial resources, US citizenship status, and positive experiences with police institutions benefited the most from this version of the VAWA.

The funding allocated toward police training, mandatory arrest laws, and criminalization policies in the VAWA were directly counter to the needs and interests of survivors of color who are often subjected to greater state-sanctioned violence and witness other types of state violence against members of their community. These experiences with state-sanctioned violence by police officers often deter women of color from reporting violence to these institutions (Bell, 2016). Survivors of color are also more aware of stereotypical implications of claiming men of color as perpetrators of violence and, as a result, lack incentives to report sexual violence to the authorities (Davis & Shaylor, 2001; Whittier, 2016). For immigrant women, reporting abusive partners can also jeopardize their residential status and legal rights (Crenshaw, 1994). As Richie (2012) points out, public policies already stigmatize poor women of color, and solutions like the VAWA, which expanded the carceral state, only intensified the impact of male violence for them. Thus, while all women are at risk of experiencing intimate partner or sexual violence, and many will encounter it across social identities, criminalization as a way to address this issue does not equally protect all women. Moreover, allocating billions of dollars to new prison construction and an expansion of police institutions (as opposed to allocating it toward resources like welfare or housing that could improve the economic positionality of all women) directly harmed survivors of color. Domestic violence arrests disproportionately incarcerated women and men of color (Richie, 2012; Whittier, 2016). By focusing on incarceration as the primary solution to gender-based violence, the VAWA led to further marginalization of the poor and people of color. Moreover, the unenforced arrests, and court cases that did not effectively criminalize abusers or only held them in jail for short periods of time, did not benefit more privileged women with better police experiences (Mink, 2001). While middle- and upper-class white women were rarely disproportionately harmed by these criminalization policies, they also did not fully benefit from the policy interventions.

Establishing immediate services in the VAWA without accounting for how intersectionally marginalized groups would access these services resulted in exclusionary practices that prevented survivors from getting the help they needed. Among immigrant women without formal citizenship, the exclusions in the VAWA were particularly detrimental. For example, in 1996, Mariella Batista was killed by her intimate partner after she was denied legal services and an order of protection based on her immigration status (Claiborne, 1996). At this time, the VAWA provided legal services to survivors of domestic abuse, but Mariella did not qualify for them. To qualify, the VAWA would need to be amended and linked to other legislation on immigration that distributed these rights to immigrant survivors of violence. In the absence of this linkage, Mariella pleaded for and was denied legal services. In 1996, her abusive partner shot and killed her on one of her many attempts to seek legal representation. Her story was captured in several newspaper headlines such as the *Washington Post* and the *New York Times*. It was also mentioned in the congressional hearings on VAWA.[17] Policy gaps such as these exacerbated inequalities among women by their race, ethnicity, and citizenship status.

The emphasis on and allocation of resources toward immediate services such as short-term counseling services, shelters, and hotlines also disproportionately benefited middle- and upper-class survivors of violence with the resources to seek long-term care afterwards. Middle-class and high-income women have access to resources that help keep their abuse private, such as private physicians that guard them from other institutions such as the police or social service agencies. Low-income women who lack these resources are more likely to be subjected to state coercion by bureaucrats and privacy invasion as they seek help from social service agencies (Chesney-Lind, 2002; Miller, 1989). Moreover, without the economic resources to afford independent housing, long-term healthcare, and food for themselves or for their children, survivors of violence are incentivized to return to their abusive partners for economic support (Coker, 2004). Among those that do not return to these abusive households, many become homeless, especially transgender survivors who could not access temporary shelters (Mottet & Ohle, 2006).

While the initial version of the VAWA in 1994 provided some funding to American Indian reservations, it did not include policy or funding interventions that fully considered the positionality of American Indian and Alaska Native women and their experiences with violence. This group are disproportionately subjected to the most sexual violence compared to other groups, and yet the resources designated to tribal governments do not match this disproportionate need (Hartman, 2021). Moreover, the VAWA did not address other issues such as tribal sovereignty or Indigenous rights that undergird American Indian and Alaska Native women's experiences with violence. For example, in the

---

[17] Hearing before the Committee on the Judiciary United States Senate, Combating Violence Against Women, May 15, 1996.

congressional hearings in 2005 advocates reference a case in Oklahoma where two unidentified American Indian women were intentionally sexually assaulted by non-Native men who blindfolded them so they would not be able to decipher if this violence took place on federal, state, or tribal land.[18] This distinction was important, because depending on what land the act took place on, the tribal government would not have the power to intervene. Moreover, the 1948 General Crimes Act extended federal jurisdiction onto an American Indian reservation when a non-Native person was involved in a crime. These other policy and legal contexts shaped recourse for American Indian and Native Alaska women who experienced violence particularly by non-Native perpetrators by either subjecting them to US federal legal requirements (as opposed to tribal responses to the issue) or not designating a legal actor to intervene whatsoever. In Oklahoma, 58 percent of cases at this time involved non-Native perpetrators (Grenier & Locker, 2007). Without addressing these other policy and legal dynamics, the VAWA in 1994 did very little to provide American Indian and Native Alaska women with resources to navigate these situations that were unique to their positionality.

The VAWA's policy boundaries excluded intersectionally marginalized groups by not accounting for how criminalization would exacerbate their circumstances and through its lack of connection with other policy areas such as welfare, immigration, and tribal rights. These are the boundaries and separations between policies that intersectional advocates[19] encountered and sought to reconfigure. To them, these boundaries were incompatible with serving intersectionally marginalized groups. The VAWA would be amended over the next twenty-five years, and I found that intersectional advocates leveraged congressional hearings to make a case for policy linkages between the VAWA and these three other policy areas by proposing amendments. These amendments would link the VAWA to policy on welfare, immigration, and tribal rights, which would fundamentally challenge its boundaries and better represent the lived experiences of intersectionally marginalized survivors.

INTERSECTIONAL ADVOCACY AND RECONFIGURATION

The enactment of the VAWA was not the end of the policymaking process; the statute included a "sunset clause" that required it to be reauthorized upon its expiration. As a result, the statute changed four times between 1994 and 2014. This process of reauthorization was accompanied by committee and subcommittee hearings where organizations had opportunities to influence the policy process. In Chapter 3, I analyze these hearings and find that a group of

---

[18] Hearing before the Committee on Indian Affairs United States Senate, Examining the Prevalence of and Solutions to Stopping Violence Against Indian Women, September 27, 2007.

[19] I use the term "intersectional advocates" to refer to organizational leaders who practice intersectional advocacy.

organizations consistently challenged the policy boundaries set in 1994 and proposed laws, policies, and programs that required amendments to other pieces of legislation outside of the VAWA. Intersectional advocates in hearings often brought up stories similar to those of Mariella's that were mentioned in this chapter to communicate how these boundaries were harmful to intersectionally marginalized women and to underscore a need for policymaking that linked issue areas together. Over time, their recommendations for policy change across issue areas were partially incorporated into later versions of the VAWA. Figure 2.3 illustrates the policy linkages that occur over time between the VAWA and other policies.

Studies of policymaking often take policy boundaries for granted (Faling et al., 2019). The few that do study boundary crossing in the policy process often focus on how advocates reframe issues to make their policy goals more convincing to legislatures or how they draw from other successful policy regimes to make their claims (Failing et al., 2019). For example, Ramanathan (2021) found that advocates of maternity leave drew on civil rights claims and, in doing so, were able to adopt (unpaid) family and medical leave policies despite an unfavorable political context for expanding social welfare policies. I build on this work by observing how advocates not only made claims across policy boundaries but also proposed policies that linked seemingly distinct, bounded policy areas together. In Chapter 3, I will return to Figure 2.3 and explain how intersectional advocates pursued these linkages between policy areas. In doing so, I argue that these policies are fundamentally reconfigured.

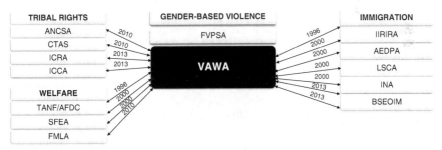

FIGURE 2.3 Intersectional advocacy policy linkages and VAWA change 1994–2014
Note. AEDPA = Anti-terrorism and Effective Death Penalty Act; ANCSA = Alaska Native Claims Settlement Act; BSEOIM = Border Security, Economic Opportunity, and Immigration Modernization Act; CTAS = Coordinated Tribal Assistance Solicitation; FMLA = Family and Medical Leave Act; FVPSA = Family Violence Prevention and Services Act; ICCA = Indian Country Crimes Act; ICRA = Indian Civil Rights Act; IIRIRA = Illegal Immigration Reform and Immigrant Responsibility Act; INA = Immigration and Nationality Act ; LSCA = Legal Services Corporation Appropriations Act; SEFA = Security and Financial Empowerment Act; TANF/AFDC = Temporary Assistance for Needy Families/Aid to Families with Dependent Children; VAWA = Violence Against Women Act

CONCLUSION

While clear boundaries around a policy that define a problem area and constrain possible policy solutions make the policy process more efficient, they can also reproduce inequalities. In this chapter, I examined how policy boundaries around gender-based violence were set during the passage of the VAWA and the role of different feminist groups in this process. The participation of mainstream organizations in the early congressional hearings before the enactment of the VAWA underscores the role these groups play in establishing and reinforcing policy boundaries that can reproduce inequities among intersectionally marginalized groups. In an effort to immediately respond to a national crisis of violence against women, these advocates focused on police intervention, public awareness, and immediate services to help women escape from their circumstances.

While we can understand why advocates focused on this approach given the political context of the time, these solutions did not account for how different positionalities by class, race, and ethnicity among women impacted their access to these policies, their experiences with police officers, their language or citizenship status, or their income level. These outcomes should provoke us to ask: Did mainstream organizations make the right compromises to pass VAWA? Was excluding intersectionally marginalized groups from VAWA and expanding funding for the mass incarceration worth the policy gains for addressing gendered-based violence? In the words of Cathy Cohen in her interview with *Signs*:

[F]eminism should also require us to think broadly and radically about what we are fighting for – the outcomes we seek to the oppression that we face. Radical black feminists, in particular, have argued that while immediate policy changes can be part of what we fight for, the structural transformation of the lived condition of marginal communities has to guide our struggle. (Cohen & Jackson, 2016)

The lived conditions of marginal communities guide intersectional advocacy. Intersectional advocates representing groups with these marginalized positionalities recognized these deficits of the VAWA in 1994. While they were minimally represented in the policy process prior to 1994, they intervened more often in later congressional hearings that occurred across reauthorization cycles. In Chapter 3, I present an analysis of these interventions and show how, over time, intersectional advocates' approach to policymaking influenced policymakers to adopt several revisions of the VAWA. While VAWA was not the ideal policy for intersectional advocates, it was an opportunity to participate in the policymaking process. As these advocates intervened, the VAWA changed remarkably between 1994 and 2014 in ways that better reflected the diversity of the US population experiencing gender-based violence.

3

Reconfiguring the Violence Against Women Act

> The truth is that the Violence Against Women Act was never about just the money ... It established protections for battered immigrant women. It required states to honor each other's protective orders. And most importantly, it brought people together to the table who had never been together before to create multi-disciplinary responses to end violence against women.
>
> National Network to End Domestic Violence, Hearing before the Subcommittee on Crime and Drugs of the Committee on the Judiciary United States Senate, April 16, 2002

Between 1994 and 2014, the Violence Against Women Act (VAWA) changed substantially to include amendments, provisions, and additional legislation that better served intersectionally marginalized survivors, people marginalized across more than one axis of their identity (e.g., gender, race, ethnicity, class). In this chapter, I show that intersectional advocacy is one important explanation for why these changes occurred. Select advocacy groups, what I call "intersectional advocates," played this important role in the policymaking process by influencing how legislators understood, discussed, and proposed to address gender-based violence. Intersectional advocates influenced these legislators through consistent testimony and statements in the congressional hearings on the VAWA that emphasized issue and policy linkages between this Act and legislation on welfare, immigration, and tribal law. By 2014, there were several linkages between these policies. While these changes certainly cannot be attributed to intersectional advocacy alone, I show clear evidence that the policy linkages intersectional advocates proposed were included in revised versions of the VAWA. In doing so, I illustrate how these groups intervened in the policymaking process. I also show how the policy linkages that were successfully established between the VAWA, welfare, immigration, and tribal law reconfigured the policy boundaries of the VAWA in ways that benefited intersectionally marginalized survivors of violence. In Chapter 2, I explained that the initial enactment of the VAWA contained policy boundaries by defining gender-based violence as a crime and addressing it as an isolated problem with reactionary services. These boundaries benefited the most advantaged survivors who are only marginalized across one axis of their identity (i.e., gender) while exasperating policy gaps for intersectionally marginalized survivors who are positioned between more than one issue area.

Examining the evolution of the VAWA through the testimony and statements from advocacy organizations, this chapter highlights the ways in which fragmented policies can be linked to create more comprehensive policy outcomes for intersectionally marginalized populations. This outcome not only better serves those at the margins in addressing the issue of gender-based violence but also expands their rights and improves their overall positionality in the United States (i.e., increasing financial security, obtaining citizenship, improving their health). These types of policy benefits not only address the issue of gender-based violence but also reduce the overall vulnerability of intersectionally marginalized groups to additional issues such as poverty, incarceration, and homelessness. Intersectional advocates have a vision for US policy that comprehensively addresses how issues overlap with one another, and this vision is partly visible in the changes that occurred between 1994 and 2014 in the VAWA.

The VAWA was able to be revised in this time period because it has a legal feature, the sunset clause, that permits the law to be revised, reauthorized, or to expire. This temporary authorization requires Congress and the president to pass a new law whenever the initial one expires. Some of these laws do expire (Fagan & Bilgel, 2015; Kouroutakis, 2016), but laws like the VAWA, the Voting Rights Act, and the Elementary and Secondary Education Act (ESEA) are traditionally renewed because they address social problems or needs that are ongoing and publicly recognized (Adler & Wilkerson, 2013). Unlike other laws, this legal feature establishes "reauthorization cycles," which are periods of time between when the law is renewed and expires. These years in between reauthorization enable Congress to evaluate a law's implementation, solicit feedback from stakeholders and practitioners, and assess the ongoing needs of the issue it seeks to address (Adler & Wilkerson, 2013). Because Congress is incentivized to engage in these activities, there are institutionalized processes for seeking this information, which include the congressional hearings.

Congressional hearings are opportunities for interest groups, advocacy organizations, practitioners, and other stakeholders to influence the content of these laws when they are renewed. All of these groups can and do leverage this streamlined policy process to influence laws such as the VAWA. The most common form of advocacy I observed in the congressional hearings was advocating for updates and changes to existing policies, programs, and laws that were already passed in previous versions of the VAWA (i.e., staying within the policy boundaries). This form of advocacy is well documented (Adler &

Wilkerson, 2013; Gover & Moore, 2020; Rivera, 1996). Alongside this advocacy, though, select groups proposed issue and policy linkages that required the VAWA not only to be renewed but also to be amended, to include the passage of new legislation, and to be connected to policies outside of it. This advocacy challenged the policy boundaries of the VAWA by making those boundaries more permeable in order to connect the Act to laws, policies, and legislation defined outside of its scope.

I identify this engagement as "intersectional advocacy," and in this chapter I show (1) how this form of advocacy differs from traditional approaches among those representing intersectionally marginalized populations, (2) how advocacy groups established relationships with legislators that supported this advocacy, (3) the policy linkages intersectional advocates proposed between the VAWA and welfare, immigration, and tribal policies, as well as the extent to which these linkages were successfully established, and (4) the types of advocacy infrastructures that served as a precedent for maintaining and promoting future linkages. At the end of this chapter, I discuss how the policy linkages that were successfully established in the VAWA fundamentally reconfigured its policy boundaries and recognize the role these organizations played in influencing the processes that led to these outcomes. In this legislative setting, reauthorization cycles are key to observing how intersectional advocates strategically pushed for issue and policy linkages.

REAUTHORIZATION CYCLES AND POLICYMAKING

The analyses presented in this chapter illustrate that the sunset clause in the VAWA created opportunities for advocacy groups to regularly engage in the legislative process and pursue policy change. Among intersectional advocates, I found this opportunity presented them with the greatest resource to persuade legislators to make policy connections between the VAWA and other policies: time. Sunset clauses are temporal, which means they allow a law to be revised, reauthorized, or to expire (Fagan & Bilgel, 2015; Kouroutakis, 2016). Very little research in political science and legal studies has examined how groups leverage sunset clauses to contest and reshape legislation even though there are numerous laws with this feature (e.g., the VAWA, the Voting Rights Act, the ESEA). Most studies on sunset clauses have focused on tax and anti-terrorist laws, which last for shorter periods of time and eventually expire (Baugus & Bose, 2015; Finn, 2010; Listokin, 2009; Tucker, 2007; Viswanathan, 2007; Warner, 1986, 1986). Meanwhile, there has been little attention to how sunset clauses through the reauthorization periods they create present opportunities for advocacy groups to influence the policymaking process.

The analyses I present in this chapter examine the participation of advocacy groups in the congressional hearings on the VAWA across reauthorization cycles. In the VAWA, reauthorization periods known as "reauthorization cycles" mark defined periods of time to observe what organizations advocated

TABLE 3.1 *Reauthorization cycles of the Violence Against Women Act (VAWA)*

Cycle	Passage and Reauthorization Year	Party of President at Reauthorization	Senate Majority at Reauthorization	House Majority at Reauthorization
1990–4	1994	Democrat	Democrat	Democrat
1995–9	2000	Democrat	Republican	Republican
2000–4	2005	Republican	Republican	Republican
2005–13	2014	Democrat	Democrat	Democrat

for and to what extent these interests were reflected in the renewed version of the Act by the end of the cycle. Testimonies and statements from the congressional hearings during these time periods then provide a running transcript of this advocacy. In this chapter, I present an analysis of all the testimonies and statements from the congressional hearings on the VAWA between 1990 and 2014, which encompass four reauthorization cycles. Table 3.1 presents these cycles and the partisanship makeup of the House, Senate, and president at the time of reauthorization.

These reauthorization cycles present three different configurations of party control of the House, Senate, and presidency. Partisanship influences the VAWA reauthorization process (see Dreveskracht, 2013; Whittier, 2016). For example, the partisanship makeup of the House and Senate influenced the number of congressional hearings on the VAWA (Whittier, 2016). Although these partisanship differences were included in my analysis of the testimonies and statements, I did not find that partisanship was related to when intersectional advocacy occurred in the hearings. For example, I found that intersectional advocacy occurred even when Republicans had control of the Senate and House. Variation in partisanship among the House, Senate, and presidency also did not account for the types of policies intersectional advocates proposed or when these proposed changes were incorporated into the revisions of the VAWA. While partisanship certainly has an overall effect on policymaking decisions, the number of hearings that occurred, and votes for VAWA (see Dreveskracht, 2013; Whittier, 2016), it does not determine when intersectional advocacy occurs. Partisanship does affect what types of relationships intersectional advocates are able to cultivate with political officials; political officials that use intersectional advocacy language are mostly affiliated with the Democratic Party. Thus, partisanship is a force that can determine resources for intersectional advocacy, but it does not explain when and why intersectional advocacy occurs in the hearings. Partisanship I observed in the hearings is also not related to the implemented policy changes that reflect intersectional advocacy goals over the course of the VAWA reauthorization cycles. More research should be done to fully tease out how the partisanship status of individual political officials influenced their decisions to support (or not support) intersectional advocacy, but in this chapter my focus is on the advocacy groups: how they strategically engage with these officials and propose both issue and policy linkages throughout the hearings. With specific attention to these groups, I do not observe that their behaviors change according to differences in partisanship.

It is also important to note, though, that these policy changes are undoubtedly influenced by a variety of additional factors that I did not observe, including intragroup coalitions, legislative interests, activism, the #MeToo movement, events and news coverage, policy windows in other legislative areas, and interest groups' advocacy beyond VAWA reauthorization. While acknowledging these other forces are cooccurring, the analyses in this chapter focus on how advocacy organizations representing intersectionally marginalized groups participated in the policymaking process on the VAWA.

To examine the participation of these groups, a subsample was drawn from the congressional hearings of all the testimonies and statements by individuals representing advocacy groups, which also included transcribed conversations between these advocates and legislators. These testimonies and statements were coded using a codebook designed to inductively capture patterns (Fereday & Muir-Cochrane, 2006) among advocacy groups representing intersectionally marginalized populations as well as a cross comparison (Merriam & Tisdell, 2015) of these approaches to other organizations that did not prioritize this population. This inductive analysis approach led to the emerging theme of "intersectional advocacy," which was the outcome of noting consistent instances of proposed issue and policy linkages among select advocates in the congressional hearings. Additional codes to capture these themes were then added to the codebook and used to code the hearings. After identifying the proposed policy linkages by advocacy groups from these analyses, I then examined the revisions of the VAWA over the four reauthorization cycles and noted when there was an amendment, new legislation, or new laws that provided evidence that these proposed linkages successfully occurred.[1]

The findings presented in this chapter are based on this analysis and focus primarily on the organizations that participated in intersectional advocacy. However, to fully understand the novelty of intersectional advocacy, I also present the findings from analyzing advocacy groups that participated in the more traditional method of proposing interventions within the policy boundaries of the VAWA. This comparison is helpful for understanding the counterfactual approach when it comes to representing intersectionally marginalized populations.

---

[1] The full codebook, subsample, list of witnesses and participants, and the description of the analysis approach are all located in the Appendices.

REPRESENTING INTERSECTIONALLY MARGINALIZED WOMEN

Intersectionally marginalized women – women who are marginalized by more than one identity (e.g., Black, Latina, Asian, American Indian, low-income, and immigrant women) – were mentioned 954 times by different organizational leaders across all four reauthorization cycles. Advocates that referenced these groups varied in how they sought to address the experiences and problems faced by women with intersectionally marginalized identities. I argue that this variance is reflected in how advocacy groups worked either within or outside the policy boundaries of the VAWA as they advanced their efforts and policy goals. Groups that worked within the VAWA to advocate for intersectionally marginalized women often focused on policies that increased their access to services, such as allocating more funding to hire bilingual staff. These are important improvements for intersectionally marginalized survivors whose native language is not English, and they stay within the scope of the VAWA. However, for intersectionally marginalized survivors whose first language is Spanish and who do not have US citizenship or a green card, bilingual services are not enough to grant them safe access to shelters, hotlines, and legal services because immigration law has not been changed. Advocacy groups that thus worked outside of the boundaries of the VAWA pushed for changes to policies such as immigration law because they saw a need to expand the boundaries of the VAWA by connecting it to other relevant policies. Figure 3.1 provides a distribution of coded testimonies according to these two approaches among organizational leaders. Testimonies that represented an intersectional advocacy approach by leaders occurred far less than those that represented a traditional approach to policymaking (i.e., staying within the bounds of the VAWA to make political claims).

Advocates that viewed the VAWA as the primary solution for their goals to serve intersectionally marginalized survivors focused on issues of access within existing programs funded in the previous VAWA – and further strengthened these policy boundaries. This advocacy was driven by grassroots and service organizations such as the Harriet Tubman Center, the House of Ruth, the Shelter for Abused Women, and UNIDOS Against Domestic Violence. These organizational leaders advocated for bilingual services to access hotlines,[2] nondiscriminatory training for service providers,[3] removal of citizenship requirements to access shelters,[4] funding for multicultural service organizations,[5]

---

[2] Hearings before the Committee on the Judiciary, Combating Violence Against Women, May 15, 1996.

[3] Hearings before the Committee on the Judiciary, U.S. Senate. 2005 Reauthorization of the Violence Against Women Act, July 19, 2005.

[4] Hearings before the Committee on the Judiciary, Domestic Violence: Not Just a Family Matter, June 30, 1994.

[5] Hearings before the Committee on the Judiciary, Reauthorization of the Violence Against Women Act, July 19, 2005.

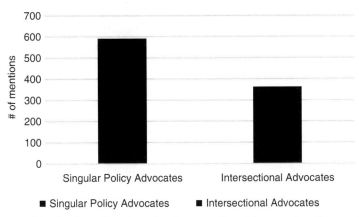

FIGURE 3.1 Distribution of testimonies that mentioned intersectionally marginalized women

and making shelters available on reservations.[6] These advocates stayed within the boundaries of the programs authorized by the previous VAWA to meet their goals and objectives, which were to improve access to these resources for women who were also marginalized by class, race, ethnicity, and citizenship status. However, this approach did not address interrelated issues such as immigration status, poverty, or tribal sovereignty. Advocates that argued for expanding access to programs that were already part of the VAWA succeeded in making each version of the VAWA more inclusive for women with intersectionally marginalized identities.

Without attention to other issues, though, these policy changes did not fully address the additional vulnerabilities these groups faced. For example, making shelters more available on reservations would not address the complexity of adjudicating on violence against American Indian women that occurred on tribal land by US citizens. The latter would require amendments and changes to tribal-related legislation. In the section "Policy Linkages and Tribal Law," I will show that some of these advocates recognized the limitations of this strategy, especially when serving American Indian survivors, and changed to an intersectional approach where they focused on sovereignty laws and tribal legislation outside of the VAWA. Meanwhile, there was another group of advocates who represented intersectionally marginalized women but did so differently by attempting to link the VAWA to policies addressing issues beyond the scope of previous versions of the Act. As these advocates encountered the boundaries of the previous VAWA, they argued that past institutional structures constrained the extent to which VAWA programs

[6] Hearings before the Committee on Indian Affairs, Examining the Prevalence of and Solutions to Stopping Violence Against Indian Women, September 27, 2007.

could serve intersectionally marginalized groups. They then brought attention to how experiences with violence were magnified by other issues such as unaffordable housing, poverty, tribal sovereignty, and lack of citizenship status. For these advocates, there was a false boundary between the VAWA and these other policies. Thus, they aimed to reinterpret these rigid boundaries and, in the process, advocate for new provisions and amendments of the VAWA that formed linkages to other policies, laws, and legislation. In the remainder of this chapter, I describe this approach at length.

INTERSECTIONAL ADVOCATES

Intersectional advocates are individuals or organizations that advocate for linkages between policies and issues that reflect the experiences of intersectionally marginalized groups positioned between more than one problem area. Groups and individuals advocate for these linkages in their testimonies and statements in the congressional hearings by making a case for connecting the VAWA to either another problem (e.g., poverty, homelessness, lack of immigration rights, unaffordable housing, lack of tribal sovereignty) and/or another policy (e.g., Temporary Assistance for Needy Families [TANF], the Illegal Immigration Reform and Immigrant Responsibility Act [IIRIRA], the Indian Country Crimes Act). Over the course of the hearings and reauthorization cycles, they build relationships with legislators, and some of these legislators make an effort to advocate for these issue and policy linkages. When policy linkages are successfully implemented by the end of one reauthorization cycle, intersectional advocates reference these linkages to set a precedent for normalizing this approach to policymaking. They also refer to these previous instances as a way to maintain these more porous boundaries of the VAWA. When advocacy groups use this strategy, I refer to it as "advocacy infrastructure" because it provides a tool kit of policy victories that they can draw on to be more persuasive when they advocate for additional linkages or expanding the scope of previous laws. An example of this strategy would be advocating for increasing the number of eligible U Visas once there was policy linkage in place between immigration law and the VAWA for granting this type of visa to survivors of violence.

Intersectional advocacy was far less common than others presented in the congressional hearings; however, I did note that there were more instances of it over time. Figure 3.2 demonstrates this increase, and there are a few reasons that explain why based on my analyses. Firstly, new organizations showed up in the congressional hearings that engaged in this practice, especially when there is a hearing dedicated to the specific group they represent (e.g., American Indian women, immigrant women). More hearings were dedicated to specific identity groups as time went on, which means there were more opportunities for these new groups to participate in the hearings. Secondly, some organizations changed their strategies over time to an intersectional advocacy approach.

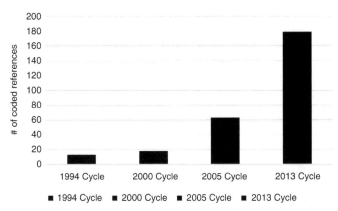

FIGURE 3.2 Intersectional advocacy over time

This shift in strategy often occurred when organizations could not achieve their policy goals by working within the VAWA alone, and I show examples of these instances. Thirdly, as more policy and issue linkages successfully occurred throughout the time of the hearings, advocates had more precedent to reference previous linkages and advocate for new ones. Together, these types of changes in organizational participation increased the visibility of intersectional advocacy in the hearings.

While I kept track of this increase in occurrences, it is important to note that the qualitative analyses of these testimonies and statements are most helpful for understanding how organizations engaged in intersectional advocacy and to what extent this advocacy was reflected in changes to the VAWA and other policies. In this chapter, I will show that consistent efforts over time to link the VAWA to other policies correspond to actual changes in amendments, provisions, and new legislation passed.

RELATIONSHIP BUILDING AND ISSUE LINKAGES

Reauthorization cycles presented all advocacy groups with several opportunities to engage with legislators that serve on committees and subcommittees on the VAWA; and for intersectional advocates, these opportunities were especially important for communicating issue linkages. US policy organizes "various social benefits operationally, fiscally, and symbolically separate from one another" (Weir et al., 1988, p. 9). The VAWA, as shown in Chapter 2, is no different than these other policies, which means that, in order for intersectional advocates to persuade legislators to rethink the policy boundaries of the VAWA, they need time to conceptually change long-standing and historical precedent to create policy change within a single Act. Time with legislators over the course of the reauthorization cycles provided intersectional advocates with opportunities to change how legislators understood, discussed, and proposed to address the issue of gender-based violence.

There were a few important examples of these exchanges between intersectional advocates and legislators in the congressional hearings. For example, some legislators like Senator Kennedy (D-MA) adopted the language used by intersectional advocates to connect citizenship rights to issues of violence. This change is especially apparent in how political officials responded to advocates pushing for new provisions in the Anti-terrorism and Effective Death Penalty Act (AEDPA) of 1996. Intersectional advocates, particularly from the NOW Legal Defense and Education Fund Immigration Program[7] and the National Network to End Violence Against Immigrant Victims, argued that this bill made women who unlawfully entered the United States ineligible for the VAWA protections. To communicate this point, organizational leaders recounted the story of Mariella, a Cuban woman without US citizenship who was killed because she did not have the appropriate protections under the Anti-terrorism bill (see Chapter 2). They went on to reference the 1996 Legal Services Corporation Appropriations bill as another piece of legislation that prevented Mariella from getting the legal help she needed.

This story is repeated by Senator Kennedy (D-MA) in the hearing to make the same point offered by organizational leaders:

She wanted protection, but there was nothing the agency could do because under the 1996 Legal Services Corporation Appropriations bill, the agency could not even use private funds to help her, since she was not yet a permanent resident. She was in the protected parole position, as is given to Cubans before there are adjustments of status. What was the result? Her husband killed her. The courthouse deputies killed her husband. Her young son is left an orphan. Steps which could have been taken to protect the woman from her abuser were not taken because Congress denied her access to the agencies which could help her. So, this is just one example of what happens when Congress passes legislation that goes too far, I believe, whether it is help and assistance for legal services programs, youth crime prevention programs, or others.[8]

In this example, intersectional advocates from the Now Legal Defense and Education Fund Immigration Program and the National Network to End Violence Against Immigrant Victims explicitly brought legislators' attention to the intersectionally marginalized identities of their supporters (i.e., gender, ethnicity, class, and citizenship status) to tell a story about how the government failed to protect them by enforcing other legislation that withheld citizenship rights. They connected this failure to the political institutions (i.e., Congress)

---

[7] Note that the organization NOW has several branches of organizations and programs that operate distinctly separately from one another. This group is not the same as the National Organization for Women's (NOW) Legal Defense and Education Fund that led the taskforce on VAWA.

[8] The hearing before the Committee on the Judiciary United States Senate, May 15, 1996.

that created laws that undermined the goals of the VAWA and suggested changes to the VAWA as an opportunity to change policy to serve their constituents who are trapped between them. Public officials like Senator Kennedy (D-MA) then used these same stories and rhetoric to make connections between immigration policy and the VAWA.

The hearings also highlight a unique opportunity that reauthorization cycles present to organizational leaders: to build relationships with committee members. Most of the relationships between intersectional advocates and legislators reported in the congressional hearings are with legislators from the Democratic Party. Republicans called fewer witnesses per hearing than Democrats and held fewer hearings altogether. Thus, relationship building predominantly occurred with Democrat legislators.

These relationships were important for engaging in intersectional advocacy, particularly during the exchanges on the floor when legislatures asked witnesses questions. For example, the following is an exchange between Ms. Rodgers, an organizational leader from the NOW Legal Defense and Education Fund, and Senator Wellstone (D-MN), on TANF:

SENATOR WELLSTONE: Let me ask you one final question, because this will probably be a very contentious issue this September, on the whole question of TANF and welfare reform and the notion of work, and then trying to reach a goal of maybe 70 percent of the mothers working outside the home 40 hours a week, or 30 hours a week. Can you spell out for us how domestic violence, and also as it spills off to the workplace, would affect this requirement that women work?

MS. RODGERS: Well, the short answer to that is that violence makes women poor and keeps women poor. It throws them into poverty because they lose their job or economic security. It keeps them in that situation because they cannot work. If the TANF reauthorization does not recognize the fact that a woman who is in a violent situation must deal with that situation first and get herself out of it to make herself workable, then it is just going to be the U.S. Government punishing that woman yet again for the crimes of somebody else. That is the U.S. Government punishing children for the crimes of somebody else. I do not think the Government should be in that business. We did in the original 1996 TANF manage to get the family violence option into the welfare reform. We had hoped it would be mandatory, but it was an option which said that these requirements could be waived for a temporary period to give the woman the kind of help and support she needs so that she can work. What Senators need to know is that these women want to work. They do not want to stay in this situation forever. But we as a society need to provide some support. The good news is that some 40-plus States have adopted either the family violence option or something very close to it. It has had some beneficial effects. We think that the States that have not done that should be required to do it.

SENATOR WELLSTONE: Senator Murray and I wrote that, and we wanted to do it that way and could not, so we are going to have to revisit it.[9]

---

[9] Hearing before the Committee on Health, Education, Labor, and Pensions United States Senate, July 25, 2002.

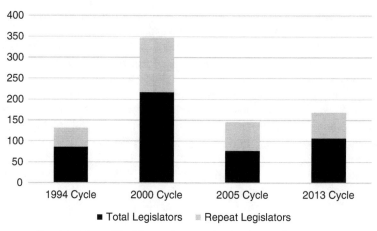

FIGURE 3.3 Participation of legislators by reauthorization cycle

In the above floor exchange, Senator Wellstone (D-MN) is asking for talking points to make a case for reforming TANF and goes on to say that he and Senator Murray (D-WA) will try again to connect these issues together outside of the VAWA hearings. Supportive committee members who are present across authorization cycles are important for maintaining the momentum for proposed policy changes, especially when organizational leaders suggest revising contested bills such as welfare. This support was not just lip service to organizations. Legislators advocated for these changes in other types of legislation. For example, Senator Smith (D-MN) in particular led efforts to connect the VAWA with immigration and welfare reform by ensuring that the IIRIRA extended welfare benefits to immigrant survivors of domestic violence.[10]

This consistency in representation is partly a function of committee appointments, which allows intersectional advocates to interact with political representatives regularly. The committee system allows advocates to develop long-standing relationships with members of Congress that can translate into these forms of allyship. In total, 232 different legislators sat on these committees for the hearings. Figure 3.3 shows how many legislators participated in the hearings for each reauthorization cycle and how many were present more than one time. Fifteen of the members sat on at least 25 percent of the hearings.

This distribution of 232 legislatures across the hearings demonstrates the breadth of legislators that organizational leaders interacted with over the span of the reauthorization cycles as well as repeat participants they could build

---

[10] Hearing before the Committee on the Judiciary United States Senate, Reauthorization of the Violence Against Women Act, July 19, 2005.

relationships with over time. Senator Kennedy (D-MA) is a good example of this relationship building. He attended the earliest hearings in the 1990s and consistently made appearances throughout the 1990s and 2000s. Kennedy did not chair the committees, and in the earlier hearings there is little record of his participation. However, in the mid-1990s and mid-2000s that changes. He uses similar language to support immigration rights in 1996, and in 2005 he submits a statement supporting the bill while championing intersectional advocates' proposals to address unaffordable housing.[11] This example illustrates how reauthorization cycles allow intersectional advocates to develop relationships with legislatures over time and gain new allies in advancing political goals outside of the VAWA.

POLICY LINKAGES AND WELFARE

The earliest examples of advocacy for policy linkages that occurred in the hearings were from organizational leaders who focused on welfare policy reform, mostly testimonies from advocates representing the NOW Legal Defense and Education Fund (28 percent). The other organizations that advocated for linking welfare and gender violence policies were primarily from national organizations such as the National Women Abuse Prevention Project and Concerned Women for America. Both primarily focus on domestic violence issues (20 percent). However, the groups that most often included welfare policy in their witness testimony came from two legal-based organizations: the National Women Abuse Prevention Project and the Harvard Legal Aid Bureau (40 percent). These two organizations also had multiple interactions with legislatures. Advocates from these two organizations focused on making legislative changes to the following welfare policies: the Aid to Families with Dependent Children (AFDC)/TANF, the Family and Medical Leave Act (FMLA), the Security and Financial Empowerment Act (SFEA), and the IIRIRA. Advocacy efforts by the National Women Abuse Prevention Project and the Harvard Legal Aid Bureau began in 1990 before the implementation of the VAWA in 1994, but linkages between these policies did not occur until later reauthorizations.

While most intersectional advocacy linking gender-based violence and welfare policy focused on increasing resources and financial rights among survivors of domestic violence, intersectional advocates in the early 1990s – especially from the National Women Abuse Prevention Project – used their testimonies and statements to advocate for greater welfare support for all Americans. They submitted budget sheets comparing the funding women received from the state to their actual needs and made a case for increasing welfare funds for all.[12]

[11] Hearing before the Committee on the Judiciary United States Senate, July 19, 2005.
[12] Committee on the Judiciary United States Senate on Legislation to Reduce the Growing Problem of Violent Crime Against Women, August 29 and December 11, 1990.

TABLE 3.2 *Social welfare policies that intersectional advocates proposed to be amended*

Social Welfare Policy	1994	2000	2005	2013
Temporary Assistance for Needy Families (TANF)/Aid to Families with Dependent Children (AFDC)	✓	✓	✓	✓
Family and Medical Leave Act (FMLA)	✓			
Illegal Immigration Reform and Immigrant Responsibility Act (IIRIRA)	✓	✓		
Security and Financial Empowerment Act (SFEA)				✓

By focusing on domestic violence survivors who were also homeless, this organization also advocated for welfare reform that was not reliant on a person's residential status.[13] As intersectional advocates explained the experiences of domestic violence survivors among low-income women to legislators, they advocated for legislative reform that was outside of the VAWA's traditional boundaries. These initiatives would benefit not only survivors of violence but also others who experienced poverty and homelessness. This advocacy steadily increased over time from the first cycle in 1994 until 2009. Table 3.2 illustrates which social welfare policies organizational leaders focused on during the hearings between these cycles. While intersectional advocates concentrated on a variety of policies, AFDC/TANF was a consistent focus, particularly because it was the most difficult to reform over time.

Leading up to the 1994 implementation of the VAWA, intersectional advocates from the National Women Abuse Prevention Project, the Center Against Sexual and Domestic Abuse, and the NOW Legal Defense and Education Fund advocated for their low-income constituents who were often reliant on their partners for financial security. The testimonies and statements of three organizations highlighted the intersection between the issues of violence and poverty. For example, a leader of the National Women Abuse Prevention Project explained the need to expand the VAWA's scope beyond violence prevention:

What rapidly became clear to all of us doing this business is that the safe shelter was the tip of the iceberg. The women coming to us needed everything. They needed legal protection. They needed food. They needed clothing. They needed medical help. They needed low-income housing. They needed job training ... Thus, domestic violence programs, which often began as small, grass-roots voluntary programs, suddenly

---

[13] Roundtable Discussion before the Special Committee on Aging United States Senate, May 4, 1994.

found themselves facing every major social issue confronting our country today: the victimization of women and children, poverty, substance abuse, homelessness ...[14]

Beginning with the hearings that started in 1990, organizational leaders from the National Women Abuse Prevention Project, the Harvard Legal Aid Bureau, and the NOW Legal Defense and Education Fund consistently brought up welfare legislation when discussing the VAWA. They often voiced their concerns that policy implementation issues associated with welfare meant survivors of violence were excluded from these benefits. One of the first issues they discussed in these hearings was homelessness among domestic abuse survivors. An organizational leader from the NOW Legal Defense and Education Fund said: "I have testified and begged and pleaded, working in the area of welfare reform – or on any women's issue – for the experts to recognize that over half the women in homeless shelters have run away from home because of violence, incest, battering, and assault."[15]

This advocate and others from these three organizations connected the issue of homelessness to welfare reform. They explained that many women who were in homeless shelters were there to escape violence from the home. But due to the restrictions in the AFDC/TANF, they could not access necessary welfare funds.[16] Organizational leaders continued to focus on the failure of these policies to highlight how their constituents were unable to access welfare programs based on their socioeconomic and residential status. In a different hearing, they also argued that even women who were eligible for welfare were not applying for the AFDC/TANF because their abusive partners could access their personal information.[17] In both these cases, these intersectional advocates sought to amend qualifications and restrictions associated with welfare to ensure that women who experienced violence had inclusive access to this policy.

Intersectional advocates utilized narratives that highlighted women's marginalization across both gender and class to advance their political goals by emphasizing how violence had differential outcomes for poor women. They argued that the VAWA alone made it impossible for these women to improve their positionality by describing how women they interacted with at shelters couldn't afford groceries or safe housing – preventing them from escaping poverty.[18,19] They then tied these stories

---

[14] Hearing before the Subcommittee on Children, Family, Drugs and Alcoholism of the Committee on Labor and Human Resources United States Senate, April 19, 1990.

[15] Roundtable Discussion before the Special Committee on Aging United States Senate, May 4, 1994.

[16] Roundtable Discussion before the Special Committee on Aging United States Senate, May 4, 1994.

[17] Hearing before the Committee on the Judiciary United States Senate, First Session on the need to concentrate the fight against an escalating blight of violence against women, February 1, 1993.

[18] Hearing before the Subcommittee on Children, Family, Drugs and Alcoholism of the Committee on Labor and Human Resources United States Senate, April 19, 1990.

[19] Hearing before the Committee on the Judiciary United States Senate, First Session on the need to concentrate the fight against an escalating blight of violence against women, February 1, 1993.

directly to welfare reform as they advocated for changes in eligibility and resource allocation in AFDC/TANF.[20]

Legislation linking AFDC/TANF and the VAWA did not happen for years. Intersectional advocates appeared to be aware of the long timeline for legislating, as they persistently advocated for TANF reform for a decade. Across this time period, advocates consistently tried to normalize linkages between the VAWA and welfare. For example, after the first authorization cycle of 1994, advocates from the NOW Legal Defense and Education Fund and the National Women Abuse Prevention Project referenced their previous efforts in 1994 to make a consistent case for welfare reform in the next cycle. Testimony referencing these consistent arguments and goals from prior reauthorization cycles highlighted the slow progression of their efforts to conceptually reconfigure the boundaries between welfare and gender-based violence policies.

Advocates also focused on smaller policy linkages alongside their commitments to reforming AFDC/TANF. For example, in the 1990s, advocates from these organizations made the case that women who left their jobs as a result of violence or abuse also deserved unemployment benefits provided by this Act.[21] At the time, they could not change TANF, but they did succeed in advocating for the revision of the FMLA, which provided partial rights to survivors of violence. In 2002, organizational leaders and senators referenced this victory to push for further reform, such as providing funding and resources for paid leave, in the next iteration of the welfare bill.[22]

In 2010, the SFEA was passed as a part of TANF, which finally granted survivors of violence a right to emergency leave. This process took time; the first revisions of AFDC/TANF took place in 2002 and the final policy granting emergency leave was not implemented until 2010. Hearings alone likely did not result in these outcomes,[23] but they do provide a running transcript of how these advocacy organizations received legislative support to reform AFDC/ TANF and link it to the VAWA over time through each reauthorization cycle. Intersectional advocates leveraged reauthorization cycles to bring up the same issues repeatedly until these changes were implemented by Congress.

Finally, organizational leaders representing those without citizenship status pursued welfare reform through changes to the IIRIRA. Organizations that pushed for this type of reform included the National Network to End Violence Against Immigrant Victims, and the NOW Legal Defense and Education Fund Immigrant Women Program. These intersectional advocates

---

[20] Hearing before the Subcommittee on Crime and Drugs of the Committee on the Judiciary United States Senate, April 16, 2002.

[21] Hearing before the Subcommittee on Children, Family, Drugs and Alcoholism of the Committee on Labor and Human Resources United States Senate, April 19, 1990.

[22] Hearing before the Committee on Health, Education, Labor, and Pensions United States Senate, July 25, 2002.

[23] It is important to note that there are other hearings, advocacy groups, and legislative interests outside of the VAWA that are also influencing TANF reform at this time.

TABLE 3.3 *Policy linkages between the VAWA and welfare policies*

Agenda Item	Hearing Year(s) Proposed	Linkage	Reauthorization Cycles				Year(s) Enacted
			1990–4	1995–9	2000–4	2005–13	
Social services for homeless people	1990, 1993, 1994, 2002	AFDC/ TANF	✘	✘	✘	✔	2013
Welfare benefits for immigrant survivors	1996, 1999, 2000, 2009	AFDC/ TANF IIRIRA	✘	✔	✔		1996/ 2000
Unemployment benefits/ emergency leave	1993, 1994, 2002, 2009	AFDC/ TANF FMLA SFEA	✘	✔	✘	✔	2000/ 2010

✘ = proposed changes to law/policy that did not take effect that cycle
✔ = proposed changes successfully enacted

emphasized that the IIRIRA meant women survivors without citizenship did not qualify for welfare and argued that a change in both welfare legislation *and* immigration legislation was required:

Restrictions on safety-net benefits also adversely affect immigrant victims' children. Many young noncitizen children are ineligible for federal means-tested public benefit programs like TANF, food stamps, housing assistance, and non-emergency Medicaid. Without adequate access to healthcare, food, clothing, and shelter, children needlessly continue to suffer the devastating effects of violence. Increasing access to safety-net benefits would provide immigrant victims and their children with the financial, medical, and social resources necessary to escape abuse and lead productive lives.[24]

Between 1996 and 2000, organizational leaders from the National Network to End Violence Against Immigrant Victims and the NOW Legal Defense and Education Fund, Immigrant Women Program advocated for the welfare reform for VAWA beneficiaries for those without citizenship status. This reform added provisions to the IIRIRA to extend welfare benefits to immigrant survivors of domestic violence.[25] For intersectional advocates representing women without citizenship, this advocacy was only one part of their broader political agenda to link policies together.

---

[24] Hearing before the Committee on the Judiciary United States Senate on the Continued Importance of the Violence Against Women Act, June 10, 2009.
[25] Subcommittee on Immigration and Claims of the Committee on the Judiciary House of Representatives, July 20, 2000.

Table 3.3 illustrates this incremental process for connecting the VAWA to policies and laws related to welfare. Advocates pushed for changes in legislation such as AFDC/TANF, and FMLA across reauthorization cycles, but the enactment of laws that would support these changes took time. Advocates that attended the VAWA congressional hearings are not the only groups that pushed for welfare reform; other coalitions and organizations also advocated for changes in unemployment benefits in the 1990s (Ramanathan, 2021). Thus, these outcomes are not the sole product of advocacy group efforts. However, by examining their advocacy across reauthorization cycles, we can observe their role in pushing for these changes and the specific policy windows that opened up to house these new linkages between policies and laws. Moreover, while intersectional advocates may not be the only actors pushing for these types of reforms, these policy victories, and their involvement in advocating for them do suggest that the policy outcomes they sought were getting implemented.

POLICY LINKAGES AND IMMIGRATION

Intersectional advocates representing Latina and Asian constituents without US citizenship often advocated for legislative change that connected to immigration policy. In addition to the IIRIRA of 1996, leaders from these organizations also advocated for changes in the AEDPA of 1996, the 1996 Legal Services Corporation Appropriations bill, Border Security, Economic Opportunity, and Immigration Modernization Act (BSEOIM), and Immigration and Nationality Act (INA). Similar to those who worked to link the VAWA to welfare policies, these intersectional advocates strategically leveraged their victories over time to try to accomplish their desired political goals. However, differing from those who focused only on welfare reform, advocates representing women without citizenship often had to advocate for revising multiple types of immigration policies because their constituents could not access resources granted by the VAWA. They argued this approach was necessary because in many cases their constituents' rights were scattered across different laws and Acts. To fully ensure the survivors they represented had protection, safety, residential status, and access to needed resources, organizations turned to immigration policy. Table 3.4 provides an illustration of the policies these advocates focused on during each reauthorization cycle.

For intersectional advocates focusing on immigration reform, the class, ethnic identity, and citizenship status of their constituents were critical identities to highlight in order to make a case for legislative reform outside of the VAWA. In 1996, a coalition of intersectional advocates began making a case for linking the VAWA to immigration policy by mentioning how other Acts, bills, and laws made it impossible for VAWA to adequately protect women without citizenship who experienced violence. These advocates predominantly represented the following organizations: American Civil Liberties Union, NOW Legal Defense Education Fund's Immigrant Women Program, the National

TABLE 3.4 *Immigration policies that intersectional advocates proposed to be amended*

Immigration Policy	1994	2000	2005	2013
Illegal Immigration Reform and Immigrant Responsibility Act (IIRIRA)	✓	✓	✓	✓
Anti-terrorism and Effective Death Penalty Act of 1996 (AEDPA)	✓	✓		
1996 Legal Services Corporation Appropriations bill (LSCA)	✓			
Immigration and Nationality Act (INA)			✓	✓
Border Security, Economic Opportunity, and Immigration Modernization Act (BSEOIM)			✓	✓

Network to End Violence Against Domestic Violence, the National Law Center on Homelessness and Poverty, and the National Network on Behalf of Battered Immigrant Women. While the NOW Legal Defense Education Fund's Immigrant Women Program made up the majority of testimonies on immigration (63 percent), these other legal organizations made up the remaining 37 percent of the testimonies. Most of these organizations or programs specifically focused on the well-being of immigrants.

When mentioning immigrant women in their testimonies, most of the organizations made parallel statements to immigration policy. For example, one leader from the National Network on Behalf of Battered Immigrant Women explained:

We submit comment on the provisions of the Violence Against Women Act which protect battered immigrant women and children (VAWA). These provisions of VAWA take great strides to assure that perpetrators of domestic violence upon immigrant women and children will not remain immune from prosecution by controlling of their victims' immigration status. However, these important protections are being dismantled by recently enacted legislation and threatened by the pending immigration bills which are going to conference. We hope that these comments will be helpful in understanding the accomplishments of VAWA as well as the threats to its continued effectiveness in protecting battered immigrant women and children. The Violence Against Women Act contains two forms of relief that allow battered immigrant women to flee marriages without risking deportation: "self-petitioning" for permanent residency or applying for suspension of deportation. The suspension provisions have been in effect since September 13, 1994, and are currently a governed public health and criminal justice issue.[26]

---

[26] The hearing before the Committee on the Judiciary United States Senate, May 15, 1996.

This testimony connects immigrant rights to the VAWA by explaining that immigrant women cannot be protected by the Act without changes in immigration legislation that provide them with "self-petitioning" for permanent residency. To bridge these issues, intersectional advocates from the National Network on Behalf of Battered Immigrant Women, the NOW Legal Defense and Education Fund's Immigrant Women Program, and the National Network to End Violence Against Immigrant Victims suggested reforming the IIRIRA of 1996 and the INA to extend citizenship and residency rights to those without citizenship status who experienced domestic abuse.[27] To do so, they advocated for the "Adjustment of Status" in the IIRIRA to be reformed so that immigrant women who applied for migrant status under the VAWA had access to visas.[28] Under the INA, they advocated for a special visa for survivors without citizenship.[29] This was a victory. Congress reauthorized the VAWA with the Battered Immigrant Women Protection Act of 2000, which created the U Visa for victims of crimes who did not have citizenship. Those without citizenship status who experienced domestic abuse were now eligible for a visa that would give them lawful status for up to four years, authorization to work, and eligibility to adjust this status to a lawful permanent resident after three years.

Once this connection existed between policies, advocates could propose expanding the rights of women without US citizenship by leveraging this policy linkage to expand immigrant survivors' benefits – and they did. Following the 2000 reauthorization cycle, these same organizations advocated for expanding eligibility under these provisions for the U Visas and adding additional protections for women without US citizenship.[30] By 2005, the second reauthorization added these protections and expanded the eligibility for the U Visa. Following 2005, advocates from these organizations, especially from the National Network on Behalf of Battered Immigrant Women, pushed for expanding the number of available U Visas in their testimony during the hearings.[31] They experienced another incremental victory in the next reauthorization cycle. By the 2013 reauthorization, the Senate approved the S.744 BSEOIM that expanded the annual number of U Visas from 10,000 to 18,000. This Act also allowed VAWA petitioners to adjust their status without being subject to the numerical limits that were part of the INA. Table 3.5 displays these incremental victories over the reauthorization cycles.

The Act also created a policy window for another policy linkage that advocates, especially those from Legal Momentum, had been working on

---

[27] The hearing before the Committee on the Judiciary United States Senate, May 15, 1996.
[28] The hearing before the Committee on the Judiciary United States Senate, May 15, 1996.
[29] The hearing before the Committee on the Judiciary United States Senate, May 15, 1996.
[30] Subcommittee on Immigration and Claims of the Committee on the Judiciary House of Representatives, July 20, 2000.
[31] Hearing before the Committee on the Judiciary United States Senate, May 5, 2010.

TABLE 3.5 *Policy linkages between the VAWA and immigration policies*

Agenda Item	Hearing Year(s) Proposed	Linkage	Reauthorization Cycles				Year(s) Enacted
			1990–4	1995–9	2000–4	2005–13	
Legal protection and work authorization (U Visa)	1993, 1994, 1996, 1999	IIRIRA LSCA INA AEDPA	✘	✘	✓		2000
Welfare benefits	1996, 1999, 2000, 2009	IIRIRA		✓	✓	✘	1996/ 2000
Expand number of U Visas	2000, 2005, 2007, 2009, 2011	BSEOIM INA			✘	✓	2013
Housing benefits	1996, 1999, 2000, 2005, 2009, 2010	BSEOIM		✘	✘	✓	2013

✘ = proposed changes to law/policy that did not take effect that cycle
✓ = proposed changes successfully enacted

since 1996 with no luck whatsoever, which was housing. Housing was often tacked on to a list of public benefits that advocates were trying to provide immigrant survivors. For example, an advocate from Legal Momentum includes housing as a safety-net benefit:

Restrictions on safety-net benefits also adversely affect immigrant victims' children. Many young noncitizen children are ineligible for federal means-tested public benefit programs like TANF, food stamps, housing assistance, and non-emergency Medicaid. Without adequate access to healthcare, food, clothing, and shelter, children needlessly continue to suffer the devastating effects of violence. Increasing access to safety-net benefits would provide immigrant victims and their children with the financial, medical, and social resources necessary to escape abuse and lead productive lives.[32]

---

[32] Hearing before the Committee on the Judiciary United States Senate on the Continued Importance of the Violence Against Women Act, June 10, 2009.

Housing often came up in this way. As Table 3.5 illustrates, housing benefits were mentioned across two reauthorization cycles without any changes to laws or policies in immigration legislation. For the issue of unaffordable housing, the BSEOIM opened up a policy window for a policy on this issue to be linked with the VAWA. Under this Act, a provision was included to permit survivors of violence without US citizenship status to access assisted housing for the first time in US history.

Leaders from the NOW Legal Defense and Education Fund's Immigrant Women Program not only leveraged the VAWA to change laws related to immigration but also proposed that the VAWA include resources to make these laws more effective. For example, these organizations advocated for creating grants through the VAWA to educate localities about the new legal rights for immigrant women survivors of violence that were established through the Immigration and Naturalization Act.[33] Thus, intersectional advocates also sought to provide the resources and needed infrastructure for other immigration policies and programs. As this analysis demonstrates, there are multiple bills and pieces of legislation that intersectional advocates had to contend with that structured the conditions of their supporters. They then advocated for linking together this legislation and VAWA by including amendments, provisions, and new Acts related to these policies. They also advocated for attaching federal resources in the VAWA to support these changes normatively: trainings for judges, funding for legal counsel, and dissemination resources for constituents.[34] These efforts appear to be successful. Across reauthorization cycles, these additional Acts, provisions, and new statutes established new funding streams for immigration rights through the VAWA, a unique visa that created a new pathway for citizenship for immigrant women survivors without citizenship, and eligibility for assisted housing and welfare for this group.

POLICY LINKAGES AND TRIBAL LAW

Intersectional advocacy was also used to link the VAWA to tribal policies. Throughout the 1990s, when American Indian women were specifically mentioned in the congressional hearings it was mostly in relation to issues of sovereignty. Organizational leaders often mentioned instances of crimes that were committed against American Indian women by Americans that were unaddressed because non-Indians could not be prosecuted on reservations.[35,36] This outcome was a result of the Supreme Court ruling in *Oliphant* v. *Suquamish*

---

[33] Hearing before the Subcommittee on Crime and Drugs of the Committee on the Judiciary United States Senate, April 2002.

[34] Hearing before the Subcommittee on Crime and Drugs of the Committee on the Judiciary United States Senate, April 2002.

[35] Hearing before the Committee on the Judiciary United States Senate, May 15, 1996.

[36] Hearing before the Subcommittee on Crime of the Committee on the Judiciary House of Representatives, September 29, 1999.

in 1978, which did not allow tribal authorities to prosecute crimes committed by non-Indian perpetrators on tribal land. To address this issue in the 1990s, organizational leaders from the American Civil Liberties Union, the National Coalition Against Domestic Violence, and the National Network to End Domestic Violence successfully advocated for amending the Omnibus Crime Control and Safe Streets Act of 1968 to include protections for American Indian women.[37,38]

Most of this early advocacy from these national organizations resembled the traditional approach of the VAWA advocates that were mentioned at the start of this chapter, those that focused on policy solutions for intersectionally marginalized groups within the VAWA. However, organizations such as the National Coalition Against Domestic Violence, for example, adopted an intersectional advocacy approach later on to push for policy linkages between tribal policy and the VAWA. These groups may have been in part influenced by the new organizations that joined the hearings in 2007: the Alaska Native Women's Coalition, the Sacred Circle, and the Native American Women's Health Education Resource Center. These organizations took on an intersectional advocacy approach by calling attention to the ways in which the VAWA was an insufficient solution to serving American Indian women who were being sexually assaulted at high and disproportionate rates compared to other racial and ethnic groups.[39] For the American Indian women they represented, issues around sovereignty and resource allocation to reservations were issues that required engagement with tribal legislation and policies. To advance these goals, they advocated for policy linkages between the VAWA and the following other statues: the Indian Civil Rights Act (ICRA), the Indian Country Crimes Act, the Alaska Native Claims Settlement Act (ANCSA), and Coordinated Tribal Assistance Solicitation (CTAS). As Table 3.6 illustrates, these efforts predominantly took place between 2004 and 2014.

TABLE 3.6 *Policies that intersectional advocates proposed to be amended*

Tribal Policy	1994	2000	2005	2013
Indian Civil Rights Act (ICRA)			✓	
Indian Country Crimes Act (ICCA)			✓	
Alaska Native Claims Settlement Act (ANCSA)			✓	
Coordinated Tribal Assistance Solicitation (CTAS)				✓

[37] Hearing before the Subcommittee on Crime of the Committee on the Judiciary House of Representatives, September 29, 1999.

[38] Hearing before the Subcommittee on Immigration and Claims of the Committee on the Judiciary House of Representatives, July 20, 2000.

[39] Hearing before the Committee on Indian Affairs United States Senate, September 27, 2007.

In the 2007 and 2009 hearings, intersectional advocates from the Alaska Native Women's Coalition advocated for revising the ICRA and Indian Country Crimes Act to give tribes more discretion to address crimes that occurred on their land.[40] These Acts limited tribal civil jurisdiction, which advocates argued was a result of the tribal justice system not being able to hold offenders accountable.[41] Even with these changes, uncertain boundaries between the United States and tribal land made it difficult to adjudicate crimes of gender-based violence. These organizational leaders then advocated for revisions of the ANCSA, which did not create clear boundaries of sovereignty. Revising and clarifying land rights in the ANCSA, advocates argued, would eliminate disputes about who had the authority to adjudicate crimes.[42]

Shifting the authority to tribal leadership to manage their own crimes needed to occur through tribal-related legislation and policies, because this lack of authority was deeply connected to land rights (see Bruyneel, 2007; Jacobs, 2009). Tribal leadership also includes different approaches to criminal justice than those typically used by the United States. An organizational leader from the Alaska Native Women's Coalition gave the following testimony in a 2007 hearing:

We are not necessarily seeking that our tribal members be cast off into jail or places like that, although there are some tribes that are seeking banishment as an option. What we are hoping for is healing, because we believe that domestic violence and sexual assault came into our communities as an effect of colonization and oppression.[43]

Intersectional advocates from the Alaska Native Women's Coalition and the Sacred Circle representing American Indian women perceived gender-based violence as a community problem that was shaped by historical colonization and oppression. Thus, they sought alternative pathways for justice that were not options under the VAWA and US criminal law. To do so, they advocated for more rights among tribes to adjudicate crimes that occurred on reservations and for stricter land rights altogether.[44,45] These intersectional advocates also requested funding outside of the VAWA that would directly support these efforts. They pushed for the CTAS, which was successfully passed in 2010 and provided independent funding of more than $273.4 million for Native tribes to decide how they wanted to respond to crimes of violence on their reservations.[46] Table 3.7 illustrates the hearings where these groups focused on these issues and that these efforts were concentrated within the last reauthorization cycle when these groups emerged.

[40] Hearing before the Committee on Indian Affairs United States Senate, September 27, 2007.
[41] Hearing before the Committee on Indian Affairs United States Senate, September 27, 2007.
[42] Hearing before the Committee on Indian Affairs United States Senate, September 27, 2007.
[43] Hearing before the Committee on Indian Affairs United States Senate, September 27, 2007.
[44] Hearing before the Committee on Indian Affairs United States Senate, September 27, 2007.
[45] Hearing before the Judiciary United States Senate, June 10, 2009.
[46] Hearing before the Committee on the Judiciary United States Senate, May 5, 2010.

TABLE 3.7 *Policy linkages between the VAWA and tribal policies*

Agenda Item	Hearing Year(s) Proposed	Linkage	Reauthorization Cycles				Year(s) Law Enacted
			1990–4	1995–9	2000–4	2005–13	
Legal authority to adjudicate crimes on reservation land	2007, 2009, 2010	ICRA ICCA				✓	2013
Social benefits to survivors on reservations	2007, 2009, 2010	ANCSA CTAS				✓	2010

✘ = proposed changes to law/policy that did not take effect that cycle
✓ = proposed changes successfully enacted

Although organizational leaders from the American Civil Liberties Union, the National Coalition Against Domestic Violence, and the National Network to End Domestic Violence were the first to bring up issues related to American Indian women, they primarily advocated for interventions that remained within the policy boundaries of the VAWA. However, by the mid-2000s, advocates from the Alaska Native Women's Coalition, Sacred Circle, and the Native American Women's Health Education Resource Center engaged in intersectional advocacy. Especially in the 2007 hearing, organizational leaders from Sacred Circle and the Alaska Native Women's Coalition communicated the problem of policy feedback. Specifically, they argued that changes within this policy were not enforceable and did not give tribal leadership any power to intervene in and adjudicate crimes of violence against American Indian women. These advocates then argued that, as citizens of tribal nations, the welfare and safety of American Indian and Alaska American Indian women were directly linked to the authority and capacity of their nations to address such violence. Around the time of these efforts, there are noticeable changes to policy that align with these advocacy goals. Congress enacted a partial *Oliphant* fix in the reauthorized version of the VAWA in 2013 while at the same time amending the provisions in the ICRA to authorize a special domestic violence criminal jurisdiction to tribal courts. This transferred legal authority to reservations allowed American Indians to adjudicate crimes against women on their own reservation land instead of deferring them to the US government.

These organizations practicing intersectional advocacy sought to create linkages between the VAWA and tribal law. This shift to tribal policy allowed for more community solutions in addressing gender-based violence, providing tribal authority to prosecute non-Indian perpetrators of violence, and establishing more resources to support American Indian women. For American Indian women, these were outcomes that they could not achieve through the VAWA alone but only by connecting the VAWA to changes in tribal policy that would provide them more autonomy and resources. In many cases, this general strategy of policy linkages was successfully implemented by Congress, as evidenced by the markups in the VAWA that included these reforms. I cannot confirm that the hearings alone contributed to these outcomes. Testimonies from these hearings may only be one component in explaining the success of these strategies, but at the very least they are written confirmation that the policy linkages these advocates pushed for were indeed occurring in the markups of these bills.

ADVOCACY INFRASTRUCTURE

As intersectional advocates pressed for connections between policies, it was important to establish an advocacy infrastructure within the VAWA that would set precedents for the US policy system to maintain and continue establishing policy linkages. Advocacy infrastructure ensured that these linkages were not temporary but instead more permanently reconfigured the boundaries between the VAWA and other issue areas. This advocacy infrastructure included establishing policies in the VAWA that were contingent on laws and policies outside of it to establish institutional entrenchment (see Starr, 2019). Institutional entrenchment provided intersectional advocates with leverage to address political backlash that could (and did) occur. In cases where there was backlash, advocacy infrastructure served as provisions that were interdependent on the VAWA and other policies outside of it. For example, intersectional advocates from the National Network for Domestic Violence and the National Network on Behalf of Battered Immigrant Women advocated for this infrastructure by making the case that the VAWA was successful because of its extension to immigration policies. Conceptually, these advocates are trying to normalize the interdependence between these two types of policies. Others contributed to this rhetoric. An organizational leader from the National Network for Domestic Violence mentioned that violence decreasing among the general female population is a direct result of protecting immigrant women's rights.[47] Therefore, this advocacy infrastructure can be both conceptual (i.e., viewing an interdependence between linked policies) and tangible (i.e., there are physical amendments in two different pieces of legislation that connect to one another).

---

[47] Subcommittee on Immigration and Claims of the Committee on the Judiciary House of Representatives, July 20, 2000.

However, despite these efforts to integrate immigration policy into the infrastructure of the VAWA, the same sunset clause and reauthorization cycles that granted opportunities to expand the rights of intersectionally marginalized groups could be taken away in the next cycle. For example, organizational leaders from the National Network on Behalf of Battered Immigrant Women defended the revisions that were made in the INA to lower the burden of proof of abuse for immigrant women survivors of violence in order to access self-petitions.[48] This was a victory in the reauthorization cycle of 2000, but in 2005 they had to defend these legislative changes, which were being contested by a divided government that lacked a consensus about immigration goals.[49] Intersectional advocates not only did this through congressional hearings; the National Network on Behalf of Battered Immigrant Women worked in partnership with the organizations Legal Momentum (affiliated with NOW), Family Violence Prevention Fund, the National Immigration Project of the National Lawyers Guild, and the Advanced Special Immigration for Survivors Technical Assistance. These groups addressed this backlash by submitting letters to allied senators that used the exact same rhetoric, language, and strategies that were mirrored in the VAWA hearings. In these letters, they explained how the protections provided by VAWA were being dismantled by the REAL ID Act and urged senators to defend the VAWA by not supporting this Act that was part of legislation on immigration.[50]

This political environment placed intersectional advocates in a difficult position: they had to contest threatening proposals and defend past victories. The sunset clause is thus a double-edged sword for intersectional advocacy. Regular reauthorization creates vast political space for reshaping and redeveloping legislation connections across policy issues but also for contesting it. Moreover, interdependence with provisions situated in separate policies increases the VAWA's vulnerability to backlash and erosion from outside legislative changes. This is certainly a challenge that organizational leaders are faced with as they engage in intersectional advocacy. To address this challenge, they strengthened the connections between these two policy issues by advocating for laws that further married them. Despite best efforts among organizational leaders to link the VAWA to immigration policies, there were always politics beyond their control, especially when legislative changes occurred outside of the VAWA.

---

[48] Hearing before the Senate Committee on the Judiciary on the "Violence Against Women Act" Building on Seventeen Years of Accomplishments, July 13, 2011.

[49] Hearing before the Senate Committee on the Judiciary on the "Violence Against Women Act" Building on Seventeen Years of Accomplishments, July 13, 2011.

[50] The letter that was distributed by the National Network to End Violence Against Immigrant Women and their partners: www.epic.org/privacy/dv/real_id_immigrant_women.pdf.

Therefore, at each renewal cycle of the VAWA, advocates had to not only push for more legislative changes in these laws but also guard their previous victories, which were constantly under siege by interest groups such as the American Immigration Control Foundation and the Federation for American Immigration Reform as well as Republican senators, such as those from Arizona who contested immigration legislation outside of the VAWA. In those cases, advocacy infrastructure was a useful tool that they used in their testimonies guarding amendments in the VAWA to prevent rollbacks in immigration reform.[51] While the sunset clause opened up space for pushback on these policy goals, intersectional advocates representing immigrants did their best to try to advocate for immigration policy to be interdependent with the VAWA through policy implementation so that, when these instances occurred, it was more difficult to separate the two from one another. Advocacy infrastructure is a helpful resource for intersectional advocates who are fundamentally pushing for changes in how gender-based violence is understood normatively. In cases of backlash, this infrastructure is even more valuable because it allows them to reference successful policy linkages that are entrenched in the structure of the VAWA. This institutional entrenchment makes these linkages appear to be fundamental to the Act, and thus threats to these linkages are consequently threats to the VAWA.

POLICY RECONFIGURATION

The cumulative effect of the policy linkages discussed in the findings is what reconfigures the institutional boundaries of the VAWA: these linkages create connections between one policy (in this case, the VAWA) and another (i.e., immigration, welfare, tribal). Table 3.8 aggregates individual Acts, laws, and statues under each policy to showcase linkages between policies across reauthorization cycles. These policy linkages illustrate the prolonged efforts by intersectional advocates to intervene in the policymaking process and influence legislators to amend and pass legislation that reconfigured these issue areas over the course of reauthorization cycles.[52] By the end of 2013, intersectional advocates proposed issue and policy linkages across three categories of policy (i.e., welfare, immigration, tribal) to advocate for laws and funding outside of the VAWA. In doing so, they played an important role in supporting the reconfiguration of the VAWA to expand into other issue areas they viewed as relevant to addressing gender-based violence.

When policy linkages were successfully established between the VAWA and these other policies, to ensure they were more permanent, intersectional

---

[51] Hearing before the Senate Committee on the Judiciary on the "Violence Against Women Act" Building on Seventeen Years of Accomplishments, July 13, 2011.

[52] There were additional policy linkages in the revised versions of the VAWA; however, in this chapter, I only present the linkages that were also mentioned in the hearings by advocacy groups.

TABLE 3.8 *Proposed policy linkages across all policies by reauthorization cycle*

	Reauthorization Cycles			
	1990–4	1995–9	2000–4	2005–13
Welfare policy (TANF) (AFDC) (FMLA)	✓	✓	✓	✓
Immigration policy (IIRIRA) (SFEA) (AEDPA) (LSCA) (INA) (BSEOIM)		✓	✓	✓
Tribal policy (ICRA) (ICCA) (ANCSA) (CTAS)			✓	✓

FIGURE 3.4 Established policy linkages in the VAWA 1996–2014

Note. AEDPA = Anti-terrorism and Effective Death Penalty Act; ANCSA = Alaska Native Claims Settlement Act; BSEOIM = Border Security, Economic Opportunity, and Immigration Modernization Act; CTAS = Coordinated Tribal Assistance Solicitation; FMLA = Family and Medical Leave Act; FVPSA = Family Violence Prevention and Services Act; ICCA = Indian Country Crimes Act; ICRA = Indian Civil Rights Act; IIRIRA = Illegal Immigration Reform and Immigrant Responsibility Act; INA = Immigration and Nationality Act ; LSCA = Legal Services Corporation Appropriations Act; SEFA = Security and Financial Empowerment Act; TANF/AFDC = Temporary Assistance for Needy Families/Aid to Families with Dependent Children; VAWA = Violence Against Women Act

advocates pushed for interdependent provisions and programs that made it more difficult to separate these policies from one another. Moreover, by focusing on multiple types of legislation and related policies in a given issue area, intersectional advocates were able to make connections more comprehensively between the VAWA and issues such as welfare, tribal rights, and immigration. By the end of 2013, several of the policy linkages that advocacy groups mentioned in their testimonies and statements were successfully implemented. Figure 3.4 provides a visualization of the years in which these policy linkages took place over the course of four reauthorization cycles. Some of the most surprisingly effective linkages occurred between the VAWA and the IIRIRA and the VAWA and TANF. The IIRIRA was an Act that largely restricted immigration rights (O'Brien, 2018), and the replacement of the AFDC with TANF restricted welfare recipients' access to the policy's benefits by instituting time limits (Gordon, 2012). Meanwhile, the policy linkages between the VAWA, IIRIRA, and TANF were expanding the rights and benefits of survivors. These examples highlight how policy linkages can expand the rights and benefits of intersectionally marginalized groups across policies.

The advocacy in the congressional hearings that I presented in this chapter is likely not the only factor that led to these policy changes. There are a variety of other components that could have contributed to these outcomes, such as actors on other committees, social movements and protesting, publicized media events, policy windows in other legislative areas, and interest groups that worked outside the hearings. Moreover, in my interviews with forty-three advocacy group leaders, which will be presented in Chapter 4, they shared with me that much of their efforts to influence the VAWA included private and strategic meetings with legislators and coalitions outside the hearings. This is a common practice that often occurs before congressional hearings (Daniels et al., 1997; Hall & Deardorff, 2006; Hansen, 1991; Holyoke, 2011). For example, I learned from a policy director from the organization the Latina Network[53] that some of the policy linkages that were discussed in the hearings connecting the VAWA to tribal law were effectively included as amendments because organizations like the Latina Network formed a coalition that pressured legislators by threatening to not support the reauthorization of the Act. Therefore, the congressional hearings only provide a snapshot of the advocacy that occurred to promote the issue and policy linkages I observed in the testimonies and statements by advocacy groups. It is nonetheless an important snapshot of the language, issue linkages, and policy linkages that advocacy groups conveyed to legislators to support intersectionally marginalized survivors. In the end, I posit that the transformations the VAWA underwent as a result of policy linkages fundamentally reconfigured its policy boundaries. Figure 3.5 provides a conceptual visualization of what this reconfiguration looks like theoretically.

Policy linkages fundamentally change the boundaries of policies like the VAWA by making them more interconnected with other policies. In doing so, these changes better addressed the needs of intersectionally marginalized groups who are situated between several of the problems these policies seek to address. This chapter demonstrates the role that intersectional advocates played in proposing and supporting policy linkages. Intersectional advocates representing women who were experiencing violence and living in poverty

---

[53] This is a pseudonym name for the organization to maintain their confidentiality.

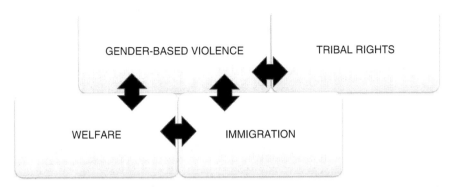

FIGURE 3.5 Policy reconfiguration

pushed for policy linkages that provided more financial resources, fewer restrictions in applying for welfare if they became homeless, and access to unemployment benefits and emergency leave. Intersectional advocates representing women without citizenship proposed policy linkages between the VAWA and anti-terrorist and immigration laws to provide women without citizenship with more pathways to citizenship and access to social services, such as assisted housing and welfare. These changes were not uncontested; legislation on immigration, especially during times of a divided government, made it difficult to maintain the reforms achieved in earlier authorization cycles. At each renewal cycle of the VAWA, advocates simultaneously needed to push for legislative changes in these laws while keeping an eye on their previous victories, which were constantly at risk of being back rolled by interest groups outside of the VAWA. Finally, among intersectional advocates representing American Indian women, sovereignty law prevented the VAWA from being a successful intervention for their constituents. Without changes in tribal law, the VAWA did not go far enough in protecting American Indian women, and so these advocates viewed policy linkages as essential for providing American Indian women with more access to recourse and the resources to heal. Intersectional advocates are concerned about the ways in which structural inequality (e.g., citizenship rights, lack of tribal sovereignty, income inequality) overlaps with experiences of violence, and intersectional advocacy provides a mechanism for reconceptualizing policy to be more reflective of these experiences.

REAUTHORIZATION AND ADVOCACY

In this legislative setting, intersectional advocates leveraged the sunset clause to engage in intersectional advocacy. While there is some research on sunset clauses in legal studies, most of the focus is on how these provisions balance power among the legislative and executive branches (see Baugus & Bose, 2015;

Fagan & Bilgel, 2015; Finn, 2010). The most relevant scholarship on sunset clauses that pertains to this analysis is by Adler and Wilkerson (2013), which finds that legislation with reauthorization features tends to get more attention by Congress and is more often successfully passed. Applying Alder and Wilkerson (2013) to this context, we can understand why advocacy groups would find these political spaces most appealing for pushing for their policy goals. However, none of these scholars study how reauthorization cycles are used over time by interest groups to advance their policy objectives.

Legislation like the VAWA that has a sunset clause creates a unique political opportunity for all advocacy groups. As this analysis demonstrates, a lot happens over the course of these cycles as advocacy organizations strategically develop statements and testimony as well as prepare for floor debates. Reauthorization cycles are set up for these strategies and engagement; committees and subcommittee hearings are planned to hear testimony and statements from these groups (Alder & Wilkerson, 2013). In many ways, reauthorization cycles streamline the policymaking process and provide advocacy groups with the greatest resource to influence legislators: time. While all advocacy groups in the congressional hearings on the VAWA took advantage of this resource, as the findings in this chapter underscore, a select group of intersectional advocates used this time strategically to advocate for policy linkages. For these groups, structured time with legislators was valuable because it provided them with opportunities to persuade legislators to adopt issue linkages between gender-based violence and welfare, immigration, and tribal rights. Having regular access to these legislators, they could also build relationships with them outside of the hearings, which was important if these legislators were going to advocate for policy linkages outside of the VAWA. Reauthorization cycles also provided a structure for reflecting on the previous iteration of the Act. This reflection period allowed intersectional advocates to refer back to successful policy linkages or point out problems in the implementation of the VAWA that corresponded to other policy areas. Ultimately, reauthorization cycles and the congressional hearings that accompanied them provided a unique space for influencing the policymaking of the VAWA. The ways in which intersectional advocates took advantage of this space in part explain some of the changes that occurred in the VAWA between 1994 and 2014 that better supported and served intersectionally marginalized groups.

Intersectional advocacy is an approach to political engagement, which means it encompasses a variety of different strategies depending on the actors, context, time period, constraints, and resources available to organizations. As future scholars, decision makers, and activists consider applying intersectional advocacy to policymaking, it is thus important to note that this engagement will not always encompass the strategies showcased in this book. In this chapter, advocates engaged intersectional advocacy by taking advantage of the reauthorization cycles to persuade legislators to connect policies by using provisions, amendments, and shaping new legislation. But, at other levels (e.g., state, city, municipal), and with different organizations who may view the policy process as too constrained for their political goals, these strategies will look very different. While the VAWA is the predominant political arena for understanding intersectional politics among women's groups in movements to address gender-based violence, their advocacy goes beyond this piece of legislation. Intersectional advocacy is thus an important framework for understanding these varying forms of advocacy and the strategies that undergird them. In Chapter 4, I delve deeper into who these advocacy groups are, why they engage in this practice (or don't), and what strategies they use to make policy connections between gender-based violence and other interrelated issue areas such as housing, incarceration, and healthcare.

REWRITING HISTORY

In the case of the VAWA, intersectional advocates work with the existing structure and policy boundaries to reconfigure the Act through issue and policy linkages; but what if intersectional advocates influenced the policymaking process earlier? What might the VAWA of 1994 have looked like instead? In the congressional hearings, intersectional advocates emphasize welfare benefits, public housing, immigrants' rights, and tribal rights. We can imagine what the VAWA might have looked like in 1994 if these connections were made earlier. Instead of investing millions of dollars in expanding the prison system and the carceral state (Richie, 2012; Whittier, 2016), much of these resources could have been reallocated toward welfare benefits, public housing options, U Visa infrastructure, resources and support toward American Indian tribes, and legal services for noncitizen survivors of violence.

Investing in these policy linkages earlier would have addressed the underlying power dynamics of gender-based violence. When groups and individuals lack economic independence, legal rights, and safe places to live they are more vulnerable to acts of violence because others that *do* have these resources and rights can abuse this power. While penal and incarceration policies in the 1990s effectively stigmatized gender-based violence (Arnold, 1992), mass incarceration approaches in which perpetrators of violence themselves can be subjected to sexual violence in the prison system (Jones & Pratt, 2008) do very little to change the dynamics between the powerful and the powerless. These investments in carceral punishment have only expanded disparities among people of color, who are disproportionate targets of the prison system, rather than fully stop gender-based violence from occurring (Richie, 2012; Whittier, 2016). The advocates presented in this chapter are resourceful and work with the existing policy space they have (i.e., the VAWA), but it is important to consider what this approach might look like if they were given structures earlier on that supported issue and policy linkages. The history of VAWA in 1994 cannot be rewritten, but as we consider the development of future Acts and policies, this is a helpful exercise for imagining how these Acts can be written in different ways that take on an intersectional advocacy approach.

INTERSECTIONAL ADVOCACY BEYOND THE VAWA

The findings in this chapter provoke the question of who separate policies benefit. Based on this analysis, I posit that the most privileged groups who are only marginalized across one axis (e.g., gender) are the primary beneficiaries of the VAWA. For them, most of their needs can be addressed with either this single piece of legislation or corresponding legislation in the same policy. But for others for whom marginalization occurs across multiple social issues, other forms of legislative change that occur across policies need to accompany the VAWA. Studying the evolution of the VAWA through testimony and statements from women's organizational leaders highlights the ways in which fragmented policies can be linked to create more comprehensive policy outcomes. This outcome not only better serves those at the margins in addressing the issue of violence but also expands their rights and improves their overall positionality in the United States (i.e., increasing financial security, obtaining US citizenship). This is the potential of utilizing intersectional advocacy as an approach to policymaking.

Intersectional advocacy is not necessarily confined to the issue of gender-based violence. While this issue area is a key observation site for this type of advocacy because it affects women across different identities, most policy issues would benefit from this comprehensive approach. For example, poverty, racism, unaffordable housing, police brutality, incarceration, and welfare are issues experienced differently by Americans who hold multiple identities. For those who hold multiple, marginalized identities, addressing one of these problems alone is an impossible task when many of the issues are interlocking (Cohen, 1999; Collins, 1998a; Crenshaw, 1997; McCall, 2001; Nadasen, 2012; Parker, 2019; Richie, 2012; Springer, 2005; Williams, 2004). These singular policies have differential effects, especially among women with multiple marginalized identities, as they often are caught between overlapping experiences of oppression (Michener & Brower, 2020). Women's organizational leaders who are engaging in intersectional advocacy are at the forefront of political innovation as they seek *not* to disentangle issues but instead to connect them across policies.

CONCLUSION

This chapter has shown that a select group of advocates contested the original policy boundaries of the VAWA, with the goal of ensuring legislation reflected intersectionally marginalized women's experiences and interests. Policy boundaries exist throughout US policy institutions: welfare laws and policies are bounded around economic relief, housing issues are bounded around real estate law, carceral laws are bound around crime policy. And while these boundaries make sense to a degree, as the findings in Chapter 2 demonstrate, they can be harmful to intersectionally marginalized groups and not fully serve them. For these groups that experience issues not as separate from one another but as interrelated, these policies and laws can miss the nuances of these experiences that lie somewhere in between them. Intersectional advocates recognize this disconnect in policy and propose a different approach: issue and policy linkages. This practice is intersectional advocacy.

As intersectional advocates pushed for these linkages, they encouraged political representatives to recognize false boundaries between gender-based violence and the issues of welfare, immigration, and tribal sovereignty. When policy linkages were successfully established, to maintain these connections they advocated for building infrastructure within the VAWA that would make policies inseparable from one another by establishing several types of amendments and provisions between the two policies. These transformations in policies occurred across four reauthorization cycles. Intersectional advocates may not do it alone, and these changes may not all take place within the context of the congressional hearings, but it is happening. They are part of a reconfiguration process that alters the boundaries of the VAWA to connect to other relevant policies. This outcome is important if we care about the welfare of intersectionally marginalized groups who are often positioned between issues because it recognizes this unique positionality and creates structures that accommodate it.

Despite these remarkable changes that occurred within VAWA over time, the Act has not been completely transformed to meet the needs of intersectionally marginalized survivors. At the time of writing, it still included various laws and policies that promoted a criminal justice approach to address gender-based violence. Despite victories such as the U Visa, the U Visa is still capped, leaving thousands of immigrant survivors unable to access this benefit. American Indian women continue to require more support and agency in navigating gender-based violence on their reservations. Moreover, the analyses presented in this chapter only illustrate political behaviors among a small and select group of activists, those who either are based in Washington, DC or have the resources to send a representative to the Hill, who engage in traditional legislative politics, and who view VAWA as an effective strategy for their goals.

Yet we know from Richie (2012) that for many activists with multiple marginalized identities VAWA is not a promising political space for their efforts. It still predominantly focuses on punitive measures enforced by police institutions to address the issue of gender-based violence – an approach most organizations representing queer, noncitizen, and women of color do not support (Mama, 1989; Patterson, 2016; Richie, 2012; Smith et al., 2006; Sokoloff & Dupont, 2005; Thuma, 2019). Therefore, if these organizations are not leveraging VAWA for their political goals, where are they investing their efforts? Are they too engaging in intersectional advocacy, and if so, what strategies are they using? In the following chapters, I answer these questions by discussing the findings from an in-depth qualitative sample of women's advocacy organizations, and I illustrate the breadth of intersectional advocacy – a strategy that can be used legislatively (as evidenced by this chapter) but also locally within city, state, and municipality policy venues.

4

Policy Linkages and Organizational Strategy

> I think it's important that we advocate, and this is where the leadership of women of color is really important to make sure that people [representing] government entities understand the historical oppression of particular groups, [so] that way by which we are doing the work and the way that the work is funded [allows] us to explore other ways to really think about how we can help these families holistically. So, I think that for us, we have to be more willing than we were before to point out when things are not working and demand that things be done in a way that is truly open to new ideas.
>
> Executive Director, Member Organization of
> Communities for Survivors (CFS)

Advocacy organizations engage in the policymaking process at varying governmental levels and deploy different strategies depending on these political contexts. In Chapter 3, I observed how advocacy groups intervened at the federal level to influence legislation on the Violence Against Women Act (VAWA). To better understand why and when select organizations choose an intersectional advocacy approach as opposed to other strategies, I interviewed forty-three organizational leaders who engaged in the policymaking process for the VAWA as well as in other contexts and at various levels of government. These interviews illuminate the goals, strategies, and practices that undergirded the types of policy linkages I observed in the congressional hearings on the VAWA. In this chapter, I focus on three policy areas that organizational leaders sought to connect gender-based violence with: housing, healthcare, and incarceration. I also spoke with organizational leaders that took on a more traditional approach of advocating for policies to address a single issue (i.e., sexual assault). At the end of this chapter, I compare organizations that used an intersectional advocacy approach to one that took on a single-issue approach. I also assess the impact of these policy outcomes on the intersectionally marginalized women that all of these organizations represented. In doing so,

I bring the policymaking process into full view so that we can understand how policies can embrace or further marginalize intersectionally marginalized groups.

Qualitatively examining organizational goals, strategies, policy wins, institutional challenges, and compromises, I found that intersectional advocates intervened in the policymaking process in a variety of ways to create connections between policies. These behaviors, which are well-studied in the social sciences, include forming intragroup coalitions (Lorenz, 2020), developing newly proposed bills (Andrews & Edwards, 2004), establishing informal agreements between political actors (Daniels et al., 1997), adding provisions to existing laws and policies (Grossmann, 2012), and engaging in budget advocacy (Hall & Deardorff, 2006). What makes this form of advocacy unique though is how these organizations engage in these actions to establish issue linkages, policy linkages, and advocacy infrastructure to hold these connections between one issue area (e.g., gender-based violence) and another (e.g., housing, healthcare, or incarceration). Throughout this chapter, I show how intersectional advocates strategically pursued these policy outcomes. Along the way, these advocates encountered a policymaking process that at times included both policy and issue boundaries that they had to confront and contest.

CASE SELECTION AND ADVOCACY ORGANIZATIONS

I interviewed forty-three advocates from four different organizations. Each organization was selected as a case for understanding how advocacy groups participate in the policymaking process to address gender-based violence. I used the following criteria to select these organizations: (1) located in cities that were represented by Democratic mayors and governors at the time of the study; (2) focused on the issue of domestic violence or sexual assault as a primary advocacy issue; (3) founded either in the early 1980s when these types of professional organizations first emerged or were the first organization of their kind; (4) variation in the level of government targeted for advocacy efforts; and (5) variation in the population the organization represented by race and ethnicity. Using this criterion, I selected the following organizations: Communities for Survivors (CFS), Sisters Against Violence (SAV), the Latina Network (LN), and Women Against Violence Everyday (WAVE). These organizations are summarized in Table 4.1.

First, to compare advocacy strategies within relatively similar political contexts, I selected organizations located in cities that were governed by mayors from the Democratic Party the entire time they were in operation. By holding this partisanship feature constant, I was able to better focus on the policymaking processes and policy terrain these groups encountered. The states these organizations operated in also had Democratic governors. It is difficult to engage in the practice of intersectional advocacy under all political

TABLE 4.1 *Advocacy organizations*

Organization	Issue Area Focus	Primary Ethnoracial Representation	Institutional Level of Advocacy	Years of Operation
Women Against Violence Everyday (WAVE)	Sexual violence	White women, Latinas	National, state, & municipality	1981 to present
Communities for Survivors (CFS)	Domestic violence	Black women	State & municipality	1985 to present
Sisters Against Violence (SAV)	Sexual violence	Black, Latina, and Asian women	National & municipality	2003 to present
The Latina Network (LN)	Domestic violence	Latinas	State & national	1982 to present

Note. Organization names are pseudonyms to keep the identities of the organizations that participated in this study confidential. Confidentiality motivated organizations to participate in the project and for staff to be truthful about their experiences with the organization.

circumstances. This qualitative study aims to observe intersectional advocacy in contexts with the fewest political barriers. At the time of the study though, there was a Republican President (President Trump), a Senate Republican majority, and a House Republican majority. This context is important for the national advocacy groups engaged in.

Second, these organizations are all relatively old. Most professionalized nonprofit organizations focusing on gender-based violence emerged in the early 1980s (Ake & Arnold, 2017). Studying organizations with this history allowed for an examination of strategies, missions, and infrastructure over time. The youngest organization in this study is SAV, which was established in 2003. It was included in this study because it was the first nationally recognized organization representing women of color on the issue of sexual violence. The other two organizations began as shelter and service-focused groups that institutionalized their advocacy over time.

Third, I selected organizations representing two issue areas that are considered as the primary types of gender-based violence: domestic violence and sexual violence. Both issues fall into the gender-based violence policy area, and yet there is a degree of separation in terms of how these issues are supported and addressed by policies. For example, the Family Violence Prevention Services Act primarily funds domestic violence initiatives whereas the Victims of Crime Act provides funding to both domestic violence and sexual assault. Studying organizations that represented both issues within gender-based violence allowed me to observe advocacy on different scales: advocacy to expand efforts within a policy area and efforts to link it to other issues and policies. Two of these organizations primarily focus on domestic violence (LN, CFS) and the other two primarily focused on sexual assault (SAV, WAVE).

Fourth, these four organizations varied in the levels of government they target for their advocacy. The organizations CFS and LN both focused on state policy, but CFS also focused on municipality policies. Both LN and SAV worked on national policy, and WAVE engaged in advocacy at all three levels of government. These organizations provided areas of overlap and divergence in their policymaking efforts allowing for the examination of their advocacy across governmental levels.

Finally, I selected four organizations that all claimed to take an intersectional approach to their advocacy efforts but varied in the race and ethnicity of the population they primarily served. I was interested in understanding to what extent the "intersectional approach" mapped onto the practices I observed in the congressional hearings and if it occurred at other levels of government and within different political contexts. As a reminder, intersectional advocacy is *advocacy for linkages between policies and issues that reflect the experiences of intersectionally marginalized groups positioned between more than one problem area.* Both CFS and WAVE appeared to be mainstream organizations serving a general population. Upon screening, before proceeding with interviews, I learned that while CFS served a broader population, it focused its efforts on supporting Black survivors. I also learned that while WAVE predominantly served white survivors, it increasingly worked with Latina survivors. So WAVE and CFS represented mainstream organizations meant to serve the general population while also directing some of their efforts to represent a specific intersectionally marginalized group (i.e., Black women, Latinas). Comparatively, SAV and LN were considered "culturally specific" organizations, a term designated to organizations representing a specific cultural group of survivors: SAV represented Black, Latina, and Asian American women; LN represented one culturally specific group – Latinas.

These organizations provided a rich gradient for understanding when and how groups attempted to link issues and policies to gender-based violence. I found that LN, SAV, and CFS all participated in intersectional advocacy to link gender-based violence to issues of housing, healthcare, and incarceration. Meanwhile, WAVE's advocacy remained focused solely on sexual assault policies despite opportunities to link these policies to other issue areas. By explaining what motivated the linkages pursued by LN, SAV, and CFS and the strategies they used to establish these policy outcomes, I explain how organizations use intersectional advocacy as a strategy. In Chapter 5, I delve deeper into these organizations and the individual experiences of advocates to tell a more comprehensive story of why these groups take on an intersectional advocacy approach, and how it can vary depending on their organizational structures. In this chapter, the primary focus is on how LN, SAV, and CFS all similarly established issue linkages, advocacy infrastructure, and policy linkages across three very different policy contexts and at varying levels of government.

LINKAGES AND ADVOCACY INFRASTRUCTURE

Issue linkages, policy linkages, and advocacy infrastructure are three outcomes of intersectional advocacy that I identified by analyzing the interviews I conducted with forty-three organizational leaders that represent the four organizational case studies. The interviews presented in this chapter were analyzed using a codebook to capture organizational goals, motivations, tactics, and the outcomes of advocacy in the policymaking process.[1] Table 4.2 provides a summary of the codebook approach used to identify how advocacy groups intervened in the policymaking process, the strategies they deployed, at what levels they engaged in these practices, and to what end.

Based on this analysis, issue linkages, policy linkages, and advocacy infrastructure are three key policy outcomes that resulted from the intersectional

TABLE 4.2 *Codebook and analysis approach*

Code Category	Description of Codes and Analysis
Organization	Features of the organization (e.g., mission, founders, organizational structure) that are related to the advocacy pursued by these groups.
Representation	The identity groups (e.g., race, ethnicity, sexual orientation, class, gender) the organization represents.
Leadership	The vision of the organization and the actors that make decisions about advocacy, approach, and strategies.
Strategies	The strategies that were deployed by the organization, at what part of the policy process, and the extent to which they failed or were successful in reaching their goals.
Resources	The resources (e.g., funding, partnerships, allies, buildings) that were used for each strategy and goal of the organization.
Networks	The networks of other individuals, political officials, and additional organizations that shared the goals of the organization or were a part of their strategies to advance their goals.
Issue definitions	How organizations defined gender-based violence and strategically presented the issue to other stakeholders.
Policy linkages	The connections organizations made between the issue of gender-based violence and other issue areas through rhetoric, policies, and practices.
Level and boundary	The governmental-level organizations targeted for their advocacy and the types of issue boundaries they faced at this level.
Reconfiguration	When a goal or strategy successfully linked together two issue areas using policies, practices, or legal precedent.

[1] The methods used to analyze these interviews and the codebook are located in the Appendices.

TABLE 4.3 *Policy outcomes of intersectional advocacy and definitions*

	Issue Linkage	Advocacy Infrastructure	Policy Linkage
Definition	Rhetoric, framing, and problem definitions that identify one issue in relation to another	Networks, coalitions, previous policy victories, and working policy drafts that bring people and organizations together to advocate for issue and policy linkages	Amendments, new policies, and funding that link one policy to another
Stage of the policy process	Agenda setting	Policy proposal debate and enactment	Implementation

Note. Policy stages are broadly categorized here based on Jones and Baumgartner (2005) and Béland and Waddan (2012).

advocacy efforts of LN, SAV, and CFS. Table 4.3 presents the definitions of these policy outcomes and at what broad stages of the policy process (Béland & Waddan, 2012; Jones & Baumgartner, 2005) intersectional advocates sought to establish them. Issue linkages are rhetoric, framing devices, and problem definitions that identify one issue in relation to another. In Chapter 3, issue linkages in the congressional hearings on the VAWA were primarily new definitions and framing of gender-based violence as an issue that crosscuts other problems such as poverty, immigration rights, and tribal sovereignty. In this chapter, issue linkages are additionally frames and definitions that connect gender-based violence to affordable housing, access to healthcare, and mass incarceration.

Intersectional advocates also aim to establish policy linkages. Policy linkages are amendments, new policies, and funding that link one policy to another. In Chapter 3, there were many examples of policy linkages, and most of them were presented as legislative amendments and provisions that connected welfare, immigration, or tribal policy to the VAWA. In this chapter, policy linkages are additionally illustrated as informal policies at the local level, changes to funding eligibility, and policy implementation that address interlocking problems. Establishing both issue and policy linkages is difficult for intersectional advocates. Depending on the policy stage, intersectional advocates encounter varying institutional boundaries as they make an effort to advance these policy goals. In this chapter, I bring attention to these boundaries to highlight the challenges intersectional advocates face at different stages of the policy process. One of the key tools intersectional advocates used to confront these boundaries and advance these efforts is what I call advocacy infrastructure. Advocacy infrastructure includes networks, coalitions, previous policy victories or precedent set for policy linkages, and working policy drafts that bring people and organizations together to advocate for issue and policy linkages.

In the remaining sections, I explain how the LN, SAV, and CFS strategically pursue and successfully advocate for issue and policy linkages. I also explain how advocacy infrastructure provides them with support for advocating for issue and policy linkages. Finally, the chapter ends with a discussion of WAVE's approach to policymaking, which illustrates a counterfactual form of advocacy that does not follow this process and instead stays within the single policy area of gender-based violence.

INSTITUTIONAL BOUNDARIES AND ISSUE LINKAGES

Intersectional advocates work at varying governmental levels to pursue issue linkages between gender-based violence and other problems. While these different levels present a unique policy terrain for intersectional advocates depending on the issues they are aiming to connect, they face similar types of challenges in navigating institutional boundaries at the stages of the policy process where problem definitions are determined and agenda setting is occurring. At this broad stage of the policy process, some institutional boundaries intersectional advocates face when linking issues are financial: legislative restrictions and eligibility that determine the allocation of funding streams. Other boundaries are definitional: how existing and proposed legislation demarcate issue areas as separate from one another. And other institutional challenges are matters of political organization, such as coalitions that are issue-specific. Finally, some boundaries are normative, including precedents or practices among policymaking actors to address issues within well-defined policies. The content of the law creates and exacerbates separate issue definitions.

Intersectional advocates strategically confront these boundaries that separate the issue of gender-based violence from housing, healthcare, and mass incarceration.[2] They do so by making compelling cases for issue linkages that change how policymakers and funders define these issues, organize agenda setting to address more than one issue at a time, and evaluate the eligibility of policy beneficiaries across issue areas. Each organization advocates for these issue linkages within their own unique policy terrain and governmental level.

[2] Other issue and policy linkages also emerged from this analysis (i.e., migrant worker rights, immigration rights, economic inequality, legal advocacy, other types of police reform, educational disparities). In this chapter, I only selected one type of linked issue from each organization to illustrate how intersectional advocacy is used to advance it, but there were many other examples that are not included in this chapter.

The Latina Network (LN): Housing and Violence

Organizational leaders from LN often discussed the challenges they faced in linking the issue of gender-based violence with unaffordable housing, especially when it came to defining these problems. According to these leaders, housing policies at the state and city levels are conceived and administered separately from initiatives that address gender-based violence. Valeria, the executive director of LN, explains that this separation often leads policymakers to fail to see a connection between unaffordable housing and gender-based violence. Valeria works hard to link these issues. She explains: "when [a funder or policymaker] says, 'Oh, you don't – you don't really qualify for the money we have, or the grants that we have because we focus on housing.' And we go, 'Oh, let me tell you something. What do you think we do? We focus on housing.'"

To organizational leaders, the relevance of housing to the issue of gender-based violence is apparent. Carmen, LN's development director, recounted: "most women who leave a partner often do end up being homeless. [O]ne of the largest contributing factors to women experiencing homelessness is domestic abuse." Legal advocates like Gabriela and Daniela explained the difficulties that low-income Latinas who left their households to escape domestic violence face in finding housing because they cannot afford rent. Many of these survivors of domestic violence also do not want their partners to look up their housing information, which is legally available to them (Hazen & Soriano, 2007). For women without citizenship, the lack of a Social Security number is a significant barrier to applying for housing in the rental market. Moreover, landlords that do provide housing to these groups can engage in predatory financial practices: refusing to make repairs, entering the property without notice or permission, charging illegal fees or interest, and conducting illegal evictions (Desmond, 2016; Lopez et al., 2009; Oliveri, 2009; Purcell, 2002). The challenges faced by Latina survivors without citizenship are not limited to the private housing market: applications for public housing also do not acknowledge the specific vulnerabilities of this population. Although, public housing programs cannot require applicants to have a Social Security number or deny an application for failure to include this information, many of these programs do anyway (Desmond, 2016).

Despite these specific housing-related vulnerabilities faced by immigrant survivors of domestic abuse, housing policies and laws in the city in which LN is located do not acknowledge this connection. As Gabriela explained, this is a common issue among immigrant survivors of domestic violence who come to the local shelter. Undocumented survivors are left with transitional housing options that receive funding from domestic violence programs. Unfortunately, transitional housing is temporary and does not provide survivors with a sustainable long-term option. There were no resources at the federal, state, or city level to provide affordable and permanent housing options for survivors who phase out of transitional housing.

The issue distinctions between the housing and gender-based violence policies are reinforced by the structure of state advocacy coalitions. State advocacy coalitions establish a critical bridge between local advocates and statewide policymakers by providing a structure to communicate with one another to develop and evaluate policy. However, according to Valeria, there were two separate advocacy coalitions for housing domestic violence at the state level; these two coalitions did not communicate with one another prior to their advocacy efforts.

Advocates from LN also have to navigate tensions that arise when their efforts go beyond the perceived scope of the issue area of gender-based violence. The organization must be very careful about how it presents these issues, which sometimes means not being able to communicate the structural inequalities the organization is trying to address. Maria, the research director, explains this challenge:

> [We] hav[e] to be really careful about what language we use, and we can't say that we're serving a particular group. We have to use some other word for that group. Even in the work that I'm doing with the Children's Bureau project. I can't call out the system as causing this structural harm and violence to families that are engaged with child welfare. When I do, I get called out [by the government]. We can't say that because it's going to be reviewed by the federal funder.

Maria is candid about the political biases LN faces when its leaders engage in this work. These institutional restrictions do not deter people like Maria from engaging in intersectional advocacy to propose issue linkages, but these restrictions do require that organizational leaders like her are careful about how they communicate their advocacy to the federal government. The LN's advocacy on housing is no different. Instead of pushing more visibly for housing reform at the federal level, LN advocates find ways to work locally to change processes for applying for housing, collaborate at the state level with other organizations with similar interests, and influence the Hispanic National Policy Agenda to take on these types of initiatives. In sum, as LN advocates pursue efforts to address the housing vulnerabilities experienced by Latina and immigrant survivors of domestic violence, they contest a variety of institutional boundaries that enforce the view that "housing" and "gender-based violence" are separate sets of policies.

Sisters Against Violence (SAV): Healthcare and Violence

Advocates from SAV face similar challenges when they express issue linkages between healthcare and gender-based violence. They primarily pursue federal-level advocacy to establish these linkages and encounter institutional boundaries in how eligibility for healthcare funding is defined. They face these boundaries when they advocate for adjusting eligibility requirements in healthcare policies that determine which groups can access resources.

Healthcare is connected to gender-based violence in immediate ways: hospitals administer rape kits, shelters and organizations provide temporary counseling services, and hospitals treat immediate injuries related to violence (García-Moreno et al., 2015; Kalra et al., 2017; Plichta, 2007). However, according to Jada, the executive director of SAV, healthcare policies and interventions are designed under the assumption that all women will trust and can afford mainstream hospitals and counseling services.

The prevalence of the assumption that people trust healthcare providers among policymakers and other advocacy organizations makes it difficult for Jada to advocate for policy that would support alternatives to mainstream hospitals. Advocates like Jada point to community health centers as an important alternative to these mainstream hospitals for survivors of color. Yet these centers are poorly funded and do not have the capacity to offer these services. Jada explains:

So, part of our advocacy is within [healthcare policy] to push that, as well as – one of the tangential things is we're also trying to push for more funding for community-based health centers, because we understand that for communities of color that's where many of them go for help. And it's not even – sometimes it's about money, but sometimes it's about access [and trust] because community health centers, folks know them, you know what I mean? Folks go there . . . And so, we want forensic exams to be able to be done at community health centers because that's where our community goes.

Community health centers are more affordable, more accessible, and more reliable for survivors of color and LGBTQ survivors (Mayer et al., 2001). Thus, providing these types of centers with more resources is a way that advocates from SAV try to connect their advocacy around sexual assault to healthcare issues. For advocates like Jada, racial, class, and gender inequalities in healthcare are significant because they prevent survivors of color from receiving the care and attention they need.

Advocates from SAV also consider how access to healthcare is a long-term issue linked to the experiences of gender-based violence for survivors of color. Survivors of color and organizations serving them often identify alternative methods for healing that do not involve traditional mainstream approaches to mental counseling services, such as healing circles, artistic therapy, and more (Baker, 2006; Kallivayalil, 2007; Mehl-Madrona & Mainguy, 2014). Advocates like Ebony from SAV push for more resources for such "culturally specific" health services. However, when seeking to provide these services, advocates from organizations like SAV encounter institutional boundaries in healthcare policy that define healthcare according to mainstream models of care. Funding for health services to address gender-based violence is designated to mainstream hospital care, or immediate resources for counseling are only available under mainstream structures (i.e., visiting a counseling therapist). Thus, as advocates like Jada and Ebony try to support grassroots groups and community health centers, they encounter political and financial issue definitions that distinguish healthcare as a separate issue from gender-based violence in a manner that disadvantages survivors of color. Therefore, to provide survivors of color with access to affordable and culturally specific health services, SAV has to first change how policymakers define funding criteria. To influence this change, SAV establishes an issue linkage between healthcare and gender-based violence that illuminates how intersectionally marginalized groups are positioned simultaneously between these problems.

Communities for Survivors (CFS): Criminal Justice and Violence

Like advocates from LN and SAV, advocates from CFS encounter institutionalized issue definitions that they need to redefine with issue linkages between criminal justice reform and gender-based violence. A well-established issue frame defines punitive and carceral policies as a solution to gender-based violence rather than a problem exasperating it. This frame that incarceration is a solution to gender-based violence is reflected in legislation that attaches prison sentencing to the crime of gender-based violence (Gottschalk, 2006; Rabuy & Kopf, 2016; Richie, 2012; Thuma, 2019). For example, the VAWA allocated approximately US$268 million yearly to courts, police, and prosecutors to incentivize criminalizing gender-based violence and thus imprisoning perpetrators of violence (Sacco, 2015). Thus, the efforts advocates from CFS are leading to eliminate punitive criminal justice policies, such as cash bail bonds, appear contrary to the conceptual framing of punishment as a solution to violence. This framing is entrenched in legislation and is commonly used by other organizations and politicians that influence policy on gender-based violence. Angela, the executive director of CFS, explains that they receive pushback from political officials and other organizations as they campaign to end cash bail bonds:

We have ongoing conversations with [the organization we are collaborating] with to get ahead of the potential backlash to ending money bond, which of course is a concern of, "Oh, it's going to harm victims. People aren't going to be safe." [Political actors], when you try to do criminal justice reform, generally point to the Domestic Violence community and use us as a scapegoat [to support incarceration efforts]. So, we [are] support[ing] that [bail bond] bill and really have just said that the money bond, doesn't actually keep people safe ... We can tell stories of survivors who the person who caused them harm was let go because they had the money to pay their bail, and then ended up causing additional harm. So, we've been involved [in writing this bill] and that means just showing our support and showing how these systems [of incarceration] don't really keep survivors safe, and how making them better for everyone also helps survivors as well. That's also tied into our work with looking at the incarceration of survivors and how they're hurt by [this] cruel system, by being incarcerated due to actions they take to survive over self-defense actions or coping mechanisms ... So, we're both supporting some of the actions and ideas that many in the criminal justice reform world are trying to initiate.

For advocates like Angela, linking these issues involves providing counternarratives of survivor experiences with incarceration. These counternarratives are largely drawn from the experiences of women of color, especially Black women, with reporting incidents of violence. Black women survivors are disproportionately arrested compared to other groups when domestic or sexual violence is reported to the police (Mama, 1989; Richie, 1996). Advocates from CFS challenge incarceration as an intervention that ensures the safety of Black women and argue instead that punitive laws further endanger them. Bail bonds, in particular, disproportionately burden Black women who are either the victims of this practice or the primary group responsible for paying this debt when members of their family are arrested (Rabuy & Kopf, 2016; Richie, 2012). Thus, eliminating bail bonds is one of CFS's primary goals.

Eliminating this practice requires issue and policy linkages. Bail bond policies at the state level are defined in the Bail Reform Act of 1984 and are not at all connected to laws and policies related to gender-based violence. If policymakers begin a process to reform bail bond policies, involving an organization that focuses on domestic violence would seem counterintuitive to them. Moreover, framing this law to support survivors of domestic or sexual violence sets a new precedent for writing and enforcing laws that eliminate cash bail bonds. This is the institutionalized boundary that advocates from CFS face as they try to get involved in writing, framing, and advocating for the elimination of bail bonds in their state.

Bail bonds are only one part of CFS's agenda to address how mass incarceration is interrelated with survivor justice. Advocates from CFS are also leading their own efforts to defund police institutions and reallocate these resources to social services. Reallocating these services is important for survivors; Blanca, the communications director, explains why survivors need alternatives for help other than the police. She says:

Survivors don't necessarily feel safe calling the police. Oftentimes, they're in neighborhoods where [there] is just a history of police brutality. So, the police [are] not the first person they want to call when they're in those situations. Studies show that the best person to call is the relative or friend or a neighbor. But we often push [calling the police when they contact] the hotline. As someone who worked at the hotline for six months, the protocol is, when someone calls us that is in a crisis, we have to hang up. We can't help them, which I think is really problematic. If they call us and they're like, my abuser is here and he's in the house and I don't feel safe right now, we have to tell them, sorry, call 911, bye. And hang up the phone. That's the protocol.

Especially for survivors of color, police are not an ideal first responder because these survivors are more often part of communities that are overly policed and arrested (Thuma, 2019). Leaders of CFS have several ideas regarding where to reallocate these funds to help survivors. Blanca wants to create a new group of first responders who are social workers. Angela wants to reallocate funds to local groups addressing community violence more broadly. Alba, the policy director, wants to reallocate funds to social services and public benefits.

Unfortunately, defunding police institutions and reallocating these resources to social services is not an easy task. At the time of these interviews, the local police force had an annual budget of $1.75 billion and an overtime allocation of $35 million. This set of circumstances helps reinforce the political and financial issue definitions that advocates from CFS aim to overcome. Politically, police institutions are viewed by local politicians as a necessary expense. Financially, there is an existing budget that supports the jobs of thousands of police officers – and there is no precedent for relocating this budget to other services. Advocates like Angela, Alba, and Blanca, though, are up for the challenge, and they come up with creative strategies to start setting new precedents for budget reallocation while building a network of supporters for these interventions.

LINKING ISSUES TO POLICIES AND ADVOCACY INFRASTRUCTURE

How do these three advocacy organizations successfully advocate for linkages between issues and policies that policymakers see as separate? Advocates strategically intervene in different parts of the policymaking process to make these connections. These interventions reveal the strength of the issue definitions they encounter, where they view opportunities for linkages between policies, and what types of advocacy infrastructure ground their efforts. In this section, I explain how each advocacy group works within its own unique policy context and governmental level to strategically establish issue and policy linkages. These connections vary and come in different forms depending on where the organization is intervening in the policy process, the advocacy infrastructure they build, and the types of constraints that distinct issue definitions and policies pose for their advocacy.

The Latina Network (LN): Housing and Violence

Advocates from LN participate in intersectional advocacy by linking the issues of housing and gender-based violence together. To do so, they challenge the institutions that separate these two issues. The LN's leadership has several strategies for linking issues at the local, state, and federal levels. What is distinct about intersectional advocacy led by these policy entrepreneurs is not these strategies themselves but rather the goals that they serve: in this case, changing how political actors recognize and define the issue of gender-based violence in relation to unaffordable housing. Advocates from LN are strategic about making these connections by instituting informal policies at the local level.

At this level, advocates from LN work directly with landlords and community partners to change rent expectations and the norms around requiring Social Security numbers for housing. They do so by implementing localized and informal policies on the ground. Valeria explains LN's strategy for this local work: "we have to work with all kinds of partners. We work with landlords, we work with transitional housing programs, in addition to the fact that we have our own program that does scattered sites housing ... And there are certain programs our participants [without] a social security [number] – if they are not a US citizen – can access."

To scale up these local practices into city and state policies, LN advocates such as Francisca work with several other organizations in a series of one-on-one partnerships. Francisca is the community director, and she explains that these organizations regularly convene on Latines' affairs,[3] affordable housing, and healthcare. Francisca shares that:

[these organizations] don't just concentrate on domestic violence and gender-based violence, but they are looking at [other issues]: driver licenses for all, affordable housing, and health. Any bills, any policies that are coming from [these groups], [we support them by sharing] anecdotes that are helpful for them when they go to lobby and when they go to propose new bills, we collaborate with them as well.

These partnerships serve as a form of advocacy infrastructure for intersectional advocacy by providing an organizing space for groups to collaborate on agendas that establish issue linkages.

Francisca also utilizes these partnerships to change an existing structure of a state coalition to focus on multiple issues. Policy changes at the state level are important for addressing broader inequities within the housing market. Francisca explains this:

The state can play a big role in making changes around affordable housing and then eliminating some of the restrictions to rent and buy a home. By now, you need a social security number, so it's harder to buy a home or rent, if you are an undocumented immigrant, which, that means many times, as an undocumented immigrant, you end up renting a basement or renting a room and then, if there is an unsafe situation there, you're going to be less likely to complain or find support because then, you may not have more housing. Undocumented populations are less likely to report abuse around paying rent or landlord abuse or anything like that.

Advocates like Francisca focus on unfordable and inaccessible housing within a state coalition that was originally designed only to address gender-based violence. As advocates from LN assumed a leadership role within this

---

[3] Latine/es (pronounced as "latin-eh") is used as a gender-neutral term to refer to people with a Latin American cultural background. The term originates from Latin American activists (Salinas & Lozano, 2021; Zentella, 2017) who advocated for replacing the end of the term "Latin" with an –e/–es to be inclusive to all groups using the Spanish ending –es (Galvez, 2022; Limlingan et al., 2022; Slemp, 2020). While "Latinx" is another recently adopted gender-neutral term in the United States, I refer to the term "Latine/es" in this book because it is better recognized by Spanish-speaking Latin American communities as it more accurately reflects the Spanish language and is easier to pronounce than Latinx.

coalition, they brought housing-related concerns onto the agenda and expanded the coalition to include other organizations with similar interests. At the state level, advocates such as Valeria, Maria, and Luz are working on making housing more affordable for all city residents, while Francisca is trying to change renting protocols that require Social Security numbers. The organization successfully used this platform to increase funding and resources for survivors to access affordable housing. Advocates from LN share this strategy with other groups across the country. One of the program managers, Juana, explained that she was working with a community college with a high proportion of homeless students. She explains that she encouraged them to work with the housing coalition to institute housing for students who needed it. Juana said:

One of the campuses that I work with in Daytona Beach in Florida, they have a large number of homeless students. And I told them, "You know what, there are coalitions for homeless people on all the states, they have funding. Have you talked with them?" And they were like, "No." They don't know anything about DV [domestic violence] or sexual assault. And I was like, "Yeah, but they're experts on homeless people. You need to bring them to your coordinated community response team. You need to invite them. You need to partner." And so, while it was weird for them, they did that. I mean, I don't know where they are at this point, but they were going to build a house on campus to provide shelter for students. And the campus did not have those resources, but the coalition did. And it helps both of them meet a need in the community. So, I believe that those partnerships are very important.

At the national level, LN advocates strategically push to uplift these localized experiences into a political agenda. To do so, they intervene during the agenda-setting process to influence federal policymaking. Valeria explains how local experiences with housing issues inform how LN's policy team engages with federal agencies:

What we pay attention to across the country is when someone raises what's going on in their community or in their area that says, "You know, we've been trying to get housing for some of our participants, and the housing programs say they don't have to serve them." And [our policy director] will say, "I'll go speak to HUD [Department of Housing and Urban Development]." So it's really about [changing] what's in place. Like, what are the immigration remedies that people should have access to so that if we're hearing they're not getting access to it, it's like – how can our policy team actually provide support and get individuals what they need?

The organization also works to transform the agenda of national interest group coalitions. It was recently promoted to co-chair of the leadership committee for the National Hispanic Leadership Agenda, an association of forty-five of the largest Latine organizations in the country. Advocates from LN also currently colead the Latina taskforce, which directly influences the eight policy areas the coalition focuses on each year. Valeria explains how LN uses its role in this coalition to persuade other organizations about the importance of advocacy that links together issues:

And our influence has been [creating] intersections [between] domestic violence – with all of the other [issues that it] impacts – Latinas and their children – whether it be housing, immigration, civil rights, health – reproductive rights, et cetera … And so that back and forth really lifts up, then, the local realities, and the local stories, so that we can better represent that at the congressional level.

To what extent are these strategies successful in linking gender-based violence to housing policy? At the local level, advocates from LN are changing protocols and procedures around renting and affordable housing informally. According to Gabriela and Daniela on the ground, LN has established consistent practices with a network of landlords of not using Social Security numbers to determine housing eligibility. These changes do not alter the legal definitions, but they do impact localized understandings of the connections between the issues of gender-based violence and housing. These practices started to change a series of standardized procedures and processes for determining housing eligibility that did not originally consider the unique vulnerability of survivors who are dependent financially on their abusers and their immigration status. Advocates from LN linked the issues of gender-based violence to housing and immigration by expanding and changing nonstatutory policies for determining housing eligibility that resulted in tangible outcomes – survivors of violence without citizenship can now apply for long-term housing without fear of deportation. Low-income survivors without a renting history or bank account are also eligible for this type of long-term housing.

At the state level, advocates like Maria, Valeria, and Luz from LN are advocating for policymakers to allocate more resources in the state budget to housing for survivors of violence and, in the process, are leading efforts to pass policies that make housing affordable for everyone. At the federal level, advocates from LN are still creating an infrastructure for changing the conceptual issue definitions about which policies fall into the issue area of gender-based violence by influencing the national Hispanic policy agenda. They have not fully achieved their policy goals to eliminate the requirement for prospective renters to provide Social Security numbers, but they successfully changed how the National Hispanic Leadership Agenda coalition advocates for issues like housing, immigration, healthcare, and gender-based violence. The National Hispanic Agenda proposed in 2020 (after these interviews took place) a list of recommendations that included increasing access to affordable rental housing and homeownership, advocating for the passage of the Equality Act to expand and enforce anti-discrimination law when Latinas apply for housing, and expanding Section 8 for public housing vouchers to survivors of sex trafficking and violence, especially LGBTQ youth. Thus, advocates from LN are experiencing incremental victories in repurposing an existing coalition on

Latine issues for intersectional advocacy as they achieve issue linkages between gender-based violence and unaffordable housing in these agendas that legislators will read and consider as they create policy.

Sisters Against Violence (SAV): Healthcare and Violence

Advocates from SAV participate in intersectional advocacy to link the issues of healthcare and gender-based violence by changing how people of color access healthcare services and what the acceptable healing services are for survivors of violence. For advocates from SAV, changing access to healthcare means redefining how community health centers are viewed, funded, and supported by the federal government. Community health centers are underfunded, understaffed, and under-resourced (Rosenblatt et al., 2006). Yet they provide affordable care to patients and reduce racial disparities in access to healthcare (Mayer et al., 2001; Seymour et al., 2017). They are also the providers that people of color most trust and feel comfortable visiting (Seymour et al., 2017). These experiences are not surprising: community health centers were born out of the civil rights movement to provide healthcare to people of color, especially African Americans (Hall, 2005; Pérez & Martinez, 2008). Advocates from SAV like Jada strategically aim to expand and better support community health centers. Investing in community health centers for advocates like Jada means providing women of color who experience sexual violence with more accessible and affordable services, thus incentivizing them to seek out those services. Among these advocates, the Public Health Service Act (PHSA) provides a working policy document that acts as a form of advocacy infrastructure for SAV because it is a working document that this organization and their partners can target for their efforts.

This working document, though, contains a rigid legal boundary in how the Act allocates funding that these groups need to redefine. Jada explains that:

[We are trying to] push to have [this Act] address domestic violence; we are pushing for it to address sexual assault as well. And then, we are also pushing for it to be specific to communities of color. But that money, it's not specifically [set aside right now] to domestic violence or sexual assault. So, when we have these agencies that are not including that, you're not looking at the whole person. So, part of our advocacy is within [HSRA] to push that, as well as – one of the tangential things is we're also trying to push for more funding for community-based health centers, because we understand that for communities of color that's where many of them go for help. The community health centers are very much underfunded ... We're supporting legislation to increase funding to community health centers. And at the same time, trying to put in funding for gender-based violence staff and training at community health centers.

Advocates like Jada are trying to change how the HSRA allocates funding to both community health centers and groups representing survivors of color. Reallocating funding to both types of entities ensures that survivors of color have different options for care, support, and healing. This strategy was successful at the federal level. Through budget advocacy, Jada and other advocates from SAV intervened at the policy proposal and implementation stages to create new revenue streams directed toward community health centers and organizations serving survivors of color through the Public Health Service Act that determines the Health Resources & Services Administration (HRSA) budget.

Advocates from SAV also changed the criteria for how this funding can be used – modifying the definition of what constitutes "healthcare" or "mental health services" for survivors of violence. They persuaded legislators to add provisions to the Public Health Service Act that allowed for a change in funding distribution; these provisions also included increased line items in the budget. Before this change, the federal government identified mental health services as counseling services occurring in mainstream therapy offices. Advocates from SAV persuaded legislators who were deciding the criteria of what constituted healthcare funding to take into account funding for "culturally specific" practices for mental health therapy. Ebony discusses how grassroots groups and community health centers can now access this funding for culturally specific healing services:

I can give you an example of an organization that did a support group [for] LGBT [youth of color]. For example, this is from [one of the US territory islands that] I've seen. One of the things they did is weaving, and they weave mats and stuff. They were teaching the LGBT youth how to weave and when they were weaving, they kind of talked about [issues of violence and asked]: what was going on; what [were] they are seeing; how did they feel, as a different way to do therapy. What I hear sometimes [from] some communities of color [is]: "We don't go to therapy," or "Therapy is not for us." So, [these groups] do therapy [in a] totally different [way] from mainstream [organizations]. Because when you go to a mainstream therapist, you [sit] in front of a person. They're asking you all these questions [and] it might be your first time that you're there, and you're like, "Why is he asking me all these things? What is this? What am I getting out of this?" Then, [in comparison] you have [groups] in the Native community, [that] do a lot of what they call "healing circles" where they [gather as a community] and they do these different activities [for] therapy. For some [survivors of color], it's more therapeutic; they feel like they're healing, which is different than how a mainstream person or how a mainstream therapist does it.

Before leaders like Jada and Ebony advocated for a change in how the HRSA recognized and provided funding to these groups, these alternative practices for healing and therapy were rare and not widely available. This policy change has allowed groups representing women of color and LGBTQ survivors to provide alternative interventions for healing and recourse. These alternatives are important because they make physical and mental health services more accessible to intersectionally marginalized groups. Therefore, bringing together the issues of healthcare and gender-based violence through this policy linkage better represented the needs and interests of the intersectionally marginalized groups.

Communities for Survivors (CFS): Criminal Justice and Violence

Advocates from CFS participate in intersectional advocacy to change how city and state governments engage in criminal justice reform. The organization aims to illustrate the connections between mass incarceration and the interests of survivors of violence, especially survivors of color. Angela explains that, to engage in this form of advocacy, there are a variety of strategies she leads:

We use traditional methods of achieving these goals, whether it's city budget advocacy, which is really wonky, and oddly time-consuming, I'm learning, or legislative reform, and those sorts of things, which is a unique activity, in that you've got to know a lot of different folks across the state and balance a lot of interests. Or, just simply that community building, where you want to develop a culture where people are allied around this issue, and it's a real culture shift in the way that people view the issue of gender-based violence.

In this interview segment, Angela highlights that the organization uses budget advocacy and community building to colead or collaborate on these policy interventions that link issues together. Efforts by CFS to eliminate bail bonds are part of these community-building strategies. Advocates like Angela from CFS helped write up the bill to eliminate bail bonds in their state, but they did not initiate these efforts. The efforts were part of a different coalition that focused on ending bail bonds.

We want to, through our legislative advocacy, [to] really shift the thinking around, "What does it mean to be a supporter of domestic violence victims as an elected official?" So, we're supporting bond reform in [our state] with the Coalition [to end bail bond]. We're a second-tier supporter of this ... They crafted the legislation, but I've reviewed quite a few drafts of the legislation, I've made recommendations, some of which they took on, some of which they didn't, to really make sure victims' perspectives and the voice of domestic violence victims, in particular, was in that legislation, that there were protections put in place for survivors that would allow us to have a good bill that would make the criminal justice system fairer for people of color, overall, and people who don't have the economic means to bail themselves out.

The intragroup coalition that formed between CFS and this bail bond reform group served as an important form of advocacy infrastructure. This intragroup coalition provided an organized structure for coming up with strategies for issue and policy linkages. For example, one of these strategies included sending CFS advocates to town halls to intentionally redefine the issue linkages between gender-based violence and criminal justice. Efforts such as these helped curb some of the criticism this linkage faced from political officials and law enforcement. Angela says:

This is new for a domestic violence organization in [our state], but it's important to us at [CFS] to really put some credibility behind our claim that racial justice is part of survivor justice. And so, being able to do this is great. It also helps us fight back against the narrative that tough on crime is supportive of victims. And so, at first hearing, a sheriff from somewhere else in the state said, "What about victims?" and it was great that the Coalition [to end bail bonds] could say, "Actually, we're working with this organization. They've inputted into the bill. They think this is a good bill for survivors."

The organization was an important collaborator for this bill. Advocates from CFS attended town hall meetings where the bill was discussed, appeared at meetings with policymakers in the state legislature, and reviewed the bill on several occasions. This intragroup coalition and the combined legislative efforts it led were successful. The bill was passed and signed into law, making the state the first in the country to abolish cash bail payments for jail release for people who have been arrested and are waiting for their cases to be heard.

Another strategy that advocates from CFS pursue is collaborations with other local organizations to identify further areas for criminal justice reform. One of these initiatives is defunding their city's police department. The city has seen substantial organizing around the issue of police brutality, and several grassroots and community groups are advocating for police abolition. The CFS is divided among its leadership and affiliated organizations on how to advocate for police-related policies. Alba administered a survey to the organization and affiliated groups to ask if the organization should advocate for police reform, defunding the police, or police abolition. Among this group, 30 percent selected abolition, 33 percent selected defunding the police, and 37 percent selected reform. Because about 63 percent of the group selected either abolition or defunding the police, CFS moved forward with advocacy that would aim to defund the police and reallocate these funds to social services. This action did not satisfy everyone, but Alba explained she felt it was the closest compromise she could find for the time being: advocacy that was aimed to reduce the power of policing bodies in the city but that did not dismantle them entirely. Alba and other organization leaders, such as Maria, Blanca, and Rosa, aim to radicalize these efforts over time by increasingly defunding the police budget until there are very few to no resources left for police institutions.

Advocates from CFS lead their own initiative to support these efforts; the organization is currently advocating for reallocating the police budget to social services and services more generally for survivors of violence. This is a difficult goal to achieve, and advocates from CFS are aware of the challenges of using budget advocacy to change these types of institutions. Alba explains that they have not been able to defund these institutions but have been trying to set a new precedent for moving funds from one area of the city budget to another. Alba explains how CFS was successful in reallocating funds from public health to domestic violence services:

I would say as far as specifically getting money from [the police department], I don't think there has been a lot of progress. I think most of the city officials recognize that there needs to be some work done with [the police department] and reevaluating how [the police department] is structured, but it's also very complicated with the police union, so they start cutting that budget. Also, it's my political reasons not to. That being said, I do think we are making progress in other ways in just getting more support for the issue from the city. We were added into a line-item budget from the Department of Public Health.

Advocates from CFS acknowledge that they won't be able to defund the police immediately but are attempting to set new precedents for reallocating funds in the city budget and establishing strong partnerships with local political officials who support defunding the police. These partnerships are another form of advocacy infrastructure because they provide a wide range of support for the issue and policy linkages that CFS is trying to establish. Alba says:

Obviously, we can't get everything we want this year, but I think a lot of it, too, has been about just building partnerships this year, and building those connections and relationships. Hopefully, in future years, we can get more of a budget increase, but at least having the support of [local political] offices, [the] recognition of the importance of this issue, their support [for] these efforts and hopefully maybe launch[ing] some new programs that take into consideration some of the problems with the current services and how we can improve on that moving forward.

Not all groups and political officials in the city are supportive. Alba explains that some politicians refuse to support these efforts. She says: "Because our ask was also about taking money from [the city police], there were some other people who were like, 'Yes, I'd love to see you get more money, but I can't support any ask that involves defunding the police.'" At the time of this interview, CFS leaders were contacting local politicians and groups to determine what network would support their efforts to defund the police in their city, but they had not been successful at this point in making this change. After these interviews, I learned that the mayor introduced a new budget that reduced the police department's funds by $58.9 million, cutting all vacant positions to help meet the substantial debt the city faced in 2020 due to the pandemic. This action does not meet the demands of the city's defund the police movement. Still, it does prevent a further expansion of the police budget and potentially opens a policy window for CFS to advocate for additional changes to the budget. This window provides the organization with momentum moving forward in its goals to defund the police and reallocate funds to other resources and services for survivors of violence.

INTERSECTIONAL ADVOCACY AND POLICY OUTCOMES

The LN, SAV, and CFS each encountered different policy terrains depending on the level of government they targeted for their efforts, the institutional boundaries they faced at the policy stage they intervened in, and the issue they sought to connect with gender-based violence. Despite these varying contexts and range of strategies they deployed, all three organizations sought to establish issue linkages, advocacy infrastructure, and policy linkages. Table 4.4 provides a summary of these efforts by each of these policy outcomes.

TABLE 4.4 *Policy outcomes of intersectional advocacy by organization*

Organization	Issue Linkages	Advocacy Infrastructure	Policy Linkages
Latina Network (LN)	- State coalition proposes that housing laws, policies, and procedures account for the challenges faced by survivors of violence and immigrant women in particular - National Hispanic Agenda includes gender-based violence, housing, and immigration as joint policy-making efforts	- An intergroup state coalition is established to address housing, immigration, and gender-based violence - New policies drafts are considered by the state to improve housing for survivors of violence - The housing coalition at the state level no longer meets without representation from LN/advocates that address gender-based violence	- Informal policies established locally to increase accessibility and affordability to housing among immigrant survivors of violence
Sisters Against Violence (SAV)	- Identified community health centers in the policy as legitimate healthcare providers for survivors of violence - Changed what is constituted as "healthcare" and "healing" under the law	- Proposed amendments to existing laws on healthcare that would change the criteria for funding healthcare providers/ explicitly identifying groups that serve survivors of violence	- Healthcare policy includes amendments designated for survivors and community health centers - Allocated funding directly to community health centers
Communities for Survivors (CFS)	- Contests the established expectation that cash bail bonds help survivors of violence	- Works in a coalition with bail bond reform organizations to propose legislation that links bail	- Successful adoption of legislation ending cash bail in the state

(*continued*)

- Successfully changed how state policymakers framed bail bonds in relation to gender-based violence

- bond reform to gender-based violence
- Participates in network of organizations and political officials all aiming to defend the police and reallocate funds to survivors and social services
- New legal precedent at the state level set for laws on bail bond/incarceration to be directly stated as connected to gender-based violence

- Funding was reallocated in the city budget, setting the precedent that funds can be moved to meet the needs of survivors of violence

These three organizations all advocated for issue linkages and encountered institutional boundaries in the process. Most of these boundaries they faced at the policy stage of defining the problem of gender-based violence and agenda setting to address it. According to LN advocates, grant foundations, state coalitions, policymakers, and landlords all viewed unaffordable housing and gender-based violence as separate issues. Advocates from SAV similarly encountered funding criteria, healthcare policies, and designated healthcare providers that did not account for the differential healthcare service needs of survivors of color. To appropriately serve these groups, original definitions and criteria for funding needed to be challenged and to hold new issue linkages between healthcare and gender-based violence. Advocates from CFS possibly encountered the strongest definitional boundaries. They had to challenge the existing linkage between criminal justice and gender-based violence. These issues were linked to one another but in a way that reinforced inequalities among intersectionally marginalized groups, especially Black women. The CFS advocates had to redefine the connections between these issues; instead of gender-based violence reinforcing mass incarceration, it instead had to be linked to advancing criminal justice. At the policy stages when these problems are being defined, agendas are being set to address these problems, and policy debates are occurring around existing proposals – these intersectional advocates intervene by advocating for issue linkages.

Establishing these issue linkages often requires an advocacy infrastructure for supporting these efforts and ultimately transforming them into policy linkages. To challenge definitions and establish linkages between gender-based violence and housing, LN advocates established advocacy infrastructures that comprised (1) building a state coalition that included housing *and* gender-based violence on its agenda, (2) coleading the agenda-setting process for the Hispanic Caucus to bring stakeholders across issue areas together, and (3) drafting new policies with the state coalition that acted as working documents to bring together advocates from housing and gender-based violence. Because LN is contesting well-established issue definitions, intersectional advocates rely on this advocacy infrastructure to establish issue and policy linkages. This infrastructure positions them to work on the ground with individual landlords to change renting practices, alter policies and laws around eligibility for public housing, establish a state coalition, assume a leadership position within the Hispanic Caucus, and advance a political agenda that connects issues of unfordable housing to gender-based violence. Advocacy infrastructure is especially important at the policy stages of agenda setting, policy proposals, and debates. These are all opportunities during the policy process to suggest revisions and new policies, and advocacy infrastructure provides reinforcements, resources, and organized spaces to make a case for issue and policy linkages.

The organizations SAV and CFS also established their own versions of advocacy infrastructure to facilitate issue and policy linkages. Similar to LN,

CFS relies on advocacy infrastructures that include intragroup coalitions and networks of advocates and political officials that likewise support issue and policy linkages. Advocates from CFS relied on these strategic partnerships, especially for its successful campaign on bail bond reform. This advocacy infrastructure provided CFS with the support to confront a legal boundary that made it difficult for them to establish an issue linkage: bail bonds were reinforced by laws criminalizing gender-based violence. These advocates and their partners had to propose changing the law that permitted bail bonds and explicitly rewrite the legislation around the law that connected it to survivor justice. Advocates from CFS and advocates from their partner organizations were successful in linking these issues. The CFS advocates helped cowrite the bill that the state government adopted to abolish cash bail payments for jail release for people arrested and waiting for their cases to be heard. Advocates from CFS are using this policy victory as momentum to reform other laws and policies related to criminal justice. Advocacy infrastructure supports these goals, especially at the stages of policymaking where these advocates are attempting to influence the development and implementation of policy proposals.

Among SAV advocates, advocacy infrastructure includes proposed amendments to drafts of new policies that are endorsed by SAV and other organizations. For this reason, SAV predominantly intervenes at stages of the policy process when policy proposals and debates occur to change established funding criterion: altering how the federal government assesses what type of organization deserves funding/resources. The organizations to which SAV advocates are reallocating funds are often considered ineligible for this funding. For advocates from SAV, engaging in intersectional advocacy entails changing how the government recognizes grassroots and community organizations so that these groups are better positioned to serve intersectionally marginalized populations. This isn't easy, and it also comes with concessions. For SAV advocates to successfully convince policymakers to reallocate funding to these groups, organizational leaders like Jada had to determine organizational categories that were "palatable" to political officials. This is why "culturally specific organizations" is used as an identifier for community groups serving survivors of color, even though Jada originally advocated for the language of "groups serving communities of color." Advocates from SAV cannot fully transform the norms and standards held by public officials but rather chip away at them through incremental changes. Even though advocates from SAV are effective in changing the resources allocated to these groups and the issues they can address using these funds, how these groups are conceptualized remains an ongoing political battle. Advocacy infrastructure thus is an important stabilizer for these efforts.

Each of these organizations successfully advocated for policy linkages. For example, LN established informal policies locally that increased accessibility and affordability to housing among immigrant survivors of violence; SAV revised healthcare policy with amendments that designated funding to community health centers to provide affordable care for survivors of violence; and CFS in partnership with another organization successfully passed a new law on bail bond reform. The organization also successfully reallocated city funding that provides a precedent for changing city resource allocation policies moving forward. By linking these issues and policies, organizations seek to change how policies serve intersectionally marginalized populations by reconfiguring policies to address the problems they can be positioned between at the same time.

SINGLE-ISSUE ADVOCACY

Unlike LN, SAV, and CFS, other advocacy organizations take on a more traditional approach to their advocacy by proposing that policies address a single issue. My interviews with advocates from WAVE provide insights for understanding these types of organizations. Most of WAVE's advocacy is concentrated around the single policy area of sexual assault, with very few instances of linkages with other issue areas, including domestic violence, an issue that is within the scope of gender-based violence. Several factors explain why WAVE has taken this approach. First, WAVE was founded in the 1980s when gender-based violence was considered a private matter, not a public concern. Similar to the advocates I described in Chapter 2, those representing WAVE were determined at that time to add gender-based violence to the list of violent crimes occurring in the United States. Since its founding, WAVE has defined the issue of gender-based violence in a similar way to how VAWA did in 1994: as a crime that requires law enforcement, legal action, and immediate services to survivors. Second, WAVE advocates regularly work with survivors of sexual violence directly. Susan, the executive director of WAVE, explained that survivors continue to come forward and need help reporting sexual assault as a crime. She said: "this isn't like you take a bite out of crime, and it goes down. This is an epidemic that the more awareness and the more you speak about it, the more clients come forward." Helping survivors report incidents of sexual assault has revealed to WAVE the challenges survivors face in this area, which is why WAVE advocates engage in the policy process to advocate for policies that help survivors report sexual assault. Third, WAVE staff also do not see differences in reporting a crime when marginalized by class, race, ethnicity, or sexual orientation. When I asked advocates if they thought survivors required varying policies, practices, or services based on how they are marginalized across multiple identity characteristics, advocates consistently replied that they felt all women would benefit from these policies irrespective of these differences. Advocates from WAVE concentrate their advocacy on the reporting of sexual violence as a crime. Thus, they typically advocate for policies within the normalized issue definition of sexual assault. They also primarily intervene in the policymaking process at the stage of suggesting proposals.

Under these conditions, WAVE advocates for policies almost identical to its state coalition's. The assistant director of WAVE confirms this is the case. She says: "we all are on board with every law that comes through [the state coalition] that they're pushing legislatively that year." When I asked Christina, the policy assistant director, for the proposal of policies the state coalition and WAVE were advocating for, I combed through its hundreds of suggested policies to see how many times there was a connection between sexual assault and another issue area. Among the hundreds of proposed policies, there was only one. This outlier policy proposed keeping families together during cases of sexual assault under the purview of the child welfare system. This law would create a policy linkage between sexual assault and welfare. The hundreds of other policy priorities focused on improving the reporting of sexual assault cases, expanding the sex offender registry, increasing the statute of limitations for reporting sexual assault, and educational programs for increasing awareness of sexual assault. In other words, WAVE advocates concentrate their efforts on thoroughly pursuing singularly defined goals: addressing sexual assault through crime control measures and access to reporting. They meet with the state coalition regularly to influence the policymaking process. This coalition then advocates for these policies at the state level on behalf of WAVE and others.

However, one policy effort did not completely fall into this pattern and seemed to in part reflect the policy linkages that I observed among the other advocacy groups discussed in this chapter. Christina explained that WAVE was involved in developing and advocating for SUCCEEDA,[4] a sexual assault emergency treatment Act, which was first passed in 2017. This state statute provides additional legal rights to survivors who choose to report the incident and provide evidence of their assault at a hospital. According to Christina, they advocated for additional legal rights to be added to the statute that provided survivors with the legal right to an advocate during their hospital exam, to have a sexual assault examiner present during the exam, and to allow survivors to shower afterward. In this instance, there is a connection between healthcare and gender-based violence as WAVE intervenes in policymaking that changes hospital practices. This policy requires that the Nurse Practice Act be reinterpreted (though they did not advocate for revising it) by the International Association of Forensic Nurses to include new guidelines on how nurses qualify as sexual assault nurse examiners. This loose connection to the Nurse Practice Act resembles some of the policy linkages that SAV initiated with healthcare policy. However, unlike the policy linkages established by SAV advocates that connected healthcare to sexual assault, the policy initiative by WAVE is not using this linkage to make healthcare more accessible to an intersectionally marginalized group. Therefore, this is an

---

[4] This is a pseudonym name of the Act to protect the identity of the organization.

example of a connection between two policies that would not change how intersectionally marginalized populations access or experience the policy.

However, some advocates within WAVE, like Christina, did advocate for an additional policy under SUCCEEDA that does more closely resemble intersectional advocacy. She explained that she advocated for adding a policy that provides a "voucher that allows survivors of sexual assault to legally request financial compensation for activities related to them reporting the crime." According to her, these expenses include emergency room costs or new clothes they bought to replace the ones they discarded. This voucher would be provided by hospitals to make medical forensic services affordable for a survivor, and it would also offer follow-up healthcare. By providing resources for follow-up healthcare for those who cannot afford it, this policy initiative addresses how low-income women survivors are positioned between the issues of sexual assault, poverty, and unaffordable healthcare. This policy initiative, though, could go further in being more accessible, inclusive, and representative of intersectionally marginalized survivors.

If advocates like Christina fully pursued an intersectional advocacy approach here, what might this policy proposal look like? How might she advocate for it? Applying the strategies and goals we learned from LN, SAV, and CFS, we can imagine a counterfactual policy that Christina and other WAVE advocates might have developed and pursued under an intersectional advocacy approach. First, learning from SAV, WAVE could advocate that the voucher needs to be part of the PHSA to ensure that not only hospitals provide the voucher but also community health centers. To strengthen this connection, WAVE might also want to work outside the state coalition and directly with legislatures that influence the HSRA to link this voucher program more permanently to healthcare policy. Second, learning from LN, WAVE might want to expand the voucher program's benefits to include translators to accompany survivors where English is not their first language. The organization might also want to engage with immigration law to advocate for survivors of violence without a Social Security number or formal citizenship status to access these benefits. To make these connections, we can imagine WAVE developing a new coalition that brings together advocates of different organizations that work on immigration policy to help shape this new proposal. Learning from CFS, which pushes against policies that reaffirm a crime approach and support mass incarceration, WAVE might advocate for a voucher program that covers medical expenses of all survivors irrespective of whether or not they decide to report the violence as a crime or collect forensic evidence. Advocates might also push for connecting this policy to welfare policy to provide survivors of violence with additional resources and funding to care for survivors who may need to take time off their jobs and heal from major trauma. These types of changes and the advocacy that would move it through the policymaking process result in outcomes that are inclusive and representative of the diverse range of survivors that would rely on it.

Advocates from organizations like WAVE have the capacity and potential to apply an intersectional advocacy approach to their policymaking efforts. To do so requires additional strategies, approaches, and priorities. Chapter 5 explores why some organizations practice intersectional advocacy (i.e., LN, SAV, CFS) while others primarily do not.

CONCLUSION

In this chapter, I showed how advocacy organizations participated in intersectional advocacy to establish issue and policy linkages and, in doing so, contributed to changes that directly impacted the experiences of intersectionally marginalized people. The policy linkages they advocated for required strategies for linking issues, building advocacy infrastructure, and creating connections between issue areas in different ways. In the end, these policy linkages fundamentally changed the experiences of intersectionally marginalized survivors. New housing practices at the local level provided opportunities for Latinas without a Social Security number to secure affordable housing without relying on an abusive partner. New funding streams supporting community health centers, and alternative healing services allowed women of color survivors to access affordable healthcare services and opportunities for healing that mapped onto their cultural practices. Removing money bail bonds provided all survivors, especially Black women convicted for crimes of self-defense against their abuser, time outside of jail to seek legal representation. All of these policies and practices made a difference in the lives of intersectionally marginalized survivors. Organizations like WAVE are advocating for policies that help protect and guide survivors of sexual assault through the reporting process. With some shifts in their approaches, these efforts can also substantially better serve intersectionally marginalized groups. In Chapter 5, I present four organizational features that explain why and when groups practice intersectional advocacy. I also explain how variance across four organizational features helps us understand the differences in how these groups apply this practice. Finally, I discuss how organizations with ambitions and commitments to serving intersectionally marginalized groups can take on an intersectional advocacy approach by changing their organizational characteristics.

5

Intersectional Advocates and Organizations

> [Our organization was founded on] the spirit [and] the amazing ability of women of color ... [Our organization] was really created on the backs of sisters, with the spirit of sisters. And it was created because we wanted to have our own voice. We wanted to have a women of color organization that would have its own voice that could stand in places.
>
> Jada, Executive Director, Sisters Against Violence (SAV)

What explains why groups practice intersectional advocacy to facilitate connections between policies? Increasingly, advocacy groups and nonprofit organizations more broadly are adopting the language of "intersectionality" to signal their commitments to intersectionally marginalized populations such as Black women, LGBTQ people of color, immigrant women, and so on (Nash, 2018). In many ways, "intersectionality" has become a buzzword, and its common usage makes it difficult to distinguish between groups that are adopting an intersectional advocacy approach and groups that are using this terminology as an aspiration to reflect new commitments to intersectionally marginalized populations. Meanwhile, there are other organizations that have been serving intersectionally marginalized groups for a long time, such as those that were discussed in Chapter 3, that have strong commitments to these populations but organize their advocacy around a single axis of marginalization (e.g., gender, race, class, or sexual orientation). In this chapter, I examine the relationship between the organizational structure and the advocacy of Women Against Violence Everyday (WAVE), Communities for Survivors (CFS), Sisters Against Violence (SAV), and the Latina Network (LN). All four of these organizations expressed a commitment to representing women of color, but as Chapter 4 illustrated, not all of them practice intersectional advocacy. In this chapter, I explain the underlying organizational features that undergird the advocacy of these groups to understand when and why they will use intersectional advocacy as a strategy for their policymaking goals.

Although I examined a range of organizational features,[1] I identify only four constitutive features that help explain why organizations practice intersectional advocacy: (1) leadership that emphasizes interrelated issues as a part of the mission and work of the organization, (2) direct input from intersectionally marginalized groups, (3) broad networks outside of the direct issue area, and (4) funding from other issue areas through either budget advocacy or pooled resources from partners. The organizations that I identify in this study as intersectional advocates (i.e., CFS, SAV, and LN) differ from one another in a variety of ways: in the populations they serve, their location, how they emerged, the resources they have, the issue and policy linkages they pursue, and their political strategies. Yet, despite these fundamental differences, these four features emerged across all three organizations and were directly related to advocating for issue and policy linkages on behalf of intersectionally marginalized groups. That is why I claim that they are constitutive features that help explain why organizations practice intersectional advocacy.

To capture both this broad characterization and the variation at the individual level, this chapter is organized by discussing each individual organization according to these four characteristics. Advocacy organizations differ in considerable ways from one another including but not limited to their fiscal budgets, staff capacity, geographic region, mission statement, leadership, transparency, hierarchies, funding sources, partnerships, branches, and whether or not they are part of a national coalition. Because advocacy organizations differ in these types of ways, we should not expect them to hold identical traits. For this reason, the four constitutive characteristics that consistently emerged among CFS, SAV, and LN are broad and do differ according to the unique attributes of these advocacy groups. Table 5.1 presents each of these characteristics and their definitions.

In the remaining sections, I present an analysis of each organization according to these four characteristics to explain why select organizations engage in intersectional advocacy and why others take on a more traditional approach to policymaking. After presenting each organization individually, I cross-compare them to show how organizations can vary across these characteristics. At the end of this chapter, I present a typology that describes how intersectional advocacy fits within these varying organizational structures. I then discuss how a range of advocacy organizations (e.g., culturally specific, mainstream, state coalition, networked organizations, and national organizations) seeking to address gender-based violence can locate themselves within this typology to adopt an intersectional advocacy practice that fits their existing structures.

[1] See Appendices for full range of organizational features that were captured by the codebook.

TABLE 5.1 *Organizational characteristics for intersectional advocacy*

Origins and Leadership	Representation	Networks	Funding and Resource Allocation
The political context and motivations for establishing the organization/the leadership of the organization	How the organization represents and advocates for people across differences in marginalized identities	What types of issues the organization's network represents/how the organization engages its network for advocacy	How the organization advocates for funding/how funding is allocated to which issues

WOMEN AGAINST VIOLENCE EVERYDAY (WAVE)

During my interviews with advocates from WAVE, "intersectional feminism" came up often to describe how they sought to address gender-based violence. Although the leaders of WAVE have commitments to intersectionality, their advocacy resembles a traditional approach to policymaking. That is not to say that WAVE advocates do not care about diversity, intersectionality, or improving these organizational features to better represent intersectionally marginalized groups. Instead, their commitments to "intersectional feminism" are not reflected fully through an intersectional advocacy approach. In the remaining sections, I present an analysis of WAVE's (1) origin and leadership, (2) representation, (3) networks, and (4) funding and resource allocation. Each organizational feature highlights how the organization is arranged around a traditional advocacy approach to address one primary issue (i.e., sexual assault). These organizational features enabled WAVE to serve hundreds of survivors over the years, advocate for more legal protections on behalf of survivors, and improve hospital practices for those that report instances of sexual assault. However, at times, these structures counteracted their goals to serve an intersectionally marginalized population: Latinas. These organizational characteristics help us understand why most advocacy organizations, including WAVE, engage in a traditional approach to policymaking and, at times, how these structures are at odds with their commitments to intersectional feminism.

Origins and Leadership

The origins of WAVE date back to the 1980s when its initial approach to addressing gender-based violence was grounded in reaching a general population of women. While their staff and resource capacity has grown over the past forty years, their mission, approach, and tactics have largely remained the same. What were these organizational features in the 1980s and what political context shaped them? The organization emerged during the anti-rape movement in the 1980s when there were no governmental policies in place to adjudicate gender-based violence (Arnold, 2017). This was also a time when advocates were shifting from grassroots community-based activism to professionalized organizations that directly engaged with political institutions (Bumiller, 2009; Richie, 2000). As these groups were professionalizing, their advocacy was organized to reform male-dominated institutions such as courts, law enforcement, and medical practices that revictimized women and excused rape (Koss & Harvey, 1991). During the early 1980s, when WAVE was established, laws did not exist condemning marital rape, and it was an issue delegated to the private sphere where there was no recourse available for survivors (Bumiller, 2009). During this time, making these experiences visible to the public and focusing on women as a group was radical. Susan, the executive director, explains the early goals of WAVE that she founded:

In the early days, again, rape and incest were words that really, I was not allowed to say in public. It just was relegated to a group of crazy women in those early days, was not taken seriously. There were crazy myths around who it is that gets assaulted, provocation, et cetera. I'm sure you know all those things. So, in those early days, it was all about visibility and voice and being heard and just working really hard to establish ourselves in some kind of mainstream thinking. That required me back then to be a real fighter and a real scrapper for everything. We had no money, no funding, no visibility, very little legislative support.

Susan says it herself that the goals of the organization were to establish "mainstream thinking," and with very little resources or legislative support the goals of the organization were to offer services to women who had experienced sexual assault and to advocate for harsher laws that criminalized it. At this point and time, advocates like those at WAVE believed that all women were in danger from gender-based violence irrespective of their differences and that foundational statues, laws, and policies urgently needed to be implemented to serve them all. These advocates worked hard for these changes. Susan says: "when [they] say, 'You can't do that,' I'm like, 'Okay. Watch me. We will do it. We will make it happen.' I believe in manifesting what you think about and what you say out loud. And that's how we did it – brick by brick." "Brick by brick" to her meant advocating for changes in how the government addressed sexual assault (e.g., mandating laws against sexual assault, funding shelters and counseling services, and developing policies for reporting gender-based violence) and establishing her own organization that would bring visibility to the issue of sexual assault. Susan adds: "I'm not going to take the basement somewhere. I'm not going to do it. And we're going to raise money, and we're going to be as visible in the community as the fire department is, as the library is, as the school." In many ways, the visibility of their organization is a metaphor for their targeted efforts to make gender-based violence a visible public issue. Amanda adds that, since these efforts, "I've seen the crime taken more seriously, given the attention that it deserves, laws being changed, and survivors coming forward more than they ever have, because we can't keep up with the people who are coming forward." From Amanda and Susan's perspective, a mainstream approach that focuses on the singular issue of sexual assault has resulted in tangible changes to laws and policies that help all survivors.

This feminist mainstream approach is rooted in the organization's mission, staff structure, and strategies that all revolve around the single issue of sexual assault as a collective experience. Amanda says: "There isn't a soul on Earth that doesn't have a family member or a best friend or themselves isn't a survivor. So, it's everywhere. It's everywhere." This perspective is perhaps one reason why WAVE does not differentiate its advocacy according to different intersectionally marginalized populations that experience sexual assault. That is not to say that WAVE advocates do not recognize the overlapping forms of oppression intersectionally marginalized survivors navigate. Susan says: "I want there to be dots connected with oppression, racial injustice, inequality, and all those isms that we know of that sexual violence be a part and is seen as a part of that oppression and for people to really be able to connect those dots, understand them." These interviews took place in September 2020 right after the surge of Black Lives Matter protests that predominantly occurred between May and August 2020. Although advocates like Amanda and Susan are cognizant of the connections between racial justice, inequality, and sexual assault, their advocacy practices only newly reflected commitments to these issues at this time.

One of the few practices and infrastructure established within WAVE to expand their advocacy beyond sexual violence and into the issue area of racial justice was a committee they formed. Amanda shared: "we've created not only a social justice but racial justice committee in house to make sure that we're always paying attention to folks that are out there ... it's probably over the last six months to a year that it started to kind of narrow and funnel down into something we want that has real strategic plans and goals." The committee's emergence maps onto the timeline of the Black Lives Matter protests in the summer of 2020, and within those six months one of the major practices they implemented was a book club where all advocates had to read books on anti-racism. This committee and in-house practices have provoked questions by advocates like Amanda such as "how do we make sure that we're addressing [social unrest]? Do people feel comfortable still coming here? How do we stand with that? Are we putting things on our Facebook pages and on social media that lets people know we stand with [the Black Lives Matter movement]?" Because I interviewed these advocates when this committee and these efforts were relatively new, I cannot decipher if the organization's mission, activities, and staff engagement changed as a result. What I can point out, though, is that, regardless of their commitments to diversity, intersectionally marginalized groups, and other issues like racial justice, the advocacy they engaged in at the time of the interviews resembled their advocacy in the 1980s.

Even though there have been considerable changes in laws condemning sexual assault and public awareness, WAVE advocates remained committed to advocating for a singular policy goal. Amanda, who has been working alongside Susan for more than twenty years, discusses their current policy priorities:

So, I would say that [our state] is one of the states that really leads when it comes to survivors and removing barriers so that they can access services, say what they need to in a counseling session, and that's not going to get pulled out into a court of law. I think our change to the statute of limitations [has made it] so people could come forward at any time and start getting some justice in ways that they didn't have before.

As Amanda highlights, much of their advocacy today continues to focus on increasing access to services (e.g., counseling, medical advocacy, legal advocacy) and focusing on policies that increase the statute of limitations so that people who experience sexual violence have greater legal recourse. Moreover, despite substantial changes in funding and resources over time, the organization still maintains its mainstream focus to serve all women, even though all the organizational leaders interviewed reported that WAVE is increasingly serving a Latina population of survivors and many of them state that they want to better represent intersectionally marginalized groups. Its policy advocacy also continues to singularly focus on the issue of sexual assault from a mainstream perspective. For example, some of the priorities advocates like Amanda highlighted are to increase the statute of limitations for prosecuting sexual assault and collaborate with corporations to improve responses to sexual assault and harassment in the white-collar workforce. These priorities do not take into account the unique positionality and needs of women marginalized across additional identity characteristics such as ethnicity. Why does WAVE maintain this mainstream structure when there are new incentives to serve more diverse populations, more available resources to broaden its efforts, and additional opportunities for collaborating on policies outside of sexual assault?

There are a couple of explanations for this static structure and corresponding mainstream approach to advocacy. The organization continues to be led by the same founding executive director today (Susan); she has been with the organization for more than thirty years. By her side, Amanda has served for more than twenty years. When both of these leaders discussed the organization, they often referred back to its founding principles, which has shaped its strategic plans, funding, mission, hiring decisions, and activities. This longevity of leadership may in part account for why the organization hasn't changed or evolved over the years. Moreover, the mission and goals of the organization are bounded around the issue of sexual assault. Therefore, while the organization is committed to serving all people that experience sexual assault, advocates do not differentiate these experiences by intersectionally marginalized characteristics.

The population the organization primarily serves are also not intersectionally marginalized, despite recent changes in increasingly serving a Latina population. When asked about who the organization served, even though Susan wants her organization to represent all women across differences in social identity, she did highlight in her interview this more advantaged group of survivors. She said: "I really think that we talk about inclusivity all the time and the need for diversity all the time, and we need that. And I think one area that we forget about are the very wealthy who are trapped – their trappings look very different than poor people." In another part of our interview, she referenced the importance of changing white-collar professional areas. She said: "We have really had to fight for just about everything and slowly but surely become a topic that men and other CEO roles in the corporate world are actually able to talk about and provide finance and resources. That didn't happen in the '80s and '90s. That was unheard of." White-collar and wealthy survivors certainly also need protection from sexual assault, but these groups are already disproportionately advantaged (Breines, 2002) and the resources advocates like WAVE direct to these areas then don't go toward more disadvantaged groups, such as intersectionally marginalized populations. These are the tradeoffs of a feminist mainstream approach that organizations like WAVE have to be aware of as they make choices about their advocacy.

Representation

What populations each organization prioritized mapped onto their advocacy approaches. As mentioned, WAVE does not prioritize particular groups; it is structured to serve all of them equally, which means intersectionally marginalized groups are not prioritized in its advocacy. That being said, some of its advocates do identify with an "intersectional feminist" approach to the work they do. The director of community services, Kendra, elaborates on what this approach means to her:

We come from the perspective of that intersectional feminist viewpoint that you can't really address sexual harm without also addressing racism and homophobia and class issues and all the many inequalities in society. They all somehow overlap with what we're doing. So yeah, we definitely do address that ... So, part of that is more diversity within our staff, more bilingual staff, more bilingual materials. Part of it is our participation in community events, whether it's the Pride drive or the Pride parade or Black Lives Matter protest. We do definitely try to be a part of that.

To Kendra, an "intersectional feminist" approach to the work they do is diversifying their staff, offering bilingual services, and supporting other groups that work on additional issues related to but also traditionally distinct from sexual assault. Over the course of interviews with leaders from WAVE, there were several instances where the staff spoke to intersecting issues such as incarceration, immigration, and homophobia. However, when they were asked if they were addressing these issues with their advocacy and work, leaders consistently said they "outsourced" these problems to other organizations. Susan explained this process of referring intersectionally marginalized groups to other organizations and services:

I think that if there's a situation, especially with an immigrant, for example, who would like to find a pathway to citizenship, that we would connect – we have an attorney that we've worked with in the past, an immigration attorney. We have other organizations that we can collaborate with, but that's only if the client chooses that. Otherwise, our main primary focus is on sexual violence, knowing that there's a menu of possibilities that they are bringing into the relationship and then resources that we can have that we can either use on site with our people or that we can work in tandem with another organization. So, we try to be as resourceful as possible both in house and out.

Susan is not alone. All of the other members of the leadership team that were interviewed underscored this approach and similarly mentioned that if groups had other issues related to immigration status, homelessness, poverty, or incarceration that they would have to rely on other organizations for these needs. Under this organizational model, multiple issues such as citizenship rights, poverty, and homelessness are viewed as separate from sexual violence and out of scope. This approach is not necessarily ineffective – if the organization does not have the expertise in these areas or does not understand these populations, perhaps referring them to other organizations is the best form of care they can provide. However, this approach of outsourcing people's experiences with interrelated issues is not intersectional advocacy, which builds these issue and policy linkages into the fabric of its political agendas and services.

To what extent should an organization like WAVE consider taking on an intersectional advocacy approach by expanding its services and advocacy into these other issue areas in order to effectively serve intersectionally marginalized groups? Based on interviews with their advocates, it seems that their singular approach to addressing sexual violence coupled with their mainstream focus on women is to some extent preventing intersectionally marginalized groups from seeking their services and representation. For example, as the Latine population in the area increasingly grows, advocates are concerned that WAVE remains inaccessible to them. Kendra shared:

We definitely would like to serve more of the Latina population, especially because [the part of the city the organization is located in] is kind of sandwiched between two very large Spanish-speaking communities. We're right in the middle of [two neighborhoods], and those are both areas that have a lot of Spanish speakers. But we know from our staff that we're not getting a lot of those. So, we don't know if it's maybe a cultural stigma or some sort of religious stigma or if maybe we need to do more outreach to be more welcoming and maybe have a lot of more Spanish-speaking staff.

It is not just Latines in the area that these leaders are concerned about. The community services director added: "We had a guest speaker who was talking about doing outreach to the LGBTQIA population in [the area]. And she maintained just kind of offhandedly that ... [WAVE] does not necessarily have a really welcoming reputation with that community." To address these challenges, WAVE takes a traditional approach to advocacy by increasing outreach to these communities, while maintaining the same services, policy advocacy, and organizational activities.

This approach is not intersectional advocacy, because this advocacy stays within the issue boundaries of sexual assault and does not link this issue to other related problems that intersectionally marginalized populations can be positioned between. Just because WAVE does not take an intersectional advocacy approach does not mean its advocates are not trying to better serve and advocate for the surrounding Latine population. Instead, this analysis illustrates that advocates like Kendra are in some ways constrained by the inertia and historical practices of the organization to stay within the boundaries of sexual assault and represent all survivors.

Networks

The networks of an organization can influence its advocacy, policy goals, and approach (Stone, 2019), and WAVE's narrow networks on sexual assault reinforce its traditional approach to advocacy. The groups that leaders often mentioned were part of their network included the state coalition on sexual assault, service providers such as hospitals or counselors that were directly involved in sexual assault cases, and other nearby groups in the area that similarly advocated for this issue. When asked if their goals or objectives ever diverged from the state coalition, leaders would often insist this was a rarity and that they held similar if not identical objectives to those of the state coalition. When organizations were mentioned outside of sexual assault, they were discussed as allies or places they might refer their participants to if they had additional needs or challenges (e.g., immigration, housing, welfare). Advocates from WAVE also occasionally mentioned showing symbolic support for these organizations by participating in a parade or putting up a solidarity message on their website. When WAVE created a narrow and specified network around the issue of sexual assault, it was unlikely that collaborations would emerge to address intersecting issues. Its network underscores the boundaries of sexual assault as an isolated problem that is treated separately from other related issues such as domestic violence, poverty, and homelessness.

Funding and Resource Allocation

Some of the challenges WAVE faces in both expanding its advocacy to other issue areas and representing intersectionally marginalized groups can be understood by examining how the organization receives and allocates its funding. For WAVE, establishing its reputation as a premier institution for addressing sexual assault is a funding priority – which means the organization singularly continues to invest all its resources toward this one issue. Funding opportunities through the government and private foundations only emphasize this approach by providing resources according to singularly defined issue areas (INCITE!, 2017). This funding priority also means that allocating funds to other issues areas detracts from WAVE's organizational niche. For example, even though leaders mention the majority population they serve are mothers, which are more likely to experience sexual assault in the context of domestic violence (Liang et al., 2005), the organization does not include domestic violence in its policy or service efforts. Domestic violence and other issues like immigration, homelessness, incarceration, and poverty are instead relegated to other organizations.

While WAVE supports some of these organizations by referring individual participants to them, and occasionally showing symbolic support, there are no collaborations between these groups. Susan says:

[W]e can't be everything to everyone. And many people fall in the trap in the kind of work that we do, thinking that they can do that. Took me a long time to realize I couldn't, that there are people better than I in different arenas, in different areas that were just better at whatever it was at the time than I was or that staff was. And I think it's important to know the difference.

Susan is in some ways referring to "mission creep" where nonprofit organizations take on too much and don't specialize in a given area (Fox & Maes, 2013). She would rather invest the organization's funds in their area of expertise: sexual assault – and she's not alone. Many other organizations try to avoid mission creep, because they believe it makes them less effective (Fox & Maes, 2013).

The organization maintains rigid issue boundaries around sexual assault – in the policies it advocates for, the services it provides, the lack of collaboration with other issue groups, and how it allocates funding. Unlike the other organizations in this study, WAVE has the unique financial position of having an endowment. Susan says:

Well, I certainly want to sustain what we have, and we are lucky that we were as forward thinking as we were 25 years ago when we started our endowment major gifts fund. So, we actually have a significant reserve fund, which I'm so grateful for, especially at a time like this when we're not sure about funds and how we're going to get them.

Only one-third of WAVE's funding comes from the government. The rest of its funding comes from private donations and foundation grants. This distribution of resources means that WAVE has more discretionary funds compared to the other organizations included in this study that primarily receive federal funding. It has a surplus of resources and the capacity to broaden how it addresses the issue of sexual assault, but its structure, goals, and leadership do not support this expansion. Thus, despite WAVE's financial

TABLE 5.2 *Organizational characteristics of Women Against Violence Everyday (WAVE)*

Organization	Origin and Leadership	Representation	Networks	Funding Issue and Allocation
Women Against Violence Everyday (WAVE)	One-size-fits-all model to addressing sexual assault; leadership grounded in the bounded crime policymaking of the 1980s; goals are static; leadership is unchanging	Represents intersectionally marginalized groups and is invested in them but outsources their issues to other organizations; policies and advocacy do not prioritize intersectionally marginalized groups	Localized and limited networks; networks include mostly service providers and allies that focus on sexual assault	Allocates all funding to sexual assault policy interventions and services

capacity to engage in intersectional advocacy and expand its issue boundaries and services, organizational leaders choose not to engage in this practice. Funding remains in surplus and is only directed to interventions that address sexual assault for the mainstream population of women.

Women Against Violence Everyday (WAVE) is an example of an organization that specializes in one issue area and enforces financial, policy, and service boundaries around this area. The organization does not cross boundaries even within its issue area to address domestic violence, and if you follow the trail of funding and resources these all are crafted around this single issue. It does not ignore interrelated issues; advocates try to find ways to support other organizations and refer intersectionally marginalized groups to them when they believe they are a better fit. This is one approach to advocacy, an approach that is most common among organizations addressing gender-based violence. Table 5.2 illustrates WAVE's four characteristics that were highlighted in these sections.

COMMUNITIES FOR SURVIVORS (CFS)

Communities for Survivors (CFS) is an example of a feminist mainstream organization that is transitioning from a traditional to an intersectional advocacy approach. Its origins and history are rooted in a mainstream model, but in the last five years its infrastructure has changed dramatically: its leadership, representation of intersectionally marginalized groups, network of partnerships, and interpretation of issue boundaries are no longer the same. These shifts in activities and representation align with an intersectional advocacy approach. I identify CFS as an organization that is in a transitional phase to intersectional advocacy because these changes are recent and are not necessarily permanent. A new executive director and change in its leadership structure might shift it back to a traditional policymaking approach. In this section, I explain the changes CFS has undergone and why these illustrate an intersectional advocacy approach.

Origins and Leadership

The organization emerged around the same time as WAVE and had a similar initial mainstream infrastructure. Like WAVE, CFS started as a shelter model that grew into a professionalized nonprofit organization over the years. It sought to serve all women and did not differentiate services or advocacy among this group by race, ethnicity, sexual orientation, or income level. However, over the years CFS changed to prioritize intersectionally marginalized groups and advocated for policies outside of their primary issue area: domestic violence. Much of these changes can be explained by shifts in leadership and partnerships with outside groups. In the last five years, CFS consistently crossed issue boundaries outside of gender-based violence to address interrelated problems such as housing, mass incarceration, and immigration. This shift aligns more with an intersectional advocacy approach, and it can in part be explained by changes in leadership at the executive director level.

According to CFS's leadership staff, there was a drastic change in leadership between former executive directors and the current one. The preceding executive director, Kathy, was not supportive of diversity. Three of the leadership members explained how the director resisted their efforts to support other issues that were pertinent to people of color. The communications director, Blanca, left under her leadership and came back years later under the new and current executive leadership. She explains why she left and then returned:

I left because the Executive Director at the time was racist and I couldn't be volunteering two-and-a-half years of my time anymore to an agency that was led by a racist career woman, white woman ... Now I think it is on its way up again ... That's why I'm [back] in this position and I'm hopeful that the [CFS] will truly align with those goals that are truly inspired by transformative justice advocates in the city.

Kathy also refused to support issues that impacted intersectionally marginalized groups. The director of community services, Shonda, explains:

There was a lot of tension from the previous ED before [our current executive director], who did not want to have these conversations or did not believe in working with undocumented people, or with the Black Lives Matter movement. I think that's when stuff stopped ... [Our policy director] helped create our policy on how we are now – before, if there was an issue, for example, Black Lives Matter. When we had asked our previous executive director for us to make a statement on it, she refused. After we kept on pushing, she said that she wasn't sure how other organizations felt about it. And so, she didn't want to say anything if it was going to upset some of our agencies.

Kathy pursued and supported initiatives that relied on law enforcement. This priority affected the organizations that partnered with CFS, and according to Shonda resulted in a loss of partnerships with previous organizations that represented intersectionally marginalized groups. Leadership staff referred to a history of executive directors with these types of objectives and underscored how the current director contrasts substantially from these previous leaders. The current director was hired using the same process of board approval as the previous directors. Because Kathy lost affiliated members and funding, staff believe the current executive director, Angela, was purposefully hired to change the perception of the organization and how CFS was received by the broader urban community.

Angela's perspective on the changing landscape of gender-based violence illuminates how CFS adapted in ways WAVE was unable to under its leadership. She says:

I think in our mission statement, we say, "We want to end domestic violence and the oppression that underpins it." When you start talking about the oppression that allows gender-based violence to exist, you start really talking about how one person feels about the worth of another person. And so, when we talk about the evolution of domestic violence services, moving from shelters, for instance, to now where we're at a place where we aren't so dependent on the shelter model as a service model, what we're really talking about is that we don't need it as much because women can be on an apartment lease, have their own checking account, have a credit card, work independently, where they couldn't 40 years ago when our services were designed.

Less like WAVE, the leadership staff from CFS adapted to its local context a little more. As indicated by Angela, CFS underscores a need for the organization to adapt and change especially at a local level, which is why she makes a case for engaging in criminal justice reform to improve the state and city's response to violence among survivors. The organization is located in an urban city, where high-profile incidents of police brutality occurred and mass organizing of the Black Lives Matter movement has taken place. The city also has a coalition of grassroots organizations advocating for bail bond reform. CFS is very much influenced by the Black Lives Matter movement and by the localized advocacy within the surrounding city to reform police institutions and the criminal justice system more broadly. Angela discusses these goals within the context of organizational change:

I would say that we're in a really aspirational phase, a building phase, where we seek to create a city that has a strong safety net for survivors of domestic and sexual violence. We believe that the city needs to invest more in domestic violence services and sexual violence services. We believe the state could be doing more. And we see those as our big picture items. We also see larger issues of social justice and equity as big picture items, as well. In terms of creating a community, and a culture, and a society where all survivors have equal access to services, and all survivors are able to receive healing and support and the response that they would benefit from or that they desire, that we have survivor-led criminal justice reform, that we have survivor-led service development, and survivor-led responses to crime victims' rights, or victims' issues.

For Angela, addressing gender-based violence means eliminating the boundaries between sexual assault and domestic violence and addressing interrelated issues such as criminal justice reform. This is an intersectional advocacy approach and nonprofit mainstream organizations are not built for these types of initiatives. The director of the training department, Jaimina, explains this challenge, and yet why it is important for these organizations to cross issue boundaries in this way. She says:

I think the decarceration work, indicting non-profits as pretty significant tools in perpetuating violence against survivors, as well as people that harm, and bringing in an anti-violence abolitionist perspective to this work is not something that's inherent to DV [domestic violence] advocacy, institutionalized DV advocacy. I think DV advocacy when it first started was underground, was at kitchen sinks in people's homes and was not using institutions. But domestic violence advocacy now is so rooted in the courts and in incarceration and with the police. And so, we need to be able to have domestic violence advocacy that doesn't rely on calling 911 or getting an order of protection.

Jaimina points out that CFS is very much an institutionalized domestic violence advocacy organization that is rooted in the courts, incarceration, and law enforcement. Thus, the organization's shifts to confront these institutional roles and advocate for alternative solutions to domestic violence that involve advocacy in other policy areas such as criminal justice reform are challenging. For CFS, a new executive director has in part allowed the organization to pursue this form of advocacy. However, her leadership only accounts for some of these shifts. In the next section, I explain how a covert group of staff strategically influenced Angela and established partnerships with other organizations that together shifted the priorities and structures of CFS.

Representation

Angela's strategies on criminal justice reform and decisions to expand CFS's broader efforts to other interrelated issues are largely driven by a covert group of mid-level leadership staff. They are represented structurally in the organization as mid-level leadership because they are not represented at the top of organization (i.e., executive director, CEO, assistant director) or the bottom (i.e., administrators, program coordinators). Instead, they hold mid-level positions, such as directors of subareas of the organization (i.e., policy director) and leaders of specific programs (i.e., manager of organizational partnerships). This organizational positionality doesn't provide this group with the power and influence of an executive director, but it does give each role significant influence within the parameters of their specialty area.

Among this mid-level leadership, there is a covert group of predominantly women of color who are using their individual positions of influence to expand the organization's reach and service to intersectionally marginalized groups. This group started informally about five or six years ago and included previous directors of the organization who have since left. The group meets secretly to protect their jobs within the organization, and they believe their coordinated efforts are more effective without being seen as a "diverse" initiative by people of color. Because they also hold positions that span the organization's different programmatic and policy areas, they also believe that they can reinforce each other within their own areas of expertise without drawing attention to the underlying changes they are making structurally to the organization. They often call this "managing up," and these efforts are very strategic. Currently, the group meets formally every week to push the organization in the direction of decarceration efforts. Jaimina shares:

We have this secret decarceration meeting happening weekly now … We're starting to open it up to folks, but it's been a secret for a couple of months to really talk about – to really problematize the network and figure out – and problematize the structure, our ED Executive Director, the work that we do, and figure out how to move forward from there. And I think that there are other people, other staff at other agencies that are similar to us because we're starting to find them when we bring this up in conversation with people we trust.

This group has expanded beyond CFS and now includes other women of color leaders who are working under other mainstream models outside their organization. When I asked what types of policy interventions this group is leading, Jaimina explained:

The creation of a 24-hour crisis line that does not use the police at all for de-escalation and intervention. Maybe more rape crisis care. Again, trying to funnel the work outside of the police I think is really what our interventions are looking like. And then, pushing for the defunding of the police and using those funds towards domestic and sexual violence services.

To advance these interventions, the group sets a consistent agenda, and each person in their respective role brings up these approaches. The communications director, Alba, explains how she tries to do this in her position. Alba shares: "In my position, I'm trying to figure out ways to help [CFS] out in terms of being more radical, more woke. It's just it goes hand in hand with DV and Black Lives Matter and defunding and all these things that need to happen to make this world a safer place for everybody." Influencing the organization isn't easy and has taken years. Jaimina explained when she first brought up bail bond reform to the executive director two years ago that there was no support for this advocacy. She says: "I remember bringing [up] the bond reform in a staff meeting and [the executive director] was like, that is not something [CFS] will ever support." Now, bail bond reform is one of the top priorities of CFS, and it has been a policy Angela has been advocating for more than a year since she started.

The women who are a part of this covert group explain that while the organization serves many different types of women, they are advocating for an organization that centers Black women's experiences. This approach, according to them, necessitates advocacy around bail bond and criminal justice reform. The communications director, Blanca, says:

I think ultimately, we serve a Black woman. We serve a Black woman who's dealing with domestic violence. I'm not saying that's because Black women experience the most domestic violence ... It's dealing with so many messed up systemic violence. That ends up harming the Black woman the most in [this city] ... [we're] supporting the bond fund because being that Black folks are the ones that are with the highest rates of incarceration, and Black survivors are the ones that are experiencing their abusers who are also partners that they might care about, interacting with the prison industrial complex and these systems, we have to actually talk with them more about what are all of the things that you want. We're just assuming this one track, which is a high bond, holding them and then putting them in jail. And when you actually talk to Black survivors, and a lot of times they are criminalized for their own intersections with poverty and race, you see that they have other – there's an expanse in the desire for solutions.

As Blanca explains, Black women's experience with violence necessitate criminal justice reform. Black women are more likely to be arrested when they experience domestic and sexual violence compared to other groups (Fox & Maes, 2013). They are also often part of Black communities that are overly policed and detained, which disincentives them from reporting crimes that increase incarceration among communities of color (Thuma, 2019). Finally, bail bonds, in particular, disproportionately burden Black women who are the primary breadwinners of their families as they often have to carry the financial burden of paying for bail bonds (Rabuy & Kopf, 2016; Richie, 2012).

This covert group of mid-level leadership staff has over time started to change CFS's mainstream model to focus more on intersectionally marginalized populations and, in particular, Black women. These strategies also appear to be especially effective under the new leadership. Although the current executive director at first resisted advocating for bail bond reform, over time she changed the organization's priorities to support this policy goal. These priorities appear to have changed due to both this secret leadership group and changes in the affiliated organizations.

Networks

Although WAVE and CFS were similar in their original mainstream structures, CFS differs organizationally in one important way. It is structured to have member organizations. Member organizations pay an annual fee to be a part of CFS's network. This network allows organizations to share resources with one another, fundraise together, and learn from each other. The composition of this membership group influences the priorities of CFS, which in part explains why the organization has shifted to an intersectional advocacy approach. Previous training directors and directors of community service made an effort to diversify its affiliates by including groups that approached gender-based violence as a multifaceted issue. This was an effective strategy only under the current executive director, Angela, who was more open to these changes. Under Kathy's leadership, member organizations that would be identified as "intersectional advocates" left this network. When I asked Shonda about the impact of this previous executive director on the network of affiliated organizations she explained:

[We lost] credibility among membership organizations, [and] among funders. Not [because we had] any money issues, but [because we were not doing] the work that [was] expected of [CFS]. [We are supposed to be] the leading organization for [our urban] community [that is inclusive and representative of diverse groups]. That was not happening … [Under her leadership we] definitely, [did] not think about the other intersections, [and were] not being more inclusive. When I say inclusive I don't mean race, color, all those things, I mean inclusive in terms of other service areas which, if you're a domestic violence victim, you would – housing, legal, so many other areas that are just as important to you, so including all of those allied service providers that are very important to the comprehensive service that needs to be provided to a victim or a survivor. Or, resources that need to be available to them. So, not including them in the conversation, that's very important.

When I asked Shonda if and how this membership changed under Angela, she explained: "She's started conversations with all of them, our membership now reflects not just DV providers, but many of the other allied providers. Those things. She has reached out, got onto committees of other service areas that are outside of the DV work, so herself got involved, and then invited people to get involved with [CFS]."

Angela explains how this was a necessary strategy to reengage and expand the membership: "so, reengaging membership was one of the first things that I focused on, and I visited members, I saw where they worked. We talked about different committee structures, so we shifted the committee structure of [CFS] to make sure that engaged members in the activities that they really felt the [CFS] could add value for." As she reached out to members, she also made concerted efforts to expand the membership by including community grassroots organizations that focused on intersectionally marginalized populations (e.g., Puerto Rican women) or interrelated issues (e.g., food scarcity, poverty, housing). Under a new executive director, it was possible to reestablish these connections with other organizations and to expand CFS's network.

This network of organizations largely shapes CFS's advocacy, activities, and goals. Directors from these organizations meet monthly. This membership also includes a policy committee that works together to develop their advocacy strategies. As the membership changed to include more organizations that focused on intersectionally marginalized groups, it shifted the priorities of CFS. For example, organizational members were concerned about the city's budget for law enforcement and how police officers intervened in cases of gender-based violence. The organization surveyed their members, asking them if they supported police abolition, defunding the police, or reforming the police (see also Chapter 4). The majority of members said they supported either police abolition or defunding the police. Alba, who surveyed members in this way, is part of the covert leadership group that is leading the efforts to focus on criminal justice. Jaimina recognized the role membership plays in supporting their goals to broaden CFS's policy efforts:

The policy director put out a survey earlier this year, and a lot of people were like, we should be doing more abolition work, we would like to see [CFS] do that. And that was really validating because I think when [our executive director] hears me say these things she doesn't take it seriously, but when the membership says these things, it's like, "Well, we exist to serve the membership, so we have to do what they're asking for."

Jaimina is correct. With membership signaling to CFS that they were on board with defunding the police, Angela moved forward with budget advocacy efforts aimed at reallocating police funding to services for sexual assault and domestic violence. From Jaimina's perspective, CFS still has a long way to go and has yet to win the support of more radical grassroots groups that will continue to transform the organization. Shonda, however, believes that over time, as CFS moves forward, supporting policies such as bail bond reform and defunding the police will help it gain credibility among these other groups. For this covert group of leaders, changing CFS to be an organization that engages in intersectional advocacy includes managing up and expanding the scope of their member organizations.

Funding and Resource Allocation

How does this new and evolving infrastructure support efforts to engage in intersectional advocacy? Focusing on defunding the police has incentivized CFS to try and reconfigure the city budget. To do so, the organization relies on budget advocacy. Angela explains how she uses budget advocacy at the city level to "articulat[e] why an overinvestment in law enforcement services does a great disservice to victims of gender-based violence, and why investing, instead, in services, to a certain extent, would make a lot more sense in terms of public safety." She is requesting that the police department's budget be reallocated to sexual assault and domestic violence services and go toward efforts to address community violence. Although CFS has not yet successfully defunded the police force, the organization has reconfigured the city budget in their favor in other ways. According to Alba, by using budget advocacy CFS alone added a line item to the budget of the Department of Public Health that increased funding to domestic violence services, organizations focusing on community violence, and mental health services. When CFS experiences these types of wins, these resources are shared with their membership network.

Budget advocacy has been an important strategy for CFS because, as Angela points out, these organizations are often underfunded and left out of city budgets. Budget advocacy in and of itself is not intersectional advocacy – but how CFS uses it to expand the funding boundaries for domestic violence aligns with an intersectional advocacy approach. For example, Angela explained how last time there was an emergency budget in their city "DV programs were completely left out of the budget. They just were left out of the emergency budget that funded everything but DV programs. Providers were furious. Then, once you're left out of a budget, it's an uphill climb to get back in a budget." The leadership staff at CFS underscored the importance of reconfiguring financial institutions not only to increase resources for domestic violence services but also to reallocate funds from other institutions, such as the police force, to these issue areas.

Although CFS engages in most of its budget advocacy at the city-governmental level, it has multiple funding streams and it is not majority government funding. Instead, it is majority private funding, which includes a large percentage of unrestricted resources. The organization is using these resources to expand its efforts and advocacy – and this is an intersectional advocacy approach. One way that CFS is able to address these interrelated issues is by applying for funding in issue areas outside of violence prevention. The director of development, Laura, says:

Yes, we are branching out. We started our work, and now we are being able to – previously, our funders were mostly funders who focused on domestic violence, and now we are able to go to other funders where their focus area is also housing, is also social justice issues, and things like that. We were very limited in the funding opportunities we had, before, but now, we're able to go and request for funding in these other areas, which were out of our realm in the past.

As Laura points out, CFS applies to private foundations for grants in interrelated issue areas and then makes connections between these issues and gender-based violence. These funding streams allow it to be able to hire staff, recruit new membership organizations, and engage in advocacy efforts across issue areas. These funding streams also encourage the organization to consistently cross issue boundaries and pursue advocacy outside of domestic violence. Thus, the ways that CFS advocates for budget changes, uses its private donations, and applies to foundation grants across issue areas establish a financial infrastructure that supports intersectional advocacy. It does so by

TABLE 5.3 *Organizational characteristics of Communities for Survivors (CFS)*

Organization	Origin and Leadership	Representation	Networks	Funding Issue and Allocation
Communities for Survivors (CFS)	One-size-fits-all model, with a built-in network of providers and partners; mid-level leadership advocates for prioritizing intersectionally marginalized groups	Advocates for different policies by race and gender; prioritizes interventions that most impact Black women	Several partnerships; has a built-in network of members and collaborative partnerships with organizations outside of gender-based violence	Local budget advocacy to alter how the city determines funding/distributes funding across issue areas

creating financial resources and pathways to advocate for issues that overlap with domestic violence that are not squarely within this policy area. Table 5.3 illustrates each of the organizational characteristics presented in this section that describe CFS.

SISTERS AGAINST VIOLENCE (SAV)

Organizations like Sisters Against Violence (SAV) have built-in structures for addressing several policy issues together and their leadership prioritizes the interests of intersectionally marginalized groups, but they do not directly inform the advocacy of the organization. Some of these organizations represent the interests of intersectionally marginalized populations to broader mainstream audiences. These audiences include mainstream coalitions and organizations, legislatures, and the general population. Early examples of similar organizations emerged in the 1980s in the form of tasks forces and projects that were part of wider mainstream coalitions. For example, a Women of Color Task Force was founded in 1985 by professional leaders of the mainstream organization Georgia Coalition Against Domestic Violence to increase visibility and outreach to communities of color (Aszman, 2011). This was one of the first institutionalized efforts to address sexual violence against women of color (Schechter, 1982). According to interviewees from this study, it wasn't until the late 1990s and early 2000s that national organizations were established to advocate on behalf of women of color to address issues of sexual and domestic violence. Sisters Against Violence (SAV) is the first national organization with this institutionalized role and focus on women of color. The history behind its leadership explains why it emerged and in part why SAV practices intersectional advocacy.

Origins and Leadership

The organization was created as an alternative approach to mainstream organizations that prioritized the interests of Black, Indigenous, and people of color (BIPOC) women. This organization was established by two Black women, Stella and Jada,[2] who thought the mainstream model overlooked the different ways that intersectionally marginalized populations experienced sexual violence, the resources they needed for healing, and the types of recourses they preferred for addressing this issue. As employees of these mainstream coalitions, both founders felt that women of color were underrepresented by these agencies and organizations. The cofounder and now executive director of SAV, Jada, shared these experiences of exclusion and how they motivated these two women to formulate a plan for changing how women of color were represented in these spaces:

You could be in a room of about two representatives each state territory of a hundred people. And there would be maybe five, if we're lucky, women of color, people of color, just period, in the room. And we were like, this is ridiculous. I mean, we would laugh and say we found each other because we were the only brown spots … and that was really a frustration for us. And so, both of us were at management level and had good relationships with the executive directors of our coalitions. And so, because of that, we were able to formulate this plan to begin to look at having more women of color in leadership.

Similar to the Women of Color Task Force in 1985, SAV started as an independent project to increase the representation of women of color in leadership among organizations focusing on sexual violence. The program coordinator, Uche, explains why this type of program and leadership initiative was important:

At the time, what they were seeing is that they weren't allowed women of color in leadership, so they started seeing if they could look at increasing the voices of women of color and increasing their access to leadership positions … A lot of the times when we're at meetings, we don't see a lot of women of color at the table, especially when it comes to mainstream organizations or when it comes to an event where they have a leaders' thing. A lot of the times, if you see a person of color, you only see one person of color at that table. A lot of times, I've noticed that you have a non-person of color or non-person from that community talking for that community.

---

[2] These names are pseudonyms. Organizational leaders did not want to be identified so that they could speak freely about their political advocacy. They felt if they were identified their governmental funding could be jeopardized.

While this early project provided training for women of color that aspired to assume leadership positions in their organization, this leadership was also limited under a mainstream model. This was the feedback that participants of these trainings gave to the founders of SAV. This feedback motivated Jada and Stella to leave their respective coalitions and expand this project to be a standalone organization. Jada said:

If we are going to stand for communities of color without having to feel like we need to ask permission to take that space and be able to fully use that space, we needed to stand on our Island. So, I then decided that I was going to leave my organization, leave the coalition. So, we stepped out of the coalition, and I had negotiated with the executive director that since the project was conceived by us, that we would take the project out of the coalition, and it would be a standalone agency.

Leaving the coalition meant losing a professionalized infrastructure that came with consistent funding, substantial resources, and connections. Stella and Jada had to create and establish their own infrastructure. To do so, they relied on their networks: organizations led by women of color, funders that supported their mission, and the national relationships they had established through the mainstream coalition. Jada explains how support from women of color helped them build an organization that would represent their interests:

I cannot tell you the spirit, the amazing ability of women of color. I mean, we really were – [SAV] was really created on the backs of sisters, with the spirit of sisters. And it was created because we wanted to have our own voice. We wanted to have women of color organization that would have its own voice that could stand in places. We were fortunate, my colleague and I, in founding [SAV]. We were fortunate in that we had already paved some ways, so we knew people on the national level, we knew funders. We were fortunate in that. We had a reputation for doing really good work, so we used that to begin to see how do we put our foot into meetings. And I tell you, as I reflect, I think the spirit of community and collective community with women, I mean, I think it is very difficult to start an organization, but we were able to have such support from women of color across the country that it worked, right?

Organizations led by and for women of color were more than structures of support for SAV; they were also their soundboards for deciding what type of advocacy SAV would lead. As SAV worked with organizations individually to help them increase their capacity for services and support their leadership, the organization also reached out to these groups to learn what advocacy work they needed from SAV. Uche explains this process:

We went out and we assisted them to build up their capacity of services and looked at them and really worked with them on what they needed at the time. We worked with them throughout the territories and worked with different entities there … Another thing that we do is that because we are working with different populations as well and we are a different community, we get to see the community first-hand because a lot of the times, we go to those communities, we're on the ground. We get to know the communities and see what is really going on. That also helps us to see what we want to do. A lot of times what will also affect us is what's going on in terms of sometimes what is maybe going on with policy.

This advocacy aligns with SAV's original mission and purpose – which is to be an institution that supports organizations representing women of color. For SAV, supporting these organizations means taking on an intersectional advocacy approach of expanding funding criteria for these organizations to address interrelated issues and by engaging in partnerships with them to advance agendas and interventions with issue and policy linkages.

Representation

According to the leadership staff at SAV, engaging in intersectional advocacy was necessary to address sexual assault among communities of color, which the organization saw in connection with other issues such as housing, poverty, and healthcare. Similar to CFS, SAV used budget advocacy as a tool to support this approach. Jada explained that the current structure of federal funding was detrimental to these efforts because it excluded community and grassroots organizations. According to her, addressing sexual assault is part of the intertwining and broader movements that tackle other issues. Unfortunately, the way funding is currently structured prevents groups that focus on these multiple issue areas from accessing governmental funds because they lack the professionalized structures of mainstream organizations. Jada explains:

When you talk about other social justice, we were always connected – we were always working with, always connected with other social justice movements. And we say movements because there weren't many organizations as much as there were movements ... What you end up having and what, unfortunately, even now we continue to see it, is that there is this phenomena where there is a lot of funding that is given out to address issues that impact heavily on communities of color. Whether we're talking about economic issues, housing, even health care, but it's not given to communities of color organizations. So, the leadership of communities of color organizations and many of these other areas is ... there's a lot of limitations because you don't have infrastructure.

Jada sees opportunities for funding to address issues that heavily impact communities of color, but because it is restricted to nonprofit organizations, leaders representing grassroots or community groups cannot access these funds. Yet these are the groups that most represent intersectionally marginalized populations and most often work on intersecting issue areas (e.g., healthcare, violence, housing).

The organization recognizes these limitations in funding are leading to the monopoly of mainstream organizations to hold all the resources aimed at addressing sexual and domestic violence. It engages in budget advocacy to create line items for these groups to access funding with fewer restrictions, which provides them with more opportunities to pursue issue and policy linkages. Without this support, intersectionally marginalized groups are limited to mainstream models of funding that do not account for cultural differences or the ways in which issues can be interrelated with sexual assault for these populations. Jada explains that this is why flexible funding is an important outcome of their intersectional advocacy efforts:

You have sisters that work in places that are committed to these issues, so you would work with them but they're doing this and the other job. Or they're doing, they're struggling to lift these issues in their organization, but they might be the only one. And so that's a struggle. It was one of the reasons why [SAV] started, so we could not only be able to look at responding to incidents of sexual assault and providing services and responses for sexual assault survivors, but also [get] to look at the areas where issues [impact survivors from] being able to access healthy lives and [focus on additional] issues that lead to a vulnerability [of] sexual assault [among] women of color. So [that's] always been a part of our grounding because we knew that we had to be talking about those issues, and they couldn't be an extra, it couldn't be an add on, it had to be something that if you're going to be talking about sexual assault, you also had to talk about all these other areas and all these other things that intersect, that impact, that create a barrier to services, et cetera.

For SAV, representing intersectionally marginalized populations means supporting organizations across issue areas such as housing, poverty, incarceration, and immigration. One of the ways to support these organizations is to increase their access to resources and funding. Thus, SAV spends much of its advocacy in the federal policymaking space advocating for changes in how the state identifies organizations representing intersectionally marginalized populations and how it funds them.

Networks

Partnerships with other organizations serving intersectionally marginalized populations are part of SAV's infrastructure. These partnerships have allowed the organization to share resources and networks. These shared commodities have also meant that SAV can employ staff and engage in advocacy. These networks are also vital to SAV's engagement in intersectional advocacy work.

Sisters Against Violence (SAV) receives federal funding to be a technical assistance provider for culturally specific organizations. This means that SAV distributes funding to these organizations from the federal government, which requires them to follow up with these organizations about how they are using the resources. Advocates strategically use these follow-up sessions with organizations to check-in about advocacy and policy. Jada explains:

These amazing women of color and advocates that are doing work across the country, we stay very connected to them. We stay and engage with them; we provide training for technical systems. They can call on SAV and say, hey, we need help with A, B, or C. We reach out to them on a regular basis to say, how are you doing? What's going on? How's the agency? What are you seeing? What's happening? What are some of the challenges? All of that information then feeds into our policy and advocacy levels at the federal level. Because when they tell us what's happening, where are the gaps, what they need.

The program specialist, Ebony, leads these meetings regularly. The meetings offer organizations a space to identify policy areas they need SAV to focus on at the federal level. They are also structured to create networking opportunities among organizations representing intersectionally marginalized populations. Ebony explains this goal:

So, we'll have a Black African, we have the Native Alaskan, Latinx, and Asian-Pacific islander. And so again, that just gives them a different opportunity to just pretty much connect with all the grantees. So, I think I mentioned before, so we have meetings based on fiscal year, regional, and then based off of ethnic communities, just trying to get them to network. And so ideally, the hope is that when they know that there are other organizations that they collaborate with, whether it's state or by ethnic community, we really do encourage them to reach out and create those networks because we don't really have that within organizations of color, so we really want to encourage that with our grantees.

These partnerships are important and explain how SAV and these other culturally specific organizations engage in intersectional advocacy to support each other outside of their issue area. For example, SAV collaborated with organizations focusing on the Black Lives Matter movement to push for the Breathe Act, which is an omnibus bill that proposes to divest taxpayer dollars from policing to invest in new approaches to public safety. Jada explains that it is important for their advocacy to transcend from sexual violence to issues such as police brutality and reproductive rights. She says:

And so it's for women of color, women of color have a very – we have a very difficult road because we're always caught in between. And so even as – like right now, currently, we work with folks that are doing the movement for black lives that's trying to push the Breathe Act. Have you heard of the Breathe Act? We do meetings with them to help understand that. At the same time that we are really interested in racial justice, we cannot have racial justice without gender justice, right? . . . And so one of the things that [SAV] is really trying hard to do is at the same time we're working at these overall systems, is also trying to work within our communities to – so partnering with people like Sister Song, there's amazing work in the reproductive justice sphere. And Black Women's Blueprint, they do amazing work as well. Trying to partner with folks to say – and Black Women's Blueprint, they get it. Sister Song, they're more on the reproductive justice side, so we're trying to have them lift up more of the sexual assault side. You know what I mean? And so partnering with our colleagues to say, we need you all when you're talking about women of color, we need you to be saying SA [sexual assault] and DV [domestic violence]. Just like when we're talking about SA and DV, we're saying all these other issues. Does that make sense? But it's hard. It's really – it's very – it can be very difficult, but it's worthwhile. And if we're truly ever going to get our hand around, not only responding to survivors, but ultimately putting an end to this atrocity and the vulnerabilities that lead, and that can support it continuing, then we need to be doing all the work, right?

For SAV, networks that connect them to organizations addressing issues that crosscut both gender and racial justice are an important part of the work that they do. These networks provide them with resources they can then share among themselves, as well as intersection points for collaboration. Being a part of these networks informs the intersectional advocacy efforts that SAV engages in – which is to support funding initiatives and policies that allow organizations to address issues of sexual assault in relation to other problems experienced by their communities.

Funding and Resource Allocation

The leadership staff from SAV often mentioned the challenges they faced when advocating for federal funding on behalf of other organizations. The staff described these financial institutions as rigid: only funding services and activities that are squarely in the areas of sexual violence or domestic violence. Jada explains:

[T]he funding that they get is very focused on service response, and it doesn't allow money for them to build infrastructure and for them to do policy. So oftentimes, they're just doing what they can, their total focus is that. And we hear that a lot from our agencies that we need you, [SAV], to be the voice for us, we need you to help pay attention to policy for us, we need you to do that because we're not able to.

Therefore, the way that governmental funding is structured and allocated makes it difficult for organizations serving intersectionally marginalized groups to grow organizationally and to practice intersectional advocacy. It is difficult to engage in this type of advocacy because these funding restrictions make it challenging for these organizations to focus on interrelated issues such as housing or female genital cutting, for example. Jada shares her frustration about these boundaries:

I had to push back on one of the federal agencies because one of the agencies that was funded to do that cultural-specific work is funded to do sexual assault, and they were told they got a sexual assault grant. They were told, well, you can't use your money to address FGC, female genital cutting, because that's not sexual assault.

These boundaries are often even more restrictive for certain intersectionally marginalized populations. Ebony shared with me that the organizations she works with representing Asian women often struggle with how the federal government funds sexual assault separately from domestic violence, yet she says: "I know with that community as well, we usually have to talk about domestic violence and sexual assault because those are usually intertwined."

Ebony recognizes that these financial boundaries are preventing her organization and others from comprehensively representing intersectionally marginalized populations. Thus, SAV uses intersectional advocacy to reconfigure these financial boundaries and make them more inclusive of interrelated issues that are identified outside the issue area of sexual assault (i.e., female genital cutting, domestic violence, police abolition). Advocates of SAV do so by modifying and expanding the financial criteria to fund these interrelated issues, and SAV uses federal budget advocacy to expand funding streams both within gender-based violence policy and outside of it. They created a new funding stream with fewer restrictions just for organizations representing intersectionally marginalized populations. Jada explains:

What if we were getting money directly from the feds, but didn't have to go through all the state loopholes? So, we said, okay. So then in the Violence Against Women Act [VAWA], we put in two funding streams, directly funding money that the communities of color organizations apply directly to the federal government for that money. And right now, the vast majority of communities of color organizations funded across this country doing domestic violence and sexual assault work, fund it through that funding stream that comes directly from the federal government. When we write the legislation we said, you need to – you're providing culturally specific services to survivors of domestic violence and sexual assault, that's it. And the culture-specific services is defined by your communities of color, your cultural way of healing.

Creating a funding stream just for "culturally specific organizations" was difficult. The SAV leadership staff mentioned they received pushback, especially from senators and the Republican Party. Originally, SAV advocated for designating these funds to "communities of color" or "racial and ethnic minority groups," but the only phrasing that was "palatable to congressional folks was to say culturally specific." While advocates like Jada compromised by accepting this terminology to categorize eligible policy beneficiaries, they addressed this constraint by strategically defining the statute "culturally specific" to mean communities of color. In both 2005 and 2013, SAV was successful in creating and expanding funding streams through VAWA. These funds are less restricted and allow culturally specific organizations to use them more at their discretion. In the next section, I explain how a culturally specific organization also creatively allocates funding to work on policy advocacy that expands the issue area of domestic violence to include issues such as immigration, housing, and education.

Finally, SAV also uses budget advocacy to engage in intersectional advocacy outside of its traditional policy scope. The leadership staff are currently advocating to change policies and funding by the Department of Health and Human Services (HHS). Jada explains why this is an important funding and advocacy area for their work. She says:

Department of Health and Human Services, HHS is like – HHS doesn't even do a sliver of what it needs to be doing in terms [of] communities of color and domestic violence and sexual, it just doesn't, it really doesn't . . . I mean, I am constantly at tables. They have money for runaway and homeless youth. Do you know that that money, 80 percent of that money goes to organizations that are not addressing domestic violence and sexual assault, did I ever tell you that? Or not focusing on sexual assault. One of the keyways that kids are running away is because of sexual assault. No sexual assault programs get that money. So, stuff like that . . . So, there's not this real integration of looking at where sexual assault intersects with some of these other issues.

Thus, SAV is currently working on changing HHS to fund sexual assault and domestic violence. Within this issue arena, they found that funding was not being directed to communities of color because the government did not recognize community health centers as legitimate hospital structures. Much of SAV's intersectional advocacy efforts include changing the ways that federal policy within and outside of the VAWA allocates funding to organizations focusing on women of color – a clear example of the practice of intersectional advocacy. The organization makes funding less restrictive so that these organizations can address not only their core issue (e.g., healthcare, sexual assault, domestic violence) but also other issues that are interrelated (e.g., community violence, immigration, welfare, reproductive rights).

However, these efforts come with important challenges that must be recognized. Federal funding can be an important source of support for this type of work, but even with SAV's advocacy, federal funds can be unreliable and remain restrictive. For example, Ebony explained to me that in 2019 there was an executive order from the president that stated federal funding could not be used to teach about sex, people of color, or white supremacy. For advocacy organizations that were providing training on these issues, which were the majority of culturally specific organizations that offer technical assistance, they were in jeopardy of losing their federal funding. Funding from the federal government creates tight boundaries around what constitutes an issue (e.g., sexual assault), who gets to address these issues (e.g., mainstream organizations), and how the issues are resolved (e.g., executive orders that prohibit anti-racism approaches). Thus, intersectional advocates like SAV are constantly involved in this political arena, aiming to reconfigure these financial institutions to be more representative of organizations serving intersectionally marginalized groups. Table 5.4 illustrates the four organizational characteristics described in this section that are unique to SAV.

THE LATINA NETWORK (LN)

The Latina Network (LN) is an organization with built-in structures for addressing several policy issues together, has leadership that prioritizes intersectionally marginalized group interests, and includes these groups in the process of informing its advocacy. Most of the organizations like LN started as US shelters that emerged from organized grassroots or community-based efforts. Women's Advocates in St. Paul, Minnesota, for example, was one of

TABLE 5.4 *Organizational characteristics of Sisters Against Violence (SAV)*

Organization	Origin and Leadership	Representation	Networks	Funding Issue and Allocation
Sisters Against Violence (SAV)	Focuses only on women of color, with a network of culturally specific organizations; leadership is represented by all women of color and the mission/vision of the organization is around the experiences of intersectionally marginalized groups	Advocates for policies and funding for culturally specific organizations and centers advocacy around women of color	Has a built-in network of culturally specific organizations; was founded in collaboration with partner organizations and coalitions outside of gender-based violence	Federal budget advocacy for culturally specific organizations that expands use of services to cover other issue areas

the first shelter organizations established in 1973 (Wilkes, 2019). The executive director of SAV, who has led the recognition of these organizations as "culturally specific," explains that "we differentiate between mainstream agency, which is, mainstream is just a generalist agency and ... we refer to [organizations] as culture-specific agencies when we think about communities of color agencies. Those agencies are for and by communities of color." Culturally specific organizations that focus on gender-based violence are traditionally service-based organizations (Gillum, 2009). Many of them began as a shelter and developed their organizations over time to include more staff, technical assistance training, and advocacy (Arnold, 2017). The Latina Network (LN) has these features. It started as a shelter organization and with changes in federal and local funding, the organization grew to include an advocacy staff (Markowitz & Tice, 2002) while expanding its scope of work. Similar to SAV and CFS, this organization practices intersectional advocacy and has some of the same organizational characteristics – localized communities of color as soundboards for advocacy, networks with organizations across issue areas – and it aims to identify flexible and unrestrictive funding streams. However, while LN shares broad similarities to the other organizations practicing intersectional advocacy discussed thus far, its strategies, approaches to advocacy, and interventions are all rooted in its service to localized communities of color.

Origins and Leadership

The Latina Network (LN) has existed for nearly forty years, and it began as an emergency shelter to take in Latina women experiencing violence. Over these years, LN has expanded its mission and goals. When the organization was first conceived, it was led by five Latinas and had very little funding. The goals then were modest and service-related. The current CEO, Valeria, tells this story:

We had five feisty Latina activists who said, "Enough is enough, and we're going to start this." So, they started something with volunteers. They started something with a little bit of money to – for some rents. And they grew the organization from there, but it was a cooperative structure for the first year to two years. Maybe the first director coming on, I think as they were getting ready to formally get a shelter on board, to buy the house. But there was never – like a lot of organizations, there was never this circle of big supporters, right? That were helping to fund a startup or helping to pay the day-to-day.

At this time, the organization sought to provide an alternative shelter for Latinas that was designed to be culturally specific to their needs. This included bilingual services, Latina staff, and options for recourses that acknowledged the unique positionality of those who were undocumented and who often wanted to avoid reporting violence to the authorities because of the risk of deportation. Differentiating the organization from mainstream models was important because, for LN, it meant underscoring a tailored model for serving communities of color. One of the project managers, Margarita, shared:

I see some of the challenges of working with organizations that might be considered more mainstream. Even though they might share some of our values or most of our values, there's still some things in their approach that are different to us. We do not believe that there are master recipes or one-size-fits-all type of solution to the issue of domestic violence. When other folks come up with those type of models or type of solutions, we're skeptical from the get-go because we know that most likely will not work. Especially they have not done their homework to figure out what is it that would make this model better when we're working with communities of color.

Since then, the organization has professionalized into a nonprofit organization under the category of "culturally specific." It has grown to include state and national advocacy efforts in its organizational priorities. It structured its growth in staff, activities, and funding around its local roots. Valeria believes this approach differentiates LN from organizations such as SAV or CFS. She says: "A lot of resource centers are national, but they may not have – and they may have individuals who have worked on the ground somewhere, but we have our whole history of having worked on the ground. And evolving over the years." When LN applied for its first Office of Violence Against Women (OVW) grant in 2004, it began its state and national policy advocacy, but these efforts were always informed by their experiences on the ground via the shelter. The family advocacy director, Margie, explains:

> But one of the things that we know for sure is that the local work informs the national work because it's based on a Latin[e] Advocacy framework. I think some of those realities come to really start thinking about how can we inform our communities across the country what we have learned, being one of the first organizations working with Latina communities on domestic violence? Again, doing that strategic process, we changed from being a domestic violence organization working in Latinx communities to being Latina organization working with domestic violence innovation affecting our community. The main thing is we are a Latina organization.

When I asked her why it was so important that localized Latine experiences shape the direction of LN, Margie responded: "Because the issues affecting our community [are] not just domestic violence. We need to see it in a very holistic way." The organization's initial infrastructure was that of a community organization serving the local Latine population.

Even though LN has scaled up its efforts since its initial establishment, its advocacy remains rooted and connected to its local work on the ground. Margarita sees this advocacy as an investment in local communities and leadership among grassroots groups. She says:

> [There is] this real understanding of the value and the strengths that community members already possess, and its process to help build on that, and to build that leadership, and to guide and support community leaders in taking on either the work of ending gender-based violence or taking on the work of addressing issues that are pertinent to them in their individual communities.

This approach is instituted throughout the organization via the "Latin[e] Advocacy Framework." Valeria, who currently leads the organization, has been involved with it for almost twenty years, and when she came on board she developed her own "Latin[e] Advocacy Framework." This framework has informed the direction of the organization and helps explain why LN practices intersectional advocacy.

Representation

The "Latin[e] Advocacy Framework" is the strategic document that guides LN's policy advocacy and activities. This framework was developed collaboratively among the leadership staff in 2006, but it was inspired by Valeria's metaphoric approach of "the last person standing." This strategic approach is meant to consider the most marginalized populations within the

Latine community. The CEO describes what she means by the "last person standing":

The last [person] is someone that maybe people don't see. She's there, but she might not be seen. Maybe she's hidden. And I was thinking about the trafficked girl that might be hidden somewhere, so people don't know where she's at, or that she needs our support. But it's the responsibility that we have to keep looking at – how do we reach – is this the girl that we see every day but don't recognize what she's going through? It is the girl that's hidden, and we have to go find? What does that – who is that last person? And then the question that I ask in this scenario is, but what about the rest of us? Aren't we important, too? And I say, of course. Everyone's important. But when we reach the last person, we will have already learned how to reach everybody else . . . it's kind of that concept of the last person. It's kind of looking at who have we missed and where do we need to lift up?

This perspective informed the "Latin[e] Advocacy Framework," which highlights LN's objective to "possess an understanding (and deep appreciation) of Latin[e] cultures, histories, religions, and oppression in the USA. This knowledge informs the entire advocacy approach with women." This framework and commitment to focusing on the most marginalized populations has informed what types of advocacy LN prioritizes. For example, in 2013, Valeria explains that the organization's efforts were about "lifting up more supports for LGBTQ [survivors] of violence, as well as native tribal [survivors] of violence, as well as immigrant communities."

When they were advocating for national legislation, there was a pressure to remove policies and programs that would benefit LGBTQ and Indigenous survivors from the VAWA. The LN advocates explain how important it was to hold their ground and prioritize these groups in national policymaking. Valeria continued to explain:

[I]t's real easy to sometimes give up and just go with, well what's going to cause the least resistance. But the last round, the programs held firm, and so we are not tossing any – we are not leaving anybody behind. And that takes extra work and leadership on behalf of all the programs that are working at this. And so – it passed. It passed with the amendments and the work that we wanted to include in the VAWA reauthorization.

This focus on intersectionally marginalized groups has also informed the types of local and state policy initiatives LN leads. It conducted a series of "listening circles" with local members of their community. As part of these sessions, it often came up that Latinas struggled to be economically independent, especially those who were undocumented, which positioned them to be financially dependent on their intimate partners. The organization worked with its city officials and a local organization that worked with business owners to start the "Mujeres Economic Project." This project provided training, services, and seed money to Latinas to start and promote their own businesses. Margie explained: "When people ask me what does that have do with domestic violence? [I say] it does in a lot of ways. Because we're thinking about empowerment; we're thinking about creativity; we're thinking about those are the women and moms that support their children when the father or the abusive partner is deported." The LN advocates continue to work with other organizations in the state to provide funding for these types of projects. By focusing on the ways in which Latinas are marginalized across other categories such as citizenship status, income level, sexual orientation, and Indigeneity, LN structures its policy efforts to focus on how these positionalities make some groups more vulnerable to intersecting issues such as sex trafficking, poverty, and deportation. It is this approach to policy efforts that is identified as intersectional advocacy – addressing multiple issues that intersectionally marginalized groups experience. For LN, this is a natural practice when it comes to serving people through their organizational framework.

The Latina Network (LN) also seeks to redistribute power back to the communities it serves. It often transitions the management of its interventions and programming at the local level to community members. Projects such as the "Mujeres Economic Project" are designed to provide local community members with leadership skills, so that they can help lead these types of intersectional advocacy initiatives. Thus, LN localizes this practice of intersectional advocacy by ensuring that people in their immediate community are able to take charge of these efforts in ways that are authentic to their intersectionally marginalized experiences.

Networks

Similar to CFS and SAV, networks are a crucial resource for LN. It often leverages its networks at the local, state, and national levels to practice intersectional advocacy. For example, at the local level, LN is involved in policy advocacy around income inequality. Valeria explains it is a misconception that income inequality is not interrelated with domestic violence, particularly at the city and state levels. She says her organization often had to change how the state views the connection between these issues. Because income inequality is a priority for LN, it established the "Neighborhood Development Alliance" at the state level. This alliance created a partnership of organizations across the state to pool resources and propose a set of economic policies at the city level that would improve the economic well-being for Latines and other communities of color that the city had divested from over time. When asked why LN coleads these types of initiatives that are outside of their policy area, Valeria responded: "[when funders, political officials, and other groups ask] Why would you do that? ... Well, we say, Well, we work with other DV programs, but we need partners that are outside the DV arena if we're going to deal with issues of housing and employment and education and et cetera, et cetera, etcetera."

For LN, partnerships with other organizations to address interrelated issues such as income inequality and housing are key to effectively practicing intersectional advocacy at the state and city level. However, this is only one example. It also has deep partnerships with school systems, national parks, and immigration organizations. The community director, Francisca, shares:

We collaborate a lot with state parks, county parks, departments of public health – not only the state one, but the county ones; [program] for mental health. Youth healthcare clinics, several schools, and many other organizations that are working with the Latinx community that don't necessarily address domestic violence, but that work in areas that intersect with the realities of survivors and children that witness violence.

The organization uses these partnerships in the same way, to change policies and funding to account for other issues that intersect with domestic violence. It also advocates at the national level and leverages its networks in similar ways there. At this level, LN partners with the National Hispanic Leadership Agenda, which is an association of forty-five of the largest Latine national organizations in the country. Advocates from LN co-chair the policy committee with another Latina organization to ensure gender is included in all eight policy areas that the group focuses on. These policy areas are then included in a comprehensive agenda that is then shared with every member of Congress and the president. Valeria explains that being involved in this way allows LN to build a policy infrastructure that accounts for intersectional experiences. She says: "our influence has been much as far as the intersections of domestic violence – with all of the other impacts – everything else it impacts – Latinas and their children – whether it be housing, immigration, civil rights, health – reproductive rights, et cetera." The Congressional Hispanic Caucus was a similar type of partnership. The Latina Network (LN) collaborated with this group to advocate for the CARE Act, which was an economic relief bill that was first introduced in 2019. Advocates from LN spearheaded this policy.

Beyond this coalition, similarly to SAV, LN also has national advocacy partners. For example, the organization has partnered with the National Alliance of Farmworker Women and Justice for Migrant Women. Together, these groups are working with each other to reform policies in the workplace, particularly in industries that have high concentrations of migrant workers. When I asked why LN chooses to forge these types of partnerships, the policy director, Maria, explained: "because Latinas make [up] such a substantial part of the workforce. When you start talking to them as workers and you're like, 'What do you need?' Protection from sexual assault and sexual harassment on the job becomes a priority. It becomes a priority when we're talking about climate change and migration patterns." The leadership staff at LN describe this partnership as a necessary collaboration. All groups focus on the different vulnerabilities that Latina women face in the workforce, and thus they claim that only together can they imagine policies that will comprehensively address these vulnerabilities. Similar to CFS and SAV, networks of partnerships with organizations outside of gender-based violence lead LN to pursue and steer intersectional advocacy efforts (i.e., issue linkages, policy linkages, cross-cutting policies).

Funding and Resource Allocation

Practicing intersectional advocacy and leading these types of issue and policy linkages are not easy for LN, which is 85 percent funded by the government and 95 percent of their total funding is restricted. According to the development director, Carmen, this budget leaves LN with only 5 percent of its funding available for discretionary expenses. The CEO of LN says: "[with] unrestricted dollars, we could maybe even step out a little bit more boldly where we want to." In lieu of this type of funding, LN is creative with its resources. Partnering with other organizations allows LN to share resources such as staff, transportation, and facilities. In many ways, LN is able to cross issue boundaries in its advocacy because it shares resources with other organizations to move this work forward.

Similar to CFS and SAV, LN also looks for revenue streams outside of its policy area. For example, the organization has increasingly advocated against human trafficking, which is not supported by OVW federal funding. To engage in this advocacy, Valeria looks to the Department of Health for funding:

[F]or [human] trafficking support in dollars ... primarily they flow through the Department of Health – State Department of Health – so that there are additional programs for the Safe Harbor Initiative, which is the state initiative focused on trafficking for victims 24 and under. So, we always participate on anything that relates to the work that we do, or the intersections.

Thus, to cross boundaries and expand its policy focuses, LN often goes outside its issue area to find funding.

The Latina Network (LN) is also creative in how it uses governmental resources. Even for funding designated for domestic violence services, such as "technical assistance training," the organization leverages it to engage in policy advocacy. For example, the technical assistant director, Rosa, while designing and leading technical assistance trainings, leveraged an executive order by Bill Clinton that mandated language access as a federal requirement to create a point of entry with health service providers, shelters, and mainstream organizations. Reminding them that they could lose federal funding if they do not meet this requirement, this executive order helped LN to pressure other organizations, state coalitions, and service providers to train their staff to be more culturally responsive not just to survivors but also to people of color more broadly. This, in turn, created pathways into these structures to more broadly address issues of sexism, racism, and classism. These types of interventions are how LN strategically elevates its existing funding model (i.e., federal funds for technical assistance training) to engage in intersectional advocacy. This funding gives LN access to police officers, judges, and other social service providers. Advocates then leverage these interactions to address other issues they perceive are interrelated to domestic violence.

Staff thus often wear two hats in the organization: a service hat and a political hat. Services are often accompanied by much-needed policy advocacy at all levels, from the local to the national. However, governmental funding does come with its restrictions. Leadership staff often mentioned needing to walk a careful line with their advocacy, especially during the Trump administration. Maria shares: "there's constantly different announcements of different interim, you know, rules, proposed rules being put out whether it's about asylum or public charge or fees or access to – you know, whether sanctuary cities, quote on quote, 'can access federal dollars.'" The organization must stay up to date on these restrictions, as these affect its ability to advocate.

Advocates from LN must also walk a fine line in their advocacy because it is primarily funded by the government. They have a newsletter to communicate their advocacy and policy efforts to their supporters, and even in this space they sometimes need to censor their work. The project specialist, Martha, explains:

Because this is a federal grant that we are pushing this newsletter out through, we can't disparage the current administration. So, I do have to do some playing around ... Just because it's – the funding game, it is hard with working with the federal government because you're censored in some ways [about] what you can and can't say, even though we're not saying the federal government [explicitly, it doesn't matter] because this is funding under the federal government.

The Latina Network (LN) is the most restricted organization in terms of its funding, and yet it is also the one that engages in intersectional advocacy at every governmental policy level. The ways that LN utilizes its resources and overlaps its staff activities across service and policy in part explain this breadth of advocacy. Table 5.5 illustrates LN's unique organizational characteristics that contribute to this approach.

IDENTIFYING AND DIFFERENTIATING INTERSECTIONAL ADVOCATES

By examining organizational features of these advocacy groups, I identified four constitutive features that help explain why CFS, SAV, and LN take on an intersectional advocacy approach and why WAVE takes on a more traditional approach. Table 5.6 illustrates how these attributes broadly map onto to these organizational structures. These descriptions showcase the organizational similarities among CFS, SAV, and LN.

Leadership approach is one of these key characteristics. Valeria, the CEO of LN, referred to reaching "the last person" as the framework that motivates her organization, which was to organize programming and advocacy that would impact the most marginalized and invisible group of women affected by violence. In doing so, the organization attempts to avoid "secondary marginalization" (Cohen, 1999), which privileges subgroups of the intersectionally marginalized population they serve (i.e., Latina women) and

TABLE 5.5 *Organizational characteristics of the Latina Network (LN)*

Organization	Origin and Leadership	Representation	Networks	Funding Issue and Allocation
The Latina Network (LN)	Focuses on Latinas, originally a culturally specific service model; leadership is guided by a framework that critically examines secondary marginalization	Advocacy and policy interventions are guided by the principle of reaching those who are most intersectionally marginalized; to do so often requires boundary crossing	Broad localized, state, and national partnerships with different groups outside of gender-based violence and with different social and political institutions	Resource sharing with partner organizations to expand advocacy and services to other issue areas and institutions

disadvantages others (i.e., Latine children, LGBTQ, sex workers, noncitizens). This approach motivated LN's leadership to pursue advocacy outside of domestic violence to include migrant worker rights, immigration law, sex trafficking policies, housing state policies, and criminal justice reform. This framework also informed their initiatives, programs, and interventions to support local leadership within their immediate community while hiring members of these groups to represent and shape the advocacy led by LN.

Similarly, Jada, SAV's executive director, focused on the most underserved organizations (e.g., community health centers, community organizations) that are working with intersectionally marginalized populations. These organizations did not singularly focus on sexual assault but instead aimed to address several issues in their communities that overlapped. To support these groups, SAV advocated for discretionary funding to support these organizations and developed a program that would create more opportunities for women of color to assume leadership roles in their organizations. These programs would be helpful for the types of efforts the women of color at CFS are leading. Much of the leadership driving intersectional advocacy among CFS was the result of women of color in mid-level leadership positions managing up. While a few of them aspired to be an executive director someday, most did not feel they would be considered for this role.

Yet we can imagine that if they had more power and more substantial leadership roles within these organizations we would see more efforts to engage in intersectional advocacy. Thus, SAV's leadership programs for women of color are creating important pipelines for this kind of advocacy. These are important

TABLE 5.6 *Organizational characteristics and advocacy*

Four Characteristics	Women Against Violence Everyday (WAVE)	Communities for Survivors (CFS)	Sisters Against Violence (SAV)	The Latina Network (LN)
Leadership	Executive leadership focuses on a single issue and does not expand into others	Executive leadership promotes agendas with issue and policy linkages and collaborates with other groups to advance this policy change		
Representation	Represents and serves all groups the same way	Directly receives input from intersectionally marginalized groups, and the organization's advocacy is centered and developed around the needs of intersectionally marginalized populations		
Networks	Smaller and more niche networks around its main issue area	Broad networks with groups outside the issue domain that are used to develop partnerships, collaborations, and resource sharing		
Funding	Funding is restricted to primary issue area	Funding from other issue areas through either budget advocacy or pooled resources from partner organizations		

investments that should be continued and that also should emphasize substantive representation – meaning that these leaders will substantively prioritize the lived conditions of intersectionally marginalized groups in their advocacy. Leaders from marginalized groups can also play a role in perpetuating inequalities among more disadvantaged people within these identity groups (Cohen, 1999). Therefore, it should not be assumed that diverse leaders will automatically be inclined to lead intersectional advocacy efforts, which is why substantive representation is such an important feature of this work.

The leadership of SAV, CFS, and LN were substantively representative of intersectionally marginalized groups, which guided their decisions to pursue advocacy outside of their main issue. Although these organizations prioritized different intersectionally marginalized groups, they used similar methods for identifying their interests. These included relying on community organizations that worked directly with these populations as soundboards for their advocacy, organizing advocacy and practices around intersectionally marginalized populations, and identifying the additional issues these groups face as a consequence of their positionality, such as housing, healthcare, incarceration, and immigration. This engagement with and representation of these groups align with an intersectional advocacy approach, which aims to create linkages between policies that reflect the experiences of intersectionally marginalized groups positioned between more than one problem area. Though organizations used different methods to engage with these populations (e.g., listening circles versus reaching out to grassroots organizations), their engagement with and prioritization of these groups were consistent with their policy advocacy.

The networks that these organizations built illustrate a clear strategy for practicing intersectional advocacy, which is bringing actors across policies together to make connections between interrelated issue areas. The organizations SAV, LN, and CFS all had extensive networks with groups that were outside of their main issue, which resulted in collaborations across issues: SAV participated in efforts to push for the Breathe Act with groups focusing on criminal justice reform and police abolition; LN established a coalition on economic inequality, immigration, and gender-based violence with an alliance of local organizations; and CFS supported a bail bond reform policy with a criminal justice reform group. Although the interventions were different, networks and relationships with groups outside their primary issue incentivized these organizations to pursue policies that crosscut these issue areas.

The three organizations also had very different funding capacities: CFS had the most private funding from foundations; SAV was evenly split between governmental and private funding but had the smallest operational budget; and LN was majority government funded, with almost no discretionary funding. Yet, despite these structural differences in funding, all three organizations used strategies to allocate their funding toward interventions that included issue and policy linkages. Both SAV and CFS relied on budget advocacy to change funding streams, and LN shared resources with other organizations to colead initiatives with issue and policy linkages. All three organizations sought funding from issue areas outside of their own to conduct advocacy that would bridge the two issues together (e.g., human trafficking and gender-based violence).

While these advocacy organizations shared these core similarities across leadership, representation, networks, and funding, as I have shown throughout this chapter, these features are not identical. Nor should we expect them to be, given how different these organizations are from one another. Table 5.7 illustrates how these characteristics varied across organizations to represent the range of structures that can support intersectional advocacy practices. Finally, WAVE has commitments to intersectionally marginalized populations and advocates stated they care about addressing interrelated issues like racial oppression, economic inequality, immigration rights, and poverty. Up until my interviews with them, though, the best way they believed in supporting these interrelated issues was through symbolic support for other organizations (e.g., solidarity messages on websites, participating in other organizations events) and outsourcing survivors to organizations outside their network when they had

TABLE 5.7 *Unique organizational context and advocacy*

Organization	Intersectional Advocacy	Origin and Leadership	Representation	Networks	Funding and Issue Allocation
Women Against Violence Everyday (WAVE)		One-size-fits-all model to addressing sexual assault, originally a service model; leadership grounded in the bounded crime policymaking of the 1980s	Represents intersectionally marginalized groups and is invested in them but outsources their issues to other organizations; policies and advocacy do not prioritize intersectionally marginalized groups	Localized and limited networks; networks include mostly service providers and allies that focus on sexual assault	Allocates all funding to sexual assault policy interventions and services
Communities for Survivors (CFS)	✔	One-size-fits-all model, with a built-in network of providers and partners; mid-level leadership advocates for prioritizing intersectionally marginalized groups	Advocates for different policies by race and gender; prioritizes interventions that most impact Black women	Several partnerships; has a built-in network of members and collaborative partnerships with organizations outside of gender-based violence	Local budget advocacy to alter how the city determines funding/distributes funding across issue areas
Sisters Against Violence (SAV)	✔	Focuses only on women of color, with a network of culturally specific organizations; leadership is	Advocates for policies and funding for culturally specific organizations and	Has a built-in network of culturally specific organizations; was founded in collaboration with	Federal budget advocacy for culturally specific organizations that expands use of

(continued)

TABLE 5.7 (*continued*)

Organization	Intersectional Advocacy	Origin and Leadership	Representation	Networks	Funding and Issue Allocation
		represented by all women of color and the mission/vision of the organization is around the experiences of intersectionally marginalized groups	centers advocacy around women of color	partner organizations and coalitions outside of gender-based violence	services to cover other issue areas
The Latina Network (LN)	✓	Focuses on Latinas, originally a culturally specific service model; leadership is guided by a framework that critically examines secondary marginalization	Advocacy and policy interventions are guided by the principle of reaching those who are most intersectionally marginalized; to do so often requires boundary crossing	Broad localized, state, and national partnerships with different groups outside of gender-based violence and with different social and political institutions	Resource sharing with partner organizations to expand advocacy and services to other issue areas and institutions

additional issues beyond sexual assault that were impacting them. These actions illustrate care for these groups.

However, WAVE does not fully take on an intersectional advocacy approach. What if organizations like WAVE want to shift away from more traditional approaches to practice intersectional advocacy? What might that look like? WAVE holds broadly a similar organizational structure to LN in that it provides direct services to survivors while also performing an advocacy role at the state and federal levels. Even though WAVE is not considered a "culturally specific" organization, it is increasingly serving a Latina population. Applying LN's organizational features to WAVE, we can visualize how the organization could make some changes that would better position it to take on an intersectional advocacy approach.

First, instead of relying on only organizational leaders and advocates to inform its policy and organizational work, WAVE could establish new practices that enable intersectionally marginalized survivors to directly influence their organization. It is already aware that the Latina population it serves is also dealing with immigration issues. Instead, of outsourcing Latina survivors who are experiencing immigration issues to other organizations, WAVE can reevaluate its strategic plans, staff, and resource allocation to see if there are ways it can advocate for this group across the issues of sexual assault and immigration. The organization has an advocate in-house with experience with Latine populations and immigration: Kendra. Second, as Kendra engages in outreach to these communities, she could hold "listening circles" to learn more about the policy gaps survivors of violence are trapped between. Third, WAVE can provide leadership opportunities for members of these communities to not only shape WAVE's agenda but also participate in advocating for policies and practices they think are necessary based on their collective experiences. Fourth, WAVE, like LN, could establish a guiding framework as a built-in process for critically questioning if its advocacy is serving all the groups it means to represent given their varying positionalities across gender, age, race, ethnicity, class, and sexual orientation. Finally, WAVE may feel it does not have the expertise at present to establish this type of framework or lead these efforts. If that is the case, new leadership could join the organization, similar to CFS's mid-level leadership team, to guide these new directions.

While WAVE has the potential to fully transform into an intersectional advocacy organization, its leaders may ultimately decide not to change because this approach may not align with their goals. While intersectional advocacy certainly has its advantages and undeniable benefits to intersectionally marginalized groups, as shown in Chapter 4, engaging in this practice often means setting incremental goals and traversing through difficult and rigid boundaries. Depending on how many policies advocates are hoping to connect together across issue areas, policy linkages can be especially difficult and, in some cases, nearly impossible to establish if it means bringing several different stakeholders to the policy table. Organizations like WAVE may view this approach as ineffective when compared to a traditional advocacy approach, where like-minded groups come together around one issue. There is also more infrastructure, support, and precedent for working on issues this way, which is why WAVE's advocacy neatly ties into the state coalition's policy agenda.

What organizations like WAVE then need to consider is what are the tradeoffs of this approach? If only select and under-resourced groups are engaging in intersectional advocacy, will intersectionally marginalized populations be fairly and equitably represented in policymaking? The advocates from CFS, SAV, and LN all used language like "surviving," "over-capacity," and "under-resourced" to describe their financial status. Opting out of this practice can mean that these groups are alone, working with minimal resources. Moreover, if WAVE continues to only focus on the issue of sexual assault without addressing how it intersects with other issues, will the intersectionally marginalized groups it is committed to serving receive the same care and protection as the other survivors? These are the potential tradeoffs that organizations taking on a traditional advocacy approach need to consider.

What about other organizations? Those addressing gender-based violence predominantly take on a traditional approach to policy advocacy (Andrews & Edwards, 2004; Bordt, 1997; Markowtiz & Tice, 2002). How might organizations addressing gender-based violence that differ by organizational type identify a structure presented in this chapter that they can use to adapt to an intersectional advocacy approach? Communities for Survivors (CFS) offers a model for networked organizations that rely on a network of other groups to make decisions about advocacy, policy, and work. The organization demonstrates the types of changes that can lead to an intersectional advocacy approach: growing and diversifying its networks, creating mid-level leadership opportunities for women of color and people with expertise serving intersectionally marginalized groups, and engaging in budget advocacy efforts that distribute funding across issue areas. Among feminist mainstream organizations with varying structures, CFS also provides an example of how these organizations can change by leading policy efforts that directly represent intersectionally marginalized groups and includes inviting more diverse partners that focus on related issue areas to collaborate with the organization.

Sisters Against Violence (SAV) is a model for national and coalition-based organizations that seek to apply an intersectional advocacy approach. It is an outgrowth of a national coalition model and in many ways still holds similar organizational characteristics: hierarchical leadership, representation of other organizations across the nation, and a primary focus on federal and state policy agendas. For national and coalition-based organizations seeking to take on an intersectional advocacy approach, SAV models how to ensure that culturally specific organizations and those led by women of color are represented nationally in these efforts. Symbolic representation does not alone equate to intersectional advocacy; leaders from these organizations need to also have experience working with and substantively representing intersectionally marginalized populations. That is why SAV creates leadership opportunities for people who come from these backgrounds and have these priorities. It also illustrates how these organizations can focus on one primary policy area for linkage (e.g., healthcare) and lead considerable federal changes in how this policy area connects to gender-based violence.

Finally, LN is a model for culturally specific and predominantly service-model organizations that want to expand their advocacy and policy work. It illustrates how an organization can utilize its proximity to survivors of violence to include them in policymaking and advocacy processes. The organization uses tools like an advocacy framework to ensure its policy work not only prioritizes intersectionally marginalized groups but also does not disadvantage members of these groups across additional characteristics of marginalization. Moreover, LN models different ways that localized programs and efforts can be led by survivors themselves. Organizations that conduct a lot of service and face-to-face work with survivors of gender-based violence can learn from how LN integrates this role into its advocacy and policy work.

Finally, some organizations may never take on an intersectional advocacy approach. That is not to say that they will not continue to lead important work. These committed advocates will continue to devote their time advocating for survivors of gender-based violence. However, even if organizations do not shift into this form of advocacy themselves, there are other ways to support it. These groups can validate policy linkages when presented to them. They can share resources collaboratively with intersectional advocates when they have mutual interests or populations of survivors they serve. These groups can circulate and sign petitions for agendas that include issue and policy linkages presented by intersectional advocates. They can also share these types of policy proposals with their state coalitions and legislative partners. In other words, there is a wide gradient of ways that organizations can support intersectional advocacy or participate in it themselves.

CONCLUSION

In this chapter, I focused on the four constitutive organizational characteristics (i.e., leadership, representation, networks, and funding resource and allocation) that I identified as being related to the practice of intersectional advocacy by CFS, SAV, and LN. Understanding how these characteristics relate to and support the practice of intersectional advocacy illuminates tangible ways that advocacy groups can identify themselves and adopt this approach if they do not already engage in this practice. These analyses provide a road map for how to transform aspects of the organization to support intersectional advocacy. In Chapter 6, I discuss another form of organizational capacity: supporters. Specifically, I examine whether or not intersectional advocacy mobilizes supporters, and I answer the final question of whether an intersectional advocacy approach actually resonates with the people it is intended to serve.

6

Mobilization and Intersectional Advocacy

> Our supporters are the key to our success. As an advocacy organization, it is critically important that we engage the community in our work. We cannot make meaningful systemic changes without a committed base of people who are willing to learn more about the issues by subscribing to our emails and attending events, to call on their elected officials to improve public policies, to spread the word with their personal and professional networks, and to provide their financial support to advance our mission. We are grateful to have so many allies standing with us in this movement.
>
> Senior Director, Women Employed

In Chapter 5, I examined the infrastructure of organizations that can support intersectional advocacy and there is another key resource these groups rely on to engage in these efforts: supporters. Formal membership in advocacy groups has steadily decreased over the years (Putnam & Putnam, 2000; Silver & Clark, 2016), especially among women's organizations (Skocpol, 2013). However, my experiences volunteering on the advocacy council for Women Employed (WE) over the years underscored how important supporters are to the work, mission, and advocacy of these groups. Because these supporters are not formal members of these organizations, though, their participation in these groups has largely been overlooked by scholars (see Bosso, 2003) and mostly understood within an online context (Guo & Saxton, 2014; Hart et al., 2005).

Women Employed (WE) is a great example of an organization that is intentionally incorporating an intersectional advocacy approach into their messaging with supporters. Historically, similar to most advocacy organizations, WE often referenced one issue at a time to supporters to communicate their policy efforts. However, as the organization increasingly has explicitly prioritized Black and Latina women in its advocacy, WE is adapting its messaging to accurately reflect how these groups are more likely to experience issues simultaneously such as sexual harassment, predatory working conditions, and poverty. Unlike the other organizations presented in this book for which gender-based violence is a primary issue that connects with additional issues, WE focuses on economic empowerment, and gender-based violence is a distinct issue that is folded into this advocacy. The organization also connects issues together outside of gender-based violence, such as paid leave with caregiving. Its advocacy is presented in this chapter to offer a different vantage point of intersectional advocacy that shows (1) how intersectional advocacy is applied when gender-based violence is an issue of connection, rather than a primary organizing issue; (2) how it is received when issues not related to gender-based violence are connected (i.e., caregiving and paid leave); (3) what types of context can help frame it to make it a more effective approach for mobilizing supporters across these types of issue pairings; and finally (4) how supporters respond to policy platforms when organizations make the change from a single-issue approach to one of intersectional advocacy.

In this chapter, I present the results of two survey experiments that compare a traditional policy platform to a multi-issue policy platform (i.e., an agenda with an issue and policy linkage) in how each mobilizes supporters of WE to sign online petitions and to get more involved in the organization. The findings from these experiments showcase when intersectional advocacy efforts are successful and when they fail to resonate with and mobilize supporters around policy agendas. To triangulate the results of these experiments, I conducted a textual analysis of the messages supporters provided with their signed petitions from both experiments. The content of these messages underscores why it is important that *supporters* view connections between the issues that organizations are creating policy linkages between.

I argue that when supporters perceive a policy linkage between two distinct issues this is when they will be mobilized by these types of agendas compared to single-issue appeals. Policy platforms are only one strategy for communicating policy linkages between issues to supporters; if advocacy organizations continue to connect seemingly separate issues, they can also consider other ways of drawing out these connections for their supporters using alternative outlets such as fundraising events, email communications, and strategic meetings. These platforms are only one part of the policymaking process that intersectional advocates intervene in to create policy linkages. However, these policy proposals are one of the main ways that advocacy groups mobilize their broader supporters – and thus this is an important strategy to evaluate and understand. Policy change can be complicated and confusing for supporters, and testing how intersectional advocacy platforms are communicated to these groups helps us understand how platforms can be effective tools for supporting these efforts. Moreover, in this chapter, actual policy platforms and online petitions are presented, which provide tangible examples of the types of messaging and framing organizations can use in their efforts to engage in intersectional advocacy.

MESSAGING AND POLICY PLATFORMS

Policy platforms are a common tool that women's advocacy groups use to communicate their expertise to both their supporters and their political stakeholders (Goss, 2012). However, this approach is relatively new and underexamined. Scholars study how advocacy groups advance broad political agendas in legislative contexts (see Clemens, 1997; Kessler-Harris, 2003); the ways in which these organizations have structurally changed to include professional staff while reducing their membership base (see Skocpol, 1995, 2013); and how these groups evolved to focus on policy expertise as a substitute for their political influence (Goss, 2012). All these aspects of change explain why women's advocacy groups today develop policy platforms to gain broader support, and we know very little about how these platforms are received by their supporters.

Yet supporters can play a substantive role in advancing these policy platforms. They can sign petitions or witness slips in support of new policies, contact their legislatures directly, donate to the organization to give it the resources it needs to advocate for its agenda, and share this information with their networks to broaden and increase overall support (Berry, 2003; Crutchfield & Grant, 2012; Gen & Wright, 2020e; Sargeant et al., 2007). Groups that are practicing intersectional advocacy, like most nonprofit organizations, are heavily underfunded and operate with limited resources (Johnson et al., 2021). Tapping into these broad support networks is thus an important resource for advocacy organizations to advance agendas with policy and issue linkages that they believe will benefit these groups. Policy platforms are a key method of communicating with these supporters – they provide clear, short, and understandable goals (Simonofski et al., 2021). The ways that the policy platforms are framed determine their effectiveness.

Framing has long been studied by political scientists, mainly as a political tool that elites use to communicate with the public (Chong & Druckman, 2007; Druckman, 2004; Druckman et al., 2013; Matthes, 2012; Slothuus & de Vreese, 2010). Framing is an art; elites, like advocacy leaders, carefully and intentionally frame political issues by selecting "some aspects of a perceived reality and mak[ing] them more salient in a communicating text, in such a way as to promote a particular problem definition, causal interpretation, moral evaluation, and/or treatment recommendation for the item described" (Entman, 1993, p. 52). Framing of political issues can affect support for social policies. For example, some scholars have found that when the framing of an issue varied in how it portrayed or impacted different identity groups (i.e., low-income women), there were different levels of support for these issues among the public (Gross, 2008; Iyengar, 1990; Winter, 2008). Although identity framing clearly matters for understanding public opinion, especially framing that includes the experiences of intersectionally marginalized groups (see Taylor

& Haider-Markel, 2014), less research has focused on its application to advocacy group engagement (see Polletta & Ho, 2006).

Among organizations practicing intersectional advocacy, framing is particularly important. By presenting policy interventions that address multiple issues at the same time, these groups are challenging traditional notions of policymaking, which can be confusing, atypical, and uncomfortable for supporters who are used to the status quo approach. Because this is a presentation of policy initiatives that run counter to the status quo, these platforms may require additional framing devices that help make the policy linkages clearer to their supporters. One framing device that can be used to make these linkages more explicit is an availability heuristic. Availability heuristics are mental shortcuts that rely on immediate examples that come to a person's mind when they are evaluating a policy initiative or platform (Schwarz & Vaughn, 2002). Availability heuristics can make framing more explicit (see Donohue et al., 2011; Dubard Barbosa & Alain, 2007; Schwarz & Vaughn, 2002). In this study, I include a framing of the COVID-19 pandemic in both the single-issue and the multi-issue policy agendas to act as an availability heuristic for participants to identify connections between issues.

The COVID-19 pandemic has been widely discussed by media, politicians, and organizations as a problem that is connected with other issues such as unaffordable healthcare, unsafe work environments, poverty, racial injustice, and violence (Tisdell, 2020), especially among intersectionally marginalized populations (Gray et al., 2020). Thus, the pandemic is included in the second experiment to examine if this context strengthens the policy linkages between the issues presented in the multi-issue platform for supporters. In this chapter, I examine how the framing of policy platforms using an intersectional advocacy approach can be differently received by a range of supporters in order to evaluate if this is an effective strategy for mobilizing them.

WOMEN EMPLOYED (WE)

Women Employed (WE) practices intersectional advocacy while also engaging in mainstream practices such as single-issue policy advocacy. In some ways, WE is similar to Communities for Survivors (CFS), discussed in Chapter 5, because it has changed over the years to prioritize intersectionally marginalized groups in its policy efforts. It was established in 1973 as a feminist mainstream organization: its early strategies, policy efforts, and political action were all geared toward representing the general, mainstream population of working women. However, even when it represented the general population of women, WE always crossed policy boundaries by focusing on interrelated issues of access to higher education, poverty, sexual harassment, and pay inequity.

In the last decade or so, WE increasingly changed its leadership representation, focus, and policy efforts to prioritize the interests of Black and Latina women working in low-wage industries. These interests are prioritized through WE's advocacy for policy initiatives such as eliminating the subminimum wage, instituting paid leave in the state, and increasing financial aid for college students – all policy areas that disproportionately impact Black and Latina women. The leadership team over the years has also diversified. For example, at the time of the study, WE was led by a woman of color CEO.

Amidst these changes, WE involves its supporters in shaping the direction of the organization, leading its advocacy, and participating in a range of policy efforts. For example, as a member of its advocacy council, I participated in its strategic planning process. All supporters were invited to attend virtual meetings and offer feedback to the organization. During my meeting, we discussed prioritizing Black and Latina women in WE policy efforts and messaging because this is the group that are most vulnerable in the workplace and have the least access to safety-net policies (Browne, 2000; Kilbourne et al., 1994; Woody, 1992). While there was a back-and-forth about how this prioritization would influence wealthier and white donors of the organization, WE ultimately moved forward with a plan to emphasize Black and Latina women more explicitly in its policy and advocacy work. As a woman of color in these spaces, I felt heard by WE staff and personally watched the organization continue to transform over the years to adopt what I now call an "intersectional advocacy" approach.

Supporters play an important role in these organizations. In a given year, between 111 and 153 supporters serve on different councils and working groups to advance WE's advocacy efforts. These are the most involved supporters who volunteer their time regularly to the organization. In addition, WE has a network of 4,425 supporters who subscribe to a newsletter that specifically presents them with opportunities to sign online petitions and to write letters to their legislatures advocating for policy changes the organization is leading. Finally, WE has a wider group of 6,450 supporters who subscribe to its general newsletter for updates, events, and opportunities to get involved with the organization. Supporters, of course, overlap across these groups; however, at any given time there are thousands of people available to participate in WE's advocacy efforts. For example, in 2020, when WE sent out a petition related to paid sick leave to its supporters, 2,887 signed it. Given the role that supporters play in WE's organization, it was the ideal advocacy group to partner with to explore how supporters respond to different types of policy platforms.

One of the policy priorities of the organization at the time of this project was sexual harassment and assault in the workplace. Although WE had a multi-issue agenda to address economic issues such as the subminimum wage and sexual harassment and assault in low-wage industries, advocates weren't sure if it made sense to present these policy issues together to supporters. Even though they saw the connections between these issues and were advocating for policies that would address them in this way, they were unsure if this presentation of platforms with issue and policy linkages would be confusing to supporters because it is an untraditional policy approach. At the same time, this organization was also working on a policy agenda around paid leave and caregiving with the same types of concerns. This real challenge that the organization was facing in the field of advocacy presented an opportunity to (1) test out intersectional advocacy strategies on supporters and (2) explore intersectional advocacy strategies on issues outside of gender-based violence.

Women Employed (WE) was an ideal organization with which to collaborate for the purposes of this study. The organization presents both traditional and intersectional advocacy approaches to its supporters. This context allowed for a manipulation of its policy agendas: the experimental control accurately displayed the organization's traditional approach in presenting its policy agendas to its supporters (i.e., as single issues) and the treatment accurately displayed the way the organization communicates multi-issue policy platforms (i.e., agenda with an issue and policy linkage). Thus, varying policy agendas in these two ways allowed for a rich comparison of the two approaches on the mobilization of supporters. These findings are helpful for organizations in the field that are trying to adopt intersectional advocacy and pursue agendas with issue and policy linkages. Because WE also regularly engages its supporters in signing online petitions for its policy efforts, supporters are accustomed to getting alerts asking them to sign an online petition that will sway their legislators to support a policy intervention led by WE. To ensure the survey experiments were authentically representative of WE, I used their actual online petitions to measure supporters' responses to the experimental conditions. Thus, WE provided a unique opportunity to design field survey experiments that had the benefits of random assignment while also remaining authentic to the experiences of supporters in a real advocacy context.

EXPERIMENTAL DESIGNS

Experiment 1: Policy Disconnect

Based on the analysis presented in the previous chapters of this book, policy platforms that present multiple issues together – such as sexual violence and economic inequality – should better represent the ways that intersectionally marginalized groups experience these issues. This framing of a policy agenda should then appear to be more authentic and representative of these experiences and, in doing so, motivate all supporters to get more involved in advocating for these efforts.[1] Women of color, the primary target group of these efforts, should

---

[1] (Hypothesis 1) Supporters of a women's advocacy organization will take action to support an issue more when they receive an agenda that is framed to address multiple, related issues relative to an agenda that is framed to address a single issue.

be most supportive of these agendas because these interventions are designed to represent them as a group (Kristen et al., 2015).[2] However, we should not expect these outcomes if participants do not view policy linkages between these types of issues. In other words, even if a participant views poor working conditions (i.e., industries that rely on subminimum wages) as an environment that makes women more vulnerable to sexual harassment and assault, this does not mean they see a *policy* connection between these issues. If participants do not view these issues as interconnected in the policy agenda, a multi-policy platform will mobilize them less than a single-issue one. They will be less motivated to support this initiative because it is not clear to them how the policy will effectively address both issues.

The first experiment presented in this analysis allows for this examination. It randomly presented two types of policy platforms to participants supporting WE. The control condition includes a policy platform that focuses solely on one issue and subsequent policy solution. The language framing the problem of the policy platform mentions focusing on sexual violence. The phrasing at the end that I used to communicate that the policy agenda will solely address sexual violence was the following: WE *believe that sexual violence in the workplace will only be eradicated if we prioritize policy interventions that fully address it.*

Figure 6.1 includes the stimuli presented to participants who received the control for addressing sexual violence. The treatment condition included a policy platform that includes two issues and a policy solution to address them together. At the end of the treatment, to communicate an issue and policy linkage in the agenda, the following language included: WE *believe that sexual violence in the workplace can only be eradicated if we prioritize multi-issue policy interventions that address both this issue and interrelated ones like pay inequality.* Figure 6.2 shows the stimuli that were presented to participants who received the treatment for addressing sexual violence.

Because the treatment introduces a second issue, it was important to design an experiment that would not introduce a confounding observation (i.e., that the second issue introduced in the treatment explained the increase in support and not the actual framing strategy of connecting issues together). To avoid this outcome, respondents were asked to rank the importance of all issues the organization focused on and then to select which issue was most important to them. In the first experiment, these issues included sexual violence or the minimum wage. Whichever issue they selected, they received a control and treatment for that issue. Therefore, if they reported minimum wage was a more important issue to them than sexual violence, they were either randomly assigned a control with a policy platform for *only a* minimum wage (i.e., subminimum wage) or a treatment with a platform for *both* minimum wage and sexual violence. The same assignment occurred if they reported that

[2] (Hypothesis 2) Supporters with intersectionally, marginalized identities (i.e., women of color) will take action to support a multi-issue policy platform more often relative to all supporters.

The Challenge

Sexual violence is a serious issue in the workplace. Women in low-paid industries, especially those who rely on tips, report this issue at the highest rates. Women of color, LGBTQ+ folks, people with disabilities, immigrants, and refugees are especially vulnerable and have fewer protections available to them. That is why we need to focus on increasing their protections by strengthening the laws around sexual harassment and assault in the workplace.

What We're Doing

WE fight to ensure that working women, especially those who are most marginalized in the workforce (i.e., women of color, low-paid workers, immigrants) are protected. To do so, we focus directly on laws that address sexual harassment and assault in the workforce. <u>WE believe that sexual violence in the workplace will only be eradicated if we prioritize policy interventions that fully address it.</u>

FIGURE 6.1 Sexual violence (control)

sexual violence was more important to them. For those that ranked the minimum wage issue above sexual violence, they were assigned a control and treatment using the same type of language highlighting the subminimum wage as the primary issue. Figure 6.3 includes the stimuli presented to participants who were randomly assigned the control condition after ranking the minimum wage as more important to them than sexual violence in their issue preferences.

As Figure 6.3 demonstrates, I used the same exact wording to identify the single issue in the control for the subminimum wage that I used for the issue sexual violence. The problem statement includes *we need to focus on* with the single-policy solution. It then also ends with the same language of *WE believe [the problem] will only be eradicated if we prioritize policy interventions that fully address it*. The target group in these policy agendas is a broad intersectionally marginalized population: women of color, LGBTQ+ folks, people with disabilities, immigrants, and refugees. Even though WE is prioritizing Black and Latina women in its advocacy efforts, the organization and I wanted to test how a broader group of intersectionally marginalized people responded to this messaging. This target group was held constant in all the policy platforms.

The only change between the control and treatment stimuli is the last sentence identifying the problem statement and the last sentence presenting the policy solution. Both use the same language to convey severity (i.e., we

The Challenge

Sexual violence is a serious issue among vulnerable workers. Women in low-paid industries who rely on tips experience this issue at the highest rates. Women of color, LGBTQ+ folks, people with disabilities, immigrants, and refugees are especially vulnerable and have fewer protections available to them. That is why we need a multifaceted approach to solving this issue that includes addressing sexual harassment and assault in the workplace **AND** eliminating the subminimum wage for tipped workers.

What We're Doing

WE fight to ensure that working women, especially those who are most marginalized in the workforce (i.e., women of color, low-paid workers, immigrants) are protected. To do so, we focus on multiple issues that exacerbate this problem. WE are advocating for laws that protect workers from sexual harassment and assault while ALSO pushing to eliminate the subminimum wage for tipped workers, a practice that leaves them especially vulnerable to harassment and abuse. **WE believe that sexual violence in the workplace can only be eradicated if we prioritize multi-issue policy interventions that address both this issue and interrelated ones like pay inequality.**

FIGURE 6.2 Sexual violence + subminimum wage (treatment)

need to focus on) and action (i.e., the problem will be eradicated if we prioritize). The only difference between the conditions is that one focuses on a single problem/policy issue and the other suggests a multifaceted approach/ multi-policy initiative.

After receiving either the control or the treatment policy platform, participants were asked if they would like to sign a petition supporting the agenda. Those that chose to sign the petition were then asked to write a message to their legislators to be included with the petition, which is a standard practice for WE when it asks supporters to sign their petitions. These qualitative messages provide an opportunity to examine whether participants viewed a policy linkage between the issues that were presented to them.

Experiment 2: Policy Linkages

In the next experiment, I considered if a framing device, an availability heuristic (i.e., the COVID-19 pandemic) that would prime participants to read the policy agenda while thinking about interrelated issues, would increase the signing of

The Challenge

The minimum wage is a serious issue and one of its most damaging aspects is the subminimum wage paid to tipped workers. Women in low-paid industries, especially those who rely on tips, are the most underpaid. Women of color, LGBTQ+ folks, people with disabilities, immigrants, and refugees are especially vulnerable and have fewer protections available to them. That is why we need a to focus on increasing their protections by eliminating the subminimum minimum wage.

What We're Doing

WE fight to ensure that working women, especially those who are most marginalized in the workforce (i.e., women of color, low-paid working people, immigrants) are protected. To do so, we focus directly on laws that eliminate the subminimum wage for tipped workers. <u>WE believe pay inequality will only be eradicated if we prioritize policy interventions that fully address it.</u>

FIGURE 6.3 Subminimum wage (second control)

petitions for multi-issue interventions relative to single-issue ones. This experiment was fielded at the same time with the same survey participants, although participants were randomly assigned to the conditions again. This context can act as heuristic for supporters to think about issues interrelatedly, as opposed to separately. Thus, we should expect supporters to be most responsive to policy platforms that provide multi-issue solutions (i.e., issue and policy linkages) to these problems.[3] Among intersectionally marginalized populations, especially women of color who represent the group that is most concentrated in industries that were affected by COVID-19 (Brower & Michener, 2021), there should be even greater support for multi-issue agendas that better represent these workplace experiences.[4] This experiment used the same exact design and process for randomly assigning the control and treatment conditions. However, the second experiment framed the issues of paid family leave and

---

[3] (Hypothesis 3) Supporters of a women's advocacy organization will take greater action to support an issue more when framed in the context of the global pandemic when they receive an agenda that is framed to address multiple, related issues, relative to an agenda that is framed to address a single issue.

[4] (Hypothesis 4) Supporters with intersectionally, marginalized identities (i.e., women of color) will take action to support a multi-issue policy platform more often relative to all supporters.

The Challenge

COVID-19 has made it clear that working people need time off from work to care for themselves and their families so that they don't have to choose between their paycheck and their health. Unfortunately, 80% of the lowest-paid working people do not have access to a single paid sick day, and only 15% have access to paid family and medical leave through their employers. That is why we need to focus on getting paid leave for all working people.

What We're Doing

WE fight to ensure that women, especially those who are most marginalized in the workforce (i.e., women of color, low-paid workers, immigrants) are eligible for paid family and sick leave. To do so, WE are pushing to pass laws in Illinois that would give working people up to 12 weeks of paid family and medical leave, and up to 5 permanent paid sick days for use in COVID and beyond. <u>WE believe we can only address this issue if we prioritize policy interventions that fully address it.</u>

FIGURE 6.4 Paid leave (control)

caregiving within the context of the pandemic. Figure 6.4 shows the stimuli I used for the control.

The control, similar to the treatment, has the same availability heuristic for COVID-19 framing the entire policy initiative. It reads: *COVID-19 has made it clear that working people need time off from work to care for themselves and their families, so they don't have to choose between their paycheck and their health*. What follows this framing is a sentence that reads: *we need to focus on [single issue]*. The control condition then ends with a sentence that says we need to explicitly prioritize this single policy intervention.

The policy agenda targets an intersectionally marginalized group population in both conditions (i.e., women of color, low-paid workers, and immigrants). The treatment includes the exact same language framing the COVID-19 pandemic. As Figure 6.5 demonstrates, the only change is in the last sentence of the problem statement that says paid leave needs to include caregiving for children and adults and the last sentence of the action statement that suggests prioritizing *multi-issue policy interventions that address both sick and medical leave as well as interrelated needs such as caregiving*. These changes reflect the experimental intervention to observe whether a single- or multi-issue solution

The Challenge

COVID-19 has made it clear that working people need time off from work to care for themselves and their families so that they don't have to choose between their paycheck and their health. Unfortunately, 80% of the lowest-paid working people do not have access to a single paid sick day, and only 15% have access to paid family and medical leave through their employers. For those who have caregiving roles both as part of their professional lives and their home lives, the public health crisis has increased their caretaking responsibilities exponentially. That is why we are advocating for workers to be able to use these days to ALSO care for children or adults.

What We're Doing

WE fight to ensure that women, especially those who are most marginalized in the workforce (i.e., women of color, low-paid workers, immigrants) are eligible for paid family and sick leave. To do so, WE are pushing to pass laws in Illinois that would give working people up to 12 weeks of paid family and medical leave and up to 5 permanent paid sick days for use in COVID and beyond. To ALSO address caregiving needs we are advocating for these days to be eligible for taking care of children out of school, elderly, and young children. <u>WE believe we can only address this issue if we prioritize multi-issue policy interventions that address both sick and medical leave as well as interrelated needs such as caregiving.</u>

FIGURE 6.5 Paid leave + caregiving (treatment)

will mobilize supporters. The same types of stimuli are used for participants who ranked caregiving as a more important issue compared to paid leave.

I designed the survey experiments to be affiliated with WE. Their logo appeared throughout the survey, and the policy platforms used their branding, font colors, styles, and graphics. Policy platforms were also authentic to WE and represented real platforms the organization is advancing. Finally, the focus of this study is intersectional advocacy. Thus, all policy frames focus on intersectionally marginalized groups as the main target group for these efforts. This focus is held constant throughout all the conditions presented across the two experiments. To view all the stimuli that I used in this study, see the Appendices.

EXPERIMENTAL METHODS AND SUPPORTERS

Framing is used in these experiments to communicate the difference between a single-policy and a multi-policy approach that would be associated with intersectional advocacy. Experiments are frequently used to test the

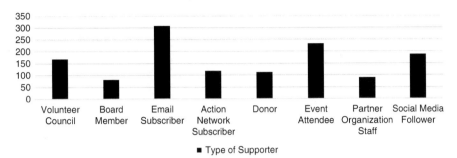

FIGURE 6.6 Sample by type of supporter

effectiveness of framing on attitudes (Iyengar, 1990; Matthes, 2012; Slothuus & de Vreese, 2010; Winter, 2008). Some work tests the impact of framing in support for political candidates (Burns & Kinder, 2012; Simien & Clawson, 2004), but very few studies investigate the effects of policy framing that center the experiences of intersectionally marginalized groups (see Brower, 2022). Cassese et al. (2015) examine policy support by race and gender, but they do not consider the actual framing of policy agendas. The analysis of the experiments presented in this chapter focuses on the framing of policies that highlight intersectionally marginalized groups' experiences with social issues. These are the types of agendas that intersectional advocates are advancing – and to what extent supporters are part of these mobilization efforts I investigate in this analysis. To study these effects, survey participants needed to identify as supporters of the organization WE. Participants in both survey experiments were recruited directly by the organization via email and targeted social media ads/posts. In total, 755 people participated in both experiments (though they were randomly assigned each time). These participants represented a range of different types of supporters. Figure 6.6 provides a distribution of these supporters to show the range of people who took the survey and their varying affiliations to the organization. These identifications were self-reported by participants.

Participants were recruited by WE directly. The organization sent supporters an email asking them to take a survey that would improve their advocacy efforts. Supporters were aware that they would be shown WE's current policy initiatives and that they would be asked to provide feedback. After the experiment was administered, supporters were asked additional questions about the organization to genuinely receive their feedback. These questions were added as a service to the organization but also made the survey more authentic to avoid it looking like a research study. Participants were further entered in a lottery to win a gift card of their choosing for twenty dollars.

I fielded the survey between the end of November 2020 and early March 2021. Because the goal was to recruit a diverse group of supporters,

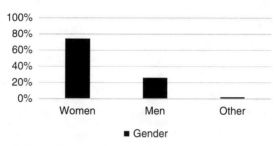

FIGURE 6.7 Sample by gender

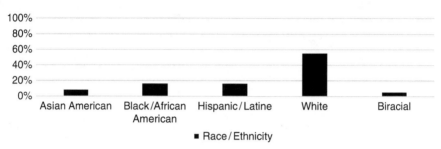

FIGURE 6.8 Sample by race/ethnicity

especially women of color, the survey could not be closed until it included a diversity of respondents. All analyses presented in this chapter include a time series ordinary least squares (OLS) model to account for this long period of time. When the duration of the survey is factored into this analysis, it does not change the findings presented in it.

As indicated by Figure 6.7, the sample is 74 percent women, 1 percent other, and 25 percent men. Women's advocacy organizations are majority-led and majority-supported by cis women. Thus, this distribution is representative of the gender of supporters who are affiliated with these types of organizations.

Finally, to observe the effects of the policy platforms on women of color specifically, it was important that the sample was racially/ethnically diverse. Figure 6.8 provides the distribution of the sample by race and ethnicity. The sample includes 8 percent Asian Americans, 16 percent Black/African Americans, 16 percent Hispanic/Latine, 55 percent white, and 5 percent biracial respondents. Women of color were identified in this study as respondents who selected "female" as their gender and any of the racial/ethnic categories that were not "white." In total, 755 survey participants were randomly assigned to the conditions in the first and second experiment.

As Figure 6.9 illustrates, for the first experiment, 366 were randomly assigned by the program Qualtrics to the treatment and 389 were randomly assigned to the control.

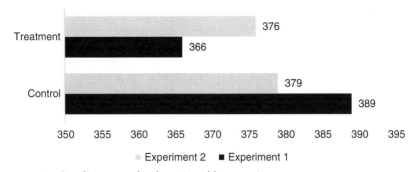

FIGURE 6.9 Conditions randomly assigned by experiment

In the same survey, Qualtrics then randomly assigned participants to the conditions in the second experiment, which resulted in 376 participants assigned to the treatment and 379 assigned to the control. After each experiment, participants were asked posttreatment to either select to "sign a petition in support of this policy platform" or select "no thanks, continue with the survey." They were then led to an actual petition used by WE. The actual petitions used for these experiments are included in Research Appendix 3 on the experimental methods. The petition for the control group similarly focused on the single-issue/single-policy solution presented in the policy platform. The petition for the treatment group focused on the same policy solution but presented it as a policy that could address the two issues presented in the treatment platform. After reading the petition, the survey asked the participants to provide a signature and to write a message for legislators to read. I coded and analyzed these written responses to examine patterns in rationale between the control and the treatment groups.

Written responses additionally provided a robustness check to ensure the experimental conditions were read accurately by respondents. Following the petition, respondents were asked in the survey if they wanted to get more involved in addressing the issue(s) presented to them via the policy platform. Specifically, they were asked: There are many opportunities to get more involved with WE to address [policy issue or issues]. Which of the following activities are you interested in participating in or would continue participating in to address the issue? They were then able to select as many of these options as they wanted; in total, there were ten options. Table 6.1 shows these different options.

To study the effect of the experimental conditions on willingness to get more involved politically with the issues in the policy platforms, I created a variable to capture the sum of the nine activities each respondent selected. In the second experiment on policy linkages, there was a significant effect of the treatment on women of color's future participation in these issues. When this analysis is presented, I also discuss which specific participation items were significant

TABLE 6.1 *Participation options*

1.	Joining for in-person visits (when it is safe to do so)
2.	Working with us to connect with your legislator virtually or by email
3.	Attending a virtual community event
4.	Attending an in-person community event (when it is safe to do so)
5.	Buying a ticket to the annual fundraiser
6.	Joining a volunteer council
7.	Subscribing to the legislative action alert email from the Action Network
8.	Making a donation
9.	Subscribing to the e-newsletter
10.	None of these activities

among this group to highlight the activities that most mobilized women of color. The analyses presented in the next sections include a simple comparison of means across treatment and control groups for each experiment. Significant results are reported based on a two-tail analysis, unless otherwise noted.

EXPERIMENT I: POLICY DISCONNECT

The findings from the first experiment illustrate that when supporters do not view the issues in the multi-policy platform as interconnected, they will be more mobilized by single-issue appeals instead. As shown by the comparison of means presented in Figure 6.10, choosing to sign a petition is more popular among supporters who received a single-issue policy platform (i.e., the control) relative to the multi-issue platform (i.e., the treatment) ($p < 0.05$).[5]

These results indicate that when supporters received a policy agenda for sexual violence or the subminimum wage as stand-alone issues with single-policy solutions, they more often selected to sign a petition in support of this platform rather than continuing with the survey. Among women of color, their willingness to sign a petition in support of a policy platform with this single focus was even greater. Figure 6.11 illustrates a comparison of means between women of color who received the control condition and the treatment. Among women of color, there is a significant and greater effect of the control condition on their selection to sign a petition relative to all supporters ($p < 0.01$).

The results from this experiment show that intersectional advocacy policy frames will not always mobilize supporters more than single-issue appeals, even among the target groups that we would most expect they will appeal to (i.e., women of color). Supporters need to view the issues presented in the policy platform as interconnected for multi-policy agendas to effectively mobilize

---

[5] The findings from the first experiment do not support the first hypothesis.

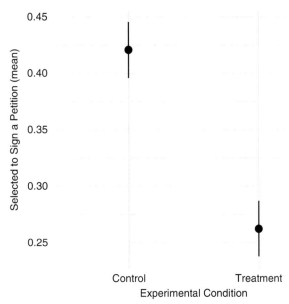

FIGURE 6.10 Selecting to sign a petition among all supporters

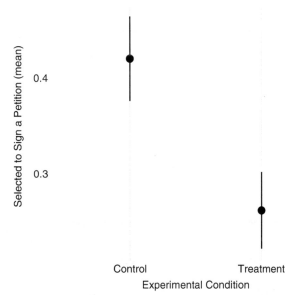

FIGURE 6.11 Selecting to sign a petition among women of color

them. Because participants were asked which issue was more important to them (i.e., sexual violence or subminimum wage) before they took the survey, the control presented to them highlighted the more salient issue. Thus, without a connection between the more salient issue and the secondary issue, it makes sense that participants were more mobilized by the control, which presented the issue to them in a way that highlighted it as most important. The qualitative analysis of the messages supporters included with their signed petitions is presented in the section "Policy Disconnect and Petitions" to provide evidence that participants did not view a policy linkage between sexual violence and the subminimum wage when they received the treatment in this experiment. In the next section, I discuss the results of the other experiment, which demonstrates when multi-issue agendas can be effective for mobilizing supporters, especially women of color. The added heuristic for thinking about issues as interrelated, the COVID-19 pandemic, to the framing of multi-issue agendas was more effective in mobilizing supporters to sign the petition compared to single-issue appeals that included the same framing of the pandemic.

EXPERIMENT 2: POLICY LINKAGES

During the same survey experiment, when supporters were randomly assigned to two different policy agendas that were contextualized by the COVID-19 pandemic, these agendas most effectively mobilized them when they received the treatment, the multi-issue intervention.[6] Supporters selected to sign a petition after receiving the treatment policy platform that included a multi-issue policy platform (i.e., for paid leave and caregiving) more often than when they received the control, which included a single-issue platform (i.e., paid leave or caregiving). As shown by the comparison of means presented in Figure 6.12, choosing to sign a petition is more popular among supporters that received a multi-issue policy platform (i.e., the treatment) relative to the single-issue platform (i.e., the control) ($p < 0.0001$).

When additional engagement in this issue was considered, there was a heterogenous effect among women of color. As demonstrated by Figure 6.13, women of color's willingness to engage in political actions after receiving the treatment increased and was statistically significant ($p < 0.01$).[7]

Among all supporters and white women, these political actions were not significant. Figure 6.14 demonstrates these results. Participants were able to select from nine different political activities. I conducted a *t*-test for each political activity among women of color who received either the control or the treatment policy agenda. The bars in this figure illustrate the mean of the sum of all the political actions that participants selected they would take after receiving

---

[6] The findings from the second experiment support the third hypothesis.

[7] These results support the final hypothesis that there will be a heterogenous treatment effect among women of color that received the treatment condition.

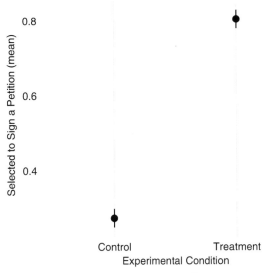

FIGURE 6.12 Selecting to sign a petition among all supporters

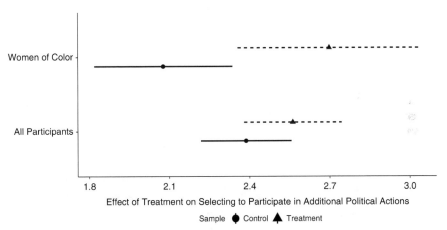

FIGURE 6.13 Selecting to participate in additional political actions among women of color

the policy platform. Figure 6.14 displays the political activities that were statistically significant: subscribing to the Action Network, which is how WE sends new online petitions to supporters ($p < 0.05$); participating in the annual fundraiser ($p < 0.05$); attending community events ($p < 0.05$); and calling legislators ($p < 0.05$). The last two political activities were significant according to a one-tail t-test. The bars in this figure are the mean of the

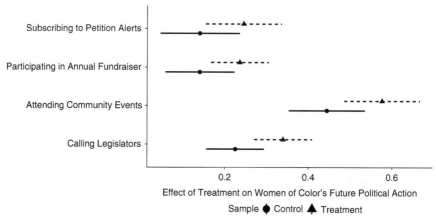

FIGURE 6.14 Significant political actions women of color selected posttreatment

number of times each woman of color selected a particular action when they received the treatment versus the control. Each of these political activities were also compared among all supporters and white women. None were statistically significant, even when I included a one-tail *t*-test.

Although women of color and white women were equally mobilized to sign an immediate petition after receiving the treatment policy condition, these results demonstrate that multi-issue policy treatments may have long-term effects on mobilizing women of color, especially engaging them through community events. These results highlight the effectiveness of multi-policy agendas where the linkages between the issues are apparent to supporters, especially women of color. It is possible that the framing device of the COVID-19 pandemic is not the only factor contributing to these results; paid family leave and caregiving may simply be issues supporters naturally see in connection to one another. A robust check in the future would include providing the same policy platforms without the COVID-19 framing and viewing the differences. However, for the purpose of this study, this potentially confounding result is less concerning. The major takeaway from this research is that platforms that effectively demonstrate policy linkages between issues to supporters will be most effective in mobilizing them. Whether or not it is the selection of issues or an availability heuristic that is bolstering these connections is tangential to the actual outcome of viewing these issues as interconnected.

Finally, I consider how these policy platforms were received by only Black and Latina women, because this is the primary intersectionally marginalized population WE prioritizes in its advocacy efforts. Among just Black and Latina women supporters, they selected to sign a petition after receiving the treatment that included a multi-issue policy platform more often than when they received

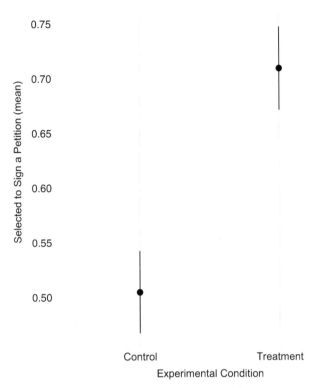

FIGURE 6.15 Selecting to sign a petition among Black and Latina women

the control, which included a single-issue platform. As shown by the comparison of means presented in Figure 6.15, choosing to sign a petition is much higher among Black and Latina women who received a multi-issue policy platform (i.e., the treatment) relative to the single-issue platform (i.e., the control) ($p < 0.0001$).

While the multi-issue platform mobilizes women of color across race and ethnic differences to get more involved in organizational activities, Latina women in particular are significantly motivated. Among Latinas, their willingness to engage in political actions after receiving the treatment increased and was statistically significant as shown in Figure 6.16 ($p < 0.01$).

There was not a statistically significant difference among Black women supporters. These findings illustrate not only that WE is reaching a diverse group of women of color with its intersectional advocacy efforts but that this messaging also specifically aligns with the interests of the group they are most concerned with: Black and Latina women. Among Latinas, this messaging is particularly mobilizing in that it motivates them to select more participation options to get involved with the organization's advocacy efforts.

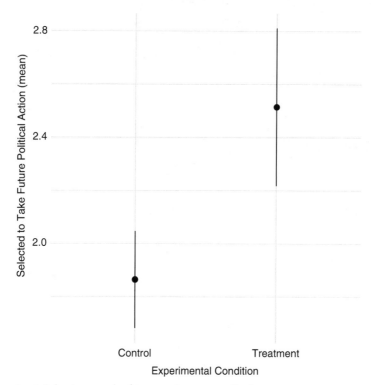

FIGURE 6.16 Selecting to take future action among Latina women

In the next section, I discuss the results from a qualitative analysis of the petition messages that supporters provided. These results underscore this consistent takeaway – which is that, in order for multi-issue platforms with policy linkages to successfully mobilize supporters, especially women of color, people need to be able to identify the connections between the issues presented to them.

PETITIONS AND POLICY LINKAGES

Petitions are an important way that supporters can not only contribute to organizational policy efforts but also engage in the political process more directly to state their interests and needs. Petitions are a historical and contemporary tool that marginalized groups in particular use to advocate for their policy preferences (Blackhawk et al., 2021; Carpenter, 2016; Carpenter & Moore, 2014). Petitioning plays a central role in American law and policymaking (Carpenter, 2016), and these petitions can be particularly revealing in how marginalized groups evaluate policy institutions (Blackhawk et al., 2021). Because the petition is an important tool in communicating policy interests, I conducted a qualitative analysis of all the messages that supporters wrote accompanying their signatures. All participants that opted to sign the petition were asked to write a message to their legislators that would be included with their signature. This option was available to all participants in both experiments.

I analyzed these messages to understand which characteristics of the policy platforms were most motivating to participants. Using an inductive coding process (Small, 2011; Vaismoradi et al., 2013), I noted patterns that were consistently appearing in the messages accompanying the signed petitions. I then cross-compared (Fereday & Muir-Cochrane, 2006) the messages between the control and treatment groups for each experiment and then compared the control and treatment messages in the first experiment to those in the second experiment. In this section, I present the qualitative findings that emerged from comparing petition messages among participants who supported either the policy linkage in the first experiment or the second (i.e., the two treatment groups that agreed to sign a petition). These qualitative analyses help to identify why intersectional advocacy approaches are more effective than others.

After coding and analyzing the messages, I find that the COVID-19 pandemic heuristic did help supporters identify connections between the issues presented to them in the multi-issue initiative. I also find that participants who did support the multi-issue initiative in the first experiment for sexual harassment and the subminimum wage did not view these issues as interconnected and the majority of participants supported the platform because one of the issues was particularly salient to them. In other words, when participants view connections between issues they are more motivated to support policy linkages. But when these connections are less obvious, traditional approaches to address a singular issue are more effective.

POLICY DISCONNECT AND PETITIONS

For the first experiment, among those who received a multi-issue platform and opted to write a message about the issue that they wanted their legislators to address, 71 percent discussed either subminimum wage or sexual violence as a separate issue of concern. In comparison, among this same treatment group, only 29 percent wrote a message that explicitly discussed these two issues together. Figure 6.17 illustrates these differences among participants who wrote a message with their petition.

Participants assigned to the multi-issue platform who provided a message often focused on one issue or the other. For example, one person wrote:

[R]eal wages have fallen behind while [the] cost o[f] everything else continues to climb. The sub-minimum wage for service workers creates even more inequities. Just because they should make up the difference in tips doesn't mean it is realistic and employers are[n't]

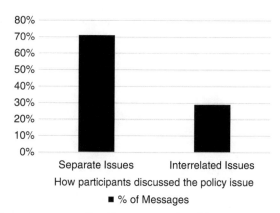

FIGURE 6.17 Experiment 1: policy disconnect and petition messages

taking advantage. The workers are too desperate to continue making anything to complain. They need to feed their families. This needs to be fixed. We've waited too long already.

In this message, the person is only focusing on the subminimum wage issue. Meanwhile another person wrote: "a good friend of mine was sexually harassed while working at McDonalds." In general, people who wrote a petition message most often referenced the working conditions/pay inequities part of the policy treatment and did not often mention sexual violence at all. This attention to the subminimum wage is perhaps because this issue was popular in 2021 at the tail end of the survey experiment; minimum wage was being discussed by President Biden and Congress at this time. However, when a time series OLS model was conducted for selecting to sign a petition, the time of the survey was not significant (results are presented in the Appendices), whereas the treatment variable remained significant in this analysis. Thus, while this issue may have been front of mind for survey participants, it does not appear that this political context was a confounding factor.

Not all messages focused on one issue. Some people did write about a connection between the two issues. One participant wrote: "respect for a human being's work and freedom from sexual violence are two sides of the same coin. It's astonishing that in the 21st century these are still urgent issues." Others were more specific about how these conditions overlapped with one another. One person wrote:

It is impossible for someone to take pride in their work and enjoy it unless they feel heard, respected, and valued. Every person has a right to feel safe from assault in their workplace, no matter what. We must protect women and especially woman of color in the workforce. Think about how many women of color you see on a daily basis when you're out to eat, grocery shopping, etc. These "essential" workers we've been calling them. They deserve a fair wage and protection from all forms of sexual harassment.

This person's message explicitly reflects the connections between wage conditions and vulnerabilities to sexual assault, especially among women of color. These are the types of linkages that these policy agendas are intended to create between these issues. Unfortunately, these messages were far less common. The analyses of all these messages demonstrate that those who received a treatment policy platform via the first experiment and wrote a message less often interpreted the two issues together – even though this was the goal of the policy initiative.

Thus, one explanation for why participants in the first experiment were not as motivated to sign a petition after receiving a multi-issue policy platform compared to those that received a single-issue one is that the two issues presented to them were not obviously interconnected. However, when these connections are more apparent, it seems an intersectional advocacy approach was effective for mobilizing supporters. The second experiment provides evidence that this is the case. Participants in the second experiment more often signed a petition when they received a multi-issue policy treatment, especially women of color. The qualitative analysis of their messages that were included with their petitions further confirms that this group viewed these connections between issues.

POLICY LINKAGES AND PETITIONS

In the second experiment, among those who received a multi-issue policy platform and opted to write a message about the issue they wanted their legislators to address, 29 percent discussed either paid leave or caregiving as a separate issue of concern. In comparison, among this same treatment group, 71 percent wrote a message that explicitly discussed these two issues together. Figure 6.18 compares

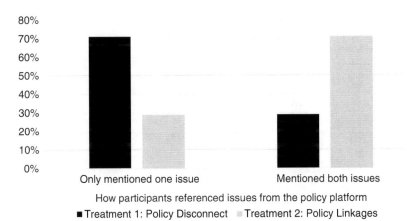

FIGURE 6.18 Comparing petition messages among treatment groups by Experiments 1 and 2

the two treatment groups from Experiment 1 to Experiment 2 to demonstrate the difference in how they wrote a petition message for the multi-policy platform that they received. As Figure 6.18 demonstrates, there is a notable difference between the messages that people from the treatment group in the first experiment provided compared to those from the treatment group in Experiment 2. Those in the treatment group who wrote a message with their petition in the second experiment tended to write messages that discussed the policy issues as interrelated.

For example, one participant wrote: "women as parents and caregivers are being forced to leave the workplace in droves because of the coronavirus. Please provide greater support to parents in resources for caregiving, paid time off, and expanded leave programs that come with job protections." In this message, the person is emphasizing how the pandemic affects women in terms of both caregiving responsibilities and their working vulnerabilities. Another person wrote:

[The Family and Medical Leave Act (FMLA)] is helpful but one must use their own sick or annual time to still receive compensation. 12 weeks of paid FMLA that doesn't require using one's own sick leave our annual leave bank would ease the anxiety that so many single parents endure when taking care of both elderly parents and a sick child at home. The current FMLA isn't enough in today, for the current COVID crisis. We should expect that stressors caused by this pandemic will have long lasting effects on families who take care of generational families.

These messages demonstrate the connections people are making between the issues of paid leave and caregiving responsibilities and the ways that COVID contextualizes these experiences.

Even people who wrote messages only focusing on one of these issues often discussed it in relation to other problems such as homelessness. For example, one person wrote:

I work in the nonprofit sector providing emergency financial assistance and have seen so many families at risk of homelessness simply because they have no access to paid leave. This lack of paid leave and its implications can no longer be ignored[;] the pandemic has made it clear that lack of paid leave perpetuates inequality and harms Americans. COVID-19 is hitting low-income families harder, who are less likely to have access to paid leave. This problem can be fixed through legislation[,] and it is time we did so.

Therefore, introducing COVID-19 into the policy platforms appears to have been an important context for viewing the issues linked together in the multi-issue platform as interconnected for the 67 percent of the treatment group who wrote a message in the second experiment.

COMPARING POLICY MESSAGING

I constructed a variable to capture these qualitative differences. I included it in the dataset to compare these messages across treatment groups. If the petition

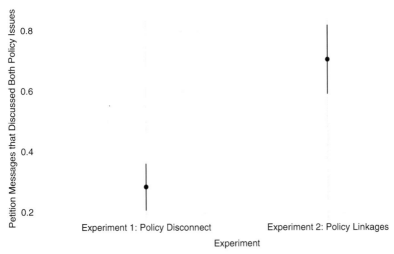

FIGURE 6.19 Comparing petition messages among treatment groups by Experiments 1 and 2

message referenced both of the two issues in the policy platform together, their response was assigned a 1. If the petition message only referenced one of the issues mentioned in the policy platform, their response was assigned a 2. If the message included other subtext that did not include these messages, it was assigned as NA. I then conducted a *t*-test to compare this variable among the two treatments, and the difference was significant ($p < 0.001$). Figure 6.19 demonstrates this difference. Participants who provided a petition message from the treatment group in the first experiment did not reference both issues in their platform as often as those in the treatment group from the second experiment. These findings demonstrate that those in the first experiment who signed the petition in the treatment group did not view the issues as interconnected as often as those in the second experiment who similarly received a multi-issue treatment policy platform.

This analysis has an important limitation: it does not account for those who chose not to sign the petition. However, it does provide some additional insights that are helpful for better understanding the supporters who the treatment policy platform mobilized and who are the primary interest of this study.

MOMENTS OF CRISIS AND ISSUES OF STRUGGLE

The global pandemic has illuminated to the broader public the ways in which inequality is multidimensional. In 2021, Vice President Kamala Harris declared a state of national emergency for women – especially among low-income women and women of color who were most vulnerable to layoffs and

COVID-19 exposure in the workplace (Rogers, 2021). Many other scholars, media reporters, and political leaders referenced how the pandemic exasperated gender, racial, and income inequality (Brower & Michener, 2021; Gray et al., 2020; Tisdell, 2020). Scholars of race and gender have always viewed these issues as interconnected (Browne, 2000; Conley, 2010; Hegewisch et al., 2010; Michener & Brower, 2020; Sum et al., 2010), and likewise organizations on the ground practicing intersectional advocacy have organized their political efforts around these multiple struggles. Media coverage of the COVID-19 pandemic and the ripple effect of issues that this health crisis has induced appears to provide a salient frame for viewing multi-issue agendas with issue and policy linkages.

The second experiment presents large and significant effects of selecting to sign a petition when supporters received a multi-issue policy platform. When it came to engaging in additional political actions beyond the petition, the effects among women of color were large and significant. These results are the ideal outcome for organizations practicing intersectional advocacy: their supporters are mobilized by messaging and platforms that aim to address the ways in which their experiences can be positioned between multiple struggles. Introducing the pandemic into these forms of messaging underscores these connections for supporters who organizations are hoping to mobilize. This is not to say that all messaging from these groups should tie back to the pandemic. Instead, these findings provoke us to consider what contextual framing devices are useful for helping supporters view the connections between issues that advocacy groups are attempting to marry together in their political efforts. There are additional availability heuristics that we could imagine which would also frame these connections, such as salient and publicized court cases that emphasize two issues, examples of laws or policies that effectively connected issues together, social movements like the Black Lives Matter movement that underscore interrelated problems, and other national events such as financial recessions or natural disasters that can illuminate interlocking issues experienced by intersectionally marginalized groups. The findings presented here demonstrate most importantly that organizations need to find ways to explicitly communicate connections between issues to their supporters if they are to effectively mobilize them around these agendas with issue and policy linkages.

INTERSECTIONAL ADVOCACY AND OVERLAPPING ISSUES

The findings from the experiments presented in this chapter encourage us to consider when intersectional advocacy efforts will be effective in mobilizing supporters around agendas with issue and policy linkages (i.e., here referred to as multi-issue agendas). Part of this consideration is what framing contexts help illustrate these connections (i.e., the COVID-19 pandemic). The other is a question of which issues are viewed as overlapping by supporters. In the first experiment presented in this chapter, supporters did not select to sign a petition more often when it displayed a multi-issue policy platform compared to one with a single-issue. In this experiment, participants who received a treatment were asked to consider a policy intervention addressing both sexual violence and the subminimum wage. Although there is substantial research that connects low-wage working conditions and low wages to environments where women, especially women of color, are more vulnerable to sexual violence (Aizer, 2010; Browne, 2000; Kilbourne et al., 1994; Tangri et al., 1982), and this is a connection that advocacy organizations on the ground are trying to establish, their supporters may not view these issues in this way. These findings demonstrate when multi-issue agendas with policy linkages can be counterproductive to the efforts intersectional advocates are leading.

These results also leave intersectional advocates with important questions to consider when they use these strategies in the form of policy agendas: Are there more effective ways to communicate the interrelatedness of issues to supporters that better establish these connections? Are some issues incompatible with one another when it comes to developing compelling policy agendas? Does there need to be a political context (i.e., the COVID-19 pandemic) to make these issue connections salient? The next experiment presented in this chapter provides some answers to these questions.

The results of this second experiment demonstrated that, when caregiving and paid leave were presented together in a policy intervention, this grouping had a large and positive effect on supporters selecting to sign a petition in support of this agenda. The qualitative analysis of participants who signed a petition for this agenda indicated that they viewed connections between these issues; these connections were important enough to participants that they noted the connections in their messages to legislators. It is possible that the political context of COVID-19 made these connections more apparent – COVID-19 was also mentioned in these messages. However, to fully draw this conclusion we would need to present a multi-policy agenda within this context that holds the issues of the subminimum wage and sexual violence constant. Without this additional research, though, these findings still indicate that, when issues are viewed as interrelated (regardless of what part of the framing device is shaping these connections), multi-issue agendas with policy linkages are more often supported by people.

Women Employed (WE) includes a diverse range of supporters by class, race, ethnicity, sexual orientation, and job occupation – and in the second experiment all of these supporters were more likely to sign a petition when they received a policy platform connecting paid leave and caregiving. This result shows general public support for intersectional advocacy approaches, which means that even groups not marginalized across more than one identity category can also see the benefit of this approach for better public policymaking. Additionally, WE's primary group for its advocacy efforts, Black and Latina women, were especially mobilized by this approach. Women of color across differences in race, ethnicity, and class were particularly motivated to sign up for actions to support the policy platform. These findings are reassuring for organizations practicing intersectional advocacy that aim to mobilize their participants as part of their strategy for moving their agendas forward. The findings from this research suggest that these groups need to be confident that the issues they are linking together under these policy initiatives are similarly perceived in this way by supporters.

The results of this research also highlight the practice of intersectional advocacy among organizations that focus on different policy areas from gender-based violence. Women Employed (WE) showcases an example of organizations that are working in additional distinct policy areas (in this case, economic social policies) that are also making connections between these areas and gender-based violence. The lack of support for connecting the subminimum wage to sexual harassment in a policy agenda reveals the challenges of making these connections when the primary organizing feature of advocacy is not gender-based violence. Meanwhile, the support for policy connections between caregiving and paid leave highlights the potential for intersectional advocacy to be applied across issue areas outside of gender-based violence.

There are many opportunities to forge issue linkages beyond adapting the framing of these policy agendas. Organizations have several points of contacts with their supporters: fundraising events, campaign events, email updates, newsletters, social media posts, and in-person gatherings. If these groups want to mobilize their participants around agendas with issue and policy linkages, these many forms of contact each present an opportunity to make the connections apparent and salient for their supporters. Thus, while this study focused on framing explicitly because it is an element of intersectional advocacy that lends itself to empirical exploration, there are other activities and outreach strategies that can augment the policy initiatives these organizations share with their supporters. The most important conclusions to draw from this study is that multi-issue platforms with policy linkages can be effective for mobilizing supporters – as long as they view the issues presented to them as interconnected, which of course is the core component of intersectional advocacy.

CONCLUSION

In this chapter, supporters of advocacy organizations are the vocal point because they are a key and overlooked resource for advancing policy efforts. The study presented in this chapter incorporated authentic policy agendas that WE used to motivate supporters to sign online petitions, write letters to their legislatures, and volunteer their time to the organization. This design allowed me to share in this chapter realistic models of the types of policy agendas that work and do not work for mobilizing supporters around intersectional advocacy. By conducting a textual analysis of the comments submitted by supporters with their online petitions, I also was able to provide some insights about what makes these policy agendas effective or lacking when it comes to communicating policy linkages. As advocacy groups take on an intersectional advocacy approach and pursue multi-policy agendas, the findings presented in this chapter caution them to thoughtfully consider how they communicate connections between distinct policies.

Those that can effectively illustrate these linkages to their supporters will be able to mobilize them considerably more than comparative single-issue appeal approaches. Women of color in particular may be even more motivated to sign petitions and get more involved with these organizations. Multi-issue agendas with issue and policy linkages resonate more with these groups because they better reflect the lived experiences of women who are intersectionally marginalized and positioned between more than one problem. While these groups are mobilized more by these agendas, all supporters across differences in identity and marginalization were also more motivated to sign petitions in support of intersectional advocacy. When issue and policy linkages are clear and internalized, intersectional advocacy has the potential to mobilize all different types of groups to change traditional policymaking and make it more inclusive, comprehensive, and equitable. In other words, how supporters responded to these policy agendas should reassure intersectional advocacy organizations that they are leading us in the right direction.

7

The Challenges and Possibilities Ahead

[O]ur national work [is] to uplift what we're seeing on the ground and taking that [up] nationally. And think that's just the question we've been [asking] for a while now, how do we do this national work? [We] continue to sustain it with our own organizational growing pains and leadership changes, but also with[in] the environment that we're living in politically ... I think [if] we had more support at the federal level, as a priority area of this culturally specific, anti-violence work, our work [would be] able to really be groundbreaking.

                                   Assistant Director, the Latina Network (LN)

In the words of Audre Lorde, people "do not live single-issue lives." Why then, are US policy institutions designed as if they do? Organizing public policies into neatly defined categories such as welfare, housing, gender-based violence, criminal justice, healthcare, tribal rights, and immigration is efficient. But this approach cannot fully address the persistent problems people experience, particularly when they differ in their gender, race, ethnicity, class citizenship status, sexual orientation, and age. Throughout this book, I emphasize "policy boundaries," which encompasses the many ways policymakers demarcate issues and policies separately from one another. Without deeper and more thoughtful attention to the differences among the US population during the policymaking process, it is likely that these types of boundaries and the gaps they inevitably create will continue to further marginalize people who experience issues across these policies. This outcome is very visible by observing and examining policymaking on gender-based violence. In Chapter 2, I presented evidence that shows how singularly defined policies designed for mainstream populations can overlook important differences among intersectionally marginalized groups that lead to greater inequality and harm. While I showed in Chapter 3 how intersectional advocates played an important role in revising the Violence Against Women Act (VAWA) to address these policy gaps by establishing issue and policy linkages, policies like the VAWA still have further to go before they embrace the diverse population of people that depend on it.

Advocates continue to try and improve the VAWA because it is still attached to several of the crime bill policies (Gover & Moore, 2020), is limited in the number of U Visas it grants to immigrant survivors of violence (Chen, 2000), does not offer enough protections for tribes to prosecute non-Indian perpetrators of gender-based violence (Le May, 2018), and does not provide adequate immediate and long-term healthcare services (García-Moreno et al., 2015). In other words, even examples of successful policies like the VAWA that have issue and policy linkages need to be improved if they are to completely meet the needs of intersectionally marginalized survivors. Gender-based violence as a problem is not going away and continues to be a relevant issue in the United States. It was the focus of national attention especially between 2017 and 2018 when the #MeToo movement peaked in visibility (Manikonda et al., 2018); a series of sexual assault allegations led to the resignations of several public figures (Detrow, 2017; Ettachfini & Beusman, 2018; Stolberg et al., 2018); more than two dozen women alleged that former president Trump engaged in sexual misconduct (Shear, 2017); and allegations of sexual assault dominated the confirmation proceedings of Supreme Court nominee Brett Kavanaugh (Hauser, 2018). Amid these events, policymakers are grappling with how to handle and combat gender-based violence. Unfortunately, most policymakers continue to pursue piecemeal measures as quick fixes to this problem without more holistic responses to address the full range of underlying problems. To do so would require considering women's differing vulnerabilities to and experiences with violence that are contingent on their other identities – especially race, ethnicity, immigrant status, and class.

Gender-based violence is particularly high among women of color. American Indian, Black, and multiracial women experience the highest percentage of intimate partner violence, compared to other races/ethnicities (The National Center for Victims of Crime, 2018). These outcomes are not random; as I have highlighted in the Introduction and Chapter 1, they are deeply connected to systems of oppression such as colonialization, slavery, migration, patriarchy, racism, and sexism. The subjugation of women who are marginalized by their race, ethnicity, citizenship status, and class is shaped by these distinct historical processes of oppression, which in turn shape the modern conditions for gender-based violence. This subjugation of intersectionally marginalized women, though, is unfortunately largely ignored by policies in the United States.

This book theorizes and examines how select advocacy organizations are leading an approach to policymaking that prioritizes intersectionally marginalized populations in ways that improve policies for everyone. By advocating for issue and policy linkages, intersectional advocates pave the way for policymaking that more authentically addresses problems in the way that people experience them in their multi-issue lives. I identify this approach as "intersectional advocacy," from examining the strategies, actions, and policy victories among these advocacy organizations that orient their approach around intersectionally marginalized groups.

ADVOCACY ORGANIZATIONS AND INTERSECTIONAL ADVOCATES

Throughout this book, different advocacy approaches are explored and examined. Some organizations take on a more traditional policy approach by focusing all of their efforts on a single issue and a single identity (i.e., gender). Examples of some of these organizations presented in this book were Women Against Violence Everyday (WAVE), the National Organization for Women (NOW), the National Coalition Against Domestic Violence, and the Iowa Coalition Against Sexual Assault. To be clear, just because these organizations focused on a single issue does not mean their efforts do not substantially change our political institutions in remarkable ways – these groups have led efforts to establish and enforce orders of protection for survivors of violence, secured federal funding for rape crisis centers, shelters, and hotlines, and more. Despite these incredible efforts, without a focus on how these changes would impact women differently by race, ethnicity, and class, some of these policy outcomes reinforced and reproduced inequities among women. For example, even policies that would ostensibly benefit all women, such as establishing rape crisis centers, were not accessible at first to all groups of women; many of the first shelters and counseling services that were secured by this advocacy were only provided to English-speaking, heterosexual, female passing, US citizens. Making these types of services inaccessible to certain groups of women was not the intention of these advocacy groups and in many ways was a product of their participation in a policymaking process that enforced norms and practices of addressing single issues among the mainstream population.

Advocacy groups that prioritize the experiences and interests of intersectionally marginalized groups intervene in the policymaking process to address these gaps. Evidence from the VAWA hearings show that organizations such as the House of Ruth, the Harriet Tubman Center, and UNIDOS Against Domestic Violence advocate for bilingual services so that non-English speakers could access hotlines, included nondiscretionary training for service providers, and made shelters available on reservations. All of these efforts and initiatives improved intersectionally marginalized groups' access to federal services and resources – but none of these challenged the laws or policies undergirding these services. By not challenging the policy boundaries of VAWA and instead making existing mainstream services more accessible to women of color, immigrants, and LGBTQ people, these efforts could not fully meet the needs of intersectionally marginalized groups that were experiencing gender-based violence in combination with other issues such as poverty, lack of immigration rights, and unaffordable housing. As shown in this book, all of these advocacy organizations care deeply about intersectionally marginalized groups and have commitments to intersectional feminism. It is my hope that these types of organizations with these commitments will improve their existing efforts to take on a more intersectional advocacy approach in the future.

Intersectional advocates illuminate the radical shift this form of advocacy can have on policies and the people that depend on them. Intersectional advocates contest policies that create distinct boundaries around what is considered "gender-based violence" and the standard policy solutions proposed to address it. This contestation and boundary-crossing is what distinguishes them as intersectional advocates. I report findings from an in-depth qualitative study of three such organizations: the Latina Network (LN), Sisters Against Violence (SAV), and Communities for Survivors (CFS). By talking to organizational leaders, I learned more about what motivates their engagement in intersectional advocacy and what constitutive features are needed to advance and sustain this practice. Intersectional advocates promote issue and policy linkages, center the needs of intersectionally marginalized populations in their mission and priorities, include broad networks outside their issue area, and allocate funding to interrelated issues that intersect with gender-based violence. Each organization that practices intersectional advocacy varies uniquely across these characteristics, but each one shares these broader similarities. Though they have different goals and serve varying populations, all intersectional advocates pursue issue and policy linkages, and they build some form of advocacy infrastructure to help them reach these goals. Intersectional advocates intervene in this way to reduce the vulnerabilities intersectionally marginalized groups face and in the process are reconfiguring policies to better represent their needs and interests.

While I focus selectively on a handful of organizations practicing intersectional advocacy, there is a wide landscape of advocacy groups representing intersectionally marginalized people that we can learn from moving forward. Although I cannot confirm these groups are fully practicing intersectional advocacy, I can underscore the range of organizations that are promoting the types of issue linkages that were observed throughout this book. Some of these organizations include Love and Protect, INCITE!, and Survived and Punished, which focus on how women, transgender, and gender-nonconforming people of color are harmed by both state and interpersonal violence. These organizations confront how forms of gender violence experienced by people of color are bound up with systems of incarceration, deportation, and police violence. Black Women's Blueprint, Ujima, and Black Women for Wellness work to advance policies that better address the struggles of Black women as they face gender-based violence, which for them often includes multi-issue initiatives that also promote reproductive justice.

The National LGBTQ Institute on Intimate Partner Violence, the Northwest Network of Bi, Trans, Lesbian and Gay Survivors of Abuse, and the Sylvia Rivera Law Project center the experiences of LGBTQ people as they seek to change the United States' capacity for addressing domestic violence and sexual assault among these communities. The National Indigenous Women's Resource Center, the Alliance of Tribal Coalitions to End Violence, and the First Nation's Alliance bring attention to how colonialization has led to harmful policies and laws that prevent American Indian women from being protected from gender-based violence and exclude them from essential services to heal from violence. These organizations seek to contest how the United States interprets tribal sovereignty when it comes to adjudicating and responding to violence against American Indian women.

The Immigrant Battered Network, Las Americas Immigrant Advocacy Center, and the Alliance for Immigrant Survivors advocate for addressing the ways in which citizenship status prevents immigrant women from escaping violence and accessing social services that would allow them to be financially independent from their abusers. Manavi, the Asian Pacific Institute on Gender-Based Violence, and Womankind bring attention to how specific subgroups of Asian American women need not only immigration services but culturally specific options for healing from gender-based violence. Mujeres Latinas en Acción, Sepa Mujer Inc., and Coordinadora Paz para la Mujer advocate for policies at the intersections of immigration, welfare, and violence that will directly serve Latina survivors.

As policymakers consider who is included in the policymaking process, what expertise is valuable in designing policy, and what types of connections need to be formed between issues, *I encourage them to seek out these types of advocacy organizations*. Advocacy organizations are a hugely important resource for policymaking. These groups are often "client-facing," which means they are on the ground and often face to face with the people who are experiencing the issues we hope to solve. Advocacy organizations such as the examples given in this section are led by people with extraordinary expertise and understandings of the experiences of intersectionally marginalized people. They are familiar with the systems of oppression these groups face, the vulnerabilities these systems create, and how policy systems can sometimes magnify and exacerbate these conditions. Finally, the advocates I spoke with hold refreshing visions of a policy system that protects, supports, and liberates all people, especially those who have spent most of their lives at the margins of democratic life. These advocates are wise, imaginative, and resourceful. It is my hope that this book underscores just how important these groups are to developing policies that support the type of diverse, just, and equitable democracy in which we all want to live.

LEADING INTERSECTIONAL ADVOCACY

The organizations presented in this book illustrate the importance of "substantive" representation in leading intersectional advocacy. Several of the staff and leaders of the organizations LN, CFS, and SAV are cis women of color. But it is not the descriptive feature of this leadership alone that encourages intersectional advocacy. These leaders substantively incorporate the experiences, needs, and interests of low-income and women of color survivors into the mission, advocacy, and approach of the organization. Thus, while leaders who descriptively are marginalized by gender, race, ethnicity, and class are more likely to have lived experiences that resemble this group, descriptive representation alone will not necessarily result in intersectional advocacy practices. Substantive leadership, people who understand how groups can be positioned between multiple issues and prioritize policy solutions that address this positionality, will more likely engage in intersectional advocacy. Indeed, that is why white cis women and white LGBTQ women lead alongside women of color in the organizations CFS and Women Employed.

Across differences in race, ethnicity, class, and sexual orientation these leaders share a substantive commitment to addressing how intersectionally marginalized groups are positioned between multiple issues as a result of interlocking systems of oppression. That is not to say that organizations and policymakers should not also consider descriptive representation when applying intersectional advocacy. The organization SAV invests its resources in creating a pipeline for women of color to lead in this capacity, because they more often will understand and prioritize the needs and experiences of intersectionally marginalized groups. These are important investments that should be continued but that should also emphasize substantive representation. Because leaders from marginalized groups can also play a role in perpetuating inequalities among more disadvantaged people within these identity groups (Cohen, 1999), it should not be assumed that diverse leaders will automatically be inclined to lead intersectional advocacy efforts, which is why substantive representation is such an important feature of this work. As organizations and policymakers aim to diversify their staff, they also should evaluate existing substantive representation among their current leadership and plan how to probe perspective employees to demonstrate this commitment to intersectionally marginalized groups. These efforts incentivize leadership that can more effectively adopt and apply intersectional advocacy practices.

MOBILIZATION AND MOMENTUM

I also examine a variety of strategies intersectional advocates use to advance their multi-issue agendas and reconfigure policy institutions. Supporters are not always key to these efforts, but in some cases they are. For that reason, it was important to consider how policy platforms that communicate multi-issue agendas are received by supporters and to what extent supporters can be mobilized by these efforts. I find that multi-issue agendas can effectively mobilize supporters but only when they include policy linkages that convincingly connect issues together. Such policy platforms are especially promising for developing sustained mobilization among women of color. These platforms can motivate women of color to engage in immediate political actions (e.g., signing an online petition) and to sign up for continued future action (e.g., reaching out to their legislators).

Not all policy platforms that take on an intersectional approach will be this successful. I find that when supporters of the organization do not clearly view a policy connection between two issues presented to them, they will be more mobilized by a single-issue appeal. These findings are important for organizations practicing intersectional advocacy to consider, because they indicate that these organizations may need to carefully develop strategies to communicate the connections between ostensibly distinct issue areas to their supporters. Policy platforms are only one method of communication. Organizations are constantly engaging with their supporters via email, social media postings, community events, and through volunteer councils. These different modes of communication present numerous opportunities where organizations can be more explicit about how their policy initiatives will address interconnected issues that their supporters face.

CHALLENGES FOR ADVOCACY GROUPS

Many challenges lie ahead for intersectional advocates. One of the biggest challenges is that these organizations tend to be underfunded. Leaders from all three organizations included in the qualitative study, especially SAV and LN, communicated that finding money for policy work is extremely difficult. For example, the SAV executive director shared:

Many communities of color organizations and many women of color organizations specifically that are doing this work, that are doing violence against women work … Many of them do not have access to funds to support infrastructure, infrastructure that allows you to do the policy [work] … There's not that infrastructure, the vast majority of money that goes to us, only support services. We need more money that supports infrastructure, that can build the foundation of these organizations.

Although groups such as LN are creative with their public funding and find ways to include advocacy in their service work, they too struggle to maintain their infrastructure. Much of the funding available to these organizations is earmarked for service provision, which means that these groups have to spend considerable time and resources to find ways to overcome the financial limitations to their advocacy and policy work. These organizations also must consider the prospect that they may lose government funding *because of* their activities. Fearing that being explicit about its political work would lead to the government defunding it, LN mentioned needing to sometimes engage in censorship with its supporters.

There are also political limitations to this work. For example, as CFS pushes for the city to defund the police and reallocate these funds to survivors and social services, it encounters political pushback from a variety of actors. Not only are several local public officials opposed to the reallocation of police funds but also affiliated organizational members are divided about to what degree police institutions should be defunded or removed. Cognizant of these challenges, CFS has attempted to set a precedent for budget reallocation, survey its affiliated members to determine possible compromises, and build a network of public officials who share similar goals. Because CFS leaders understand and accept the presence of political limitations, they set incremental goals. To cross these boundaries and reconfigure them takes time. These groups have to find ways to establish new precedents in the form of laws, policies, and funding streams that bind issues together. They need time to build policy infrastructures that will act as bridges between issue areas. These infrastructures are always contested, and thus these groups have to then spend a considerable amount of time protecting these policy wins.

In the end, no matter how successful these groups are at reconfiguring and repurposing these policies, they will always be limited by the broader political institutions that encompass policymaking. Intersectional advocacy will not fully liberate the groups from the various forms of oppression they face, in that it does not dismantle the systems that produce these inequalities. Because intersectional advocacy primarily targets policy, advocates will always be limited to some degree by the institutional structures that house these policies. Thus, intersectional advocacy cannot by itself fundamentally change the broader systems of inequality. To fully dismantle these systems, intersectional advocacy needs to be accompanied with more radical transformations to these very structures.

POLICY DEVELOPMENT AND RECONFIGURATION

Intersectional advocacy is a response to how state regulation of the lives of intersectionally marginalized people creates conditions of inequality especially by gender, race, and class. Intersectional advocates intervene by strategically crossing institutional boundaries to produce new laws and policies that transcend issue areas. This is a difficult task because the state reinforces social policy boundaries that advocates seek to rearrange by maintaining these policies as operationally, fiscally, and politically separate from one another (Weir et al., 1988). Organizations practicing intersectional advocacy do not endorse these policy boundaries. For them, addressing the issue of gender-based violence necessitates some type of boundary-crossing into state structures that operate outside the scope of their core issue.

I show how intersectional advocates cross institutional boundaries to address gender-based violence in relation to issues of poverty, unaffordable housing, mass incarceration, paid-leave, the minimum wage, economic inequality, human trafficking, immigration rights, inaccessible healthcare, and tribal sovereignty. The political strategies they use are not untraditional (i.e., building coalitions, budget advocacy, lawmaking), but their ability to bring together several stakeholders around different issues is a distinct and understudied phenomenon. To advance multi-issue policy agendas that create linkages between these issues, intersectional advocates establish an advocacy infrastructure to house these efforts. This can take the form of coalitions of groups across issue areas or developing drafts of policies that explicitly connect two issues. This infrastructure serves as a concrete political space in which intersectional advocates can strengthen connections between issue areas. These connections can be achieved by changing how funding is allocated, passing new legislation, and modifying existing policies. These wins establish policy linkages between policies, which over time can reconfigure the boundaries of these policy institutions.

My analysis of congressional hearings on the VAWA over the last twenty-five years illustrates how policies can be reconfigured over time. This legislative case study showcases how intersectional advocates can incrementally change institutional boundaries by advocating for new policies that link together distinctly separate issues (i.e., welfare, immigration, and tribal rights). These changes are impactful as they have redistributed resources, provided pathways for citizenship, and established more autonomy for deciding recourse and healing among survivors of violence. For survivors who are marginalized across multiple axes of their identities, these policy changes directly reduce their vulnerabilities to homelessness, poverty, poor health outcomes, deportation, and incarceration. Reconfigured policies, as shown in these pages and chapters, can radically improve the individual lives of people who are marginalized across multiple identities.

Intersectional advocacy encompasses a variety of strategies depending on the actors, context, time period, constraints, and resources available to organizations. It is a practice that is not limited to groups advocating to end gender-based violence. Any organization representing intersectionally marginalized groups that is focusing on multiple issue areas at once has the potential to be an intersectional advocate, as long as it engages in the other behaviors discussed in this book (i.e., crossing institutional boundaries, proposing issue linkages, building advocacy infrastructure, and advocating for policy linkages). As future scholars, decision makers, and activists consider examining or applying intersectional advocacy to policymaking, it is important to note that this practice will not always take the form of the strategies discussed here. Advocacy groups represent unique populations and have varying goals and unique visions for their work. What I have provided in this book are broad frameworks to identify intersectional advocates, recognize their political behaviors, study the impact of their advocacy on policy institutions, and understand what motivates this form of engagement with the state. These broad frameworks can then be used to identify, study, and understand a diverse landscape of advocacy groups participating within and outside movements to end gender-based violence.

REEVALUATING POLICY

Intersectional advocates fundamentally challenge how we evaluate the effectiveness of public policies. When policies are designed to address social problems singularly, people who are trapped between more than one of these issues are disproportionately disadvantaged. Throughout the pages of this book, there are several examples of these policies: housing solutions that do not account for how survivors of violence are dependent on their abuser economically or for their citizenship; healthcare funding that excludes community health centers and by extension people of color; immigration status exclusions for services provided by the VAWA; or bail bond laws that further disenfranchise low-income survivors of violence and people of color. When policies largely benefit the mainstream population but disproportionately exclude or worsen circumstances for marginalized groups, is it an effective policy? Intersectional advocates would unequivocally respond "no."

The advocacy presented throughout this book should provoke us to reevaluate how we determine the effectiveness of public policy. According to the organization LN, change is not effective until "the last person standing" is reached. Instead of evaluating policies in terms of the number of people impacted, intersectional advocates encourage us to evaluate policy from the margins and to look closely for gaps between policies. This radical shift is key for designing comprehensive public policies that fully address persistent and long-standing social issues such as poverty, homelessness, gender-based violence, mass incarceration, and health disparities. Throughout this book, intersectional advocates display the connections between these issues and make the case that, to effectively address one issue, it needs to be connected to another. Designing and evaluating policy in these ways is an opportunity to draw out underlying inequities that span across social issues so that everyone can be free from their hold.

OUTCOMES OF INTERSECTIONAL ADVOCACY

What are the outcomes of intersectional advocacy and how do they look different than traditional policy solutions to gender-based violence? In a scenario where intersectional advocacy is a widely used approach to addressing gender-based violence, we should expect a range of outcomes that not only reduce instances of violence but also tend to the underlying issues that position intersectionally marginalized people to be more vulnerable to this abuse of power.

When education and gender-based violence are linked by policy, both can work together to change power dynamics early in children's development and offer healthier outlets for mental health. Linking these policy initiatives can result in children with early opportunities to learn about consent, healthy relationships, and mental health that set expectations early on in relationships for respect and care instead of abuse (Burton et al., 2023). Beyond specific curriculum related to this issue, if we take an intersectional approach seriously, then in schools we also need to evaluate the myriad ways power dynamics are enforced across the learning experiences of young people (Nuamah, 2019). How are women, trans women, people of color, low-income people, and LGBTQ people portrayed in texts and lessons on history, English, math, and science? How young people learn about power and who has it in the classroom translates to their adult understandings of how power can be abused and used against these groups (Nelsen, 2021). In a world in which we thoughtfully make connections between gender-based violence and education, the outcomes are young people who grow up with radically different understandings of power and who have healthy outlets early for mental health issues that prevent them from harming others. These linkages also close disparities in power by gender, sexual orientation, race, ethnicity, and class. It is difficult to abuse power when there is none at your disposal.

Similarly, linking gender-based violence and housing policy also reduces power disparities that in turn prevent the use of abuse. People most vulnerable to abuse, especially domestic violence, are most often economically dependent on their abusers (Coker, 2000). More funding and support for public housing options provides socioeconomically disadvantaged people with financial independence (Hinshaw, 2017). Among women with children, these options can be an alternative to homelessness or staying with an abuser. Indeed, 38 percent of homeless people in the United States are survivors of violence (Department of Justice, 2020). Providing more accessible and affordable housing options reduces incentives for people to depend on abusers for shelter. This increased supply of affordable housing means that thousands of survivors and people at risk for violence have a safe pipeline out of these scenarios. Among survivors with children, the availability of safe housing can also stop intergenerational violence and trauma (Coker, 2000).

Linking gender-based violence to policies on welfare can also reduce power disparities by facilitating economic independence especially among intersectionally marginalized groups. Among current survivors of violence, increased social welfare benefits can provide economic support while the survivor takes time off work to search for new housing, seek counseling services, receive medical attention, and break economic ties with an abuser (Abramovitz, 2017). Increasing these services while providing resources such as financial literacy trainings can also prevent violence. By ensuring that people have the resources they need to be economically independent, there are fewer incentives for them to either enter abusive relationships or become abusers themselves. Gender-based violence is ultimately about power, and linking policies together is an attempt to redistribute power and resources across issue areas that fundamentally change the positionality of intersectionally marginalized groups.

Finally, linking gender-based violence to policies addressing mass incarceration encourages us to consider alternative approaches for addressing this problem, such as restorative justice. Rather than increasing the penalties and sentencing of abusers, which often are not enforced by the legal system (Gregory & Lees, 1994), and subjecting abusers to sexual violence themselves within the prison system (Jones & Pratt, 2008), restorative justice encourages policy approaches that restore and repair both the survivor and the perpetrator of violence. The organization discussed in Chapter 3, the LN, facilitates dialogue between families around racial, ethnic, and socioeconomic trauma because they recognize that many instances of domestic violence are a result of past trauma. This approach is an example of restorative justice. Linking gender-based violence to restorative justice means cultivating policies and practices around mental health resources, addressing racial and economic oppression, and healing existing trauma among abusers. The outcomes of this approach are stopping intergenerational trauma and enabling both survivors and abusers to heal and avoid harm.

Ultimately, the outcomes of an intersectional advocacy approach are transforming power dynamics until no one is marginalized across identity categories. In other words, the final outcomes of an intersectional advocacy approach are that it leaves "no person left standing."

INTERSECTIONAL POLICYMAKING

If political officials and policymakers take seriously their tasks to develop legislation, laws, and policies that serve the entire American population they will have to critically reexamine the structures of policy institutions. Throughout these pages, I outlined the ways in which these institutions have evolved over time to separate key social issues from one another through policymaking processes as well as the consequences of these structures on the most vulnerable and marginalized groups in the United States. Put simply, policymakers will never successfully address some of the most pressing issues today, such as poverty, homelessness, immigration, mass incarceration, unaffordable healthcare, and gender-based violence, if policies remain structured to address each of these issues without looking at the ways in which they intersect.

Intersectional advocates provide a road map for us to develop policies, laws, and legislation in a way that actually represents the unique lived experiences of people, which very much are shaped by gender, race, ethnicity, citizenship status, sexual orientation, and social class. They encourage us to bring together coalitions, organizations, and stakeholders from across issue areas to develop and propose policies that address these issues together simultaneously. These advocates push us to reconsider how we allocate funding at the local, state, and federal levels, especially in how we define who is eligible to receive funding, and which issues are encompassed within these appropriations. Some of these groups illustrate the benefits of listening to people who are experiencing these issues firsthand, especially people who are intersectionally marginalized, to better understand the connections between the issues and the needs of those we most want to serve. Intersectional advocates also reveal the ways in which these institutions currently reinforce inequalities particularly through exclusionary criteria that continue to be incorporated into legislation, laws, and policies.

This study of intersectional advocacy illuminates the different opportunities that are available to political officials and policymakers to change these policy institutions if there is truly an investment in making these institutions more equitable, just, and representative. There are a variety of different ways in which policymakers, political officials, and state officials can participate in supporting intersectional advocacy. Table 7.1 breaks down the policymaking process and illustrates how intersectional advocacy can shape each of these steps in policy development for these actors. It summarizes the activities observed throughout the chapters in this book that advocates, state actors and policymakers use to

TABLE 7.1 *Intersectional advocacy guide for policymakers*

Policy Process	Intersectional Advocacy Approach
Defining and framing issues	• Consider how the problem you are addressing is experienced differently by the target population across differences in gender, race, ethnicity, citizenship status, class, sexual orientation, ability, etc. (e.g., the last person standing framework). • Based on these considerations, redefine the scope of the problem area by considering what changes need to be made to the existing definition and framing of issues. • Propose issue linkages, which are connections between overlapping issues that affect marginalized groups' experience of the problem. • Develop talking points that discuss the primary problem area in relation to other salient issues in order to make a case for expanding the scope/boundary of the policy objectives.
Setting the agenda and building coalitions	• Invite advocates serving intersectionally marginalized groups to participate in the agenda-setting process. • Build and support coalitions of advocates and policymakers whose purview covers the interrelated problems and issues identified to propose and evaluate existing policy. • Identify shared agendas and resources across the coalition that enable you to pursue issue linkages.

(*continued*)

TABLE 7.1 *(continued)*

Policy Process	Intersectional Advocacy Approach
Drafting policy proposals	• When drafting new policies, develop and include provisions that make policy accessible and relevant to the beneficiaries across differences in gender, race, ethnicity, citizenship status, class, sexual orientation, ability, etc. • When amending existing policies, propose policy linkages to other laws and policies outside of the primary issue area. • When advancing policy proposals through legislatures, organize hearings through committees or subcommittees that work across overlapping issues and ensure that testimony is provided by advocates and affected individuals with expertise across issues. • When policies come up for review (e.g., due to sunset clauses or appropriations cycles), revisit the policy parameters and consider relevant policy linkages that will expand the accessibility of the policy.
Budgeting	• Evaluate how accessible resources are to nonmainstream populations and providers. Where such populations or providers are excluded, modify budgets to ensure inclusion. • Normalize language in budgets that allows for cross-issue collaborations and solutions among implementing agencies or providers.
Implementation	• Evaluate existing infrastructure to implement the policy and assess whether it is accessible to all beneficiaries across differences in race, ethnicity, gender, class, sexual orientation, and ability. • Propose resources, staffing, and funding that will ensure all policy beneficiaries can access the policy without delays or exclusions of services. • Evaluate the expertise of officials and staff in implementing agencies or providers to distribute or enforce the policy inclusively across groups, especially those marginalized by more than one identity category.

engage in an intersectional advocacy practice. As we can see, there are several opportunities in the policymaking process for individuals to integrate this practice into everyday decisions about agendas, policy drafts, and implementation.

The organizations presented in this book *are* making an investment in intersectional advocacy, but it should not be up to these groups alone to address the ways in which our democratic institutions are failing to represent America's diverse polity. As mentioned, these organizations are under-resourced, overextended, and working at overcapacity to make these changes. They do not have the power to make all the substantive changes that are required for addressing the several different ways that these institutions are currently exacerbating and perpetuating inequality. What they can do is model a different and more equitable way of engaging in policymaking that we can support them in leading and create additional spaces for this approach to thrive. That is the call to action by intersectional advocates. The question then remains: who will join them?

BEYOND THE UNITED STATES

In this book, I focus on the practice of intersectional advocacy from a Western, US perspective. However, intersectional advocacy at its core is concerned with questions of power, inequities, state institutions, and marginalization, all of which are applicable to wider political contexts beyond the case of the United States. Studying intersectional advocacy within non-Western contexts under differing political regimes with varying hierarchies will further our collective understandings of power and the role advocacy groups can play in reconfiguring how institutions distribute this power among increasingly diverse and intersectionally marginalized populations. Feminist advocacy groups outside this context are also confronting institutional structures in regions such as Latin America, Africa, and Europe. Similarly, these groups are making the case that issues such as gender-based violence are interconnected with additional social problems that need to be resolved collectively to liberate people who are marginalized by, especially, gender, race, ethnicity, and class.

Feminist groups across the globe have been making these connections for decades. In Ecuador, activists and advocacy groups made the case that gender-based violence could not be addressed among low-income women without connecting this issue across all distinct ministry policy areas. These groups successfully pressured President Correa between 2000 and 2007 to implement a national plan around gender-based violence that was established across the four ministries of education, health, government, and economics (Cole & Phillips, 2008). There are certainly issue linkages between gender-based violence and other issue areas that intersectionally marginalized women in Ecuador face, and we can imagine how policy linkages between these ministries would strengthen this approach.

In Ghana, activists and advocacy groups faced similar institutional boundaries as those discussed in Chapter 4, as they pressured their state government to change the definition of gender-based violence to include female circumcision. Female circumcision was a cultural tradition, and thus these groups had to redefine this practice and link it to the issue of gender-based violence. To do so, they redefined the issue of genital female cutting as a "harmful traditional practice" and recategorized it as gender-based violence (Hodžić, 2010). In 1994, the practice was officially outlawed.

In Brazil, advocacy groups similarly forged connections between gender-based violence and other issue areas such as criminal justice. Between the 1970s and 1980s, feminist advocacy groups successfully instituted "women police stations," institutions that were run by women only to create safer and more comfortable spaces for women to report gender-based violence. In this example, these groups connected gender-based violence to the broader issue and structure of the criminal justice system (Santos, 2005). In Britain, during this same time period, organizations advocated for similar policy linkages that were discussed in Chapter 3. For example, advocacy groups pushed for the Housing (Homeless Persons) Act of 1977, which provided survivors of domestic violence with public housing (Elman, 2003). In this example, these groups made connections between gender-based violence and unaffordable housing, similar to the groups that participated in the VAWA hearings and like the organization LN discussed in Chapters 4 and 5.

Today, activists and advocates on the ground continue to make these connections globally. For example, in Mexico there is substantial organizing around the issue of femicide. While femicide affects a wide range of Latinas in Mexico, Indigenous women are most at risk for femicide and other gender-based issues such as human trafficking. Indigenous women, 80 percent of which experience extreme poverty, are marginalized by gender, class, and ethnicity (Eagan, 2020). Advocacy groups representing these types of populations, such as Las Libres and Psydeh, are advocating for issue connections between rural poverty, domestic and sexual violence, human trafficking, sexism, and racism (Munguía & Martínez-Zarzoso, 2021).

I mention these different examples to highlight how across state contexts and time periods advocacy groups are making connections between distinct issues and in some cases may be successfully pressuring political officials to enact policy linkages between these areas. Not all aspects of intersectional advocacy are applicable to non-Western and non-US contexts. As I have demonstrated in this book, intersectional advocacy is rooted in power hierarchies predominantly through, though not exclusively, gender, race, ethnicity, and class. These categories do not carry the same meaning in other state contexts, and institutions that respond to marginalization also vary in type of government, representation, ability of advocacy groups to intervene in political processes, and policy systems. Still, the concept of intersectional advocacy can travel across these contexts, as long as we are to study and understand how it might appear and operate differently based on these varying characteristics. Even in the United States I posit that intersectional advocacy will appear and strategically be advanced in different ways depending on the group and the political opportunities available to advocacy organizations. Therefore, intersectional advocacy is a political framework we can use to better understand how groups orient themselves when confronting state institutions (e.g., policy institutions) and challenge these structures to better serve the most marginalized populations.

REIMAGINING POLICY INSTITUTIONS: THE PATH AHEAD

Intersectional advocacy is an important practice that can tangibly reduce the vulnerabilities that intersectionally marginalized people face. It is a practice led by organizations that are on the front lines of policy innovation. These organizations are creative, inspiring, and imaginative. They envision political structures that do not exist yet in full form but are very much in the process of changing as a result of their advocacy. Intersectional advocates understand the ways that intersectionally marginalized groups become trapped between more than one issue as a product of overlapping systems of oppression. They also view the ways in which the state, vis-à-vis its policy institutions, reproduces these inequalities by designing policy areas that are distinctly separate from one another. Intersectional advocates are challenging this widely accepted tradition of separating policy issues from one another, as they make a compelling argument that this institution does not serve intersectionally marginalized groups.

Intersectional advocates are imagining a new structure – one that requires us to reconsider the boundaries of policies and facilitate issue and policy linkages between issue areas. To do so would mean to accept that social problems in the United States transcend issues areas, because inequality and oppression are multifaceted and pervasive. In the context of advocacy against gender-based violence, it means challenging widely accepted political categories for determining what is "gender-based violence" and how to address it.

Intersectional advocates highlight how these are never neutral categories but instead are deeply politicized and embedded into our political institutions that hold varying forms of inequality. They encourage us to consider what political categories might look like in a world in which policy institutions acknowledge and are designed to serve intersectionally marginalized groups. Their hope is that reconfigured policy institutions can address these multiple vulnerabilities, such that these groups will no longer experience these problems. Intersectional advocates' goals are expansive: they imagine a world where laws recognize intersectionally marginalized women as full citizens, with policies that provide them with services that increase their financial independence, services that allow them to heal in ways that align with their culture, accessible and affordable housing that enables them to take care of their families safely, opportunities available to them for reporting instances of violence without contributing to mass incarceration, and experiences with social institutions that do not discriminate against them. For intersectional advocates, with imagination, resources, and persistence, policy institutions can be transformed in ways that make our democracy more equitable and representative of a diverse polity.

Violence Against Women Act Textual Analysis

SUBSAMPLE OF TESTIMONY AND STATEMENTS

- State coalitions (e.g., Nevada coalition against domestic violence)
- Service and advocacy nonprofits (e.g., shelters, counseling services, hotlines, other service providers, advocacy groups, combination organizations like the Junior League)
- Legal services (e.g., Battered Women's Law Project)
- Nonwitnesses who have submitted letters, statements, and so on to the hearing/for the record (who meet the above criteria)
- "Participants from the audience" (see especially May 4, 1994, hearing, which makes a distinction between "Participants" a.k.a. witnesses and "Participants from the audience") who meet the above criteria

EXCLUDED FROM SUBSAMPLE

- Law enforcement (e.g., police, prosecutors, judges)
- Government agencies (e.g., Department of Health and Human Services, crime victim services)
- Survivors not explicitly affiliated with/appearing on behalf of an organization included in the confirmed organizations list
- Academics (e.g., professor of psychiatry) not a part of included organization types

ANALYSES AND CODEBOOK

The analyses of the congressional hearings were guided by the question of how advocacy groups intervene in policymaking processes to represent intersectionally marginalized populations. To answer this question, I developed a comprehensive codebook that was used to code all the testimony and statements provided by advocacy organizations in the congressional hearings between 1990 and 2013. The codebook captured advocacy group strategies and behaviors commonly used to influence legislators (see Ake & Arnold, 2017; Alex-Assensoh & Stanford, 1999; Arnold, 2017; Clemens, 1997; Cobble, 2004; Dasgupta, 2003; Markowitz & Tice, 2002; Skocpol, 2013; Strolovitch, 2007; Villalón, 2011; Weldon, 2002; Weldon & Htun, 2013; Wood, 2004). To track the differences in advocacy by who the organization represented, the codebook included specific codes by identity group, including women, low-income women, immigrations, American Indian women, children, Black women, and more (Chen, 2000; Miller et al., 2011; Mills, 1999; Raj & Silverman, 2002; Rivera, 1996; Whittier, 2016; Wood, 2004). Codes also captured when advocacy groups pointed out previous policies and programs and proposed ways to revise them (see Béland, 2009; Campbell, 2012; Pierson, 1993; Sabatier & Weible, 2007; Sheingate, 2003; Skocpol, 1992). Using an inductive approach (Aronson, 1995; Weston et al., 2001), as I coded advocacy efforts on behalf of intersectionally marginalized groups I added codes to capture emerging themes among select organizations (Vaismoradi et al., 2013): referencing related policy issues; referencing laws and bills outside of the Violence Against Women Act (VAWA); advocating to revise bills and laws outside of VAWA; policy wins that captured when advocacy groups referenced successful linkages between issues or policies; and finally compromises or concessions that occurred when groups could not establish a linkage. These codes were bundled into an overarching code that became "intersectional advocacy." I then created three categories of advocacy groups that mapped onto the three different types of advocacy approaches that I observed: intersectional, intersectionally marginalized, and single-issue to differentiate between them. With these additional new codes and schemes, I went back through the hearings and recoded with these additional codes to note patterns in issue and policy linkages on behalf of select groups that were using this approach.

Using this coding approach, I systematically compared strategies among advocacy groups while also observing the extent to which their participation changed over time. Because I coded the testimonies by organizational type, I was also able to descriptively analyze which types of women's organizations engaged in intersectional advocacy and how often this strategy was used in comparison to more traditional single-issue approaches. Moreover, I note which changes in policy and legislation occurred in each reauthorization cycle. Advocacy groups often discussed these policy changes as victories, compromises, and concessions. How they discussed these outcomes allowed me to identify which strategies they thought were effective (and thus would continue to use) and describe how their strategies changed over time based upon what they learned in earlier cycles.

Conducting this analysis according to the reauthorization cycles also provided an opportunity to observe bounded time periods to track the progress and backlash against intersectional advocacy over the years. For example, when there was a concession or when legislators attempted to roll back a provision that was included in the previous cycle, these data capture how advocacy organizations reacted to these events in the next cycle. Finally, I went through the renewed versions of VAWA after each cycle and checked the amendments, provisions, and additional passage of legislation that mapped onto the proposed changes by intersectional advocates in the congressional hearings.

TABLE A1.1 *Codebook for VAWA textual analyses*

Measure	Code Name	Definition
Ideology	Ideology	Parent code to capture all the sub-codes related to ideology
Definition of violence	Desc_violence	when a type of a violence is described
Problem of violence	Desc_problem	when a problem of violence is described
Problem with solutions	Desc_policyfeedback	when current solutions are discussed with unintended problems or additional issues to now consider
Emphasizing working solutions	Desc_solutions	when current solutions are discussed as working or needing to be expanded upon
New interventions	Desc_intervene	when new interventions are described as alternatives or additions
Intervention approach: punitive	Int_punitive	when interventions are described as punitive measures/penalizing the accused/using law enforcement
Intervention approach: restorative	Int_restore	when interventions are discussed as restorative measures for those accused of violence
Intervention approach: social services	Int_socservices	when interventions are discussed to provide immediate services to survivors
Intervention approach: support	Int_support	when interventions are discussed to provide financial or tangible support, cash, housing, shelter
Intervention approach: preventative	Int_prevent	when interventions are discussed as preventative/education and training services
Intervention approach: Federal	Int_federal	expanding a solution to other regions of the United States/places
Intervention approach: Legal	Int_Legal	When interventions are discussed that include mediating and determining legal rights

(continued)

TABLE AI.I (*continued*)

Measure	Code Name	Definition
Identity	Identity	Parent code to capture all the subcodes related to ideology
White	White	whenever the racial identity group "white" is mentioned
Black	Black	whenever the racial identity group "Black" is mentioned
Latina	Latina	whenever the ethnic identity group "Latina" is mentioned
Asian	Asian	whenever the ethnic identity group "Asian" is mentioned
Native/American Indian	Native	whenever the ethnic identity group "American Indian/Native American" is mentioned
Women of color	WOC	whenever the identity group "women of color" is mentioned
LGBTQ	LGBTQ	whenever the identity group "LGBTQ" is mentioned
Immigrants	Immigrants	whenever the identity group "immigrants" is mentioned
Intersectional Advocacy	Intersect_Advocacy	Parent code to capture all the subcodes related to ideology
References a related issue	Ref_related_issue	whenever a related issue to violence is mentioned as a problem that should also be addressed by VAWA
References another law or bill	Ref_bills&laws	whenever another law or bill is referenced as relevant to VAWA legislation
Advocates to revise other bills or laws	Recc_bills&laws	whenever there is a recommendation to link VAWA to another bill or law/revise another relevant bill or law
Backlash to policies	Backlash	whenever advocates mention backlash against a previously implemented policy
Policy wins	Victory	whenever advocates reference policy wins or the successful implementation of a law or policy they advocated for

(*continued*)

TABLE A1.1 *(continued)*

Measure	Code Name	Definition
Compromises or concessions	Compromised	whenever advocates mention having to compromise on their political goals
Type of Advocacy		
Intersectional	Intersectional	Instances of intersectional advocacy: advocating for policy change across issues
Intersectionally marginalized	Multi-issue in VAWA	Instances of multi-issue advocacy: when groups represent intersectionally marginalized groups but stay within VAWA
Single issue	Single issue	Instances of advocacy that only focus on one marginalized group and stay within VAWA
Type of Organization		
Advocacy	Advocacy	Organizations that do national advocacy
Community	Community	Organizations that are grassroots and local organizations
Legal	Legal	Organizations that focus on legal advocacy
National organization	National Organization	Organizations with national branches
Service organization	Service Organization	Organizations that provide services
State coalition	State Coalition	State coalition organizations

CODED HEARINGS, TESTIMONY, STATEMENTS, AND WITNESSES

1. (1) U.S. Senate. 1990. Domestic Violence: Terrorism in the Home. Hearings before the Subcommittee on Children, Family, Drugs and Alcoholism of the Committee on Labor and Human Relations. April 19.

- ○ Women's movement witnesses (broadly conceived):
  - ▪ Mary Pat Brygger, National Woman Abuse Prevention Project (Washington, DC)
  - ▪ Sarah Buel, Harvard Legal Aid Bureau (Cambridge, MA)/also a survivor, personal testimony interwoven with system statistics
  - ▪ Naomi Tropp, The Julian Center (Indianapolis, IN)/shelter program

- Jann Jackson, House of Ruth (Baltimore, MD)/comprehensive shelter program for battered women
- Barbara Zeek-Shaw, Project Safeguard (Denver, CO)/"a grass-roots, non-profit, activist organization which facilitated in 1983 Denver's criminal justice system change from mediation in DV cases to one of holding the criminal responsible for his behavior" via suing the police department
- Association of Junior Leagues International/provides shelter services

- Non-witnesses who also submitted material:
  - N/A

2. (2A) U.S. Senate. 1990a. Women and Violence, Part 1. Hearings before the Committee on the Judiciary. June 20.

- Women's movement witnesses (broadly conceived):
  - Helen R. Neuborne, executive director, Legal Defense and Education Fund, National Organization for Women (New York, NY)

- Non-witnesses who also submitted material:
  - N/A

3. (2B) U.S. Senate. 1990b. Women and Violence, Part 2. Hearings before the Committee on the Judiciary. August 29 and December 11.

- Women's movement witnesses (broadly conceived):
  - Erica Strohl, Cofounder, Students Together Against Acquaintance Rape (Philadelphia, PA)/UPenn student group against acquaintance rape
  - *Sarah Buel (also in the April 19, 1990, hearing) appears again as a witness but this time as the Assistant District Attorney for Massachusetts as well as the supervisor for the Harvard Law School Battered Women's Advocacy Project, indicating slippage between the women's movement/women's advocacy and law enforcement*
  - Susan Kelly-Dreiss, executive director, Pennsylvania Coalition Against Domestic Violence

- Non-witnesses who also submitted material:
  - N/A

4. (3) U.S. Senate. 1991. Domestic Violence: The Struggle for Survival. Hearings before the Subcommittee of the Committee on Appropriations. February 12.

- ○ Women's movement witnesses (broadly conceived):

  - ▪ Ellen Buckley, counselor, Domestic Violence Center/critiques police response to DV in Clark County
  - ▪ Estelle Murphy, director, Domestic Crisis Outreach Center/nonprofit with a variety of services for women experiencing DV
  - ▪ Dr. Evelyn J. Hall, supervising therapist, Temporary Assistance for Domestic Crisis (TADC) Outreach Counseling Program/therapy for DV
  - ▪ Susan Meuschke, executive director, Nevada Network Against Domestic Violence
  - ▪ Helen Foley, Association of Junior Leagues, Las Vegas, NV
  - ▪ Marynne Aaronson, Family Counseling Services
  - ▪ Marge Littlejohns, director, community relations, Committee to Aid Abused Women/community-based nonprofit offering emergency and direct client services to DV victims

- ○ Non-witnesses who also submitted material:
  - ▪ Kay Bennett, Carson City Advocates to End Domestic Violence/crisis hotline, peer counseling/support groups, community outreach, legal services, program training, economic resources, and a shelter

5. (4) U.S. Senate. 1991. Violence Against Women: Victims of the System. Hearings before the Committee on the Judiciary. April 9.

- ○ Women's movement witnesses (broadly conceived):
  - ▪ None

- ○ Non-witnesses who also submitted material:
  - ▪ Dianne Fagner, Iowa Coalition Against Domestic Violence
  - ▪ Elizabeth Bernhill, Iowa Coalition Against Sexual Assault/comprises the twenty rape crisis centers in Iowa

6. (5) U.S. Senate. 1991. Behind Closed Doors: Family Violence in the Home. Hearings before the Subcommittee on Children, Family, Drugs and Alcoholism of the Committee on Labor and Human Resources. July 9.

- ○ Women's movement witnesses (broadly conceived):
  - ▪ Denise Gamache, project director, Whisper (Saint Paul, MN)/DV prevention efforts and school curricula
  - ▪ Jann Jackson, associate director, House of Ruth (Baltimore, MD)/comprehensive DV services

- Anne Menard, executive director, Connecticut Coalition Against Domestic Violence (Hartford, CT)
- Barbara Hart, staff counsel, Pennsylvania Coalition Against Domestic Violence (Reading, PA)

○ Non-witnesses who also submitted material:
- N/A

7. (6) U.S. House. 1992. Violence Against Women. Hearings before the Committee on the Judiciary, Subcommittee on Crime and Criminal Justice. February 6.

○ Women's movement witnesses (broadly conceived):
- Sandra Jean Sands, former president of District of Columbia Coalition Against Domestic Violence (also Office of General Counsel, Department of Health and Human Services, District of Columbia)
- Sherri Sunaz, executive director, Alamo Area Rape Crisis, and president, Texas Association Against Sexual Assault

○ Non-witnesses who also submitted material:
- N/A

8. (7) U.S. Senate. 1993. Hearing on Domestic Violence. Hearings before the Committee on the Judiciary. February 1.

○ Women's movement witnesses (broadly conceived):
- Professor Clare Dalton, director, Domestic Violence Advocacy Project, Northeastern University Law School
- Sarah M. Buel *directs the DV unit at the Suffolk County DA's office but is also director of the Harvard Law School Battered Women's Advocacy Project*
- Marjorie Clapprood, cochair, Jane Doe Safety Fund/fundraising effort for violence prevention and public education

○ Non-witnesses who also submitted material:
- Ann Sanders, executive director, Human Rights Commission (Boston, MA)

9. (8) U.S. House. 1993a. Violent Crimes against Women. Hearings before the Committee on the Judiciary. April 13.

○ Women's movement witnesses (broadly conceived):
- Debra Daniels, assistant executive director, YWCA (Salt Lake City, UT)/also administers the YWCA's Battered Women's Program, is a member of the Governor's Legislative Task Force, and serves as vice chair on Utah Domestic Violence Advisory Council

- Barbara Wood, executive director, Turning Point (Ephraim, UT)/ helps women and children with DV, rape, stalking, and child abuse
- Patricia Millard, behavioral specialist/social worker with New Horizons Crisis Center and Shelter for Women and Children (Richfield, UT)
- Diane Stuart, director, Citizens Against Physical and Sexual Abuse (Logan, UT)
- Karen Nielsen, statewide coordinator for Volunteer Advocates for Victims of Domestic Violence (Salt Lake City, UT)

○ Non-witnesses who also submitted material:
  - N/A

10. (9) U.S. Senate. 1993. Violence Against Women: Fighting the Fear. Hearings before the Committee on the Judiciary. November 12.

○ Women's movement witnesses (broadly conceived):
  - Donna Baietti, director, Battered Women's Project/provides services to abused women and their children
  - Barbara Michaud, Skowhegan Outreach Officer, Augusta Family Violence Project/*marginal case: this seems to be a government crime victims service focused on providing services to victims of DV in particular*
  - Julia Vigue, Rape Crisis Center (Augusta, ME)/member organization of the Maine Coalition Against Rape; *Vigue is also a police officer*

○ Non-witnesses who also submitted material:
  - N/A

11. (10) U.S. House. 1993b. Crimes of Violence Motivated by Gender. Hearings before the Committee on the Judiciary, Subcommittee on Civil and Constitutional Rights. November 16.

○ Women's movement witnesses (broadly conceived):
  - Sally Goldfarb, senior staff attorney, NOW Legal Defense and Education Fund
  - Patricia Ireland, president, National Organization for Women
  - Eleanor Smeal, president, Fund for the Feminist Majority
  - Elizabeth Symonds, legislative counsel, American Civil Liberties Union (ACLU) Women's Rights project

○ Non-witnesses who also submitted material:
  - N/A

12. (11) U.S. Senate. 1994. Elder Abuse and Violence Against Midlife and Older Women. Hearings before the Special Committee on Aging. May 4.

- Women's movement witnesses (broadly conceived):
  - Lou Glasse, president, Older Women's League
  - Joan Kuriansky, Esq., executive director, Older Women's League
  - Pat Reuss, senior policy analyst, NOW Legal Defense and Education Fund (Washington, DC)
- Non-witness "participants from the audience":
  - Judith Bowman, Women's Initiative, AARP
  - Carol Rupel, legislative director, General Federation of Women's Clubs

13. (no # because no relevant witnesses) U.S. Senate. 1994. Fighting Family Violence: Responses of the Health Care System. Hearings before the Special Committee on Aging. June 20.

- Women's movement witnesses (broadly conceived):
  - N/A
- Non-witnesses who also submitted material:
  - N/A

14. (12) U.S. House. 1994. Domestic Violence: Not Just a Family Matter. Hearings before the Committee on the Judiciary. June 30.

- Women's movement witnesses (broadly conceived):
  - Vicki Coffey, executive director, Chicago Abused Women Coalition (Chicago, IL)
  - Debbie Lee, associate director, Family Violence Prevention Fund (San Francisco, CA)
  - Rona Roberts, volunteer, Women's Emergency Services (Salisbury, CT)
  - Joan Zorza, senior attorney, National Battered Women's Law Project of the National Center on Women and Law
- Non-witnesses who also submitted material:
  - Peggy Diggs/marginal case – her role is unclear
  - Ruth Epstein/marginal case – her role is unclear
  - Sally Goldfarb, senior staff attorney, NOW Legal Defense and Education Fund
  - Esta Soler, executive director, Family Violence Prevention Fund

15. (13) U.S. Senate. 1994. Implementation of the Violence Against Women Act. Hearings before the Committee on the Judiciary. September 29.

- ○ Women's movement witnesses (broadly conceived):
  - ▪ Louise Kindley, social worker, St. Luke's-Roosevelt Hospital Center Rape Intervention Program, Crime Victim Assessment Project (New York, NY)/the program is a collaboration between Columbia University and the hospital to provide social workers to rape victims
  - ▪ Sarah Casey, executive director, Schuylkill Women in Crisis (Pottsville, PA)/counseling center and shelter
  - ▪ Mary Beth Semerod, executive director, Rape Crisis Center of Schuylkill County (Pottsville, PA)

- ○ Non-witnesses who also submitted material:
  - ▪ N/A

16. (14) U.S. House. 1994. Domestic Violence as a Public Health Issue. Hearings before the Human Resources and Intergovernmental Relations Subcommittee of the Committee on Government Operations. October 5.

- ○ Women's movement witnesses (broadly conceived):
  - ▪ Nanette Falkenberg, on behalf of executive director, Family Violence Prevention Fund, Health Resource Center on Domestic Violence
  - ▪ Christel Nichols, executive director, House of Ruth (Washington, DC)/battered women's shelter
  - ▪ Esta Soler, executive director, Family Violence Prevention Fund

- ○ Non-witnesses who also submitted material:
  - ▪ N/A

17. (15) U.S. Senate. 1995. Health Insurance and Domestic Violence. Hearings before the Committee on Labor and Human Relations. July 28.

- ○ Women's movement witnesses (broadly conceived):
  - ▪ Nancy E. Durborow, Pennsylvania Coalition Against Domestic Violence (Harrisburg, PA)
  - ▪ Sheila Wellstone/affiliated with the Pennsylvania Coalition Against Domestic Violence; Senator Wellstone's wife

- ○ Non-witnesses who also submitted material:
  - ▪ N/A

18. (16) U.S. Senate. 1995. Violence Against Women. Hearings before a Subcommittee of the Committee on Appropriations. September 12.

   - Women's movement witnesses (broadly conceived):
     - Susan Kelly-Dreiss, the Pennsylvania Coalition Against Domestic Violence

   - Non-witnesses who also submitted material:
     - N/A

19. (17) U.S. Senate. 1996. Combating Violence Against Women. Hearings before the Committee on the Judiciary. May 15.

   - Women's movement witnesses (broadly conceived):

     - Beverly Dusso, executive director, Harriet Tubman Center, Inc.
     - Kathryn J. Rodgers, executive director, NOW Legal Defense and Education Fund

   - Non-witnesses who also submitted material:
     - Delilah Rumburg, executive director, Pennsylvania Coalition Against Rape
     - The Coalition of Labor Union Women
     - Gail Burns-Smith, National Alliance of Sexual Assault Coalitions
     - The National Network on Behalf of Battered Immigrant Women

20. (18) U.S. House. 1999. Violence Against Women Act of 1999, Stalking Prevention and Victim Protection Act of 1999. Hearings before the Committee on the Judiciary, Subcommittee on Crime. September 29.

   - Women's movement witnesses (broadly conceived):
     - Carole J. Alexander, Executive Director, House of Ruth
     - Juley Fulcher, Public Policy Director, National Coalition Against Domestic Violence

   - Non-witnesses who also submitted material:
     - N/A

21. (19) U.S. House. 2000. Battered Immigrant Women Protection Act of 1999. Hearings before the Committee on the Judiciary, Subcommittee on Immigration and Claims. July 20.

   - Women's movement witnesses (broadly conceived):
     - Bree Buchanan, director, public policy, Texas Council on Family Violence
     - Leslye Orloff, director, Immigrant Women Program, NOW Legal Defense and Education Fund
     - Maria Ortiz, Shelter for Abused Women

- ○ Non-witnesses who also submitted material:
  - ▪ N/A

22. (20) U.S. Senate. 2002. Leading the Fight: The Violence Against Women Office. Hearings before the Subcommittee on Crime and Drugs of the Committee on the Judiciary. April 16.

  - ○ Women's movement witnesses (broadly conceived):
    - ▪ Lynn Rosenthal, executive director, National Network to End Domestic Violence
  - ○ Non-witnesses who also submitted material:
    - ▪ N/A

23. (21) U.S. Senate. 2002. Violence Against Women in the Workplace: The Extent of the Problem and What Government and Business Are Doing About It. Hearings before the Committee on Health, Education, Labor, and Pensions. July 25.

  - ○ Women's movement witnesses (broadly conceived):
    - ▪ Kathy Evsich, vice president, Women Against Domestic Violence
    - ▪ Kathy Rodgers, president, NOW Legal Defense and Education Fund
  - ○ Non-witnesses who also submitted material:
    - ▪ N/A

24. (22) U.S. Senate. 2005 Reauthorization of the Violence Against Women Act. Hearings before the Committee on the Judiciary. July 19.

  - ○ Women's movement witnesses (broadly conceived):
    - ▪ Lynn Rosenthal, executive director, National Network to End Domestic Violence
  - ○ Non-witnesses who also submitted material:
    - ▪ ACLU
    - ▪ Marybeth Carter, president, National Alliance to End Sexual Violence
    - ▪ Corita R. Forster, Beloit Domestic Violence Center
    - ▪ Marie F. Kingsbury, executive director, The Women's Center, Inc.
    - ▪ Debbie Lee, managing director for health programs, Family Violence Prevention Fund (Washington, DC)
    - ▪ Elizabeth Kristen, staff attorney, The Legal Aid Society Employment Law Center
    - ▪ Legal Momentum Advancing Women's Rights
    - ▪ Carey Monreal (president, CEO) and Linda Mayfield (director of Family Violence Services), Milwaukee Women's Center
    - ▪ National Coalition Against Domestic Violence

- Deb Hansen, executive director, New Horizons Shelter and Women's Center
- Maggie McCullough, executive director, Friends Aware of Violent Relationships
- Naomi Stern, Domestic Violence Project, National Law Center on Homelessness and Poverty
- Leslye Orloff, associate vice president and director, Immigrant Women Program, Legal Momentum
- Robyn Primley, records specialist, Rainbow House Domestic Abuse Services
- Sheila Przesmicki, executive director, UNIDOS Against Domestic Violence
- Joyce M. Roché, president and CEO, Girls Incorporated
- Delilah Rumberg, executive director, Pennsylvania Coalition Against Rape
- Karen Artichoker, director, Sacred Circle
- Mary Fantanazza, executive director, Safe Harbor Domestic Abuse Shelter
- Tish Stewart, paralegal, Center Against Sexual & Domestic Abuse, Inc.
- Carmen M. Pitre, executive director, Task Force on Family Violence
- Peggy Sanchez Mills, CEO, YWCA USA

25. (23) U.S. House. 2006. Sexual Assault and Violence Against Women in the Military and at the Academies. Hearings before the Subcommittee on National Security, Emerging Threats, and International Relations of the Committee on Government Reform. June 27.

   ○ Women's movement witnesses (broadly conceived):
     - Delilah Rumberg, executive director, Pennsylvania Coalition Against Rape, National Sexual Violence Resource Center

   ○ Non-witnesses who also submitted material:
     - N/A

26. (24) U.S. Senate. 2007. Examining the Prevalence of and Solutions to Stopping Violence Against Indian Women. Hearings before the Committee on Indian Affairs. September 27.

   ○ Women's movement witnesses (broadly conceived):
     - Karen Artichoker, director, Sacred Circle National Resource Center to End Violence Against Native Women
     - Tammy M. Young, director, Alaska Native Women's Coalition

○ Non-witnesses who also submitted material:

- Charon Asetoyer, executive director, Native American Women's Health Education Resource Center
- Helen Parisien, shelter manager, Bridges Against Domestic Violence

27. (25) U.S. Senate. 2009. The Continued Importance of the Violence Against Women Act. Hearings before the Committee on the Judiciary. June 10.

○ Non-witnesses who also submitted material:
- Karen Artichoker
- Family Violence Prevention Fund
- Michelle De La Calle/marginal case – focuses on personal story but also serves as a Sexual Assault Response Team nurse
- Irasema Garza, president, Legal Momentum Advancing Women's Rights
- National Foundation for Women Legislators, Inc.
- Deirdre Raver, cofounder, Women Against Violence
- Karen Tronsgard-Scott, director, Vermont Network Against Domestic and Sexual Violence

28. (26) U.S. Senate. 2010. The Increased Importance of the Violence Against Women Act in a Time of Economic Crisis. Hearings before the Committee on the Judiciary. May 5.

○ Women's movement witnesses (broadly conceived):
- Auburn L. Watersong, economic justice specialist, Vermont Network Against Domestic and Sexual Violence

○ Non-witnesses who also submitted material:
- Wendy Pollack, director of Women's Law and Policy Project at the Sargent Shriver National Center on Policy Project
- Janice Shaw Crouse, Concerned Women for America
- Lisalyn R. Jacobs, vice president of Government Relations at Legal Momentum, Women's Legal Defense and Education Fund

29. (27) U.S. Senate. 2010. Rape in the United States: The Chronic Failure to Report and Investigate Rape Cases. Hearings before the Subcommittee on Crime and Drugs of the Committee on the Judiciary. September 14.

○ Women's movement witnesses (broadly conceived):
- Carol E. Tracy, executive director, Women's Law Project
- Scott Berkowitz, Rape Abuse and Incest National Network (RAINN)
- Lawanda Raviora, director, NCCD Center for Girls and Young Women

- Eleanor Cutri Smeal, president, Feminist Majority Foundation
- Non-witnesses who also submitted material:
  - N/A

30. (28) U.S. Senate. 2011. The Violence Against Women Act: Building on Seventeen Years of Accomplishments. Hearings before the Committee on the Judiciary. July 13.

- Women's movement witnesses (broadly conceived):
  - Jane Van Buren, executive director, Women Helping Battered Women
  - Michael Shaw, codirector, Domestic Violence and Sexual Assault Services at Waypoint Services for Women, Children and Families

RESEARCH APPENDIX 2

Qualitative Case Studies

For each of the organizations, the entire leadership team was interviewed by phone. Interviews were collected between 2019 and 2020 during the ongoing COVID-19 pandemic. Thus, the only way I could conduct these interviews was by phone. The interviews lasted between forty-five minutes and two hours. On average, interviews lasted one hour and were audio-recorded. In total, forty-three interviews were completed and transcribed verbatim. A semi-structured protocol was used that included questions about the organization's history, mission, leadership approach, representation, strategies, policy goals, challenges, and victories. This protocol is shown in the next section.

A semi-structured interview approach was used to adapt to field-specific jargon that advocates used to describe their work and goals, as well as to leave room in the study for additional information about the organization that was relevant to their advocacy efforts. Field notes were also taken during informal and staff meetings with leaders when it was possible to attend them.

In addition to these interviews, organizational documents were collected. Documents included strategic plans, previous research conducted by the organization about its advocacy efforts, and annual reports. These documents were reviewed to triangulate information provided by interviewees. Organizational documents were particularly useful when piecing together the origins and history of each of the organizations to examine when and how they changed incrementally. This study was approved by the Institutional Review Board at the University of Chicago.

INTERVIEW PROTOCOL

Thank you for agreeing to an interview with me. I'm looking forward to learning more about your experiences working for [organization name]. I'd like to take a brief moment to tell you a little about myself before we proceed. I am a doctoral candidate at the University of Chicago working on a research project that focuses on violence against women and how organizations are addressing this issue in different ways. During this interview, I will ask you questions about your organization and your experiences. So you are the expert here, and I am the learner. And if you don't like one of my questions, you do not have to answer. Do you have any questions before we get started? (Answer questions if they come up) Ok, great, let's get started. I will start the recording now.

[start recorder]

Organizational Involvement and Infrastructure

- How would you describe your position with the network, what are you responsible for and what do you do?
- How would you describe your organization and its goals?
- How long have you been involved with this organization? What is your role?
- Has the organization changed over time? How so?
- Who are the leaders of this organization? How did they emerge as leaders?
- Is there a process for developing new leaders in the organization? If so, what is it?
- Who would you say this organization represents? Has that always been the case or has that changed over time?
- How does your organization fund its efforts?
- What are the challenges with funding? Does funding affect the work you are able to do?
- What do you think your organization would do if it had more funding?

Framing and Defining Gender Violence

- How does your organization define violence against women?
- What issues of violence does your organization focus on? Why are those the areas of focus?
- Does gender violence overlap with other issues you are concerned about? If so, which ones? Why are those other issues important for addressing gender violence?
- Probe for *organizational specific issues here.*

Multi-issue Agenda Building

- How does your organization decide which issues to prioritize? What does that process look like? Has it changed over time?
- Have there been disagreements about which issues to focus on? If so, what were the different perspectives? If not, what do you think accounts for the consensus among leaders?

- What strategies do you use to pursue these issues? Do you have different strategies for different issues?
- What parts of the government (such as courts, state-level government, national government) do you believe are most optimal for advancing your political agenda? Why those areas of government?
- What parts of the government are most challenging or resistant to your efforts? Why do you think that is?
- Previously you mentioned the following overlapping issues [repeat these from above], how do you pursue political action that addresses these multiple issues? What do you find challenging about this process? What do you find rewarding about this process?
- Does your organization pursue nongovernment-related strategies to address this issue? What are these strategies and why do you think they are important?
- What compromises and/or concessions (if any) has your organization had to engage in? Why do you think those compromises were necessary? How do you think they affect your long view of your impact on the issue of gender violence?
- Who would you consider allies in this work?(such as other organizations, politicians, media)? What do they contribute to your efforts? Have these changed over time? Under what conditions?
- What about partners in this work? Who would you say are your partners, and why?
- Are there any groups or individuals that you believe are blocking or preventing your efforts? How so?
- How do you plan to sustain your efforts?

Intersectional Policymaking

- What types of policies or programs is your organization currently working on? Why are these the priority now?
- Are there issues that you think need to be addressed alongside your policy agenda? If so, what are those issues? Who is working on them?
- What do you find most challenging about policymaking? What do you find most rewarding?
- What current obstacles are preventing this policy agenda from being implemented?
- Even if it was implemented, what would be the remaining problems and challenges?
- In what ways does the current structure of our government create opportunities for your organization to advocate? In what ways does this same structure prevent or discourage your efforts?

- In what ways, if any, do you think our government has to change in order for your advocacy to be most successful?
- In what ways does government need to change to prevent violence against women?

Multi-identity Politics

- How would you describe your constituents and supporters?
- Why and how does your organization attract these individuals? Does your organization intentionally try to appeal to them, and if so, how? Why these particular individuals?
- Are there any individuals that are excluded from your focus? Who are they?
- Is there a constituent group you would like to engage more that you don't already? What value do you think their support would provide? Why is it difficult to engage them?
- What challenges do you face in appealing to a broader constituent base?
- Is there a collective identity you use to mobilize supporters? If so, how would you describe it?
- How is this identity relevant to your political efforts?

Collaboration and Interpersonal Relationships

- How does your staff communicate with one another?
- How do people work with one another in the organization? What tools or methods does your staff use to collaborate?
- What is your role in the organization? Who do you work with closely and how?
- Who sets the organizational agenda? To what extent do you participate in shaping that agenda?
- What do you find challenging about working for this organization?
- What do you find most rewarding about working for this organization?

COVID-19

- Have there been any changes to your work given COVID? If so, what are they?

CODEBOOK AND APPROACH

Transcripts were uploaded to the software NVivo for coding and analysis. A codebook was developed to capture how organizations advocated to end gender-based violence and to identify when this advocacy resembled intersectional advocacy. It included the following analysis categories: organizational features, representation, leadership, strategies, resources, networks, violence, policy linkages, level and boundary, and reconfiguration. Table A2.1 illustrates these coding categories and the descriptions of the micro-codes that were used in each category. These codes were developed deductively based on existing scholarship and the findings from the analyses of the congressional hearings in Chapter 3. Table 2.1 describes the parent codes, micro-codes, and literature that informed this codebook.

TABLE A2.1 *Codebook scholarship*

Code Category	Scholarship	Description of Codes and Analysis
Organization	Banks et al., 2015; Berry, 2003; Child & Grønbjerg, 2007; Crutchfield & Grant, 2012; Evans et al., 2005; Fox & Maes, 2013; Gen & Wright, 2020a, 2020c; Gronbjerg, 1991; Jang & Feiock, 2007; Kearns et al., 2014; Roos & Manley, 1996; Sargeant et al., 2007	Features of the organization (e.g., mission, founders, organizational structure) that are related to the advocacy pursued by these groups.
Representation	Dwidar, 2021; English, 2021; Junk, 2019; Lorenz, 2020; Marchetti, 2014; Phinney, 2017; Strolovitch, 2007	The identity groups (e.g., race, ethnicity, sexual orientation, class, gender) the organization represents.
Leadership	Andrews & Edwards, 2004; Bierria, 2017; Eisenstein, 1993; Ferree & Martin, 1995; Parker, 2019; Strolovitch, 2007; Williams, 2004	The vision of the organization and the actors that make decisions about advocacy, approach, and strategies.
Strategies	Adler & Wilkerson, 2013; Clemens, 1997; English, 2021; Goss, 2012; Junk, 2019; Mahoney & Thelen, 2010; Phinney, 2017	The strategies that were deployed by the organization, at what part of the policy process, and the extent to which they failed or were successful in reaching their goals.
Resources	Andrews & Edwards, 2004; Gen & Wright, 2020b; Grossmann, 2012; Hansen, 1991; Holyoke, 2011; Lacombe, 2021; Moulton & Eckerd, 2012; Sargeant et al., 2007	The resources (e.g., funding, partnerships, allies, buildings) that were used for each strategy and goal of the organization.

(*continued*)

TABLE A2.1 *(continued)*

Code Category	Scholarship	Description of Codes and Analysis
Networks	Andrews & Edwards, 2004; Chen & Graddy, 2010; Grossmann, 2012; Holman & Schneider, 2018; Silverman, 2008; Stone, 2019	The networks of other individuals, political officials, and additional organizations that shared the goals of the organization or were a part of their strategies to advance their goals.
Violence	Htun & Jensenius, 2020; Ingram et al., 2010; McGuire, 2010; Mills, 1999; Raphael, 2015; Richie, 2012; Smith, 2004; Thuma, 2019; Villalón, 2011	How organizations defined gender-based violence and strategically presented the issue to other stakeholders.
Policy linkages	Brower, 2021	The connections organizations made between the issue of gender-based violence and other issue areas through rhetoric, policies, and practices.
Level and boundary	Faling et al., 2019; Jochim & May, 2010; Jones & Baumgartner, 2005; Michener, 2018; Skocpol, 1992; Thurston, 2018	The governmental level organizations targeted for their advocacy and the types of boundaries they faced at this level.
Reconfiguration	Banaszak et al., 2003; Brower, 2021	When a goal or strategy successfully linked together two issue areas using policies, practices, or legal precedent.

CODEBOOK FOR INTERVIEWS

TABLE A2.2 *Interview codebook*

Identity Politics (Iden)	Parent code to capture when organizations reference specific social identity categories
Iden_Black	When Black people are mentioned
Iden_Latin	When People of Latin or Hispanic descent are mentioned
Iden_Asian	When Asians are mentioned
Iden_White	When white people are mentioned
Iden_Indig	When American Indians or Indigenous people are mentioned

(continued)

TABLE A2.2 *(continued)*

Iden_Men	When men are mentioned
Iden_Child	When children are mentioned
Iden_Noncitizen	When people without citizenship are mentioned
Iden_Poor	When low-income status is mentioned about a group or person
Iden_Disability	When a disability is mentioned about a group or person
Iden_Immigrant	When immigrants are mentioned
Iden_LGBTQ	When members of the LGBTQ are mentioned
Iden_Women	When women are mentioned
Leadership (Lead)	**Parent code to capture the organization's leadership**
Lead_Direct	When leadership roles among directors or executive directors are discussed
Lead_Decisions	How decisions are made about what the organization does and how it does it
Lead_Vision	How leaders or staff imagine the organization's long-term impacts and goals
Lead_Approach	How members describe their leadership approach generally
Strategies (Strat)	**Parent code to capture strategies organizations use**
Strat_Goals	Goals and objectives of the organization
Strat_Process	Specific strategies they mention to reach their goals and objectives
Strat_Victory	Examples of when their strategies worked or succeeded
Strat_Challenges	Challenges organizations encountered when trying to implement their strategies
Resources (Res)	**Parent code to capture the organization's resources and funding**
Res_Funding	Mention funding sources
Res_Material	Mention material resources that are not money (e.g., facilities, transportation)
Res_Shared	Mention sharing resources with another group or entity
Res_Constraints	Mention how they are constrained due to a lack of resources
Network (Net)	**Parent code to capture the networks the organization is a part of**
Net_Partners	Mention groups or individuals they view as partners or collaborators
Net_Allies	Mention groups or individuals that serve as allies for their work
Net_Supporters	Mention supporters of their work outside of the organization
Net_Donors	Mention donors

(continued)

TABLE A2.2 (*continued*)

Violence (V)	**Parent code to capture how the organization frames and describes the issue of violence**
V_defined	How the organization defines violence
V_discussed	How the organization discusses the issue of violence and who it affects
V_impacts	How the organization describes the short-term and long-term impacts of violence
V-Intersects	Whenever a leader mentions issues that intersect with violence
Reconfiguration (Reconfig)	**Parent code to capture the** institutional reconfigurations organizations engage in
Reconfig_Finance	Budget appropriations are changed in how they are presented in the budget
Reconfig_Legal	Laws are mentioned that now refer to more than one issue area
Reconfig_Policy	Policies are mentioned that address more than one issue area
Reconfig_Inst	Institutions are reformed, disbanded, or newly created that address more than one issue are
Institutional Target (Inst)	**Parent code to capture the level of government that organizations are targeting**
Inst_Local	Local government
Inst_City	City government
Inst_State	State government and federalism practices
Inst_Federal	The federal and national government
Inst_Boundaries	When leaders discuss encountering an institutional boundary
Issue Bind (Bind)	**Parent code to capture the specific issue binds that organizations advocate for**
Bind_Immigration	When VAW is connected to immigration
Bind_Housing	When VAW is connected to housing
Bind_CriminalJus	When VAW is connected to criminal justice
Bind_Welfare	When VAW is connected to welfare
Bind_Healthcare	When VAW is connected to healthcare
Bind_Tribal	When VAW is connected to tribal issues, such as land rights
Bind_Education	When VAW is connected to issues of education
Bind_Environment	When VAW is connected to the environment
Bind_Reproductive	When VAW is connected to reproductive rights
Bind_Other	When VAW is connected to other issues not mentioned above

(*continued*)

TABLE A2.2 *(continued)*

Organization (Org)	Parent code to capture organizational history and identity
Org_Start	Mentions how the organization started, its origins, and its infrastructure
Org_Change	Mentions how the organization has changed over time
Org_staff	Mentions the organizational chart, staff responsibilities, and staff roles
Org_Mission	Mentions the mission of the organization
Org_ identity	Describes the organization's role, ethos, values, and norms

QUALITATIVE ANALYSIS (CHAPTER 4)

This analysis mainly draws from an examination of the overarching code categories: identity politics, leadership, strategies, violence, institutional target, issue bind (linkage), and reconfiguration. After each analysis category was fully coded, I used matrix coding queries in NVivo to compare the excerpts from each of these coding categories across the cases of organizations in the qualitative study. Starting with the excerpts from the "issue bind" codes, I applied a within-case analysis (Aronson, 1995; Fereday & Muir-Cochrane, 2006; McFarland et al., 2012).

This analysis entailed noting which policy areas were being linked within each case and examined how this linkage mapped onto the strategies organizations were deploying, their visions for their work, and the level of government that this linkage took place. While examining the level of government that these activities occurred, I also tried to decipher where in the policy process these groups were intervening in and why. I then noted when these strategies and linkages were recorded in "reconfiguration" codes to determine to what extent these efforts were successful. Using the codes to track the boundaries advocates faced, I also noted the challenges they faced and when they failed in meeting their short-term goals. By examining the challenges and institutional boundaries, I was able to trace the incrementalism strategy that is presented in Chapter 4.

To examine themes across cases, I used cross-case axial coding to identify common strategies, approaches, and goals (Merriam & Tisdell, 2015). Although, each case included unique strategies, activities, and motivations, I needed to cross-check that each case was indeed advocating for the policy linkages I observed in the congressional hearings. Going through each individual case, I checked for (1) issue linkages, (2) policy linkages, (3) institutional boundary crossing, and (4) policy infrastructure. I then checked if these linkages were directly related to representing and advocating for multiply marginalized groups. This process of cross-case axial coding ensured that I was able to provide both a within and across analysis of the cases in this qualitative study.

QUALITATIVE ANALYSIS (CHAPTER 5)

This analysis mainly draws from an examination of the code categories: representation, organizational characteristics, leadership approach, resources, and networks. For each organization individually examined, excerpts that fell into these coding categories were organized by theme and then were compared across organizations to locate similarities and differences among them. I cross-examined advocacy strategies, approaches, leadership styles, and goals of the organization – all characteristics that explained each organization's unique approach to advocacy. This analysis allowed for the noting of commonalities and differences among the organizations to determine to what extent organizations were practicing intersectional advocacy and to what extent they were not. I then used cross-case axial coding to identify relevant structural differences and similarities among these organizations (Merriam & Tisdell, 2015).

Cross-case axial coding helped with determining four common characteristics among the organizations included in this study: (1) the origins of the organization and its accompanying leadership structure, (2) the representation of intersectionally marginalized groups, (3) their relevant networks for advocacy, and (4) their funding strategies and resource allocation. In Chapter 5, I presented an analysis of each of the organizational case studies broken down according to these four characteristics to explain the relationships between organizational structures and intersectional advocacy (or lack thereof). These findings describe the different types of organizational features that can support intersectional advocacy and the types of leadership that encourage this practice. At the end of this process, what emerged was that each organization had a unique origin and infrastructure that helped explain its overall capacity to engage in intersectional advocacy.

A typology was created based on this information to explain which organizations engage in intersectional advocacy, to what extent there were common organizational characteristics that shaped this advocacy, and the ways in which these characteristics differed by organizational context and structure. This analytical approach demonstrates both comparison and within-case variation – to illustrate the differences between organizations and across organizations.

RESEARCH APPENDIX 3

Experimental Methods

TABLE A3.1 *Random assignment by personal income*

	Experiment 1: Control	Experiment 1: Treatment	Experiment 2: Control	Experiment 2: Treatment
Under $15k	57	65	71	51
$15k–$29k	65	52	58	59
$30k–$49k	87	84	88	83
$50k–$74k	84	79	83	80
$75k–$99k	39	41	37	43
$100k–$249k	21	19	15	25
$250k+	6	6	4	8

TABLE A3.2 *Random assignment by race/ethnicity*

	Experiment 1: Control	Experiment 1: Treatment	Experiment 2: Control	Experiment 2: Treatment
Asian	27	30	27	30
Biracial	18	21	17	22
Black	60	51	58	53
Hispanic	55	61	52	64
Native American	19	17	22	14
Other	1	1	2	0
White	209	182	201	190

TABLE A3.3 *Random assignment by supporter type*

	Experiment 1: Control	Experiment 1: Treatment	Experiment 2: Control	Experiment 2: Treatment
Volunteer council	90	78	79	89
Board member	37	46	39	44
Email subscriber	229	219	221	227
Action network subscriber	65	54	53	66
Donor	63	49	60	52
Event attendee	121	114	115	120
Partner organization staff	45	44	54	35
Social media follower	101	88	95	94

ORDINARY LEAST SQUARES (OLS) TIME SERIES ANALYSES

TABLE A3.4 *Ordinary least squares (OLS) time series for selecting to sign a petition (Experiment 1)*

Variables	All Supporters
Time of survey	0.312
	(0.0004)
Treatment	−1.98*
	(0.0350)
Constant	10.521***
	(0.0374)
Observations	756
Standard errors in parentheses ***$p < 0.01$, **$p < 0.05$ *$p < 0.01$	

TABLE A3.5 *OLS time series for selecting to sign a petition (Experiment 2)*

Variables	All Supporters
Time of survey	0.819
	(0.0003)
Treatment	17.3***
	(0.0306)
Constant	7.6***
	(0.0331)
Observations	756
Standard errors in parentheses ***$p < 0.01$, **$p < 0.05$ *$p < 0.01$	

T-TEST RESULTS

TABLE A3.6 *Full* t-*test results*

Dependent Variable	Control Mean and Standard Error	Treatment Mean and Standard Error	Degrees of Freedom	Significance
Signing a petition (Figure A3.8)	0.4206349 (0.024865)	0.2622951 (0.02457366)	756	$p < 0.05$
Signing a petition [among women of color] (Figure A3.9)	0.4206349 (0.04415438)	0.2622951 (0.03998929)	244	$p < 0.01$
Signing a petition (Figure A3.10)	0.2736842 (0.02481449)	0.8047493 (0.02478723)	748	$p < 0.0001$
Selecting to participate in political actions [all participants] (Figure A3.11)	2.386842 (0.08666149)	2.562005 (0.09307911)	748	$p < 0.0001$
Selecting to participate in political actions [women of color] (Figure A3.11)	2.077465 (0.1321084)	2.698113 (0.1744038)	241	$p < 0.01$
Selecting to participate in calling legislatures (Figure A3.12)	0.1408451 (0.04183945)	0.2452830 (0.04621679)	241	$p < 0.05$
Selecting to participate in attending community events (Figure A3.12)	0.4436620 (0.04621679)	0.5754717 (0.03518629)	241	$p < 0.05$
Selecting to participate in an annual fundraiser (Figure A3.12)	0.1408451 (0.04823593)	0.2358491 (0.04823593)	241	$p < 0.05$
Selecting to subscribe to petition alerts (Figure A3.12)	0.2253521 (0.03518629)	0.3396226 (0.03518629)	241	$p < 0.05$
Selecting to take future action among Latinas (Figure A3.13)	1.923077 (0.06980655)	2.703125 (0.06296331)	107	$p < 0.01$

EXPERIMENT I: CONDITIONS

The Challenge

The minimum wage is a serious issue and one of its most damaging aspects is the subminimum wage paid to tipped workers. Women in low-paid industries, especially those who rely on tips, are the most underpaid. Women of color, LGBTQ+ folks, people with disabilities, immigrants, and refugees are especially vulnerable and have fewer protections available to them. That is why we need a to focus on increasing their protections by eliminating the subminimum wage.

What We're Doing

WE fight to ensure that working women, especially those who are most marginalized in the workforce (i.e., women of color, low-paid working people, immigrants) are protected. To do so, we focus directly on laws that eliminate the subminimum wage for tipped workers. <u>WE believe pay inequality will only be eradicated if we prioritize policy interventions that fully address it.</u>

FIGURE A3.1 Control: subminimum wage

The Challenge

Sexual violence is a serious issue in the workplace. Women in low-paid industries, especially those who rely on tips, report this issue at the highest rates. Women of color, LGBTQ+ folks, people with disabilities, immigrants, and refugees are especially vulnerable and have fewer protections available to them. That is why we need to focus on increasing their protections by strengthening the laws around sexual harassment and assault in the workplace.

What We're Doing

WE fight to ensure that working women, especially those who are most marginalized in the workforce (i.e., women of color, low-paid workers, immigrants) are protected. To do so, we focus directly on laws that address sexual harassment and assault in the workforce. <u>WE believe that sexual violence in the workplace will only be eradicated if we prioritize policy interventions that fully address it.</u>

FIGURE A3.2 Control: sexual violence

The Challenge

The minimum wage is a serious issue and one of its most damaging aspects is the subminimum wage paid to tipped workers. Women who rely on tips are not only underpaid but are also more vulnerable to other issues such as sexual violence. Women of color, LGBTQ+ folks, people with disabilities, immigrants, and refugees are especially vulnerable and have fewer protections available to them. That is why we need a multifaceted approach to solving this issue that includes eliminating the subminimum wage **AND** addressing sexual harassment and assault in these industries.

What We're Doing

WE fight to ensure that working women, especially those who are most marginalized in the workforce (i.e., women of color, low-paid working people, immigrants) are protected. To do so, we focus on multiple issues that exacerbate this problem. WE are pushing to eliminate the subminimum wage for tipped workers while ALSO advocating for laws that protect these same workers in low-paid industries from sexual harassment and assault. <u>WE believe that pay inequality can only be eradicated if we prioritize multi-issue policy interventions that address both this issue and interrelated ones like sexual violence in the workplace.</u>

FIGURE A3.3 Treatment: subminimum wage

The Challenge

Sexual violence is a serious issue among vulnerable workers. Women in low-paid industries who rely on tips experience this issue at the highest rates. Women of color, LGBTQ+ folks, people with disabilities, immigrants, and refugees are especially vulnerable and have fewer protections available to them. That is why we need a multifaceted approach to solving this issue that includes addressing sexual harassment and assault in the workplace **AND** eliminating the subminimum wage for tipped workers.

What We're Doing

WE fight to ensure that working women, especially those who are most marginalized in the workforce (i.e., women of color, low-paid workers, immigrants) are protected. To do so, we focus on multiple issues that exacerbate this problem. WE are advocating for laws that protect workers from sexual harassment and assault while ALSO pushing to eliminate the subminimum wage for tipped workers, a practice that leaves them especially vulnerable to harassment and abuse. <u>WE believe that sexual violence in the workplace can only be eradicated if we prioritize multi-issue policy interventions that address both this issue and interrelated ones like pay inequality.</u>

FIGURE A3.4 Treatment: sexual violence

The Challenge

COVID-19 has made it clear that for working people who have caregiving roles both as part of their professional lives and their home lives, the public health crisis has increased their caretaking responsibilities exponentially. Unfortunately, too many workers don't have the resources from their employers to fulfill these roles, especially those working in low-paid sectors who don't have access to paid leave. That is why we need to focus on increasing caregiving resources for these employees.

What We're Doing

WE fight to ensure that women, especially those who are most marginalized in the workforce (i.e., women of color, low-paid workers, immigrants) are eligible for paid sick time and paid family and medical leave. To do so, WE are fighting for more emergency resources for families so that they can access paid family and medical leave to be used for their caregiving needs. <u>WE believe we can only address this issue if we prioritize policy interventions that fully address it.</u>

FIGURE A3.5 Control: caregiving

The Challenge

COVID-19 has made it clear that working people need time off from work to care for themselves and their families so that they don't have to choose between their paycheck and their health. Unfortunately, 80% of the lowest-paid working people do not have access to a single paid sick day, and only 15% have access to paid family and medical leave through their employers. That is why we need to focus on getting paid leave for all working people.

What We're Doing

WE fight to ensure that women, especially those who are most marginalized in the workforce (i.e., women of color, low-paid workers, immigrants) are eligible for paid family and sick leave. To do so, WE are pushing to pass laws in Illinois that would give working people up to 12 weeks of paid family and medical leave, and up to 5 permanent paid sick days for use in COVID and beyond. <u>WE believe we can only address this issue if we prioritize policy interventions that fully address it.</u>

FIGURE A3.6 Control: paid leave

The Challenge

COVID-19 has made it clear that for working people who have caregiving roles both as part of their professional lives and their home lives, the public health crisis has increased their caretaking responsibilities exponentially. Unfortunately, too many workers don't have the resources from their employers to fulfill these roles, especially those working in low-paid sectors who don't have access to paid leave. They need paid time off from work to care their families so that they don't have to choose between their paycheck and their health. That is why we need to focus on getting workers caregiving resources <u>AND</u> paid-family and sick leave.

What We're Doing

WE fight to ensure that women, especially those who are most marginalized in the workforce (i.e., women of color, low-paid workers, immigrants) are eligible for paid sick time and paid family and medical leave. To do so, WE are pushing to pass laws in Illinois that would give working people up to 12 weeks of paid family and medical leave and up to 5 permanent paid sick days for use in COVID and beyond. To ALSO address caregiving needs we are advocating for these days to be eligible for taking care of children out of school, elderly, and young children. <u>WE believe we can only address this issue if we prioritize multi-issue policy interventions that address both sick and medical leave as well as interrelated needs such as caregiving.</u>

FIGURE A3.7 Treatment: caregiving

The Challenge

COVID-19 has made it clear that working people need time off from work to care for themselves and their families so that they don't have to choose between their paycheck and their health. Unfortunately, 80% of the lowest-paid working people do not have access to a single paid sick day, and only 15% have access to paid family and medical leave through their employers. For those who have caregiving roles both as part of their professional lives and their home lives, the public health crisis has increased their caretaking responsibilities exponentially. That is why we are advocating for workers to be able to use these days to <u>ALSO</u> care for children or adults.

What We're Doing

WE fight to ensure that women, especially those who are most marginalized in the workforce (i.e., women of color, low-paid workers, immigrants) are eligible for paid family and sick leave. To do so, WE are pushing to pass laws in Illinois that would give working people up to 12 weeks of paid family and medical leave and up to 5 permanent paid sick days for use in COVID and beyond. To ALSO address caregiving needs we are advocating for these days to be eligible for taking care of children out of school, elderly, and young children. <u>WE believe we can only address this issue if we prioritize multi-issue policy interventions that address both sick and medical leave as well as interrelated needs such as caregiving.</u>

FIGURE A3.8 Treatment: paid leave

POST-CONDITION SURVEY ITEMS

Posttreatment Survey Items/Dependent Variables (DV): Following the experimental condition, respondents were asked the following questions:

1. **DV 1:** Women Employed has put together a legislative petition for this issue. Would you be interested in signing the petition? It includes signing your name and sending a comment to your Congress representative to support this action.

   - Yes, take me to the petition
   - No thanks, continue with the survey

2. **DV 2:** There are many opportunities to get more involved with Women Employed to address the issue of sexual harassment. Which of the following activities would you be interested in participating in? (Check all that apply)

   - Making a donation
   - Subscribing to the e-newsletter
   - Subscribing to legislative action alert emails
   - Joining for in-person visits to legislators
   - Attending a community engagement event
   - Buying a ticket to the annual fundraiser luncheon
   - Joining a volunteer council
   - None of these activities
   - Other_____

If respondents, selected they wanted to sign a petition they were provided with an actual petition and asked to sign it. These were the following petitions they received. This is not the measure of the DV, because the petitions themselves act as their own control and treatment conditions. But they needed to be provided to make the petition an authentic part of the survey experiment:

POSTTREATMENT PETITIONS

Petition for the Be HEARD Act:

*I believe that ALL working people deserve access to safe and respectful workplaces that are free from sexual violence. The **BE HEARD Act** is an essential step towards ensuring equity for all. Sexual harassment and assault in the workplace keeps women from advancing in their careers in so many ways— either because they face retaliation, or because they are forced to leave jobs and careers when their harassers or perpetrators are not held accountable. It is fundamentally detrimental to equality. And yet, sexual harassment and assault remains a widespread problem, affecting women–as well as non-binary people and men – in every kind of workplace setting and at every level of employment. This is why we must pass BE HEARD, the first comprehensive federal legislation that would fix our broken laws to prevent workplace harassment and abuse.*

FIGURE A3.9 Petition for control: sexual violence

Petition for One Fair Wage:

*I believe that all working people—including women and people of color—deserve a full, fair wage, which is why I am urging my elected officials to eliminate the sub-minimum tipped wage. Subminimum wages for tipped workers keep millions in poverty. Over two-thirds of the nation's six million tipped workers are women— disproportionately women of color—and 36 percent of them are mothers. Servers are 2.6 times more likely to live in poverty than the overall workforce. Working families should be able to earn enough to afford basic necessities and seek opportunities for a better economic future. This must include passing **One Fair Wage** to eliminate the sub-minimum tipped wage in Illinois and nationwide.*

FIGURE A3.10 Petition for control: subminimum wage

Petition for the Be HEARD Act & One Fair Wage:

I believe that ALL working people should have access to workplaces where they are treated with respect and are paid fairly. It is imperative that we pass and enforce laws that protect workers from sexual violence, including passing the **BE HEARD Act**—*federal legislation that would ensure all of us are protected from sexual harassment and assault on the job, no matter who we are or where we work. And we need to pass* **One Fair Wage** *to eliminate the sub-minimum tipped wage in Illinois and nationwide, because workers are especially vulnerable to sexual harassment when they rely on tips for wages and their work requires them to please customers.*

FIGURE A3.11 Petition for treatment: sexual violence and subminimum wage

Petition for the HEROES Act:

I believe that paid leave is an essential resource all workers should have access to—especially during the ongoing coronavirus pandemic—which is why I urge my members of Congress to pass the HEROES Act. In the next major relief package, Congress must prioritize the needs of working women and families by incorporating critical paid leave policies. That means passing the **HEROES Act**, *which will:*

- *Ensure all workers have 14 emergency paid sick days and up to 12 weeks of emergency paid family and medical leave for a wider range of reasons, including COVID-19-related medical and family issues*

- *Extend paid leave benefits through 2021*

- *Provide permanent paid sick time and paid family and medical leave that mirrors the protections included in the Healthy Families Act and the FAMILY Act*

- *And include immigrants and undocumented residents, who have disproportionately been doing the essential work that's keeping our economy going*

FIGURE A3.12 Petition for control: paid leave

Petition for the HEROES Act:

I believe all working people need access to childcare and caregiving supports—especially during the ongoing coronavirus pandemic—which is why I urge my members of Congress to pass the HEROES Act. In the next major relief package, Congress must prioritize the needs of working women and families by incorporating caregiving supports. That means passing the **HEROES** *Act, which will:*

- *Extend paid leave benefits through 2021*

- *Provide $7 billion in dedicated funding for childcare*

- *Provide $850 million for child and family care for essential workers*

- *Expand the caregiving reasons for taking paid leave, including allowing for care of family members*

- *Clarify that paid leave provided in previous relief packages, taken for COVID-19 reasons, does not count against regular Family and Medical Leave Act (FMLA) leave*

FIGURE A3.13 Petition for control: caregiving

Petition for the HEROES Act:

I believe all working people need access to paid leave, childcare, and caregiving supports—especially during the ongoing coronavirus pandemic—which is why I urge my members of Congress to pass the HEROES Act. In the next major relief package, Congress must prioritize the needs of working women and families passing the HEROES Act, which will:

- *Ensure all workers have 14 emergency paid sick days and up to 12 weeks of emergency paid family and medical leave for a wider range of reasons, including COVID-19-related medical and care of family members with COVID-19-related medical issues*

- *Extend paid leave benefits through 2021*

- *Provide permanent paid sick time and paid family and medical leave that mirrors the protections included in the Healthy Families Act and the FAMILY Act,*

- *Provide $7 billion in dedicated funding for childcare,*

- *Provide $850 million for child and family care for essential workers*

- *Clarify that paid leave provided in previous relief packages, taken for COVID-19 reasons, does not count against regular Family and Medical Leave Act (FMLA) leave*

FIGURE A3.14 Petition for treatment: paid leave and caregiving

Under their signature for the petition, participants were asked:

3. **Qualitative Question:** WE will be including messages with this petition to make this advocacy more compelling. Can you write a personalized message below for us to include with your signature?

References

Abramovitz, M. (2017). *Regulating the Lives of Women: Social Welfare Policy from Colonial Times to the Present*. Routledge. https://doi.org/10.4324/9781315228150.

Ackerman, G., Anderson, B., Jensen, S., & Ludwig, R. (2001). Crime Rates and Confidence in the Police: America's Changing Attitudes toward Crime and Police, 1972–1999. *Journal of Sociology and Social Welfare*, 28, 43.

Adams, J. (2007). *The Familial State: Ruling Families and Merchant Capitalism in Early Modern Europe*. Cornell University Press.

Adler, E. S., & Wilkerson, J. D. (2013). *Congress and the Politics of Problem Solving*. Cambridge University Press.

Ahnen, R. E. (2007). The Politics of Police Violence in Democratic Brazil. *Latin American Politics and Society*, 49(1), 141–164.

Aizer, A. (2010). The Gender Wage Gap and Domestic Violence. *The American Economic Review*, 100(4), 1847–1859. https://doi.org/10.1257/aer.100.4.1847.

Ake, J., & Arnold, G. (2017). A Brief History of Anti-violence Against Women Movements in the United States. In C. Renzetti, J. L. Edleson, & R. Bergen (Eds.), *Sourcebook on Violence Against Women* (pp. 3–25). Sage.

Alexander, M. (2020). *The New Jim Crow: Mass Incarceration in the Age of Colorblindness*. New Press.

Alex-Assensoh, Y., & Stanford, K. (1999). Gender, Participation, and the Black Urban Underclass. In C. Cohen, K. Jones, & J. C. Tronto (Eds.), *Women Transforming Politics: An Alternative Reader* (pp. 398–411). New York University Press.

Alvarez, S. E. (1990). *Engendering Democracy in Brazil: Women's Movements in Transition Politics*. Princeton University Press.

Andrews, K. T., & Edwards, B. (2004). Advocacy Organizations in the U.S. Political Process. *Annual Review of Sociology*, 30(1), 479–506. https://doi.org/10.1146/annurev.soc.30.012703.110542.

Appiah, A., & Gates, H. L. (Eds.). (2005). *Africana: The Encyclopedia of the African and African American Experience*. Oxford University Press.

Arnold, G. (2017). U.S. Women's Movements to End Violence against Women, Domestic Abuse, and Rape. In H. J. McCammon, V. Taylor, J. Reger, & R. L. Einwohner (Eds.), *The Oxford Handbook of U.S. Women's Social Movement Activism* (pp. 270–290). Oxford University Press.

Arnold, R. D. (1992). *The Logic of Congressional Action.* Yale University Press.

Aronson, J. (1995). A Pragmatic View of Thematic Analysis. *The Qualitative Report,* 2 (1), 1–3.

Arvin, M., Tuck, E., & Morrill, A. (2013). Decolonizing Feminism: Challenging Connections between Settler Colonialism and Heteropatriarchy. *Feminist Formations,* 25(1), 8–34.

Aszman, J. (2011). *Going Back to Go Forward: A Brief History of Women of Color in Georgia's DC Movement.* https://d3vnvedzfq7zpv.cloudfront.net/content/uploads/20161005085917/WOC-in-DV-Movement-in-GA.pdf.

Babcox, D., & Belkin, M. (1971). *Liberation Now! Writings from the Women's Liberation Movement* (Vol. 4787). Dell Publishing Company.

Baker, B. A. (2006). Art Speaks in Healing Survivors of War: The Use of Art Therapy in Treating Trauma Survivors. *Journal of Aggression, Maltreatment & Trauma,* 12(1–2), 183–198. https://doi.org/10.1300/J146v12n01_10.

Banaszak, L. A., Beckwith, K., & Rucht, D. (Eds.). (2003). *Women's Movements Facing the Reconfigured State.* Cambridge University Press.

Banks, N., Hulme, D., & Edwards, M. (2015). NGOs, States, and Donors Revisited: Still Too Close for Comfort? *World Development,* 66, 707–718. https://doi.org/10.1016/j.worlddev.2014.09.028.

Barbosa, S. D., & Fayolle, A. (2007). Where Is the Risk? Availability, Anchoring, and Framing Effects on Entrepreneurial Risk Taking. *Frontiers of Entrepreneurship Research,* 27(6), 1–15.

Bauer, R. A., Pool, I. D. S., & Dexter, L. A. (1972). *American Business and Public Policy: The Politics of Foreign Trade.* Transaction Publishers.

Baugus, B., & Bose, F. (2015). Sunset Legislation in the States: Balancing the Legislature and the Executive. Social Science Research Network (SSRN) Paper ID No. 3211623. https://doi.org/10.2139/ssrn.3211623.

Beal, F., Norton, E., & Weisstein, N. (1970). Double Jeopardy. In R. Morgan (Ed.), *Sisterhood Is Powerful: An Anthology of Writings from the Women's Liberation Movement* (pp. 340–352). Random House.

Béland, D. (2009). Ideas, Institutions, and Policy Change. *Journal of European Public Policy,* 16(5), 701–718. https://doi.org/10.1080/13501760902983382.

Béland, D., & Waddan, A. (2012). *The Politics of Policy Change: Welfare, Medicare, and Social Security Reform in the United States.* Georgetown University Press.

Bell, M. C. (2016). Situational Trust: How Disadvantaged Mothers Reconceive Legal Cynicism. *Law & Society Review,* 50(2), 314–347. https://doi.org/10.1111/lasr.12200.

Bergen, R. K., & Barnhill, E. (2006). *Marital Rape: New Research and Directions.* National Resource Center on Domestic Violence.

Bergoffen, D., Gilbert, P. R., Harvey, T., & McNeely, C. L. (2010). *Confronting Global Gender Justice: Women's Lives, Human Rights.* Routledge.

Berry, J. M. (2003). *A Voice for Nonprofits.* Brookings Institution Press.

Bhuyan, R., & Senturia, K. (2005). Understanding Domestic Violence Resource Utilization and Survivor Solutions among Immigrant and Refugee Women: Introduction to the Special Issue. *Journal of Interpersonal Violence,* 20(8), 895–901. https://doi.org/10.1177/0886260505277676.

Bierria, A. (2017). Pursuing a Radical Anti-violence Agenda Inside/Outside a Non-profit Structure. In Andrea Smith (Ed.), *The Revolution Will Not Be Funded* (pp. 151–164).

Duke University Press. www.degruyter.com/document/doi/10.1515/9780822373001-014/html.

Blackhawk, M., Carpenter, D., Resch, T., & Schneer, B. (2021). Congressional Representation by Petition: Assessing the Voices of the Voteless in a Comprehensive New Database, 1789–1949. *Legislative Studies Quarterly*, 46(3), 817–849. https://doi.org/10.1111/lsq.12305.

Blackhawk, N. (2009). *Violence Over the Land: Indians and Empires in the Early American West*. Harvard University Press.

Blackwell, M. (2016). *¡Chicana Power! Contested Histories of Feminism in the Chicano Movement*. University of Texas Press.

Bograd, M. (1999). Strengthening Domestic Violence Theories: Intersections of Race, Class, Sexual Orientation, and Gender. *Journal of Marital and Family Therapy*, 25(3), 275–289.

Bonner, M. D. (2009). State Discourses, Police Violence and Democratisation in Argentina. *Bulletin of Latin American Research*, 28(2), 227–245. https://doi.org/10.1111/j.1470-9856.2008.00270.x.

Bordt, R. L. (1997). *The Structure of Women's Nonprofit Organizations*. Indiana University Press.

Bosso, C. J. (2003). Rethinking the Concept of Membership in Nature Advocacy Organizations. *Policy Studies Journal*, 31(3), 397–411. https://doi.org/10.1111/1541-0072.00030.

Bound, J., & Turner, S. (2002). Going to War and Going to College: Did World War II and the G.I. Bill Increase Educational Attainment for Returning Veterans? *Journal of Labor Economics*, 20(4), 784–815. https://doi.org/10.1086/342012.

Bourdieu, P. (1998). *Practical Reason: On the Theory of Action*. Stanford University Press.

Brasher, V. D. (2006). Constitutional Law-Wallace v. City of Chicago: When the Heck Do Section 1983 Claims Arising under Violations of the Fourth Amendment Accrue. *American Journal of Trial Advocacy*, 30, 433.

Breines, W. (2002). What's Love Got to Do with It? White Women, Black Women, and Feminism in the Movement Years. *Signs*, 27(4), 1095–1133. https://doi.org/10.1086/339634.

Brower, M. T. (2021). How She Reconfigures the State: Intersectional Advocacy and the Movement against Violence. PhD dissertation, University of Chicago.

Brower, M. T. (2022). Reframing Gendered Issues: Intersectional Identity Frames and Policy Agendas. *Political Behavior*, 1–23. https://doi.org/10.1007/s11109-022-09833-y.

Brower, M. T., & Michener, J. (2021). Latina and Black Women Lost Jobs in Record Numbers: Policies Designed for All Women Don't Necessarily Help. *Washington Post*, February 9. www.washingtonpost.com/politics/2021/02/09/latina-black-women-lost-jobs-record-numbers-policies-designed-all-women-dont-necessarily-help/.

Browne, I. (Ed.). (2000). *Latinas and African American Women at Work: Race, Gender, and Economic Inequality*. Russell Sage Foundation.

Bruyneel, K. (2007). *The Third Space of Sovereignty: The Postcolonial Politics of U.S.-Indigenous Relations*. University of Minnesota Press.

Bumiller, K. (2009). *In an Abusive State: How Neoliberalism Appropriated the Feminist Movement against Sexual Violence*. Duke University Press.

Burns, G. (2005). *The Moral Veto: Framing Contraception, Abortion, and Cultural Pluralism in the United States.* Cambridge University Press.

Burns, N., & Kinder, D. (2012). Categorical Politics: Gender, Race, and Public Opinion. In A. J. Berinsky (Ed.), *New Directions in Public Opinion* (1st ed.). Routledge. https://doi.org/10.4324/9780203839836.

Burns, S., Eberhardt, L., & Merolla, J. L. (2013). What Is the Difference between a Hockey Mom and a Pit Bull? Presentations of Palin and Gender Stereotypes in the 2008 Presidential Election. *Political Research Quarterly, 66*(3), 687–701. https://doi.org/10.1177/1065912912471974.

Burstein, P., & Hirsh, C. E. (2007). Interest Organizations, Information, and Policy Innovation in the U.S. Congress. *Sociological Forum, 22*(2), 174–199. https://doi.org/10.1111/j.1573-7861.2007.00012.x.

Burton, O., Rawstorne, P., Watchirs-Smith, L., Nathan, S., & Carter, A. (2023). Teaching Sexual Consent to Young People in Education Settings: A Narrative Systematic Review. *Sex Education, 23*(1), 18–34. https://doi.org/10.1080/14681811.2021.2018676.

Calton, J. M., Cattaneo, L. B., & Gebhard, K. T. (2016). Barriers to Help Seeking for Lesbian, Gay, Bisexual, Transgender, and Queer Survivors of Intimate Partner Violence. *Trauma, Violence, & Abuse, 17*(5), 585–600. https://doi.org/10.1177/1524838015585318.

Calvo, J. (2004). A Decade of Spouse-Based Immigration Laws: Coverture's Diminishment, but Not Its Demise. *Northern Illinois University Law Review, 24*(2), 153–210.

Campbell, A. L. (2012). Policy Makes Mass Politics. *Annual Review of Political Science, 15*, 333–351.

Cannuscio, C. C., Alley, D. E., Pagán, J. A., et al. (2012). Housing Strain, Mortgage Foreclosure, and Health. *Nursing Outlook, 60*(3), 134–142. https://doi.org/10.1016/j.outlook.2011.08.004.

Carpenter, D. (2016). Recruitment by Petition: American Antislavery, French Protestantism, English Suppression. *Perspectives on Politics, 14*(3), 700–723. https://doi.org/10.1017/S1537592716001134.

Carpenter, D., & Moore, C. D. (2014). When Canvassers Became Activists: Antislavery Petitioning and the Political Mobilization of American Women. *American Political Science Review, 108*(3), 479–498. https://doi.org/10.1017/S000305541400029X.

Carruthers, C. (2018). *Unapologetic: A Black, Queer, and Feminist Mandate for Radical Movements.* Beacon Press.

Cassese, E. C., Barnes, T. D., & Branton, R. P. (2015). Racializing Gender: Public Opinion at the Intersection. *Politics & Gender, 11*(01), 1–26. https://doi.org/10.1017/S1743923X14000567.

Castillo, S., & Schweitzer, I. (Eds.). (2001). *The Literatures of Colonial America: An Anthology.* Wiley. www.wiley.com/en-us/The+Literatures+of+Colonial+America%3A+An+Anthology-p-9780631211259.

Chen, B., & Graddy, E. A. (2010). The Effectiveness of Nonprofit Lead-Organization Networks for Social Service Delivery. *Nonprofit Management and Leadership, 20*(4), 405–422. https://doi.org/10.1002/nml.20002.

Chen, C.-J. (2007). The Difference That Differences Make: Asian Feminism and the Politics of Difference. *Asian Journal of Women's Studies, 13*(3), 7–36. https://doi.org/10.1080/12259276.2007.11666028.

Chen, S. W. (2000). The Immigrant Women of the Violence Against Women Act: The Role of the Asian American Consciousness in the Legislative Process. *Georgetown Journal of Gender and the Law*, *1*(3), 823–848.

Chesney-Lind, M. (2002). Criminalizing Victimization: The Unintended Consequences of Pro-Arrest Policies for Girls and Women. *Criminology & Public Policy*, *2*(1), 81–90. https://doi.org/10.1111/j.1745-9133.2002.tb00108.x.

Chetty, R., Grusky, D., Hell, M., et al. (2017). The Fading American Dream: Trends in Absolute Income Mobility since 1940. *Science*, *356*(6336), 398–406. https://doi.org/10.1126/science.aal4617.

Child, C. D., & Grønbjerg, K. A. (2007). Nonprofit Advocacy Organizations: Their Characteristics and Activities. *Social Science Quarterly*, *88*(1), 259–281. https://doi.org/10.1111/j.1540-6237.2007.00457.x.

Cho, S., Crenshaw, K. W., & McCall, L. (2013). Toward a Field of Intersectionality Studies: Theory, Applications, and Praxis. *Signs: Journal of Women in Culture and Society*, *38*(4), 785–810. https://doi.org/10.1086/669608.

Chong, D., & Druckman, J. N. (2007). Framing Theory. *Annual Review of Political Science*, *10*(1), 103–126. https://doi.org/10.1146/annurev.polisci.10.072805.103054.

Claiborne, W. (1996). Abused Immigrant Slain After Plea for Legal Services Help Is Denied. *Washington Post*, June 5. www.washingtonpost.com/archive/politics/1996/06/05/abused-immigrant-slain-after-plea-for-legal-services-help-is-denied/90af558c-a987-4026-af66-22dd2dad2a33/.

Clemens, E. S. (1997). *The People's Lobby: Organizational Innovation and the Rise of Interest Group Politics in the United States, 1890–1925*. University of Chicago Press.

Cobble, D. S. (2004). *The Other Women's Movement: Workplace Justice and Social Rights in Modern America*. Princeton University Press.

Cohen, C. J. (1999). *The Boundaries of Blackness: AIDS and the Breakdown of Black Politics*. University of Chicago Press.

Cohen, C. J. (2005). Punks, Bulldaggers, and Welfare Queens: The Radical Potential of Queer Politics? In E. P. Johnson & M. G. Henderson (Eds.), *Black Queer Studies: A Critical Anthology* (pp. 21–51). Duke University Press. www.jstor.org/stable/j.ctv11cw38r.

Cohen, C. J., & Jackson, S. J. (2016). Ask a Feminist: A Conversation with Cathy J. Cohen on Black Lives Matter, Feminism, and Contemporary Activism. *Signs: Journal of Women in Culture and Society*, *41*(4), 775–792.

Cohen, J. L. (1985). Strategy or Identity: New Theoretical Paradigms and Contemporary Social Movements. *Social Research*, *52*(4), 663–716.

Coker, D. (2000). Shifting Power for Battered Women: Law, Material Resources, and Poor Women of Color. *UC Davis Law Review*, *33*(4), 1009–1056.

Coker, D. (2004). Race, Poverty, and the Crime-Centered Response to Domestic Violence: A Comment on Linda Mills's Insult to Injury: Rethinking Our Responses to Intimate Abuse. *Violence Against Women*, *10*(11), 1331–1353. https://doi.org/10.1177/1077801204269349.

Cole, E. R. (2008). Coalitions As a Model for Intersectionality: From Practice to Theory. *Sex Roles*, *59*, 443–453.

Cole, S., & Phillips, L. (2008). The Violence Against Women Campaigns in Latin America: New Feminist Alliances. *Feminist Criminology*, *3*(2), 145–168.

Collins, P. H. (1998a). Intersections of Race, Class, Gender, and Nation: Some Implications for Black Family Studies. *Journal of Comparative Family Studies*, 29 (1), 27–36.

Collins, P. H. (1998b). The Tie That Binds: Race, Gender and US Violence. *Ethnic and Racial Studies*, 21(5), 917–938.

Collins, P. H. (2009). *Black Feminist Thought: Knowledge, Consciousness, and the Politics of Empowerment*. Routledge.

Collins, P. H., & Chepp, V. (2013). Intersectionality. In G. Waylen, K. Celis, J. Kantola, & L. Weldon (Eds.), *The Oxford Handbook of Gender and Politics* (pp. 57–87). Oxford University Press.

Conley, D. (2010). *Being Black, Living in the Red: Race, Wealth, and Social Policy in America*. University of California Press.

Corrigan, P., & Sayer, D. (1991). *The Great Arch: English State Formation As Cultural Revolution [with Preface, Postscript and Bibliographical Supplement]*. Blackwell.

Cox, G. W., & McCubbins, M. D. (2005). *Setting the Agenda: Responsible Party Government in the U.S. House of Representatives*. Cambridge University Press.

Crenshaw, K. (1991a). Demarginalizing the Intersection of Race and Sex: A Black Feminist Critique of Antidiscrimination Doctrine, Feminist Theory, and Antiracist Politics [1989]. In K. T. Bartlett & R. Kennedy (Eds.), *Feminist Legal Theory* (1st ed.). Routledge. https://doi.org/10.4324/9780429500480-5.

Crenshaw, K. (1991b). Mapping the Margins: Intersectionality, Identity Politics, and Violence against Women of Color. *Stanford Law Review*, 43(6), 1241–1299.

Crenshaw, K. (1994). Mapping the Margins: Intersectionality, Identity Politics, and Violence against Women of Color. In M. A. Fineman & R. Mykitiuk (Eds.), *The Public Nature of Private Violence: The Discovery of Domestic Abuse* (pp. 93–118). Routledge.

Crenshaw, K. (1997). Intersectionality and Identity Politics: Learning from Violence against Women of Color. In M. L. Shanley & U. Narayan (Eds.), *Reconstructing Political Theory: Feminist Perspectives* (pp. 178–193). Pennsylvania State University Press.

Crenshaw, K. (2015). Demarginalizing the Intersection of Race and Sex: A Black Feminist Critique of Antidiscrimination Doctrine, Feminist Theory and Antiracist Politics. *University of Chicago Legal Forum*, *1989*(1). https://chicagounbound .uchicago.edu/uclf/vol1989/iss1/8.

Crenshaw, K., Ritchie, A., Anspach, R., Gilmer, R., & Harris, L. (2015). *Say Her Name: Resisting Police Brutality against Black Women*. Center for Intersectionality and Social Policy Studies. https://scholarship.law.columbia.edu/faculty_scholarship/ 3226/.

Crutchfield, L. R., & Grant, H. M. (2012). *Forces for Good: The Six Practices of High-Impact Nonprofits*. John Wiley & Sons.

Curtin, N., Stewart, A. J., & Cole, E. R. (2015). Challenging the Status Quo: The Role of Intersectional Awareness in Activism for Social Change and Pro-social Intergroup Attitudes. *Psychology of Women Quarterly*, 39(4), 512–529.

Daniels, C. R., Brooks, R., & Soto, P. D. (1997). *Feminists Negotiate the State: The Politics of Domestic Violence*. University Press of America.

Dasgupta, S. D. (2003). *Safety & Justice for All: Examining the Relationship between the Women's Anti-violence Movement and the Criminal Legal System*. Ms. Foundation for Women. www.ncdsv.org/images/Ms_SafetyJusticeForAll_2003.pdf.

Davidson, R. H., Oleszek, W. J., Lee, F. E., & Schickler, E. (2019). *Congress and Its Members*. CQ Press.

Davis, A. Y. (2011). *Women, Race, and Class*. Knopf Doubleday Publishing.

Davis, A. Y., & Shaylor, C. (2001). Race, Gender, and the Prison Industrial Complex: California and Beyond. *Meridians*, 2(1), 1–25.

Dawson, M. C. (2014). The Hollow Shell: Loïc Wacquant's Vision of State, Race and Economics. *Ethnic and Racial Studies*, 37(10), 1767–1775. https://doi.org/10.1080/01419870.2014.931990.

Dawson, M. C. (2016). Hidden in Plain Sight: A Note on Legitimation Crises and the Racial Order. *Critical Historical Studies*, 3(1), 143–161. https://doi.org/10.1086/685540.

Day, T. (2002). *Fluid Iron: State Formation in Southeast Asia*. University of Hawai'i Press.

Deer, S. (2006). Federal Indian law and violent crime. In INCITE! Women of Color Against Violence (Ed.), *Color of Violence: The INCITE! Anthology* (pp. 32–41). South End Press.

Department of Justice. (2020). *National Crime Victimization Survey 2019*. Office of Justice Programs, Bureau of Justice Statistics.

Desmond, M. (2016). *Evicted: Poverty and Profit in the American City*. Crown.

Detrow, S. (2017). Roy Moore Continues to Lose GOP Support Amid Allegations of Sexual Harassment. NPR.org, November 14. www.npr.org/2017/11/14/564163449/roy-moore-continues-to-lose-gop-support-amid-allegations-of-sexual-harassment.

Donohue, W. A., Rogan, R. G., & Kaufman, S. (2011). *Framing Matters: Perspectives on Negotiation Research and Practice in Communication*. Peter Lang.

Dozier, R. (2010). The Declining Relative Status of Black Women Workers, 1980–2002 Social Stratification and Mobility. *Social Forces*, 88(4), 1833–1857.

Dreveskracht, R. D. (2013). House Republicans Add Insult to Native Women's Injury. *University of Miami Race and Social Justice Law Review*, 3(1), 1–29.

Druckman, J. N. (2004). Political Preference Formation: Competition, Deliberation, and the (Ir)relevance of Framing Effects. *American Political Science Review*, 98(4), 671–686. https://doi.org/10.1017/S0003055404041413.

Druckman, J., Peterson, E., & Slothuus, R. (2013). How Elite Partisan Polarization Affects Public Opinion Formation. *The American Political Science Review*, 107(1), 57–79.

Drutman, L. (2010). Congressional Fellowship Program: The Complexities of Lobbying: Toward a Deeper Understanding of the Profession. *PS: Political Science & Politics*, 43(4), 834–837. https://doi.org/10.1017/S1049096510001721.

Dubard Barbosa, S., & Alain, F. (2007). Where Is the Risk? Availability, Anchoring, and Framing Effects on Entrepreneurial Risk Taking. *Frontiers of Entrepreneurship Research*, 27.

Dutton, M. A., Orloff, L. E., & Hass, G. A. (2000). Characteristics of Help-Seeking Behaviors, Resources and Service Needs of Battered Immigrant Latinas: Legal and Policy Implications Symposium Briefing Papers. *Georgetown Journal on Poverty Law and Policy*, 7(2), 245–306.

Dwidar, M. A. (2021). Coalitional Lobbying and Intersectional Representation in American Rulemaking. *American Political Science Review*, 116(1), 301–321. https://doi.org/10.1017/S0003055421000794.

Eagan, M. (2020). Indigenous Women: The Invisible Victims of Femicide in Mexico. *Harvard International Review.* https://hir.harvard.edu/indigenous-women-victims-of -femicide-in-mexico/.

Eisenstein, Z. R. (1993). *The Radical Future of Liberal Feminism* (2nd ed.). Northeastern University Press.

Elman, R. A. (2003). Refuge in Reconfigured States: Shelter Movements in the United States, Britain and Sweden. In L. A. Banaszak, K. Beckwith, & D. Rucht, (Eds.), *Women's Movements Facing the Reconfigured State* (pp. 94–113). Cambridge University Press.

English, A. (2021). Implementing Intersectionality: Women's Organizations' Representation of Women of Color and Poor Women during Two Rulemakings. *Politics, Groups, and Identities, 9*(4), 739–758. https://doi.org/10.1080/21565503 .2019.1674161.

Entman, R. M. (1993). Framing: Toward Clarification of a Fractured Paradigm. *Journal of Communication, 43*(4), 51–58. https://doi.org/10.1111/j.1460-2466.1993.tb01304.x.

Erez, E., & Hartly, C. C. (2003). Battered Immigrant Women and the Legal System: A Therapeutic Jurisprudence Perspective. *Western Criminology Review, 4*(2), 155–170.

Ettachfini, L., & Beusman, C. (2018). Politicians Who've Resigned for Sexual Misconduct in the Wake of #MeToo. *Broadly,* May 9. https://broadly.vice.com /en_us/article/kzkeyv/these-9-politicians-have-resigned-for-sexual-misconduct-in-the -wake-of-metoo.

Evans, B., Richmond, T., & Shields, J. (2005). Structuring Neoliberal Governance: The Nonprofit Sector, Emerging New Modes of Control and the Marketisation of Service Delivery. *Policy and Society, 24*(1), 73–97. https://doi.org/10.1016/S1449-4035(05) 70050-3.

Fagan, F., & Bilgel, F. (2015). Sunsets and Federal Lawmaking: Evidence from the 110th Congress. *International Review of Law and Economics, 41,* 1–6. https://doi.org/10 .1016/j.irle.2014.08.002.

Faling, M., Biesbroek, R., Karlsson-Vinkhuyzen, S., & Termeer, K. (2019). Policy Entrepreneurship across Boundaries: A Systematic Literature Review. *Journal of Public Policy, 39*(2), 393–422. https://doi.org/10.1017/S0143814X18000053.

Feal, R. G. (2002). Feminism and Afro-Hispanism: The Double Bind. *Afro-Hispanic Review, 21*(1/2), 30–34.

Feinstein, R. A. (2018). *When Rape Was Legal: The Untold History of Sexual Violence during Slavery.* Routledge.

Fereday, J., & Muir-Cochrane, E. (2006). Demonstrating Rigor Using Thematic Analysis: A Hybrid Approach of Inductive and Deductive Coding and Theme Development. *International Journal of Qualitative Methods, 5*(1), 80–92. https://doi .org/10.1177/160940690600500107.

Ferraro, K. J. (1996). The Dance of Dependency: A Genealogy of Domestic Violence Discourse. *Hypatia, 11*(4), 77–91. https://doi.org/10.1111/j.1527-2001.1996.tb01036.x.

Ferree, M. M., & Martin, P. Y. (1995). *Feminist Organizations: Harvest of the New Women's Movement.* Temple University Press.

Finn, J. E. (2010). Sunset Clauses and Democratic Deliberation: Assessing the Significance of Sunset Provisions in Antiterrorism Legislation. *Columbia Journal of Transnational Law, 48*(442), 442–502.

Fleming, C. M., & Morris, A. (2015). Theorizing Ethnic and Racial Movements in the Global Age: Lessons from the Civil Rights Movement. *Sociology of Race and Ethnicity*, 1(1), 105–126. https://doi.org/10.1177/2332649214562473.

Ford, C. L., Slavin, T., Hilton, K. L., & Holt, S. L. (2013). Intimate Partner Violence Prevention Services and Resources in Los Angeles: Issues, Needs, and Challenges for Assisting Lesbian, Gay, Bisexual, and Transgender Clients. *Health Promotion Practice*, 14(6), 841–849. https://doi.org/10.1177/1524839912467645.

Fox, H., & Maes, D. J. (2013). The Promise of Organizational Development in Nonprofit Human Services Organizations. *Organization Development Journal*, 31 (2), 72–81.

Frymer, P., & Skrentny, J. D. (1998). Coalition-Building and the Politics of Electoral Capture during the Nixon Administration: African Americans, Labor, Latinos. *Studies in American Political Development*, 12(1), 131–161. https://doi.org/10.1017 /S0898588X9800131X.

Galvez, A. (2022). The Journey to a Consensus of Gender-Neutral Language in Spanish: Does -x Really Mark the Spot? *Journal of the Student Personnel Association at Indiana University*, 50, 48–56.

Garcia, A. M. (1989). The Development of Chicana Feminist Discourse, 1970–1980. *Gender & Society*, 3(2), 217–238. https://doi.org/10.1177/089124389003002004.

García-Moreno, C., Hegarty, K., d'Oliveira, A. F. L., et al. (2015). The Health-Systems Response to Violence against Women. *The Lancet*, 385(9977), 1567–1579. https://doi .org/10.1016/S0140-6736(14)61837-7.

Gen, S., & Wright, A. C. (2020a). Considerations for Strategic Policy Advocacy. In S. Gen & A. C. Wright (Eds.), *Nonprofits in Policy Advocacy: Their Strategies and Stories* (pp. 191–211). Springer International Publishing. https://doi.org/10.1007 /978-3-030-43696-4_9.

Gen, S., & Wright, A. C. (2020b). Correction to: Nonprofits in Policy Advocacy. In S. Gen & A. C. Wright (Eds.), *Nonprofits in Policy Advocacy: Their Strategies and Stories* (pp. 24–44). Springer International Publishing. https://doi.org/10.1007/978-3-030-43696-4_10.

Gen, S., & Wright, A. C. (2020c). Inside-Outside. In S. Gen & A. C. Wright (Eds.), *Nonprofits in Policy Advocacy: Their Strategies and Stories* (pp. 97–120). Springer International Publishing. https://doi.org/10.1007/978-3-030-43696-4_5.

Gen, S., & Wright, A. C. (2020d). Institutional Partnership. In S. Gen & A. C. Wright (Eds.), *Nonprofits in Policy Advocacy: Their Strategies and Stories* (pp. 73–96). Springer International Publishing. https://doi.org/10.1007/978-3-030-43696-4_4.

Gen, S., & Wright, A. C. (2020e). Nonprofit Policy Advocacy in the United States. In S. Gen & A. C. Wright (Eds.), *Nonprofits in Policy Advocacy: Their Strategies and Stories* (pp. 1–21). Springer International Publishing. https://doi.org/10.1007/978-3-030-43696-4_1.

Giddings, P. J. (2009). *When and Where I Enter: The Impact of Black Women on Race and Sex in America*. HarperCollins.

Gillum, T. L. (2009). Improving Services to African American Survivors of IPV: From the Voices of Recipients of Culturally Specific Services. *Violence Against Women*, 15(1), 57–80. https://doi.org/10.1177/1077801208328375.

Goodmark, L. (2012). *A Troubled Marriage: Domestic Violence and the Legal System*. New York University Press.

Goodmark, L. (2013). Transgender People, Intimate Partner Abuse, and the Legal System. *Harvard Civil Rights–Civil Liberties Law Review, 48*(1), 51–104.

Gordon, L. (2012). *Women, the State, and Welfare*. University of Wisconsin Pres.

Gorski, P. S. (2003). *The Disciplinary Revolution: Calvinism and the Rise of the State in Early Modern Europe*. University of Chicago Press.

Goss, K. A. (2012). *The Paradox of Gender Equality: How American Women's Groups Gained and Lost Their Public Voice*. University of Michigan Press.

Gottschalk, M. (2006). *The Prison and the Gallows: The Politics of Mass Incarceration in America*. Cambridge University Press.

Gover, A. R., & Moore, A. M. (2020). The 1994 Violence Against Women Act: A Historic Response to Gender Violence. *Violence Against Women, 27*(1), 8–29. https://doi.org/10.1177/1077801220949705.

Gray, D. M., Anyane-Yeboa, A., Balzora, S., Issaka, R. B., & May, F. P. (2020). COVID-19 and the Other Pandemic: Populations Made Vulnerable by Systemic Inequity. *Nature Reviews Gastroenterology & Hepatology, 17*(9), 520–522. https://doi.org/10.1038/s41575-020-0330-8.

Greenwood, R. M. (2008). Intersectional Political Consciousness: Appreciation for Intragroup Differences and Solidarity in Diverse Groups. *Psychology of Women Quarterly, 32*(1), 36–47. https://doi.org/10.1111/j.1471-6402.2007.00405.x.

Gregory, J., & Lees, S. (1994). In Search of Gender Justice: Sexual Assault and the Criminal Justice System. *Feminist Review, 48*(1), 80–93. https://doi.org/10.1057/fr.1994.43.

Grenier, D., & Locker, R. (2007). *The Failure to Protect Indigenous Women from Sexual Violence in the USA: (569262010–001)* [Dataset]. American Psychological Association. https://doi.org/10.1037/e569262010-001.

Gronbjerg, K. A. (1991). How Nonprofit Human Service Organizations Manage Their Funding Sources: Key Findings and Policy Implications. *Nonprofit Management and Leadership, 2*(2), 159–175. https://doi.org/10.1002/nml.4130020206.

Gross, K. (2008). Framing Persuasive Appeals: Episodic and Thematic Framing, Emotional Response, and Policy Opinion. *Political Psychology, 29*(2), 169–192. https://doi.org/10.1111/j.1467-9221.2008.00622.x.

Grossmann, M. (2012). Interest Group Influence on US Policy Change: An Assessment Based on Policy History. *Interest Groups & Advocacy, 1*(2), 171–192. https://doi.org/10.1057/iga.2012.9.

Grumbach, J. M., & Michener, J. (2022). American Federalism, Political Inequality, and Democratic Erosion. *The ANNALS of the American Academy of Political and Social Science, 699*(1), 143–155.

Guo, C., & Saxton, G. D. (2014). Tweeting Social Change: How Social Media Are Changing Nonprofit Advocacy. *Nonprofit and Voluntary Sector Quarterly, 43*(1), 57–79. https://doi.org/10.1177/0899764012471585.

Hacker, J. S. & P. Pierson. (2010). Winner-Take-All Politics: Public Policy, Political Organization, and the Precipitous Rise of Top Incomes in the United States. *Politics & Society, 38*(2), 152–204. https://doi.org/10.1177/0032329210365042.

Hall, J. D. (2005). The Long Civil Rights Movement and the Political Uses of the Past. *The Journal of American History, 91*(4), 1233–1263.

Hall, R. L., & Deardorff, A. V. (2006). Lobbying As Legislative Subsidy. *The American Political Science Review, 100*(1), 69–84.

Hancock, A.-M. (2007). When Multiplication Doesn't Equal Quick Addition: Examining Intersectionality As a Research Paradigm. *Perspectives on Politics*, 5(1), 63–79. https://doi.org/10.1017/S1537592707070065.

Hancock, A.-M. (2011). *Solidarity Politics for Millennials: A Guide to Ending the Oppression Olympics*. Springer.

Haney, L. A. (2010). *Offending Women: Power, Punishment, and the Regulation of Desire*. University of California Press.

Hansen, J. M. (1991). *Gaining Access: Congress and the Farm Lobby, 1919–1981*. University of Chicago Press.

Hart, T., Greenfield, J. M., & Johnston, M. (2005). *Nonprofit Internet Strategies: Best Practices for Marketing, Communications, and Fundraising Success*. John Wiley & Sons.

Hartman, J. L. (2021). Seeking Justice: How VAWA Reduced the Stronghold Over American Indian and Alaska Native Women. *Violence Against Women*, 27(1), 52–68. https://doi.org/10.1177/1077801220949695.

Hauser, C. (2018). The Women Who Have Accused Brett Kavanaugh. *The New York Times*, September 26. www.nytimes.com/2018/09/26/us/politics/brett-kavanaugh-accusers-women.html.

Hazen, A. L., & Soriano, F. I. (2007). Experiences with Intimate Partner Violence among Latina Women. *Violence Against Women*, 13(6), 562–582. https://doi.org/10.1177/1077801207301558.

Hegewisch, A., Liepmann, H., Hayes, J., & Hartmann, H. (2010). Separate and Not Equal? Gender Segregation in the Labor Market and the Gender Wage Gap. Institute for Women's Policy Research, Briefing Paper IWPR C377, September.

Hidalgo, R. (2015). Advancing a Human Rights Framework to Reimagine the Movement to End Gender Violence. *University of Miami Race & Social Justice Law Review*, 5(2), 559–578.

Higginbotham, E. B. (1992). African-American Women's History and the Metalanguage of Race. *Signs*, 17(2), 251–274.

Hine, D. C. (1989). Rape and the Inner Lives of Black Women in the Middle West. *Signs: Journal of Women in Culture and Society*, 14(4), 912–920. https://doi.org/10.1086/494552.

Hinshaw, R. (2017). *The Unsheltered Woman: Women and Housing*. Routledge.

Hodžić, S. (2010). Seduced by Information, Contaminated by Power: Women's Rights As a Global Panopticon. In D. Bergoffen, P. R. Gilbert, T. Harvey, & C. L. McNeely (Eds.), *Confronting Global Gender Justice: Women's Lives, Human Rights* (pp. 233–248). Routledge.

Holman, M. R., & Schneider, M. C. (2018). Gender, Race, and Political Ambition: How Intersectionality and Frames Influence Interest in Political Office. *Politics, Groups, and Identities*, 6(2), 264–280. https://doi.org/10.1080/21565503.2016.1208105.

Holyoke, T. T. (2011). *Competitive Interests: Competition and Compromise in American Interest Group Politics*. Georgetown University Press.

Hondagneu-Sotelo, P. (2007). *Doméstica: Immigrant Workers Cleaning and Caring in the Shadows of Affluence*. University of California Press.

hooks, b. (2000). *Feminist Theory: From Margin to Center*. Pluto Press.

hooks, b. (2014a). *Ain't I a Woman: Black Women and Feminism*. Routledge.

hooks, b. (2014b). *Feminism Is for Everybody: Passionate Politics*. Routledge.

Howard, C. (1997). *The Hidden Welfare State: Tax Expenditures and Social Policy in the United States*. Princeton University Press.

Htun, M., & Jensenius, F. R. (2020). Fighting Violence against Women: Laws, Norms & Challenges Ahead. *Daedalus, 149*(1), 144–159. https://doi.org/10.1162/daed_a_01779.

Htun, M., & Weldon, S. L. (2018). *The Logics of Gender Justice: State Action on Women's Rights around the World*. Cambridge University Press.

Ikegami, E. (1997). *The Taming of the Samurai: Honorific Individualism and the Making of Modern Japan*. Harvard University Press.

INCITE! (2017). *The Revolution Will Not Be Funded: Beyond the Non-profit Industrial Complex*. Duke University Press.

Ingram, M., McClelland, D. J., Martin, J., et al. (2010). Experiences of Immigrant Women Who Self-Petition Under the Violence Against Women Act. *Violence Against Women, 16*(8), 858–880. https://doi.org/10.1177/1077801210376889.

Irvine, J., Lang, S., & Montoya, C. (2019). Introduction: Gendered Mobilizations and Intersectional Challenges. In J. Irvine, S. Lang, & C. Montoya (Eds.), *Gendered Mobilizations and Intersectional Challenges: Contemporary Social Movements in Europe and North America* (pp. 1–22). Rowman & Littlefield.

Iyengar, S. (1990). Framing Responsibility for Political Issues: The Case of Poverty. *Political Behavior, 12*(1), 19–40. https://doi.org/10.1007/BF00992330.

Jacobs, H. (1861). *Incidents in the Life of a Slave Girl*. North Carolina Collection. https://docsouth.unc.edu/fpn/jacobs/jacobs.html.

Jacobs, M. D. (2009). *White Mother to a Dark Race: Settler Colonialism, Maternalism, and the Removal of Indigenous Children in the American West and Australia, 1880–1940*. University of Nebraska Press.

Jacquet, C. O. (2019). *The Injustices of Rape: How Activists Responded to Sexual Violence, 1950–1980*. University of North Carolina Press.

James, S., Herman, J., Rankin, S. et al. (2016). *The Report of the 2015 U.S. Transgender Survey*. https://ncvc.dspacedirect.org/handle/20.500.11990/1299.

Jang, H. S., & Feiock, R. C. (2007). Public versus Private Funding of Nonprofit Organizations: Implications for Collaboration. *Public Performance & Management Review, 31*(2), 174–190. https://doi.org/10.2753/PMR1530-9576310202.

Jayaraman, S. (2021). *One Fair Wage: Ending Subminimum Pay in America*. New Press.

Jennings, M. K., & Andersen, E. A. (2003). The Importance of Social and Political Context: The Case of AIDS Activism. *Political Behavior, 25*(2), 177–199. https://doi.org/10.1023/A:1023851930080.

Jochim, A. E., & May, P. J. (2010). Beyond Subsystems: Policy Regimes and Governance. *Policy Studies Journal, 38*(2), 303–327. https://doi.org/10.1111/j.1541-0072.2010.00363.x.

Johnson, A., Rauhaus, B., & Webb-Farley, K. (2021). The COVID-19 Pandemic: A Challenge for US Nonprofits' Financial Stability. *Journal of Public Budgeting, Accounting & Financial Management, 33*(1), 33–46.

Johnson, E. P., & Henderson, M. G. (2005). *Black Queer Studies: A Critical Anthology*. Duke University Press.

Jones, B. D., & Baumgartner, F. R. (2005). *The Politics of Attention: How Government Prioritizes Problems*. University of Chicago Press.

Jones, T. R., & Pratt, T. C. (2008). The Prevalence of Sexual Violence in Prison: The State of the Knowledge Base and Implications for Evidence-Based Correctional Policy

Making. *International Journal of Offender Therapy and Comparative Criminology*, 52(3), 280–295. https://doi.org/10.1177/0306624X07307631.

Jordan, S. P., Mehrotra, G. R., & Fujikawa, K. A. (2019). Mandating Inclusion: Critical Trans Perspectives on Domestic and Sexual Violence Advocacy. *Violence Against Women*, 26(6–7). https://doi.org/10.1177/1077801219836728.

Junk, W. M. (2019). When Diversity Works: The Effects of Coalition Composition on the Success of Lobbying Coalitions. *American Journal of Political Science*, 63(3), 660–674. https://doi.org/10.1111/ajps.12437.

Kallivayalil, D. (2007). Feminist Therapy. *Women & Therapy*, 30(3–4), 109–127. https://doi.org/10.1300/J015v30n03_09.

Kalra, N., Di Tanna, G. L., & García-Moreno, C. (2017). Training Healthcare Providers to Respond to Intimate Partner Violence against Women. *The Cochrane Database of Systematic Reviews*, 2017(2). https://doi.org/10.1002/14651858.CD012423.

Kasturirangan, A., Krishnan, S., & Riger, S. (2004). The Impact of Culture and Minority Status on Women's Experience of Domestic Violence. *Trauma, Violence, & Abuse*, 5 (4), 318–332. https://doi.org/10.1177/1524838004269487.

Kattari, S. K., & Begun, S. (2017). On the Margins of Marginalized: Transgender Homelessness and Survival Sex. *Affilia*, 32(1), 92–103. https://doi.org/10.1177 /0886109916651904.

Katznelson, I. (2005). *When Affirmative Action Was White: An Untold History of Racial Inequality in Twentieth-Century America*. W. W. Norton & Company.

Keane, M. P., & Wolpin, K. I. (2010). The Role of Labor and Marriage Markets, Preference Heterogeneity, and the Welfare System in the Life Cycle Decisions of Black, Hispanic, and White Women. *International Economic Review*, 51(3), 851–892.

Kearns, K. P., Bell, D., Deem, B., & McShane, L. (2014). How Nonprofit Leaders Evaluate Funding Sources: An Exploratory Study of Nonprofit Leaders. *Nonprofit and Voluntary Sector Quarterly*, 43(1), 121–143. https://doi.org/10.1177 /0899764012458038.

Kessler-Harris, A. (2003). *In Pursuit of Equity: Women, Men, and the Quest for Economic Citizenship in 20th Century America*. Oxford University Press.

Kilbourne, B., England, P., & Beron, K. (1994). Effects of Individual, Occupational, and Industrial Characteristics on Earnings: Intersections of Race and Gender. *Social Forces*, 72(4), 1149–1176. https://doi.org/10.1093/sf/72.4.1149.

King, B. G., Bentele, K. G., & Soule, S. A. (2007). Protest and Policymaking: Explaining Fluctuation in Congressional Attention to Rights Issues, 1960–1986. *Social Forces*, 86 (1), 137–163. https://doi.org/10.1353/sof.2007.0101.

King, D. K. (1988). Multiple Jeopardy, Multiple Consciousness: The Context of a Black Feminist Ideology. *Signs*, 14(1), 42–72.

Kingdon, J. W. (1995). *Agendas, Alternatives, and Public Policies* (2nd ed.). Pearson Education.

Kogan, M. D., Kotelchuck, M., Alexander, G. R., & Johnson, W. E. (1994). Racial Disparities in Reported Prenatal Care Advice from Health Care Providers. *American Journal of Public Health*, 84(1), 82–88. https://doi.org/10.2105/AJPH.84.1.82.

Koss, M. P., & Harvey, M. R. (1991). *The Rape Victim: Clinical and Community Interventions*. Thousand Oaks, CA: Sage Publications.

Kouroutakis, A. E. (2016). *The Constitutional Value of Sunset Clauses: An Historical and Normative Analysis*. Taylor & Francis.

Koyama, E. (2001). The Transfeminist Manifesto. In R. Dicker & A. Piepmeier (Eds.), *Catching a Wave: Reclaiming Feminism for the Twenty-First Century* (pp. 244–259). Northeastern University Press.

Krehbiel, K. (1991). *Information and Legislative Organization.* University of Michigan Press.

Kristen, E., Banuelos, B., & Urban, D. (2015). Workplace Violence and Harassment of Low-Wage Workers. *Berkeley Journal of Employment and Labor Law, 36*(1), 169–204.

Lacombe, M. J. (2021). Post-loss Power Building: The Feedback Effects of Policy Loss on Group Identity and Collective Action. *Policy Studies Journal, 50*(3), 507–526. https://doi.org/10.1111/psj.12446.

Lafree, G. (2000). Review: Explaining the Crime Bust of the 1990s. *Journal of Criminal Law and Criminology, 91*(1), 269–306.

Lawson, G. (1994). The Rise and Rise of the Administrative State. *Harvard Law Review, 107*(6), 1231–1254. https://doi.org/10.2307/1341842.

Le May, G. (2018). The Cycles of Violence against Native Women: An Analysis of Colonialism, Historical Legislation and the Violence Against Women Reauthorization Act of 2013. *McNair Scholars Online Journal, 12*(1). https://doi.org/10.15760/mcnair .2018.1.

Leong, N. (2013). Racial Capitalism. *Harvard Law Review, 126*(8).

Levi, M. (1989). *Of Rule and Revenue.* University of California Press.

Liang, B., Goodman, L., Tummala-Narra, P., & Weintraub, S. (2005). A Theoretical Framework for Understanding Help-Seeking Processes among Survivors of Intimate Partner Violence. *American Journal of Community Psychology, 36*(1–2), 71–84. https://doi.org/10.1007/s10464-005-6233-6.

Lieberman, R. C., & Lapinski, J. S. (2001). American Federalism, Race and the Administration of Welfare. *British Journal of Political Science, 31*(2), 303–329. https://doi.org/10.1017/S0007123401000126.

Limlingan, M. C., McWayne, C., & Hassairi, N. (2022). Habla Conmigo: Teachers' Spanish Talk and Latine Dual Language Learners' School Readiness Skills. *Early Education and Development, 33*(4), 655–674. https://doi.org/10.1080/10409289 .2021.1898227.

Linder, M. (1999). *Wars of Attrition: Vietnam, the Business Roundtable, and the Decline of Construction Unions.* Fănpihuà Press.

Listokin, Y. (2009). Learning through Policy Variation. *Yale Law Journal, 118*(480), 480–553.

Lopez, I. F. H. (1994). The Social Construction of Race: Some Observations on Illusion, Fabrication, and Choice. *Harvard Civil Rights–Civil Liberties Law Review, 29* (1), 1–62.

Lopez, M. H., Livingston, G., & Kochhar, R. (2009). *Hispanics and the Economic Downturn: Housing Woes and Remittance Cuts.* Washington, DC: Pew Hispanic Center.

Lorde, A. (2017). *A Burst of Light: And Other Essays.* Courier Dover Publications.

Lorenz, G. M. (2020). Prioritized Interests: Diverse Lobbying Coalitions and Congressional Committee Agenda Setting. *The Journal of Politics, 82*(1), 225–240. https://doi.org/10.1086/705744.

Mahoney, J., & Thelen, K. (2010). *Explaining Institutional Change: Ambiguity, Agency, and Power.* Cambridge University Press.

Mama, A. (1989). Violence against Black Women: Gender, Race and State Responses. *Feminist Review*, 32(1), 30–48. https://doi.org/10.1057/fr.1989.18.

Manikonda, L., Beigi, G., Liu, H., & Kambhampati, S. (2018). Twitter for Sparking a Movement, Reddit for Sharing the Moment: #metoo through the Lens of Social Media. *ArXiv, ArXiv:1803.08022 [Cs]*. http://arxiv.org/abs/1803.08022.

Marchetti, K. (2014). Crossing the Intersection: The Representation of Disadvantaged Identities in Advocacy. *Politics, Groups, and Identities*, 2(1), 104–119. https://doi.org /10.1080/21565503.2013.876919.

Markowitz, L., & Tice, K. W. (2002). Paradoxes of Professionalization: Parallel Dilemmas in Women's Organizations in the Americas. *Gender & Society*, 16(6), 941–958. https://doi.org/10.1177/089124302237896.

Matthes, J. (2012). Framing Politics: An Integrative Approach. *American Behavioral Scientist*, 56(3), 247–259. https://doi.org/10.1177/0002764211426324.

Mattina, A. F. (1986). Shattered Silence: The Rhetoric of an American Female Labor Reform Association. PhD dissertation, The Ohio State University.

Mayberry, R. M., Mili, F., & Ofili, E. (2000). Racial and Ethnic Differences in Access to Medical Care. *Medical Care Research and Review*, 57(1) (suppl.), 108–145. https:// doi.org/10.1177/1077558700057001S06.

Mayer, K., Appelbaum, J., Rogers, T., et al. (2001). The Evolution of the Fenway Community Health Model. *American Journal of Public Health*, 91(6), 892–894.

McCall, L. (2001). *Complex Inequality: Gender, Class and Race in the New Economy*. Routledge.

Mcclintock, A. (2013). *Imperial Leather: Race, Gender, and Sexuality in the Colonial Contest*. Routledge.

McConahay, J. B., Mullin, C. J., & Frederick, J. (1977). The Uses of Social Science in Trials with Political and Racial Overtones: The Trial of Joan Little. *Law and Contemporary Problems*, 41(1), 205–229.

Mcdonagh, E. (2002). Political Citizenship and Democratization: The Gender Paradox. *American Political Science Review*, 96(3), 535–552. https://doi.org/10.1017 /S000305540200031X.

McFarland, M. R., Mixer, S. J., Webhe-Alamah, H., & Burk, R. (2012). Ethnonursing: A Qualitative Research Method for Studying Culturally Competent Care across Disciplines. *International Journal of Qualitative Methods*, 11(3), 259–279. https://doi .org/10.1177/160940691201100306.

McGuire, D. L. (2010). *At the Dark End of the Street: Black Women, Rape, and Resistance – A New History of the Civil Rights Movement from Rosa Parks to the Rise of Black Power*. Alfred A. Knopf.

McLaurin, M. A. (1991). *Celia, a Slave*. University of Georgia Press.

Mehl-Madrona, L., & Mainguy, B. (2014). Introducing Healing Circles and Talking Circles into Primary Care. *The Permanente Journal*, 18(2), 4–9. https://doi.org/10 .7812/TPP/13-104.

Mendelberg, T. (1997). Executing Hortons: Racial Crime in the 1988 Presidential Campaign. *The Public Opinion Quarterly*, 61(1), 134–157.

Merriam, S. B., & Tisdell, E. J. (2015). *Qualitative Research: A Guide to Design and Implementation*. John Wiley & Sons.

Mettler, S. (1998). *Soldiers to Citizens: The G.I. Bill and the Making of the Greatest Generation*. Oxford University Press.

Mettler, S. (2002). Bringing the State Back in to Civic Engagement: Policy Feedback Effects of the G.I. Bill for World War II Veterans. *American Political Science Review*, 96(02), 351–365. https://doi.org/10.1017/S0003055402000217.

Mettler, S., & Soss, J. (2004). The Consequences of Public Policy for Democratic Citizenship: Bridging Policy Studies and Mass Politics. *Perspectives on Politics*, 2(1), 55–73.

Michener, J. (2018). *Fragmented Democracy: Medicaid, Federalism, and Unequal Politics*. Cambridge University Press.

Michener, J. (2019). Policy Feedback in a Racialized Polity. *Policy Studies Journal*, 47 (2), 423–450. https://doi.org/10.1111/psj.12328.

Michener, J., & Brower, M. T. (2020). What's Policy Got to Do with It? Race, Gender & Economic Inequality in the United States. *Daedalus*, 149(1), 100–118. https://doi.org /10.1162/daed_a_01776.

Miles, T. (2009). "Circular Reasoning": Recentering Cherokee Women in the Antiremoval Campaigns. *American Quarterly*, 61(2), 221–243.

Miller, B. (Ed.). (2016). *Spaces of Contention: Spatialities and Social Movements*. Routledge.

Miller, L. L. (2004). Rethinking Bureaucrats in the Policy Process: Criminal Justice Agents and the National Crime Agenda. *Policy Studies Journal*, 32(4), 569–588. https://doi.org/10.1111/j.1541-0072.2004.00081.x.

Miller, L. L. (2008). *The Perils of Federalism: Race, Poverty, and the Politics of Crime Control*. Oxford University Press.

Miller, S. L. (1989). Unintended Side-Effects of Pro-arrest Policies and Their Race and Class Implications for Battered Women: A Cautionary Note. *Criminal Justice Policy Review*, 3(3), 299–317.

Miller, S., Iovanni, L., & Kelley, K. D. (2011). Violence against Women and the Criminal Justice Response. In C. M. Renzetti, J. L. Edelson, & R. K. Bergen (Eds.), *Sourcebook on Violence against Women* (2nd ed., pp. 267–289). Sage.

Mills, L. (1999). Killing Her Softly: Intimate Abuse and the Violence of State Regulation. *Harvard Law Review*, 113(2), 550–613.

Mink, G. (2001). Violating Women: Rights Abuses in the Welfare Police State. *The ANNALS of the American Academy of Political and Social Science*, 577(1), 79–93. https://doi.org/10.1177/000271620157700107.

Montoya, C. (2016). Institutions. In L. Disch & M. Hawkesworth (Eds.), *The Oxford Handbook of Feminist Theory* (pp. 367–384). Oxford University Press.

Montoya, C., & Seminario, M. G. (2022). Guerreras y Puentes: The Theory and Praxis of Latina(x) Activism. *Politics, Groups, and Identities*, 10(2), 171–188.

Morga, C., & Anzaldua, G. (Eds.). (2015). *This Bridge Called My Back: Writings by Radical Women of Color* (4th ed.). State University of New York Press. https://books .google.com/books?id=oj2fBgAAQBAJ&printsec=frontcover&dq=This+Bridge+called+ my+back&hl=en&sa=X&ved=oahUKEwiY_peoxvDiAhVRPKoKHRFoD8wQ6AEIKj AA#v=onepage&q=This%20Bridge%20called%20my%20back&f=false.

Morgan, K. J., & Orloff, A. S. (2017). *The Many Hands of the State: Theorizing Political Authority and Social Control*. Cambridge University Press.

Morgan, R. E. (2018). *Criminal Victimization, 2018*. U.S. Department of Justice. https:// bjs.ojp.gov/content/pub/pdf/cv18.pdf.

Mottet, L., & Ohle, J. (2006). Transitioning Our Shelters: Making Homeless Shelters Safe for Transgender People. *Journal of Poverty*, *10*(2), 77–101. https://doi.org/10.1300/J134v10n02_05.

Moulton, S., & Eckerd, A. (2012). Preserving the Publicness of the Nonprofit Sector: Resources, Roles, and Public Values. *Nonprofit and Voluntary Sector Quarterly*, *41*(4), 656–685. https://doi.org/10.1177/0899764011419517.

Munguía, J. A. T., & Martínez-Zarzoso, I. (2021). Examining Gender Inequalities in Factors Associated with Income Poverty in Mexican Rural Households. *PLoS ONE*, *16*(11), e0259187. https://doi.org/10.1371/journal.pone.0259187.

Nadasen, P. (2012). *Rethinking the Welfare Rights Movement*. Routledge.

Nadasen, P. (2015). *Household Workers Unite: The Untold Story of African American Women Who Built a Movement*. Beacon Press.

Namkung, V. (2021). The Story behind the Group Tracking Anti-Asian Hate Incidents. *NBC News*, May 3. www.nbcnews.com/news/asian-america/story-group-tracking-anti-asian-hate-incidents-rcna662.

Nash, J. C. (2018). *Black Feminism Reimagined: After Intersectionality*. Duke University Press.

The National Center for Victims of Crime. (2018). *Intimate Partner Violence: 2018 National Crime Victims' Rights Week Resource Guide: Crime and Victimization Fact Sheets*. https://ovc.ojp.gov/sites/g/files/xyckuh226/files/ncvrw2018/info_flyers/fact_sheets/2018NCVRW_IPV_508_QC.pdf.

Nayak, S. (2014). *Race, Gender and the Activism of Black Feminist Theory: Working with Audre Lorde*. Routledge.

Nelsen, M. D. (2021). Cultivating Youth Engagement: Race and the Behavioral Effects of Critical Pedagogy. *Political Behavior*, *43*(2), 751–784. https://doi.org/10.1007/s11109-019-09573-6.

Nuamah, S. A. (2019). *How Girls Achieve*. Harvard University Press. https://doi.org/10.4159/9780674240131.

O'Brien, B. G. (2018). *Handcuffs and Chain Link: Criminalizing the Undocumented in America*. University of Virginia Press.

Oleszek, W. J. (2013). *Congressional Procedures and the Policy Process*. SAGE.

Oliveri, R. C. (2009). Between a Rock and a Hard Place: Landlords, Latinos, Anti-Illegal Immigrant Ordinances, and Housing Discrimination. *Vanderbilt Law Review*, *62*(53), 1–59.

Omi, M., & Winant, H. (2014). *Racial Formation in the United States*. Routledge. https://doi.org/10.4324/9780203076804.

Onkst, D. H. (1998). "First a Negro . . . Incidentally a Veteran": Black World War Two Veterans and the G. I. Bill of Rights in the Deep South, 1944–1948. *Journal of Social History*, *31*(3), 517–543.

Orloff, L. E., & Kaguyutan, J. V. (2002). Offering a Helping Hand: Legal Protections for Battered Immigrant Women: A History of Legislative Responses. *American University Journal of Gender, Social Policy & the Law*, *10*(1), 95–184.

Ortiz-Blanes, S. (2021). Puerto Rico Declares State of Emergency Over Violence against Women. *Miami Herald*, January 27. www.miamiherald.com/news/nation-world/world/americas/article248692015.html.

Parker, T. (2019). *Department Stores and the Black Freedom Movement: Workers, Consumers, and Civil Rights from the 1930s to the 1980s*. University of North Carolina Press.

Pateman, C. (2018). *The Sexual Contract*. John Wiley & Sons.

Patterson, J. (2016). *Queering Sexual Violence: Radical Voices from within the Antiviolence Movement*. Riverdale Avenue Books.

Peffer, G. A. (1999). *If They Don't Bring Their Women Here: Chinese Female Immigration before Exclusion*. University of Illinois Press.

Pérez, L. M., & Martinez, J. (2008). Community Health Workers: Social Justice and Policy Advocates for Community Health and Well-Being. *American Journal of Public Health*, 98(1), 11–14. https://doi.org/10.2105/AJPH.2006.100842.

Phinney, R. (2017). *Strange Bedfellows: Interest Group Coalitions, Diverse Partners, and Influence in American Social Policy*. Cambridge University Press.

Pierson, P. (1993). When Effect Becomes Cause: Policy Feedback and Political Change. *World Politics*, 45(4), 595–628.

Plichta, S. B. (2007). Interactions between Victims of Intimate Partner Violence against Women and the Health Care System: Policy and Practice Implications. *Trauma, Violence, & Abuse*, 8(2), 226–239. https://doi.org/10.1177/1524838007301220.

Polletta, F., & Ho, M. K. (2006). Frames and Their Consequences. In R. E. Goodin & C. Tilly (Eds.), *The Oxford Handbook of Contextual Political Analysis* (pp. 187–209). Oxford University Press.

Purcell, M. (2002). Excavating Lefebvre: The Right to the City and Its Urban Politics of the Inhabitant. *GeoJournal*, 58(2–3), 99–108. https://doi.org/10.1023/B:GEJO .0000010829.62237.8f.

Putnam, R. D. (2000). *Bowling Alone: The Collapse and Revival of American Community*. Simon & Schuster.

Rabuy, B., & Kopf, D. (2016). Detaining the Poor: How Money Bail Perpetuates an Endless Cycle of Poverty and Jail Time. Prison Policy Initiative, press release, May 10. www.jstor.org/stable/resrep27303.

Raj, A., & Silverman, J. (2002). Violence against Immigrant Women: The Roles of Culture, Context, and Legal Immigrant Status on Intimate Partner Violence. *Violence Against Women*, 8(3), 367–398. https://doi.org/10.1177/10778010222183107.

Ramanathan, K. (2021). From Civil Rights to Social Policy: The Political Development of Family and Medical Leave Policy. *Studies in American Political Development*, 35 (2), 173–193.

Randall, V., & Waylen, G. (1998). *Gender, Politics and the State*. Routledge.

Ransby, B. (2018). *Making All Black Lives Matter: Reimagining Freedom in the Twenty-First Century*. University of California Press.

Raphael, J. (2015). *Saving Bernice: Battered Women, Welfare, and Poverty*. Northeastern University Press.

Reséndez, A. (2016). *The Other Slavery: The Uncovered Story of Indian Enslavement in America*. Houghton Mifflin Harcourt.

Richie, B. E. (1996). *Compelled to Crime: The Gender Entrapment of Battered Black Women*. Routledge.

Richie, B. E. (2000). A Black Feminist Reflection on the Antiviolence Movement. *Signs: Journal of Women in Culture and Society*, 25(4), 1133–1137. https://doi.org/10.1086 /495533.

Richie, B. E. (2012). *Arrested Justice: Black Women, Violence, and America's Prison Nation*. New York University Press.

Rivera, J. (1996). The Violence Against Women Act and the Construction of Multiple Consciousness in the Civil Rights and Feminist Movements Symposium: The Violence

Against Women Act of 1994: A Promise Waiting to Be Fulfilled. *Journal of Law and Policy*, 4(2), 463–512.

Roberts, D., & Jesudason, S. (2013). Movement Intersectionality: The Case of Race, Gender, Disability, and Genetic Technologies. *Du Bois Review: Social Science Research on Race*, 10(2), 313–328.

Roberts, J., Hough, M., & Hough, M. (2005). *Understanding Public Attitudes to Criminal Justice*. McGraw-Hill Education (UK).

Robnett, B. (1997). *How Long? How Long? African American Women in the Struggle for Civil Rights*. Oxford University Press.

Rocco, P., Kelly, A. S., Béland, D., & Kinane, M. (2017). The New Politics of US Health Care Prices: Institutional Reconfiguration and the Emergence of All-Payer Claims Databases. *Journal of Health Politics, Policy and Law*, 42(1), 5–52. https://doi.org/10.1215/03616878-3702746.

Rogers, K. (2021). 2.5 Million Women Left the Work Force during the Pandemic. Harris Sees a "National Emergency." *The New York Times*, February 18. www.nytimes.com/2021/02/18/us/politics/women-pandemic-harris.html.

Roos, P., & Manley, J. E. (1996). Staffing Personnel: Feminization and Change in Human Resource Management. *Sociological Focus*, 29(3), 245–261.

Rosen, H. (2009). *Terror in the Heart of Freedom: Citizenship, Sexual Violence, and the Meaning of Race in the Postemancipation South*. University of North Carolina Press.

Rosenblatt, R. A., Andrilla, C. H. A., Curtin, T., & Hart, L. G. (2006). Shortages of Medical Personnel at Community Health Centers: Implications for Planned Expansion. *JAMA*, 295(9), 1042. https://doi.org/10.1001/jama.295.9.1042.

Roth, B. (2004). *Separate Roads to Feminism: Black, Chicana, and White Feminist Movements in America's Second Wave*. Cambridge University Press.

Roure, J. G. (2011). Gender Justice in Puerto Rico: Domestic Violence, Legal Reform, and the Use of International Human Rights Principles. *Human Rights Quarterly*, 33 (3), 790–825.

Ryan, J. G. (1977). The Memphis Riots of 1866: Terror in a Black Community during Reconstruction. *The Journal of Negro History*, 62(3), 243–257. https://doi.org/10.2307/2716953.

Sabatier, P. A. (1991). Toward Better Theories of the Policy Process. *PS: Political Science and Politics*, 24(2), 147–156. https://doi.org/10.2307/419923.

Sabatier, P. A., & Weible, C. M. (2007). The Advocacy Coalition Framework. *Theories of the Policy Process*, 2, 189–220.

Sacco, L. N. (2015). *The Violence Against Women Act: Overview, Legislation, and Federal Funding*. Congressional Research Service Report, May 26. https://sgp.fas.org/crs/misc/R42499.pdf.

Salcido, O., & Adelman, M. (2004). "He Has Me Tied with the Blessed and Damned Papers": Undocumented-Immigrant Battered Women in Phoenix, Arizona. *Human Organization*, 63(2), 162–172.

Salinas, C., & Lozano, A. (2021). The History and Evolution of the Term Latinx. In E. G. Murillo, D. D. Bernal, S. Morales et al. (Eds.), *Handbook of Latinos and Education: Theory, Research, and Practice* (2nd ed.). Routledge. https://doi.org/10.4324/9780429292026.

Santos, C. M. (2005). *Women's Police Stations: Gender, Violence, and Justice in São Paulo, Brazil*. Springer.

Sargeant, A., West, D. C., & Jay, E. (2007). The Relational Determinants of Nonprofit Web Site Fundraising Effectiveness: An Exploratory Study. *Nonprofit Management and Leadership*, 18(2), 141–156. https://doi.org/10.1002/nml.178.

Sartain, L. (2007). *Invisible Activists: Women of the Louisiana NAACP and the Struggle for Civil Rights, 1915–1945*. Louisiana State University Press.

Schechter, S. (1982). *Women and Male Violence: The Visions and Struggles of the Battered Women's Movement*. South End Press.

Schulhofer, S. J. (2000). *Unwanted Sex: The Culture of Intimidation and the Failure of Law*. Harvard University Press.

Schuller, K. (2021). *The Trouble with White Women: A Counterhistory of Feminism*. PublicAffairs.

Schwarz, N., & Vaughn, L. A. (2002). The Availability Heuristic Revisited: Ease of Recall and Content of Recall As Distinct Sources of Information. In T. Gilovich, D. Griffin, & D. Kahneman (Eds.), *Heuristics and Biases: The Psychology of Intuitive Judgment* (pp. 103–119). Cambridge University Press. https://doi.org/10.1017/CBO9780511808098.007.

Seelman, K. L. (2015). Unequal Treatment of Transgender Individuals in Domestic Violence and Rape Crisis Programs. *Journal of Social Service Research*, 41(3), 307–325. https://doi.org/10.1080/01488376.2014.987943.

Seymour, J. W., Polsky, D. E., Brown, E. J., Barbu, C. M., & Grande, D. (2017). The Role of Community Health Centers in Reducing Racial Disparities in Spatial Access to Primary Care. *Journal of Primary Care & Community Health*, 8(3), 147–152. https://doi.org/10.1177/2150131917699029.

Shear, M. (2017). Trump Sexual Misconduct Accusations Repeated by Several Women. *The New York Times*, December 11. www.nytimes.com/2017/12/11/us/politics/trump-accused-sexual-misconduct.html.

Sheingate, A. D. (2003). Political Entrepreneurship, Institutional Change, and American Political Development. *Studies in American Political Development*, 17(2), 185–203. https://doi.org/10.1017/S0898588X03000129.

Shimizu, C. P. (2007). *The Hypersexuality of Race: Performing Asian/American Women on Screen and Scene*. Duke University Press.

Shiu-Thornton, S., Senturia, K., & Sullivan, M. (2005). "Like a Bird in a Cage": Vietnamese Women Survivors Talk About Domestic Violence. *Journal of Interpersonal Violence*, 20(8), 959–976. https://doi.org/10.1177/0886260505277677.

Silva-Martínez, E. (2016). "El Silencio": Conceptualizations of Latina Immigrant Survivors of Intimate Partner Violence in the Midwest of the United States. *Violence Against Women*, 22(5), 523–544. https://doi.org/10.1177/1077801215607357.

Silver, D. A., & Clark, T. N. (2016). *Scenescapes: How Qualities of Place Shape Social Life*. University of Chicago Press.

Silverman, R. M. (2008). The Influence of Nonprofit Networks on Local Affordable Housing Funding: Findings from a National Survey of Local Public Administrators. *Urban Affairs Review*, 44(1), 126–141. https://doi.org/10.1177/1078087408316970.

Simien, E. M., & Clawson, R. A. (2004). The Intersection of Race and Gender: An Examination of Black Feminist Consciousness, Race Consciousness, and Policy Attitudes. *Social Science Quarterly*, 85(3), 793–810.

Simonofski, A., Fink, J., & Burnay, C. (2021). Supporting policy-making with social media and e-participation platforms data: A policy analytics framework. *Government Information Quarterly*, 38(3), 101590. https://doi.org/10.1016/j.giq.2021.101590.

Sjoberg, L. (2006). Gendered Realities of the Immunity Principle: Why Gender Analysis Needs Feminism. *International Studies Quarterly*, *50*(4), 889–910.

Skocpol, T. (1992). State Formation and Social Policy in the United States. *American Behavioral Scientist*, *35*(4–5), 559–584. https://doi.org/10.1177/0002764292035000412.

Skocpol, T. (1995). *Protecting Soldiers and Mothers*. Harvard University Press.

Skocpol, T. (2013). *Diminished Democracy: From Membership to Management in American Civic Life*. University of Oklahoma Press.

Skrentny, J. D. (2006). Policy-Elite Perceptions and Social Movement Success: Understanding Variations in Group Inclusion in Affirmative Action. *American Journal of Sociology*, *111*(6), 1762–1815. https://doi.org/10.1086/499910.

Slemp, K. (2020). Latino, Latina, Latin@, Latine, and Latinx: Gender Inclusive Oral Expression in Spanish. Master's thesis, The University of Western Ontario.

Slothuus, R., & de Vreese, C. H. (2010). Political Parties, Motivated Reasoning, and Issue Framing Effects. *The Journal of Politics*, *72*(3), 630–645. https://doi.org/10.1017/S002238161000006X.

Small, M. L. (2011). How to Conduct a Mixed Methods Study: Recent Trends in a Rapidly Growing Literature. *Annual Review of Sociology*, *37*(1), 57–86. https://doi.org/10.1146/annurev.soc.012809.102657.

Smith, A. (2001). The Color of Violence: Violence against Women of Color. *Meridians*, *1*(2), 65–72.

Smith, A. (2004). Beyond the Politics of Inclusion: Violence against Women of Color and Human Rights. *Meridians*, *4*(2), 120–124.

Smith, A. (2008). Looking to the Future: Domestic Violence, Women of Color, the State, and Social Change. In N. J. Sokoloff (Ed.), *Domestic Violence at the Margins* (pp. 416–434). Rutgers University Press.

Smith, A., Richie, B., Sudbury, J., White, J., & INCITE! (2006). The Color of Violence: Introduction. In INCITE! Women of Color Against Violence (Ed.), *Color of Violence: The INCITE! Anthology* (pp. 1–10). South End Press.

Smith, S. G., Zhang, X., Basile, K. G. et al. (2018). *The National Intimate Partner and Sexual Violence Survey: 2015 Data Brief – Updated Release*. National Center for Injury Prevention and Control, Centers for Disease Control and Prevention. www.cdc.gov/violenceprevention/pdf/2015data-brief508.pdf.

Sokoloff, N. J. (2004). Domestic Violence at the Crossroads: Violence against Poor Women and Women of Color. *Women's Studies Quarterly*, *32*(3/4), 139–147.

Sokoloff, N. J., & Dupont, I. (2005). Domestic Violence at the Intersections of Race, Class, and Gender: Challenges and Contributions to Understanding Violence against Marginalized Women in Diverse Communities. *Violence Against Women*, *11*(1), 38–64. https://doi.org/10.1177/1077801204271476.

Springer, K. (2005). *Living for the Revolution: Black Feminist Organizations, 1968–1980*. Duke University Press.

Star, S. L., & Griesemer, J. R. (2016). Institutional Ecology, "Translations" and Boundary Objects: Amateurs and Professionals in Berkeley's Museum of Vertebrate Zoology, 1907–39. *Social Studies of Science*, *19*(3). https://doi.org/10.1177/030631289019003001.

Starr, P. (2019). *Entrenchment: Wealth, Power, and the Constitution of Democratic Societies*. Yale University Press. https://doi.org/10.12987/9780300244823.

Stockdale, M. S. (1996). *Sexual Harassment in the Workplace*. SAGE.

Stolberg, S. G., Alcindor, Y., & Fandos, N. (2018). Al Franken to Resign from Senate amid Harassment Allegations. *The New York Times*, December 7. www.nytimes.com /2017/12/07/us/politics/al-franken-senate-sexual-harassment.html.

Stone, D. (2019). Transnational Policy Entrepreneurs and the Cultivation of Influence: Individuals, Organizations and Their Networks. *Globalizations, 16*(7), 1128–1144. https://doi.org/10.1080/14747731.2019.1567976.

Strebeigh, F. (2009). *Equal: Women Reshape American Law.* W. W. Norton & Company.

Strolovitch, D. Z. (2006). Do Interest Groups Represent the Disadvantaged? Advocacy at the Intersections of Race, Class, and Gender. *The Journal of Politics, 68*(4), 894–910. https://doi.org/10.1111/j.1468-2508.2006.00478.x.

Strolovitch, D. Z. (2007). *Affirmative Advocacy: Race, Class, and Gender in Interest Group Politics.* University of Chicago Press.

Strolovitch, D. Z. (2018). "Intersectional Advocacy and Activism in Time." Paper Presented at the Annual Meeting of the American Political Science Association, Boston, August 30 to September 2.

Sum, A., Khatiwada, I., McLaughlin, J., & Palma, S. (2010). The Great Recession of 2008–2009 and the Blue-Collar Depression. *Challenge, 53*(4), 6–24.

Tangri, S. S., Burt, M. R., & Johnson, L. B. (1982). Sexual Harassment at Work: Three Explanatory Models. *Journal of Social Issues, 38*(4), 33–54. https://doi.org/10.1111/j .1540-4560.1982.tb01909.x.

Tarrow, S. G. (2011). *Power in Movement: Social Movements and Contentious Politics.* Cambridge University Press.

Taylor, J. K., & Haider-Markel, D. P. (2014). *Transgender Rights and Politics: Groups, Issue Framing, and Policy Adoption.* University of Michigan Press.

Taylor, K.-Y. (2017). *How We Get Free: Black Feminism and the Combahee River Collective.* Haymarket Books.

Theoharis, J. (2015). *The Rebellious Life of Mrs. Rosa Parks.* Beacon Press.

Thompson, B. (2002). Multiracial Feminism: Recasting the Chronology of Second Wave Feminism. *Feminist Studies, 28*(2), 336–360. https://doi.org/10.2307/3178747.

Thuma, E. (2019). *All Our Trials: Prisons, Policing, and the Feminist Fight to End Violence.* University of Illinois Press.

Thurston, C. N. (2018). *At the Boundaries of Homeownership: Credit, Discrimination, and the American State.* Cambridge University Press.

Tilly, C. (1993). *Coercion, Capital and European States: AD 990–1992.* Wiley.

Tisdell, C. A. (2020). Economic, Social and Political Issues Raised by the COVID-19 Pandemic. *Economic Analysis and Policy, 68*, 17–28. https://doi.org/10.1016/j .eap.2020.08.002.

Tormos, F. (2017). Intersectional Solidarity. *Politics, Groups, and Identities, 5*(4), 707–720. https://doi.org/10.1080/21565503.2017.1385494.

Tormos-Aponte, F. (2019). Enacting Intersectional Solidarity in the Puerto Rican Student Movement. In J. Irvine, S. Lang, & C. Montoya (Eds.), *Gendered Mobilizations and Intersectional Challenges: Contemporary Social Movements in Europe and North America* (pp. 171–188). Rowman & Littlefield

Townsend-Bell, E. (2011). What Is Relevance? Defining Intersectional Praxis in Uruguay. *Political Research Quarterly, 64*(1), 187–199. https://doi.org/10.1177 /1065912910382301.

Tucker, J. T. (2007). The Politics of Persuasion: Passage of the Voting Rights Act Reauthorization Act of 2006. *Journal of Legislation, 33*(2), 205–267.

Vaismoradi, M., Turunen, H., & Bondas, T. (2013). Content Analysis and Thematic Analysis: Implications for Conducting a Qualitative Descriptive Study. *Nursing & Health Sciences, 15*(3), 398–405. https://doi.org/10.1111/nhs.12048.

Vanner, C., & Dugal, A. (2020). Personal, Powerful, Political: Activist Networks by, for, and with Girls and Young Women. *Girlhood Studies, 13*(2), vii–xv. https://doi.org/10.3167/ghs.2020.130202.

Villalón, R. (2010). Passage to Citizenship and the Nuances of Agency: Latina Battered Immigrants. *Women's Studies International Forum, 33*(6), 552–560. https://doi.org/10.1016/j.wsif.2010.09.010.

Villalón, R. (2011). Feminist Activist Research and Strategies from within the Battered Immigrants' Movement. *Interface, 3*(2), 246–270.

Viswanathan, M. (2007). Sunset Provisions in the Tax Code: A Critical Evaluation and Prescriptions for the Future. *New York University Law Review, 82*, 656–688.

Voegeli, W. (2012). *Never Enough: America's Limitless Welfare State*. Encounter Books.

Wacquant, L. (2009). *Punishing the Poor: The Neoliberal Government of Social Insecurity*. Duke University Press.

Wade, W. C. (1998). *The Fiery Cross: The Ku Klux Klan in America*. Oxford University Press.

Wallace, H. (2002). *Family Violence: Legal, Medical, and Social Perspectives* (3rd ed.). Allyn and Bacon.

Warner, K. E. (1986). Smoking and Health Implications of a Change in the Federal Cigarette Excise Tax. *JAMA, 255*(8), 1028–1032. https://doi.org/10.1001/jama.1986.03370080050024.

Weber, M. (1965). *Politics As a Vocation*.Fortress Press.

Websdale, N., & Johnson, B. (1997). Reducing Woman Battering: The Role of Structural Approaches. *Social Justice, 24*(1), 54–81.

Weingast, B. R., & Marshall, W. J. (1988). The Industrial Organization of Congress; or, Why Legislatures, Like Firms, Are Not Organized as Markets. *Journal of Political Economy, 96*(1), 132–163. https://doi.org/10.1086/261528.

Weir, M., Orloff, A. S., & Skocpol, T. (1988). Introduction: Understanding American Social Politics. In M. Weir, A. S. Orloff, & T. Skocpol (Eds.), *The Politics of Social Policy in the United States* (pp. 3–27). Princeton University Press.

Weisenburger, S. (1999). *Modern Medea: A Family Story of Slavery and Child-Murder from the Old South*. Macmillan.

Weissman, D. M. (2013). Law, Social Movements, and the Political Economy of Domestic Violence. *Duke Journal of Gender Law & Policy, 20*(2), 221–254.

Weldon, S. L. (2002). *Protest, Policy, and the Problem of Violence Against Women: A Cross-National Comparison*. University of Pittsburgh Press.

Weldon, S. L. (2012). *When Protest Makes Policy: How Social Movements Represent Disadvantaged Groups*. University of Michigan Press.

Weldon, S. L. (2006). Women's Movements, Identity Politics, and Policy Impacts: A Study of Policies on Violence against Women in the 50 United States. *Political Research Quarterly, 59*(1), 111–122. https://doi.org/10.1177/1065912906005900110.

Weldon, S. L., & Htun, M. (2013). Feminist Mobilisation and Progressive Policy Change: Why Governments Take Action to Combat Violence against Women. *Gender & Development, 21*(2), 231–247. https://doi.org/10.1080/13552074.2013.802158.

West, C. M. (2002). Black Battered Women: New Directions for Research and Black Feminist Theory. In J. C. Chrisler, L. H. Collins, & M. R. Dunlap (Eds.), *Charting a New Course for Feminist Psychology* (pp. 216–239). Praeger.

West, T. C. (1999). *Wounds of the Spirit: Black Women, Violence, and Resistance Ethics*. New York University Press.

Weston, C., Gandell, T., Beauchamp, J., et al. (2001). Analyzing Interview Data: The Development and Evolution of a Coding System. *Qualitative Sociology*, 24(3), 381–400. https://doi.org/10.1023/A:1010690908200.

White, D. G. (1999). *Too Heavy a Load: Black Women in Defense of Themselves, 1894–1994*. W. W. Norton & Company.

Whittier, N. (2016). Carceral and Intersectional Feminism in Congress: The Violence Against Women Act, Discourse, and Policy. *Gender & Society*, 30(5), 791–818. https://doi.org/10.1177/0891243216653381.

Wilkes, N. (2019). Shelter Movement. In F. P. Bernat & K. Frailing (Eds.), *The Encyclopedia of Women and Crime* (pp. 1–5). Wiley. https://doi.org/10.1002/9781118929803.ewac0467.

Williams, R. Y. (2004). *The Politics of Public Housing: Black Women's Struggles against Urban Inequality*. Oxford University Press.

Winter, N. J. G. (2008). *Dangerous Frames: How Ideas about Race and Gender Shape Public Opinion*. University of Chicago Press.

Wong, L. (2018). *Transpacific Attachments: Sex Work, Media Networks, and Affective Histories of Chineseness*. Columbia University Press.

Wong, R. B. (2018). *China Transformed: Historical Change and the Limits of European Experience*. Cornell University Press.

Wood, S. M. (2004). VAWA's Unfinished Business: The Immigrant Women Who Fall through the Cracks Queer Theory, Feminism, and the Law: Note. *Duke Journal of Gender Law & Policy*, 11(1), 141–156.

Woody, B. (1992). *Black Women in the Workplace: Impacts of Structural Change in the Economy*. Greenwood Press.

Wrangle, J., Fisher, J. W., & Paranjape, A. (2008). Ha Sentido Sola? Culturally Competent Screening for Intimate Partner Violence in Latina Women. *Journal of Women's Health*, 17(2), 261–268. https://doi.org/10.1089/jwh.2007.0394.

Wyatt, G. E. (1992). The Sociocultural Context of African American and White American Women's Rape. *Journal of Social Issues*, 48, 77–91.

Yuval-Davis, N. (2006). Intersectionality and Feminist Politics. *European Journal of Women's Studies*, 13(3), 193–209.

Zentella, A. C. (2017). "Limpia, fija y da esplendor": Challenging the Symbolic Violence of the Royal Spanish Academy. *Chiricú Journal: Latina/o Literatures, Arts, and Cultures*, 1(2), 21. https://doi.org/10.2979/chiricu.1.2.04.

Index

Printed in the United States
by Baker & Taylor Publisher Services